July 14, 1982

To Pop,
    Who has set such
a wonderful example
over all these years.
I love you very much.
                Lew

FELIX FRANKFURTER AND HIS TIMES

꘍꘍ THE REFORM YEARS ꘍꘍

Michael E. Parrish

THE FREE PRESS
A Division of Macmillan Publishing Co., Inc.
NEW YORK

Collier Macmillan Publishers
LONDON

THE FREE PRESS
A Division of Macmillan Publishing Co., Inc.
866 Third Avenue, New York, N.Y. 10022

Collier Macmillan Canada, Inc.

Library of Congress Catalog Card Number: 81-69263

Printed in the United States of America

printing number
1 2 3 4 5 6 7 8 9 10

Library of Congress Cataloging in Publication Data

Parrish, Michael E.
  Felix Frankfurter and his times.

  Includes bibliographical references and index.
  Contents: v. 1. The reform years.
  1. Frankfurter, Felix, 1882–1965. 2. Judges — United
States — Biography. I. Title.
KF8745.F7P37   347.73′2634   [B]   81-69263
ISBN 0-02-923740-8   347.3073534 [B]   AACR2

For Caryl Jane

CONTENTS

ACKNOWLEDGMENTS

I OWE A LARGE DEBT to many people and institutions who made this book possible, but especially to my former teacher and friend, the late Alexander M. Bickel. This imaginative, witty and brave man first inspired my interest in American law and in the life of Felix Frankfurter. Through his generosity I gained access to the latter's private judicial papers and to the incomparable resources of the Harvard Law School. I also wish to thank Paul Freund for his support and encouragement.

Gerald Gunther and Norris Darrell permitted me to quote from the papers of Judge Learned Hand, and the former's careful reading of the text spared me from several embarrassments. For their advice on matters of style and substance, I also wish to thank David J. Danelski, Earl Pomeroy, and John M. Blum.

Grant Gilmore granted me permission to quote from the papers of Oliver Wendell Holmes, Jr., and Mr. Zechariah Chafee 3rd did the same for his father's papers. I am indebted to them both.

Two very patient and devoted librarians, Charles Cooney, formerly at the Library of Congress, and Erika S. Chadbourn, Curator of Manuscripts and Archives at the Harvard Law School, provided generous assistance, including, on one occasion, a choice seat at Fenway Park.

For sharing their recollections about Felix Frankfurter, I thank especially Joe Rauh, Jr., Benjamin V. Cohen, Andrew Kaufman, Frank Sander, Al Sacks, Abram Chayes, and Jerome Cohen, although their efforts will not be rewarded entirely until the succeeding volume is published. For sharing their insight into American history and law, I am grateful to Morton Horowitz, Harry N. Scheiber, Phillip Paludan, Charles McCurdy, and Duncan Kennedy.

This study would not have been completed without the support of the Committee on Research at the University of California, San Diego; the National Endowment for the Humanities; the Harvard Law School; Jane and George Johnson; and Dieter and Christiane Schrebler. I wish to especially thank Charles E. Smith, Michael Sander, and Bessie Blum at The Free Press.

Finally, I apologize to Caryl, Scott, and Stephanie for a short temper and many distracted conversations.

MICHAEL E. PARRISH

INTRODUCTION

"THE POINT IS," Felix Frankfurter once remarked, "that I haven't any crowd — that's why Max Eastman in his *Liberator* (or *Masses*) calls me 'bourgeois' and Fred Fish thinks me 'dangerous.' I verily believe I'm an occasional target because I worship no sacred cow, and because I do regard it the business of the mind to inquire, altho neither advocating nor expecting any sudden or upsetting changes, and loving what America means passionately."[1] This skepticism and refusal to become identified with a particular creed or, as he put it, "any crowd," defined the core of Frankfurter's liberalism for half a century and made him the despair of radicals and reactionaries alike.

Every human being, Frankfurter believed, remained a hostage to "can't helps" — certain biases, habits, and ingrained predispositions that influenced how one responded to life's many choices. The key to life, however, was "to avoid the confusion between one's can't helps and an iron law of God." Frankfurter's own "can't helps" were many and not always logically consistent. Sometimes he too confused them with the commands of the deity. They included a distrust of unrestrained power, whether exercised by captains of industry or judges, but also a belief in government by a meritocracy; a concern for the underdog and the exploited, yet a dislike of socialism; a contempt for emotionalism in politics, but a fierce devotion to his adopted country; a hatred for shibboleths, but a romantic attachment to something called the rule of law.

Professors of law, even those who sometimes reach the United States Supreme Court, do not usually achieve the status of celebrities

in American society. Felix Frankfurter, however, commanded the
awe, devotion, hatred, and paranoia normally reserved for presidents,
generals, movie stars, and eccentric millionaires, although he never
held an elective office, dispensed little official patronage, and died
nearly penniless. This owlish, fastidious little man, who charmed Oliver Wendell Holmes, terrified proper Bostonians, dismayed businessmen, and often incurred the wrath of civil libertarians, played a central role in the history of modern American liberalism because he
trafficked in its newest form of power — the trained intelligence required to govern society.

Beginning in the late nineteenth century, America's universities
and professional schools, especially those of law, business, and public
administration, became important production centers for a new technical intelligentsia of men and women who staffed the growing do-
mains of private industry and government. At institutions such as the
Harvard Law School, they acquired an apprenticeship in the arcane
skills of legal draftsmanship, economic analysis, and bureaucratic manipulation that one historian has described as "the continuous management of indeterminate processes." Frankfurter, one of the earliest
products of this new intellectual world, became a principal broker of
its many opportunities from the days of Teddy Roosevelt to John F.
Kennedy. His endorsement could mean a desirable judicial clerkship,
a column in *The New Republic*, a job at the War Department, the SEC,
or even the White House; perhaps a coveted professorship at Harvard,
Yale, Chicago, or Pennsylvania.

Frankfurter's far-reaching influence, resented by many and courted by many, came from the shrewd deployment of his own considerable charm and intellectual resources. It also derived from his ability to
measure and allocate the talents of his many "boys," the gifted young
lawyers who came under his tutelage (some called it a spell) in Cambridge and Washington. By any reckoning, they were a remarkable
group, including Robert Patterson, Dean Acheson, David Lilienthal,
Alger Hiss, James Landis, Tommy Corcoran, Ben Cohen, Joe Rauh,
Jr., Philip Graham, Elliott Richardson, Alexander Bickel, Paul
Freund, and Richard Goodwin. Their conquests, in turn, expanded
his own empire within government, the legal profession, and the law
schools. He bartered intellectual property the way other people bartered votes, real estate, and common stock.

Self-interest and altruism made Frankfurter a social reformer. Like
his close friends of the progressive era, Herbert Croly, Walter Lippmann, Louis Brandeis, and Robert Valentine, he encouraged the rise

of intellectual workers in government, industry, and the professions because he believed that they, rather than ordinary politicians and businessmen, promoted rational, scientific, and humane change. A passion for efficiency, not a vision of utopia, inspired this commitment. "I try not to think of these aims in ethical terms," he once told Holmes. "It isn't a question of better or onward, and I certainly do not believe in any determinable standard of 'progress.' I do think, I do hope, that life can be finer, in the sense of a richer, more teeming sort of spectacle. . . . In other words an organized effort towards more life."[2]

A Jew and an immigrant, Frankfurter sympathized with the dreams of other outsiders in American society, especially with those of urban labor leaders such as Sidney Hillman, who aspired to form stable unions and to enter the mainstream of the nation's economic life. Above all, he placed his faith in the good sense, the educability, and the benevolence of the country's old elite, represented by Holmes, Henry Stimson, and Franklin D. Roosevelt. The gentry and the new intellectuals, he believed, would moderate the excesses of American capitalism, discipline the vulgar business classes, uplift the poor, and usher in the benign future of expanded social welfare and security. He believed, finally, in the desirability of democratic change tempered by an elite; in this respect he remained throughout his life a typical turn-of-the-century progressive.

Symbolically, his death in 1965 coincided with the end of an era of liberal hegemony in the United States — an era distinguished by a strong, popular belief in the rational control of economic progress, in social justice through incremental reforms, and in the constructive uses of American power abroad. But on the day when the man once called "the most useful lawyer in the United States" died at the age of 82, an assassin shot Malcolm X to death in the ballroom of a New York City hotel and three thousand miles away in Saigon, a military junta toppled one general from office and replaced him with another. In the United States Senate, speakers urged the president to bomb North Vietnam as a sign of the nation's resolve to resist communist aggression.

In the decade after Frankfurter's death, liberals lost their grip upon the management of American society and the rest of the world. Many of the core values, assumptions, and institutions that he had defended since the turn of the century — the role of intellectuals in government, the scientific approach to social problems, a vigorous presidency, a passive judiciary, civility and compromise in political life — all were either abandoned, discredited, or thrown on the defensive by the worst social disorders and civic confusion since the Civil War.

Some of America's most sophisticated leaders, "the best and the brightest," contributed to these disasters. Many of them, including Dean Acheson and McGeorge Bundy, had been former students and friends of Felix Frankfurter, with whom they shared a common wardrobe and quite often a common perspective on the problems of government and statecraft. On the other hand, many of their critics, including Ben Cohen, Joe Rauh, Jr., and Richard Goodwin, were also disciples of Felix Frankfurter. Posthumously, he contributed to the shaping of both the debacle of liberalism as well as its possible rehabilitation.

For over fifty years, Felix Frankfurter enlivened our politics and enriched our legal culture. His chief foibles were those of the progressive intellectuals, who believed that under wise and enlightened stewardship (their own, of course), America would experience an upward spiral of human rationality and welfare. That central myth of twentieth-century liberalism has now lost much of its old vitality, but the men and women who forged it still inspire our wonder, if not always our confidence. This is the story of one of them.

CHAPTER 1

YOUNG MAN FROM THE PROVINCES

SOMEONE ONCE ASKED his good friend, Harold Laski, why the splendidly attired professor Felix Frankfurter voted for the Democrats. "Because," Laski replied, "he is an aristocrat with an infinite sense of pity."[1] Felix Frankfurter never forgot where he came from, but he seldom brooded about it long enough to neglect where he was going. Had he been born in the age of the Tudors, the de Medicis, or the Bourbons, he might have become a courtier to kings and princes — perhaps a Thomas Cromwell, a Machiavelli, or a Cardinal Richelieu. Instead, he was born a Jew, in the most elegant of European cities, Vienna, in less than prosperous circumstances, during the twilight of Hapsburg absolutism, the birth of mass democracy, and the rise of modern anti-Semitism.

He grew up on New York's Lower East Side, where the tough Irish kids did not stop to beat him up because he was too small. Before he reached the age of thirty, he had graduated from Harvard Law School, secured a professorship there, advised presidents, and become a close friend to several members of the American gentry. Barely five feet, five inches tall, but broad shouldered, with a round, birdlike face accented by fine, bluish-grey eyes, Frankfurter was already a national legend at forty-five, a man whose name symbolized liberalism, social reform, the bureaucratic state, and endless political intrigue. At fifty-five he became one of three foreign-born Americans to serve on the United States Supreme Court and for the next twenty-five years his name stood for conservatism, the neglect of civil liberties, and endless political intrigue.

Louis Brandeis described him as America's most useful lawyer. Reinhold Niebuhr thought he was the most intelligent person he had ever met, and Lady Astor found him to be a gay and charming man. William O. Douglas, on the other hand, believed him to be crafty, self-serving, and power hungry, an opinion that was shared by others who also remarked upon his vanity, arrogance, and unscrupulousness. During the early days of the New Deal, however, he went to Oxford as a visiting professor, rather than remain in Washington close to Roosevelt, power, and influence. Archibald MacLeish called him "that rarest of God's creatures, a simon-pure, unmitigated intellectual with a limitless relish for living in a human world."[2] What many people remembered best about Frankfurter was the iron grip, right above the elbow, the laughter, the sudden bursts of rage, the sentimentality, and the loyalty. He often loved many of his friends too uncritically and hated a few enemies much too long. That he did both with enthusiasm there can be no doubt.

He wore well-tailored suits and pince-nez, enjoyed fine food, and drank expensive wines. He never learned to drive an automobile, but he defended Tom Mooney, communist-anarchists during the worst days of the Red Scare, and Sacco and Vanzetti a few years later. He loved to have breakfast with the owner of the *Washington Post*, Eugene Meyer, he once confided to a friend, because Meyer always served both melon and orange juice. When President Eisenhower entertained Queen Elizabeth II at the White House, but did not invite Mr. Justice Frankfurter, one of the nation's most unabashed Anglophiles, he organized his own party for the occasion, duplicated the swank menu, and invited old friends and law clerks to the festivities. He greeted guests at the door of his Georgetown home in a garish, red dinner jacket. "Wherever Frankfurter is," wrote Matthew Josephson during the Second World War, "there is no boredom. As soon as he bounces in — he never walks, he bounces — the talk and laughter begin, and they never let up. He brings with him the sweep of national affairs and the human interest of personal gossip."[3] He fought for Julius and Ethel Rosenberg, Caryl Chessman, and Dr. Sam Sheppard, but he believed in the death penalty for anyone who cracked the binding of a new book. He married a Congregational minister's daughter and became a Zionist, but always described himself as a reverent agnostic.

Felix Frankfurter, the outsider, became the insider, but he was never wholly comfortable there or absolutely certain that he had really made it. His self-confidence and bravado sometimes masked deep insecurities. A child of the ghetto, he read the London *Times* each day as an adult, and admired the English upper class, especially their Whiggish liberalism and their good, Tory manners. Born in the Victorian era, he resembled no one quite so much as Hyacinth Robinson, the troubled hero of Henry James's great novel, *The Princess Casamassima*. Like Robinson, the aspiring bookbinder who was torn between his belief in revolution and his taste for high culture, Frankfurter craved personal success and social justice. He believed that both were possible within a framework of regulated capitalism, democratic legality, and an aristocracy tempered with merit, symbolized by the Harvard Law School. He represented, in Lionel Trilling's famous phrase, the "young man from the provinces": "He need not come from the provinces in literal fact, his social class may constitute his province. But a provincial birth and rearing suggest the simplicity and the high hopes he begins with — he starts with a great demand upon life and a great wonder about its complexity and promise. He may be of good family but he must be poor."[4] Robinson, according to James, sprang up at him out of the London pavement. For Felix Frankfurter, life began in Vienna in 1882, the third of four sons born to Leopold and Emma Frankfurter.

The Vienna of Emperor Francis Joseph, a city of bright cafés in a nation of peasants, nourished the genius of Sigmund Freud, Gustav Mahler, Hugo von Hofmannsthal, Ernest Mach, and Arnold Schönberg. During the second half of the nineteenth century, Hapsburg Vienna experienced a burst of intellectual and artistic creativity unsurpassed by any metropolis in the world. The city became notorious for modernism in literature, the avant-garde in music, and decadence in art. Frankfurter's immediate contemporaries included the novelist, Robert Musil, the literary critic, George Lukacs, the theologian, Paul Tillich, and the philosopher Ludwig Wittgenstein. Yet this extraordinary cultural flowering took place within an economic, social, and political environment of unrelieved chaos and futility that was dominated by raw industrial growth, the hatred of warring nationalities, and the exhaustion of a governing elite mired in feudal traditions and religious mysticism. Liberal capitalism, Hapsburg style, shattered the old institutions and values of the regime, but left nothing in their place except a furious scramble for wealth, mounting social insecurity for most classes, and spreading pessimism. Vienna, wrote the critic Karl Kraus, seemed a "proving ground for world destruction."[5]

Among the many ethnic and religious groups who jostled one another in the Hapsburg Empire, the Viennese Jews occupied a unique and precarious station. Classified as Germans for the purposes of the official census (even when they spoke Yiddish), many of them converted to Christianity or practiced a vague humanism. Excluded from the highest positions in the military and state bureaucracy, they nonetheless managed to find openings in the lower civil service, as well as in the learned professions of law, medicine, and journalism. Some acquired substantial fortunes in banking, insurance, and stock speculations, but the majority of Jewish businessmen in Vienna remained petty merchants and traders, without great wealth or connections at court. Jews played a conspicuous role in the city's rich intellectual and cultural life as creators and arbiters of the newest trends in art, music, and literature. Perhaps the most assimilated and cosmopolitan in all of Europe, Vienna's Jews thrived economically under Hapsburg rule, although many of them, such as Viktor Adler, leader of the Social Democratic Party, and the journalist, Kraus, became harsh critics of their society, who rejected the absurd compromise between liberal capitalism and enlightened absolutism.

Leopold Frankfurter was not an intellectual or a radical. Nor had he prospered. Descended from six generations of rabbis, he was in fact something of a disappointment to his own family at a time when social and economic opportunities seemed most promising for Jews. They expected him to continue the rabbinical tradition, or perhaps to make a career for himself in the civil service. But during the final year of his religious studies, Leopold experienced a crisis of belief, dropped out of school, married, and announced that he was going into the bustling world of trade. Somewhat lazy, romantic, fond of the opera, but without a good head for figures, he seems to have been equally unsuited to the hard, rapacious business world of late nineteenth-century Vienna. The children — Fred, Otto, Felix, Paul, and later two daughters, Ella and Estelle — always arrived more rapidly than his income. Although not poverty stricken in comparison with many of their neighbors, the Frankfurters eked out a livelihood on the border between the city's petite bourgeoisie and working class. Most unsettling of all, while his own business career faltered, his brother Solomon rapidly ascended the academic ladder at the universities of Vienna and Berlin and received an appointment in the Vienna state library in 1884, two years after Felix's birth.

Uncle Solomon, not Leopold, became the family's success story, as director of the state library in 1919 and author of numerous scholarly articles on philology, archeology, and bibliography. The nephews, especially young Felix, worshipped him as a model of learning, culture, and successful assimilation, especially when he became a spokesman for Jewish interests in the city and a *shtadlan* (backstairs petitioner) with the gentile power structure. Their own father, in contrast, seemed adrift on a sea of vague dreams and unfulfilled expectations. During a trip to America in 1893, Leopold announced that he had fallen in love with the new country and that the family could find greater opportunity across the ocean, an idea that did not initially appeal to Emma, who made the journey very reluctantly with the children a year later. Fleeing more from personal frustration than from social persecution, Leopold nonetheless became an immigrant at a crucial turning point in the history of Vienna's Jews and of his own family.

The decade of the 1890s, climaxing a worldwide economic slump that had begun ten years earlier, altered for the worse Jewish fortunes within Vienna and Europe generally. Confronted with severe housing shortages, falling prices, rising unemployment, and business scandals that implicated imperial officials with Jewish financiers, large numbers of the city's laborers, civil servants, and small businessmen rallied to the political banner of Karl Lueger, a municipal councilman and leader of the so-called Christian Socialists, who promised to liberate Vienna from the grip of "Jewish capitalists," promote state ownership of major utilities, and combat unemployment with a vast public works program. In 1889, Lueger had helped to draw up the initial program of the United Christians that called for restrictions upon futher Jewish immigration from Eastern Europe and the expulsion of Jews from the civil service, the judiciary, the army, the professions, and even retail trades. "Handsome Karl," detested by the emperor and by the aristocracy, but feared by the liberal politicians and by the Social Democrats, achieved a stunning victory in Vienna's 1894 mayoralty election. Francis Joseph refused to confirm his appointment, but Lueger's followers still increased their strength on the city council and three years later, even the emperor capitulated after Lueger's second triumph at the polls. Over the opposition of the imperial bureaucracy, the press, and the business establishment, popular, mass-based anti-Semitism swept the Hapsburg capitol.[6]

Lueger's election took place against the spectacle of the Dreyfus trial in Paris and anti-Jewish riots by university students in Vienna, Prague, and Budapest. Outside the major cities of the empire, Georg Ritter von Schonerer, the romantic and violent son of an upstart nobleman, preached a more savage version of Lueger's anti-Semitism that combined pan-German nationalism, medieval chivalry, and radical economics. He found a sympathetic audience among German workers, hard-pressed landlords and their peasants, the lumpen clergy, and university students, who feared competition from Jews. Although the emperor named Mahler director of the Imperial Opera in 1896 and although Lueger's actual reforms proved less menacing than his anti-Semitic diatribes, Austrian liberalism had become a frail defense for the empire's Jews. Simultaneously, they received the blame for the nation's economic woes, for frustrating the hopes of other nationalities, and for subverting the social order through socialist politics and paganism in the arts.[7]

Vienna's Jews responded in many ways to the crisis of the 1890s depending upon their own social circumstances and their perceptions about the future. The journalist Theodor Herzl, observing events in Vienna from the Paris of Captain Dreyfus, concluded that Jews would never escape persecution in Europe, regardless of the regimes in power. The only safe haven, he concluded, lay in the creation of a separate Jewish homeland in Palestine. Although some wealthy Jews, who were less pessimistic than Herzl, fled from Vienna to other European cities, the majority, including Solomon Frankfurter, stayed on in the hope that Lueger and Schonerer did not represent the new order to come. Still others, believing that the liberal dreams of assimilation, opportunity, and progress had been played out in Vienna, sailed for the United States. In 1894 — the year of Lueger's initial election — Leopold Frankfurter's family entered New York harbor in steerage aboard the *Marsala*.[8]

⠶⠶⠶

The United States was hardly a paradise for Jewish immigrants in the depression-wracked nineties. Economic collapse inflamed ethnic hatreds and brought class and regional tensions to the breaking point. Farmers in the South and the West, faced with sagging commodity prices and crushing debts, declared political war against their absentee tormentors — railroads, industrialists, and Wall Street bankers — whom they regularly denounced as the tools of Great Britain and the international Jewish money cartel. In the well-appointed drawing rooms of the Anglo-Saxon elite, the Adamses, Cabots, and Lodges worried about the sinister influence of "gold bugs" upon the nation's monetary policies and feared the mongrelization of the Teutonic race by swarthy Semites. The exclusive Union League Club of New York blackballed Theodore Seligman, a prominent Jewish financier and son of one of the club's founders. Members of the city's old, German-Jewish elite suddenly found clubs, hotels, summer resorts, and private schools closed to them. For the less famous, life could be more brutal. Fourteen New York City Jewish societies protested in 1899 that "no Jew can go on the street without exposing himself to the danger of being pitilessly beaten." Although less politically organized than its European counterpart and officially rejected by the nation's egalitarian ideology, anti-Semitism nonetheless flourished mightily in the America of William McKinley and William Jennings Bryan.[9]

From the perspective of anxious patriots, most of whom viewed foreigners with suspicion in these years, the Frankfurters were model immigrants, eager to enter the society's mainstream and devoted to the social, economic, and political orthodoxies of the day. Unlike many of the *shtetl* Jews from Russia and Eastern Europe, who jammed into the dark tenement houses below Hester Street on New York's Lower East Side, the Frankfurters did not wear exotic clothing or engage in radical politics. They settled initially on Seventh Street, near Tompkins Square and Cooper Union, in the heavily German-speaking neighborhood where the sober residents voted Republican, admired their wealthy coreligionists — the Seligmans, Warburgs, and Strauses — and hoped to maintain a comfortable distance from the boisterous, Yiddish-speaking masses on Henry and Cherry Streets. "For many a rising immigrant family in this period," one historian noted, "it was judged to be a ten-year trek from Hester Street to Lexington Avenue." The Frankfurters wasted little time. They made it from Seventh Street to the middle-class environs of Yorkville on east Seventy-first Street in only five years.[10]

They made rapid progress owing largely to Emma, who emerged as the dominant influence in the household. She carefully molded her children's perceptions of the new world and overshadowed her husband's values and behavior. As might have been expected, the new land of opportunity did not change Leopold's dreamy habits and precarious fortunes. He generously carried food baskets to poorer neighbors in these years, while his own retail fur and silk business never brought the family wholly secure and comfortable circumstances. Indulgent with the children, gay, and sentimental, Leopold left a mark upon Felix through his insouciance about money and financial matters and through his fondness for music and the theatrical. He nurtured in his children a "Blue Danube side," which taught them not to take life too seriously or too strenuously, especially if it meant indifference to the welfare of other people. Much to his wife's displeasure, he also cultivated a growing distaste for formal religion and the cultural practices of the old world.

Emma struggled constantly against Leopold's secularism, his inability to provide a positive role model for the boys, and his failure to keep the family's income sufficiently ahead of the Lower East Side's grinding poverty. She solved one of these problems by sending the oldest boys — Fred and Otto — out to work, which delayed the completion of their education but added a margin of safety to the family's standard of living. A strict, disciplined homemaker, with an extensive repertoire of homilies about work, duty, and responsibility, Emma believed that her children would conquer their new environment through education. It was she who drilled into them the necessity for intellectual achievement in a brutally competitive society. "Hold yourself dear," she told Felix on many occasions, which meant two things: one should be proud of being a Jew, but as a Jew one should also expect a large share of life's insults. She saw the world as a harsh and unfriendly place, where a Jew had to be twice as smart or work twice as hard as the *goyim* in order to succeed and gain recognition. Emma outfitted her children in the tough armor of pride and ambition, with a touch of ruthlessness. The proverbial Jewish mother — warm, smothering, compliant, impossible to please, difficult to disappoint — she exercised a powerful influence over all of her children. Felix did not break from her spell until he was past the age of thirty-five.[11]

She put Felix and Paul, the youngest son, into Public School 25, where they began to master the fundamentals of English grammar, arithmetic, and patriotism under the equally stern tutelage of Miss Hogan, a redoubtable Irish lady who not only believed in corporal punishment for intellectual indolence but threatened the other students with upper cuts when they conversed with Felix in German. Like other immigrant children, he thirsted to learn the language of his adopted country because it seemed to be the magic tool of social mobility. He read newspapers avidly at the Ottendorfer branch of the

New York Public Library and attended lectures in the posh, red-chaired hall at Cooper Union, where many of the nation's most powerful orators held forth regularly on "pending social problems." There, for instance, he heard the president of Cornell University, Jacob Gould Schurmann, defend the new American empire in the Philippines by arguing that "the issue of imperialism is a tissue of etherealism," a sentence that so filled him with amazement, it remained fresh in his mind over a half-century later.[12]

New York City, the immigrants' metropolis with its sights, sounds, smells, and incredible collection of people, became Felix's richest classroom. Civilized, squalid, heroic, profane, warm, indifferent, it personified the energy and promise of America as well as the nation's mounting social problems of corporate domination, undisciplined wealth, political corruption, and proletarian misery. Felix sold newspapers after school, which permitted him to explore the wide boulevards as well as the back alleys of Manhatten. He sampled the mansions of the very rich and the hovels of the poor; factories and department stores; flop houses and museums; ferry boats and push-carts. They formed a brilliant kaleidoscope of pleasures to be tasted and misfortunes to be avoided.

Although his father professed enthusiasm for McKinley, the protective tariff, and the gold standard, young Felix ventured one afternoon to Hoboken, New Jersey, where he heard the tribune of the masses, Bryan, extoll the virtues of free silver and the need for solidarity between the farmers and the working class against bankers, stock jobbers, and greedy industrialists. Thrilled by the speech and swept away by the emotions of the crowd, he became, at least temporarily, a Populist-Democrat, who also denounced the exploitation of the poor by the rich. It was his first venture into American politics, on the side of the heart rather than the head, and not the last time he would support a lost cause of idealism and reform.[13]

For a Jewish boy of fourteen, however, education not Populism offered immediate, tangible rewards. Frankfurter excelled in school, scored near the top of his class in competitive examinations for the Pulitzer scholarships, and almost entered the exclusive Horace Mann School, a progressive teaching laboratory associated with Columbia University. The tuition, however, amounted to an additional $100 and even with his older brothers working, that sum was beyond the family's means. Instead, he returned to PS 25 and delivered a stirring recitation on graduation day, William Pitt's famous speech to the House of Commons on conciliation with the American revolutionaries: "If I were an American, as I am an Englishman, I would never lay down my arms—never, never, never!!" Bryan stirred his social conscience, but Miss Hogan instilled a robust patriotism which, when combined with an immigrant's insecurity and desire to please, sank deep, emotional roots. Years later, when MacLeish told him he was in the process of writing a play with patriotic themes, Frankfurter responded, "Good. You couldn't make it too patriotic for me."[14]

Shortly before the family moved to Yorkville, Frankfurter enrolled at the City College of New York, a red-brick building on the corner of Lexington Avenue and Twenty-third Street, where the ambitious children of immigrants combined high school and college in a five-year program that might eventually propel them into the white-collar world of education, medicine, architecture, law, and the civil service of the city. Frankfurter's 774 classmates included Irishmen, Germans, Russians, Poles, Italians, and Hungarians, many from middle-class families, but the vast majority from the city's poorest neighborhoods, who worked after school, at nights, and on weekends to put themselves through CCNY. "On Second Avenue at around eight o'clock every morning," wrote Abraham Cahan, the admiring editor of the *Jewish Daily Forward*, "one can see hundreds of Jewish boys from fourteen to eighteen or nineteen years old walking with books under their arms . . . Their clothes are mostly poor and old, but their Jewish faces often shine with spiritual joy and bear the stamp of lively, active minds . . . These are Jewish college boys."[15] Those who survived the rigorous curriculum and harsh discipline often made their mark in business, the professions, and intellectual life. Among Frankfurter's CCNY contemporaries were men destined for the highest court in New York State and Congress, as well as artists, musicians, a distinguished landscape designer, and leading members of the New York Bar.

Like other college students of his generation, Frankfurter suffered through Latin and Greek, learned some history, most of it overblown or romantic, and remained woefully ignorant of the basic sciences. He discovered, however, the richness of the Lenox Library near the campus and became an active member of the Clionia society, one of CCNY's two leading literary societies. Although only a junior, he led Clionia into debate against its arch rival, Phrenocosmia, an annual event which according to Nathaniel Phillips, clearly dwarfed in significance and raw emotion the World Series. "I shall never forget his stunning performance," Phillips recalled. "He looked so boyish, his neatness was striking. He spoke such sense. It was as though no opposition could have any significance. He was extremely courteous in manner but he pierced the arguments of his opponents with a deftness and finality that was devastating." A dashing orator, Phillips noted, Frankfurter always impressed you with his sincerity, his gaiety, and his charm. At the tender age of nineteen, he graduated from CCNY third in his class.[16]

In Frankfurter's day, the world of CCNY and the Lower East Side crackled with the intellectual and cultural electricity generated by millions of Jewish immigrants from Russia and Eastern Europe, victims of economic calamity and czarist pogroms, who had come to the United States in search of their *goldenah medinah*. Poor, ambitious, idealistic, pious, and frequently radical in their politics, they built a prosperous and exploitative economy in the narrow streets and lofts of the Lower East Side; created a vibrant Yiddish press and theatre; and embarrassed their more assimilated and acculturated neighbors, who found them to be too religious and too political. "The thoroughly acclimated American Jew," remarked the *Hebrew Standard*, "has no religious, social or intellectual sympathies with them. He is closer to the Christian sentiment around him than to the Judaism of these miserable darkened Hebrews."[17]

Having capitulated to his father's agnosticism, Frankfurter could not easily sympathize with the religious enthusiasm of the Russians. He found it much more congenial to associate with the prosperous German Jews, who measured up to his own and his mother's standards of achievement. At the same time, he remained troubled by the fact that many wealthy Jews converted to Protestantism in the hope of currying favor with those who discriminated against them. He found many of the Eastern Europeans to be fascinating, intellectually brilliant young men, who shared his interests in politics, world affairs, and current social problems. He cultivated the friendship of several of them, including Isador Goetz, "a loquacious talker and a gluttonous reader of everything," and Morris Raphael Cohen, a promising young philosophy student, with an encyclopedic mind and dazzling vocabulary. In the smoke-filled cafés of the Lower East Side, where these students debated the Talmud, Marx, Lenin, Kropotkin, and Turgenev, Frankfurter discovered another world of Jews, very different from his own. Exotic, bohemian, risqué, the conversations often turned to anarchism, revolution, Emma Goldman, dialectical materialism, and free love.[18]

He found himself fascinated, educated, and repelled by the experience, especially by what he called the "futile, speculative Russian intellectuals" who populated the coffeehouses. "They could reform the world over three glasses of tea," he recalled, "but they couldn't do anything practical to bring [it] nearer their heart's desire because that required effort, and subordination of one's own thoughts to the thoughts of other people." He was moved by the personal sincerity and ethical passion of these radical intellectuals, but dumbfounded by their apparent political naivete. Their interminable disputes over theory, their dogmatism, and their fanaticism also offended him, because they seemed to be either excessively critical of all contemporary societies or, worse yet, unduly fatalistic about the human condition. After one of these exhausting evenings, he finally decided to become a lawyer rather than a journalist, a poet, a revolutionary, or a nihilist. It was not a difficult choice, since he seemed to have a way both with people and with words. He had, after all, led Clionia to victory. He hoped, too, to do something practical about the injustices around him, something that would, in addition, make his mother proud and repay her sacrifices.[19]

He passed the city's civil service examination and worked briefly for the Tenement House Commission, a monument to progressive moralism and uplift where well-intentioned reformers, led by the famous Lawrence Veiller, attempted to solve New York's deplorable housing conditions by strict enforcement of sanitary standards and building codes. These efforts, however, encouraged landlords to abandon many properties, increased political corruption, and probably intensified the suffering of the poor. A lowly clerk, Frankfurter received $1,400 a year for processing complaints and supplemented this income by tutoring high school students. On two occasions, he began and dropped out of night classes at local law schools that neither challenged him intellectually nor offered enough prestige to an aspiring professional. With the prodding and encouragement of Sam and Meyer Rosensohn, two close friends, he enrolled at the Harvard Law School in the fall of 1902, a small package of cleverness, ambition, and innocence, who had never been far beyond the environs of New York and who, to the suppressed delight of his new Cambridge roommate, carried most of his worldly possessions in a trunk, neatly packed by his mother.[20]

☙❧☙❧☙❧

Few institutions in American society could have been more remote from the clamorous life of the Lower East Side in 1902 than the Harvard Law School. In high-ceilinged Austin Hall, festooned with Richardson's wild boars and dragons carved into its hardwood beams, the waistcoated doyens of the legal profession—James Barr Ames, Samuel Williston, John Chipman Gray, Joseph Doddridge Brannan, and Joseph Henry Beale—attempted to make gentlemen and lawyers out of the scions of the Anglo-Saxon establishment and a handful of immigrants. Harvard produced skilled mechanics for the nation's commercial machinery, men who through their mastery of procedure and substantive law could advise, influence, and defend business clients in the esoteric areas of contracts, negotiable instruments, sales, and agency. In the practice of this profession, a graduate of the school was expected to earn a large income, encourage respect for the law and the judiciary, and promote justice—roughly in that order of priority. The institution prized logical thinking, private property, and brutal competition, all within a framework of social privilege and unabashed snobbery.

Dean Ames, a scholarly gentleman who bore some resemblance to President Garfield, presided over a student body of 500 and a faculty of fifteen. They endeavored to continue a revolution in American legal education that had begun a generation earlier at the school by Christopher Columbus Langdell, who wished to move legal education forever out of lawyers' offices and judicial chambers into the academic setting of libraries and classrooms under the control of scholars and teachers. "My associates and myself," Langdell said, in his famous Harvard Celebration Address of 1887, "have constantly acted upon the view that law is a science, and that a well-equipped university is the true place for teaching and learning that science."[21]

Langdell believed that proper legal training came through rigorous intellectual labor, especially the study of cases decided by appellate courts. "The library is the proper workshop of professors and students alike," he wrote. "It is to us all what the laboratories of the university are to the chemists and physicists, the museums of natural history to the zoologists, and botanical gardens to the botanists."[22] For Langdell and many of his disciples, printed case books became the ultimate source of all legal wisdom and appellate decisions remained the raw materials from which professors and students would fashion a pure science of the law that separated true legal rules from false ones. Langdell's "case method," combined with a restructured curriculum, an improved system of examinations, and the recruitment of more full-time faculty members, had a salutary impact upon legal education at Harvard and other schools. Faculty and students abandoned the rote memorization of arid texts in favor of vigorous discussion about actual cases; historical scholarship, long ignored as useless and impractical, received greater financial support and intellectual recognition; the scientific method encouraged efforts to codify and organize the doctrinal jungle of the common law by means of modern treatises, such as Williston's voluminous *Restatement of Contracts*.[23]

On the other hand, Langdell's innovations reinforced the conservative legal values that dominated the training of most students, who learned the superiority of judge-made common law over legislation, the glories of commercial practice, and the inferiority of torts, criminal law, public administration, and constitutional law. Regarded as oracles, judges received extraordinary veneration from professors and students who aspired to become oracles themselves. By the turn of the century, the once innovative "case method" and the rhetoric of scientific inquiry had often degenerated into sterile, pedantic logic chopping, and professorial inquisitions. The students of Professor Brannan captured this dismal spirit:

> Brannan got up and put on his shoe —
> (Fifty Michigan forty-two).
> He put on his coat and went out the door —
> (Twenty Wisconsin sixty-four).

Professor Beale, responding to a student's comments, announced sarcastically that his propositions were "not law in a single State, not in one single State!" When the clever lad produced a relevant Pennsylvania decision, Beale snapped, "But Pennsylvania is not a State, it's a Commonwealth." Beale, according to the school's official historian, remained "a dialectical swordsman who played for classroom victory," and who believed that "there existed a cosmic logical sequence which could be perceived and stated if only one could think aright." He became one of Frankfurter's favorite professors.[24]

After a brief period of terror and awe during which he was dwarfed by students who seemed to be taller, wealthier, and more self-confident, Frankfurter soon came to worship the institution, its faculty, and their methods of instruction. He became adept himself at casuistic repartée, and pitied those slow-witted classmates who fell behind, such as poor Orville Frantz, a star athlete from Harvard College, who mistakenly believed that the law school classroom was a football field where "you take the ball and run with it, but he didn't have the ball." Because the school placed extraordinary emphasis upon intellectual prowess and hard work, he soon believed that it was among the most democratic of American institutions, although this perspective confused democracy with meritocracy and exhibited an unwillingness to examine too closely the procedures of an organization where he excelled more than others. Because many faculty at Harvard had given up private practice in favor of teaching and scholarship, he tended to equate their endeavors with only the purest ethical standards and "complete indifference to all the shoddiness, pettiness and silliness that occupies the concern of most people." This observation revealed more about the institution's capacity to socialize its members than about the realities of academic politics.[25]

The most important benefits conferred by the Harvard Law School probably came outside of the classrooms in the form of social contacts with those who were already powerful and those who aspired to become so. "Cultivate the society of men," Brandeis had advised a young lawyer ten years before, "particularly men of affairs. . . . Lose no opportunity of becoming acquainted with men, of learning to feel instinctively their inclinations. . . . Knowledge of decisions and power of logic are mere handmaidens — they are servants not masters. . . . No hermit can be a great lawyer. . . . " Like the youthful Brandeis, who cut a broad swath through Cambridge society in the 1870s, Frankfurter was certainly no hermit. He showed a remarkable facility for building friendships across a wide spectrum of social types and intellectual activities. He roomed with other Jews — first Sam Rosensohn and later the budding philosopher, Morris Cohen — but he also developed close ties with poor, but ambitious gentiles from the provinces, including Emory Buckner and Silas Howland, as well as with the sons of the well-to-do such as Elihu Root, Jr., Grenville Clark, and Ogden Mills, who constituted the school's social elite. During his last year at the school, Frankfurter provided free tutoring to several members of the well-connected "Gold Coast" set, an act of generosity that outraged Buckner, who depended upon these fees to support his family.[26]

Apart from his legal studies, Frankfurter found time for concerts, museums, and even a course in German literature to the point where Rosensohn worried he would disgrace himself and City College at examination time. But despite a pace of extralegal activities that would have swamped others, Frankfurter led his class academically for three years, earned a coveted position on the *Harvard Law Review*, and became a research assistant to John Gray. He also showed up regularly at Professor Charles T. Copeland's debating class where he attempted to polish his already considerable rhetorical skills. "You go off like an alarm clock," Copeland scolded him, "Don't talk so fast." This advice was apparently not heeded.[27]

In three years, Frankfurter absorbed the law schools essential social conservatism, good manners, and intellectual snobbery, but he also acquired a few heretical ideas put forth by several faculty members and two distinguished alumni — Brandeis and Oliver Wendell Holmes. Gray, Holmes, and James Bradley Thayer, who died the year Frankfurter arrived in Cambridge but whose writings had already stirred controversy, made a deep impression upon his early conceptions of American law, legal education, and the role of the judiciary in the nation's life. Gray, for instance, who had fought with Holmes in the Union army and later practiced law with him in Boston, taught a variety of legal skepticism that appealed to a great many students at the turn of the century. In contrast to those legal intellectuals who attempted to manufacture a science of American law by hiding its untidiness beneath a smokescreen of jargon, he and Holmes both advocated a robust agnosticism that often shocked a profession devoted to precedent, abstract reasoning, and judicial omniscience.

The life of the law, Holmes wrote in his epic study of the common law, had been social experience, not logic. He found it revolting to have no better reason for a particular rule than that it had been laid down in the time of Henry IV and "still more revolting if the grounds upon which it was laid down have vanished long since, and the rule simply persists from blind imitation of the past."[28] In his own distinguished lectures on *The Nature and Sources of the Law*, Gray rejected natural rights as well as John Austin's legal positivism in favor of a pragmatic interpretation of the origin of legal rules that located them in the shifting configurations of social life and the varying responses of judges to these changing circumstances. When deciding a particular dispute, Gray pointed out, a judge might be swayed by precedent, expert opinion, custom, moral principles, or legislative statutes, "but in truth all the Law is judge-made law." The rules set down by these oracles changed from one jurisdiction to another without any apparent reason apart from local convenience. For Gray, the possibilities of a unified legal "science" seemed very remote.[29]

Gray punctured the myth of legal science and exposed the potentially arbitrary power of judges. Thayer, who followed Holmes as Royall Professor at the law school, advocated strict limits upon judicial authority in the areas of social policy and constitutional litigation. At a time when, parroting the concerns of the rich, many of his colleagues looked upon the nation's judiciary as the final bulwark against radical legislation that threatened property rights, Thayer spoke out against government by judicial oligarchy. "Much which will seem unconstitutional to one man, or body of men," he told the Congress on Jurisprudence and Law Reform in 1893, "may reasonably not seem so to another. . . . the Constitution often admits of different interpretations. . . . there is often a range of choice and judgment." When passing upon the validity of any law, Thayer argued, judges should assume that the legislature contained only "competent, well-instructed, sagacious, attentive" persons who were intent upon rational, constitutional ends, not "thoughtless, reckless, incompetent" demagogues bent upon subverting the social order. Thayer's jurisprudence, although it granted broad scope to democratic, popular decision making, sprang from conservative roots. If judges continued to overturn legislative decisions on tenuous constitutional grounds, he reasoned, they endangered respect for all law-making institutions and jeopardized their own independence from political reprisals.[30]

The ideas of Gray, Holmes, and Thayer had a profound influence upon Frankfurter, who read the latter's "The Origins and Scope of the American Doctrine of Constitutional Law" so many times that he could recite whole passages from memory. Unfortunately, their concepts had little impact upon the actual behavior of the contemporary bench. As political and economic tensions increased during the 1890s, the Supreme Court of the United States escalated its offensive against new social legislation that a majority of justices deemed both unconstitutional and communistic. They sharply limited the effectiveness of the Sherman Anti-Trust Act against large, monopolistic manufacturing companies, curbed the ability of labor unions to conduct strikes, reversed one hundred years of precedent to strike down a modest federal income tax, and prevented the states from fixing utility rates without interminable judicial proceedings that favored the railroads and the power companies.[31]

During Frankfurter's last year at Harvard, moreover, the Court stunned even conservatives when it overturned a New York law that had attempted to limit the working hours of bakers to ten per day or sixty per week. The New York legislature had not adopted a reasonable health measure, Justice Peckham declared for the majority of five, but had passed instead an "unreasonable, unnecessary, and arbitrary interference" with the right of persons to make their own contracts. Holmes led the Court's four dissenters with his famous observation that the "Fourteenth Amendment does not enact Mr. Herbert Spencer's Social Statistics. . . . [A] constitution is not intended to embody a particular economic theory, whether of paternalism and the organic relation of the citizen to the State or of laissez faire. It is made for people of fundamentally differing views, and the accident of our finding certain opinions natural and familiar or novel and even shocking ought not to conclude our judgment upon the question whether statutes embodying them conflict with the Constitution of the United States."[32]

In the fetid legal atmosphere of the *Lochner* era, when many high-priced Wall Street lawyers argued against social reform, Frankfurter also absorbed the advice of Brandeis, a properous Boston attorney and progressive, who chastised his own profession in an address to Harvard students in 1905. "Instead of holding a position of independence, between the wealth and the people," he said, "prepared to curb the excesses of either, able lawyers have, to a great extent, allowed themselves to become adjuncts of great corporations and have neglected their obligation to use their powers for the protection of the people. We hear much of the 'corporation lawyer,' and far too little of the 'people's lawyer.'" Like Thayer, Brandeis feared that the legal profession's blind pursuit of corporate profits would undermine popular support for the rule of law.[33]

Filled with Harvard's customary reverence for legal institutions, Frankfurter graduated a year later, eager to join that profession but touched by many of the new ideas that battered the intellectual fortresses of the bar's self-satisfied elite. Armed with a flattering letter from Dean Ames, he secured a job with the venerable Wall Street firm of Hornblower, Byrne, Miller and Potter, where they had yet to hire a "people's lawyer," but offered him the munificent salary of $1,000 a year. Politely, he declined the advice from one junior partner who suggested that this was a fine occasion to change his name as well. The job was indeed a prize for a young lawyer, who had entered the country in steerage thirteen years earlier. He now possessed the technical abilities, the self-assurance, and some of the social polish of his new colleagues, who included Elihu Root, Jr., son of the secretary of state. And like the younger Root, also a well-honed product of the Harvard Law School, Frankfurter might have become another Wall Street counselor, skilled in the drafting of trust deeds and bond indentures. He might have become a corporation lawyer. Instead, he soon went to work for Theodore Roosevelt and Henry Lewis Stimson.[34]

CHAPTER 2

THE MAKING
OF A
REFORMER

FOR THOSE WHO NEVER felt his presence—the flashing teeth, the furious gestures, the thunderous denunciations—it is difficult to imagine Theodore Roosevelt's impact upon the men and women who rallied to his political standard in the first decades of this century. To find an emotional parallel, one would have to reach forward to Franklin Roosevelt in 1933 or John Kennedy in 1960. "What brought to Roosevelt the affection that few kings have had," wrote the journalist Mark Sullivan, "was . . . certain qualities of his temperament . . . which included his methods of combat, and the agreeable excitement that accompanied them: the din, the alarums, the thunderclaps . . . the lightning strokes of his epithets, his occasional ruthlessness of attack, his grinning acceptance of occasional setbacks, the quickness of his rally, the adroitness of his parry; the vibrations he emitted, like a master tuning-fork, setting the whole atmosphere of the country a-tingle." Roosevelt, declared Henry Adams, "showed the singular primitive quality that belongs to ultimate matter—the quality that medieval theology assigned to God—he was pure act."[1]

Part scholar, part cowboy, a politician without peer, Roosevelt inspired devotion, idealism, and a spirit of adventure in young men and women of Frankfurter's generation who wished to serve their country and their own careers on behalf of progressive Republicanism and social reform. Roosevelt, they sensed, promised to fuse politics with civic virtue and to bring to government service a fresh commitment to the public interest that might tame the unruly forces of industrial development. There hung about Roosevelt, in addition, the scent of danger and frontier bravado that appealed to the increasingly urbanized children of the Victorian middle class. "I shan't waste my time or yours defending his [Roosevelt's] many deep defects," Frankfurter wrote, "nor do I claim for him disciplined intellectual capacity. But he *is* genuinely stirred to the new social function of government, and *does* realize that it's the business of statesmanship to effect by policy what revolution effects by force." The essence of Roosevelt's leadership, he explained to Learned Hand, then a young judge on the United States District Court, "lies in his purposes and his capacity for noble expediency, stimulated by the right faith and sympathies, rather than in any formulated program."[2]

The aristocratic Roosevelt represented both the best and the worst impulses in his party and social class: the desire to harness industrial growth in the interests of social peace; the effort to utilize trained intelligence on behalf of responsible resource management; a primitive racial chauvinism; and insufferable moralism about many public issues. Deeply conservative, filled with the patrician's contempt for mere money making, Roosevelt shrewdly measured the hopes and fears coursing through an electorate eager to assert American power abroad, frightened by the prospects of class warfare, and resentful of the mysterious new influence wielded by the magnates of industry and banking. A cunning propagandist and a good administrator, he played upon these inchoate desires with the skill of a fine piano player. Adept at cajoling legislators and picking able subordinates, he pushed important social legislation through Congress and remained one step ahead of his time. A demagogue, who sometimes larded his correspondence with references to "wops," "dagos," "spicks," and "chinks," he also ratified the prejudices of his age.[3]

A student of Darwin and a believer in America's growing industrial supremacy, Roosevelt welcomed the consolidation of business enterprises into larger and larger units through mergers and holding companies. He naively equated many of these giant corporations—such as J. P. Morgan's United States Steel—with technological efficiency, the survival of the fittest, and the triumph of American virtue. At the same time, he sensed the growing frustrations of small businessmen, farmers, middle-class consumers, and industrial workers who properly blamed these new industrial titans for unfair methods of competition, inflation, monopolistic transportation rates, low wages, poor working conditions, and political corruption. Roosevelt met this conflict with a blend of "noble expediency" and statesmanship. Supported by many businessmen who desired greater predictability in their relationships with government and a reduction in cut-throat competition, he pushed through Congress new legislation that expanded the powers of the Interstate Commerce Commission over the nation's railroads, created a Bureau of Corporations to investigate business practices, and gave consumers some protection from the worst abuses of the meat packers, food processors, and drug manufacturers.

During the bitter anthracite coal strike of 1903, Roosevelt became the first president in more than a generation not to side with management against the workers. His mediation commission, although it refused to endorse the workers' demands for union recognition, awarded the miners a 10 percent pay increase. Conservative trade unions, led by John Mitchell of the United Mine workers and Samuel Gompers of the American Federation of Labor, represented for Roosevelt the inevitable growth of collectivist institutions in an economic order dominated by giant corporations. Through collective bargaining, he believed, they could provide a wholesome check on the power of the industrialists and also contain the virus of socialism by focusing their members' attention upon wages, hours, and working conditions. He regularly denounced reactionary businessmen who refused to concede the right of unions to exist as well as the militant, syndicalist-oriented Industrial Workers of the World, who preached the necessity of increasing class warfare. From Roosevelt's perspective, George F. Baer and "Big Bill" Haywood both threatened progress and order.

In addition to trade unionism and collective bargaining, Roosevelt endorsed other heresies: minimum-wage laws, an eight-hour day, workmen's compensation, and a curb on *ex parte* injunctions freely issued by federal courts against striking workers. He reserved many of his sharpest barbs for the nation's judiciary, especially for the Supreme Court, where a majority of the justices rebuffed legislative efforts to correct oppressive working conditions. In 1908, for example, a 5 – 4 majority of the Court struck down the Federal Employers' Lia-

bility Act which had been passed at Roosevelt's urging to provide
compensation for workers who sustained injuries on interstate railroads.[4] The justices also overturned labor provisions in the Erdman
Act of 1898, which Congress hoped would eliminate the use of "yellow dog" contracts on the interstate carriers.[5] And they affirmed the
conviction of the United Hatters Union (including damages of
$80,000) in a civil action brought by a Connecticut manufacturer who
refused to negotiate with the union and vowed to destroy it.[6] These
and other decisions led Roosevelt to remark that "in many American
courts property is more sacred than life," and by 1912 he endorsed the
subversive concept of reversing judicial decisions in the state courts by
means of popular referenda.[7]

Roosevelt attracted an untidy coalition: old-line Republican politicians, most of whom abhorred his programs but drifted with the tide
of popular sentiment; trigger-happy militarists, who enjoyed launch-
ing more battleships and bullying Latin Americans; conservative labor
leaders, anxious for respectability and a growing membership that only legal protection could guarantee; progressive businessmen, eager
for a respite from the competitive wars and willing to enter a new
partnership with big government; social workers like Jane Addams,
moved by his support for wages and hours legislation; members of the
gentry, who relished his occasional forays against corporate parvenus;
frightened members of the middle class, who looked to him to discipline labor and to protect them from the ravages of big business as
well; intellectuals and other professionals who believed that Roosevelt
shared their passion for ideas and their concern to raise the level of
public service by recruiting people much like themselves. Among
these followers, few became more devoted to the man or to the cause
of progressive Republicanism than Henry Stimson, United States Attorney for the Southern District of New York.

❧❧❧❧❧

Roosevelt remained at heart a romantic individualist, prone to out-
bursts of anger, impetuosity, and daring innovation. Henry Stimson,
on the contrary, was taciturn and methodical, with a good lawyer's
passion for accumulating details and navigating the well-worn grooves
of precedent. Although he used profanity and cracked an occasional
joke, Henry Stimson struck few people as excitable or humorous. But
he and Roosevelt shared a great deal, including the ability to trace
their ancestors back to the colonial period. Both men had been raised

in New York families of gentility and inherited wealth, where time had dimmed the memory of ancient plunder and enabled third generation males to become public servants rather than shopkeepers. Henry's father, Lewis Atterbury Stimson, abandoned a seat on the New York Stock Exchange in order to practice medicine. The Stimsons and the Roosevelts sent their offspring to the best schools (Phillips Academy, Groton, Yale, and Harvard) and expected them to lead useful lives, fearing God, slothfulness, and the Democratic Party. "We were so American and Presbyterian," Stimson's mother once remarked, "that we did not go to church at all on Christmas day, but I think it is a mistake."[8]

Following his reelection in 1904, Roosevelt anticipated more skirmishes with "the malefactors of great wealth," especially in the areas of railroad regulation and antitrust enforcement. In addition to applying existing federal statutes, he intended to support new legislation that would strengthen the Interstate Commerce Commission and the Bureau of Corporations. Faced with the certainty of opposition, much of it in the form of complex legal maneuvers in the federal courts, Roosevelt needed intelligent and reliable subordinates on the frontiers of law enforcement who matched in ability the representatives of the corporate bar. At the suggestion of Elihu Root, he tapped Stimson from the blue-chip Wall Street firm of Root and Clark for the New York post. His associate, Root assured the president, voted Republican, was reasonably progressive, totally incorruptible, and enjoyed the confidence of responsible businessmen.

Roosevelt offered Stimson the job on the condition that he accept a fixed salary of $10,000, live within a meager annual budget of $100,000, handle important litigation himself, and abandon the system of contingency fees, through which previous United States attorneys had earned huge incomes by prosecuting only the most lucrative violations of federal law (especially customs frauds) and continuing private practice on the side. Stimson accepted on the condition that he would have complete independence in recruiting his associates and in prosecuting offenses without political interference from Washington. Unable to hire seasoned lawyers at salaries that ranged from $750 to $1,500 per year, he secured the names of top-ranked, recent graduates from Harvard, Yale, Columbia, and Cornell. On the basis of these recommendations, he hired Frankfurter, Buckner, Thomas Thacher, Winfred Dennison, Goldthwaite Dorr, Wolcott Pitkin, and Francis Bird, but rejected the son of Admiral Alfred Mahan and the nominees of patronage-hungry congressmen. No one was acceptable, he noted, "whom I cannot implicitly rely upon to refuse a $10 bill when an Italian offers it to him, as will happen almost every day."⁹

Frankfurter joined Stimson, although he suffered an immediate cut in salary and outraged at least one member of the Hornblower firm who thought him ungrateful and rather stupid to be taking a government position in dingy quarters where the operating budget was smaller than New York City's corporation counsel. In fact, the decision was quite easy. As the only Jew in a staid, gentile office, he had looked upon the Hornblower opening initially as a challenge and a glorious opportunity, but he soon realized that progress would be slow and his legal responsibilities minimal. In addition, his fierce pride, shyness, and lingering sense of social inferiority made it diffi-cult for him to accept the necessity for fawning upon the firm's rich patrons in order to build up a clientele. Stimson's offer solved that problem. "I could," he later recalled, "practice law without having a client." In order to defend this decision, he also developed an exces-sive scorn for the conventional measurement of success at the bar. "Money," he told his future wife several years later, "is not sordid and disgusting. But it is wholly irrelevant. I mean this literally." Working for Stimson, he reflected, "I was paid seven hundred and fifty dollars a year. In money that is. I was paid much more than that in life."¹⁰

Joining Stimson's office meant greater personal independence, the likelihood of creative legal responsibilities, plus the exhilarating possi-bility of becoming connected, however tangentially, with Roosevelt himself and with the stream of reform percolating through the Repub-lican Party and his own profession. He had already joined the Citi-zen's Union, ostensibly a nonpartisan organization devoted to good government, but in reality part of the perennial Republican effort to discredit the Democratic Party and rescue New York City from the sins of Tammany Hall. In Boston, he followed with enthusiasm the career of Brandeis, who struggled against the grasping influence of traction companies and utility monopolists. In the fall of 1906, Cha-rles Evans Hughes also became governor of the Empire State. The dashing Hughes, who had exposed misfeasance and corruption in the gas and life insurance industries, entered Albany on a platform that promised additional reforms to control the state's business corpora-tions. As for Stimson, himself a product of the Harvard Law School, he demonstrated that one could simultaneously practice law, serve the public interest, and belong to the establishment. For Frankfurter, the combination was simply irresistible. The laconic Stimson — disciplined, iron willed, a model of the gentry's successful accommodation to the new forces of industrialism—became one of Frankfurter's many surrogate fathers. Like his Harvard professors—Ames, Gray, Beale—but unlike his real father, Stimson gave the impression of a man who had mastered life rather than become one of its victims.

The shift from Hornblower to Stimson temporarily reduced Frankfurter's cash income, but it did not thwart his rapid accumulation of other forms of social capital. He soon became a frequent weekend guest at Stimson's well-manicured Long Island estate, where the chief enjoyed watching his young lawyers run foot races around the grounds. Frankfurter, huffing and puffing, usually finished far back in the pack, behind the fleet-footed Thacher and the others. He cut a better figure on the dinner circuit and the dance floor, introduced Buckner to the best New York cuisine, and wooed the promising young lawyer away from the Cravath firm when Stimson needed another addition to the staff.

Stimson's assistants formed a close-knit professional family. Along with the Buckners, Frankfurter vacationed at Goldthwaite Dorr's Fire Island cottage in the summers, where they swam, sailed, and read plays, a practice that continued during the winter months in the city. "We were what was called in those days cultured people," Dorr recalled. "We cared about books and art." They cared about each other, too, and cemented these friendships through long hours of preparing briefs, sharing court appearances, writing doggerel verse, singing, drinking, and dancing. As one of the group's only bachelors, Frankfurter's many courtships attracted special notice and teasing. He was not interested in any girl, Buckner noted, but rather in the sex as a whole.[11]

Despite the camaraderie and the intoxicating feeling that one was somehow a part of Roosevelt's Square Deal, Frankfurter soon discovered that the daily affairs of the U.S. Attorney's office, even when commanded by a band of progressives, did not provide regular legal jousts with J. P. Morgan and the other titans of the business world. Swamped in the minutia of federal law enforcement, Stimson and his assistants prosecuted petty smugglers, white slavers, counterfeiters, gun runners, gambling touts, and labor factors who imported diseased immigrants.[12] In addition, they secured the conviction of James Gordon Bennett, publisher of the *New York World*, whose personal columns Judge Charles Hough once described as "a potent aid to local libertines, and a directory of local harlots."[13] Frankfurter's initial assignments took him to Ellis Island, where, because of his immigrant background, Stimson believed he was ideally suited to vindicating the majesty of American law by representing the government in *habeas corpus* actions. In his first courtroom appearance on behalf of the United States, he prosecuted Emil Sonner, a small-time hoodlum and confidence man who earned his living by impersonating Secret Service agents and bilking gullible Yorkville merchants. Although all of these transgressions violated some federal statute and no doubt offended the moral sensibilities of many progressives, they were not at the center of what Brandeis called the "continuing and ever-increasing contest between those who have and those who have not."[14]

Very soon, however, Stimson's staff began more spectacular litigation. They secured the conviction of the New York Central Railroad and its traffic manager for violating antirebating provisions of the Elkins Act, one of Roosevelt's early attempts to strengthen the regulatory powers of the Interstate Commerce Commission. The fines imposed by the court were trivial in comparison with the years of illegal rebating, but the case served as a warning to other carriers that the law would be enforced and established the important precedent that a corporation as well as its agents could be subjected to the statute's criminal penalties.[15] Stimson and his young men also jailed Charles W. Morse, the notorious ice king and shipping magnate, for his role in looting the Mercantile National Bank during the stock market panic of 1907, and they almost bagged Morse's associate, the predatory F. Augustus Heinze, with whom he had fleeced depositors in a futile effort to corner the copper market.[16]

Frankfurter found himself at the center of Stimson's most famous revenue fraud case, where they exposed the systematic and long-term corruption of the New York custom house by the powerful American Sugar Refining Company, a firm controlled by Henry Havemeyer, which had a well-deserved reputation for monopolistic behavior, extorting rebates from railroads, gouging consumers, and purchasing politicians. Like the meat packers and the Standard Oil Company, Havemeyer's firm symbolized the unchecked power of big business preying upon the American public. Through bribes, gratuities, and other favors, the refiners had easily purchased the loyalty of miserably paid government inspectors, weighters, and laborers in the custom house, who in turn reduced the companies' tariff duties by weighing unrepresentative samples and installing rigged scales.

In a long, heavily documented report to the president, Stimson and Frankfurter exposed the sordid details: "False weights according to the invoice were returned by the assistant weigher and the resulting profit divided half and half between the importer and the assistant weigher. Half of the assistant weigher's share was then paid to the foreman weigher, who in turn paid half of his share to the head weigher in charge of the district." Over a ten-year period, they estimated, one refiner received the benefit of false weights amounting to over half a million dollars. Unfortunately for the architects of the scheme, the firms kept two sets of books, one bearing the fraudulent entries and the other fixing the true weights for purposes of resale. These incriminating records, plus the confessions of frightened weighers and other company hirelings, enabled Stimson, Frankfurter, Thacher, and their accountant to secure civil and criminal convictions against most of the violators.[17]

"I believe . . . that there is great need in this matter for the 'punishment of publicity,'" Stimson wrote. The officers of the corporation, he noted, "even if not convicted criminally, should at least be pilloried before the American public as the maintainers of this debauching system of 'house money' . . . [and] a thorough ventilation of the administration of the Custom House would greatly assist the efforts of those officials who are trying now to reform it." To Stimson's credit, however, he was not content merely with "punishment of publicity" or the imprisonment of lowly government bureaucrats. In addition to filing civil suits against the refiners, which forced them to make restitution, he and Frankfurter brought criminal charges against Charles Heike, the secretary and treasurer of the American Sugar Refining Company and they would have filed a similar complaint against Havemeyer himself, but that ancient robber baron died two weeks before the case had been broken by the investigators. Heike waged a furious three-year battle in the federal courts, but Stimson and Frankfurter finally secured his conviction for conspiracy to defraud the United States after the Supreme Court rejected his plea of immunity.[18]

Not all of their battles with the corporate barons turned out as successfully as those waged against Morse and Heike. The largest quarry—railroad tycoon E. H. Harriman and investment banker Otto Kahn—escaped from Stimson's net entirely. Called to testify before the ICC, both magnates refused to answer questions concerning the joint purchase of railroad securities, the relationship between Harriman's Union Pacific Company and Kahn's bank, and allegations that they manipulated stock prices for personal gain. Stimson and his young men secured their conviction for contempt, but the Supreme Court reversed this judgment when Holmes and a bare majority of the justices drastically curtailed the ICC's subpoena powers and rescued these two helpless capitalists from the grip of governmental oppression.[19]

The protracted Heike and Harriman litigations gave Frankfurter a memorable lesson in the substance of American justice during the progressive era. He discovered that even in situations of flagrant illegality, the corporate barons had more than enough legal resources to defy the government of the United States, represented by an overworked prosecutor and his tiny staff. The behavior of Harriman's lawyers, many of them such luminaries of the New York Bar as John G. Milburn and Robert S. Lovett, repelled him, because of their "bootlicking deference" to the railroad organizer. These years with Stimson convinced Frankfurter that he probably would not become a conventional "leader" of the American Bar, especially when attorneys like Mulburn and Lovett paid such a high price in terms of independence and self respect.[20]

Arrogant corporate officials who abused their powers stirred Frankfurter's ire. So, too, did high-priced lawyers who fought Roosevelt's mild reforms. He did not display comparable outrage, however, when Stimson and Roosevelt, using their own considerable influence, made extraordinary claims of executive authority and perpetrated injustice. In 1908, for example, Joseph Pulitzer's *New York World* accused Roosevelt of negotiating an inflated Panama Canal financial settlement with the French government that enriched American investors, including some of the president's closest friends and his own brother-in-law. Smarting from these attacks, Roosevelt instructed the attorney general to bring an unprecedented charge of criminal libel against the newspaper and its publisher. Stimson's office helped to draft the indictments and manufactured the jurisdictional arguments used by the government to secure a hearing in federal court. Copies of the offending newspapers, they argued, had been mailed to military installations and the president had statutory authority to protect all harbor defense or other fortifications from "malicious mischief." Fortunately for the First Amendment, federal judges quashed the indictments and frustrated the legal ingenuity of Stimson's staff.[21]

Stimson and the president achieved greater success defending executive power against protesting black Americans and "shortsighted white sentimentalists," who deplored Roosevelt's behavior in the Brownsville affair.[22] Following a superficial military inquiry, based upon flimsy testimony from bigoted witnesses, Roosevelt blamed black soldiers for a shooting mélée in the Texas town and when none of the accused came forward to confess guilt, he discharged all 167 men with dishonor. Perhaps only two of the companies of soldiers had been actually involved, he remarked, but "all coons look alike to me."[23] When Pfc. Oliver Reid filed a breach of contract suit against the United States to recover his military pay lost as a result of the discharge, Stimson defended the president's actions in the district court.

Reid's attorneys argued that their client had been condemned and his career ruined without a finding of guilty by a military court. The Articles of War, they noted, permitted the president to discharge soldiers before their term of enlistment expired, but they did not permit a "dishonorable" discharge simply at the whim of the commander-in-chief. Judge Hough, however, followed Stimson's arguments, rejected all of these contentions, and upheld the president's authority in sweeping terms: "The exact method of this soldier's discharge and the quantum or kind of character that should be given him . . . must necessarily be left in the discretion of the executive officer having power to grant some kind of discharge." The Supreme Court, speaking through Holmes, declined even to hear Reid's appeal, because, as the justice argued, the nation's highest tribunal lacked jurisdiction in suits against the United States where the claim amounted to less than $3,000. Pfc. Reid's lost pay totalled only $122.26.[24] Like the Brownsville affair itself, the disposition of Oliver Reid's case reflected little credit upon the Roosevelt administration or the United States Attorney for the Southern District of New York, who, like the president, believed that all coons looked alike, a sentiment widely shared among other white, middle-class progressives.

During these years, Frankfurter participated in and witnessed the best and the worst of federal law enforcement: the sugar frauds, characterized by patient investigation, scrupulous prosecution, and high idealism; *Reid* v. *United States*, marred by public fear and race prejudice, where legal technicalities could not disguise a moral disaster. Frankfurter, like many other progressives, hoped to expand the powers of government against entrenched corporate abuses, but he was not always sensitive to the long-term consequences of actions that swelled the authority of the executive branch. Anxious to restore the scope of public power which had been allowed to atrophy for more than a generation, Frankfurter and his allies did not always display a keen regard for the claims of civil liberties that, more often than not, were then asserted on behalf of entrepreneurial freedom, not on behalf of other, less powerful interests.

During those years, Frankfurter forged important friendships that

lasted a lifetime. Thacher, his roommate, became solicitor general of
the United States; Buckner, a superb trial lawyer, quickly followed
Stimson's example as a government prosecutor and Wall Street power
broker. In addition to these immediate colleagues, he became close
friends with Learned Hand, the youthful, witty, and sardonic lawyer,
whom Taft elevated to the district court in 1909. But it was Stimson
who remained the principal intellectual and social force in Frankfurter's life. The older man came to rely upon the younger's quick legal
mind and sure political instincts. Frankfurter seemed to know everybody, which often proved to be a bigger resource than knowing the
correct precedent or statute. The younger man in turn looked to the
older as a model of calm intelligence and rectitude. He absorbed Stimson's essential conservatism, which worshipped orderly, measured
progress and eschewed sudden, violent change. Stimson did not lack
compassion for the poor and the disinherited, but he usually approached their problems from the standpoint of the patrician's concern for philanthropic efficiency and social peace. A similar concern
for stability led him to condemn those captains of industry and high
finance who, heedless of the larger public welfare, manipulated railroad rates, watered securities, undermined commercial banks, and ruined innocent investors in the pursuit of personal gain. Unless
checked, he believed, these manifestations of corporate irresponsibility threatened to destroy confidence in capitalism generally and would
stoke the fires of revolution.

Frankfurter also learned from Stimson that the best lawyer was
not always the one with the largest arsenal of theory, but sometimes
the one with the most relevant information. Stimson's office defeated
many of the city's ablest law firms in these years not with eloquence in
the courtroom, but with reams of facts, depositions, and statistics that
were patiently acquired through hours of labor by the staff. In many
of their cases, the sheer weight of social and economic data triumphed
over legal doctrine when they utilized a method of research made popular by muckraking journalists and also by Brandeis during his successful defense of Oregon's ten-hour law before the Supreme Court in
1908. Unlike many prosecutors, Stimson did not seek indictments until he had gathered enough evidence to convict a suspect. He did not
tolerate brutal interrogations, searches without proper judicial war-
rant, or wiretapping. Whatever his social and economic limitations,
Stimson as a prosecutor remained essentially old fashioned, decent,
and fair, a set of standards that he passed along to his young associates.[25]

In three years Frankfurter and Stimson both learned the limitations of legal action in promoting social and economic reforms. Their victories over Morse and Heike, the efforts to convict Harriman and Kahn, did little to dent the great industrial and financial empires built up over more than twenty-five years. Nor could federal law enforcement have much impact upon other areas that touched the conscience of progressives: slum housing, exploitative factory conditions, ravaged timber lands, or the huge gap in income that separated the corporate elite from the middle classes and the poor. After 1908, moreover, lethargy fell over the White House. Roosevelt's hand-picked successor, William Howard Taft, seemed well intentioned but lazy and prone to make enemies without accomplishing results—a fatal defect in a leader without blinding ambitions or a coherent program. Although he could have remained much longer, Stimson stayed in office only for a few months after Taft's inauguration in order to wind up pending litigation. He briefly returned to private practice and took Frankfurter with him, but the route to change, they believed, lay through politics and Albany.

※※※

In the summer of 1910, with Roosevelt's blessing and political influence, Henry Stimson ran on the Republican ticket for governor of New York. Frankfurter became his speech writer, sounding board, general strategist, and advance man in a campaign that served as a dress rehearsal for Roosevelt's own third-term ambitions. Heartened by Taft's political ineptitude and enraged by the latter's reversal of his own policies in many areas, Roosevelt set forth in 1910 to define their differences, to cement his grip upon the party's progressive forces, and to make known his own availability for 1912. Stimson became Roosevelt's stalking horse in New York.

At Osawatomie, Kansas in August, Roosevelt delivered his famous New Nationalism address, a blend of Alexander Hamilton's call for a strong, central government and Horatio Alger's paeans to individual success and initiative. He alarmed conservatives by calling for comprehensive regulation of all interstate corporations, including supervision of their capitalization; graduated taxes on personal income and inheritances; minimum wage and maximum hours legislation; workmen's compensation; and scientific management of the nation's natural resources. "The New Nationalism," he declared, "puts the national need before sectional or personal advantage. . . . This New

Nationalism regards the executive power as the steward of the public welfare." He singled out the judiciary for sharp attack because, he argued, they placed property above human welfare. "I am for men," he concluded, "and not for property."[26]

Stimson and Frankfurter shared Roosevelt's public philosophy, especially with respect to critical issues of corporate regulation and executive power. Three years of litigation had convinced them that individual antitrust suits provided dubious results in terms of preventing unfair methods of competition, stock watering, and the abuses of management. Corporate mergers, they believed, sometimes promoted greater efficiency, but also reduced the effectiveness of the marketplace as a safeguard for consumers. The answer to this dilemma lay in more vigorous regulation by the national government through an administrative tribunal. Stimson believed in federal incorporation of all interstate firms, legislative clarification of the Sherman Act's prohibition against "restraint of trade" in order to assist honest businessmen who wished to observe the law, and a federal regulatory commission with authority to approve or veto proposed mergers.[27]

Sharing Roosevelt's basic agenda of reforms, Stimson and Frankfurter also inherited many of the colonel's political problems as well: a state party structure that was bitterly divided among conservative regulars, Taftites, and Roosevelt supporters; a resurgence of popular support for the Democratic Party; and the fact that many New Yorkers regarded Stimson as a tool of the former president, who would abjectly do the Rough Rider's bidding in Albany. As one campaign ditty expressed it:

> If Stimson came from Africa
> If he was a Zulu Chief
> If he wore a feather in his hair
> And dressed in a fig leaf
> We'd vote for Henry just the same
> And carry out the plan
> Because he's Roosevelt's man.[28]

Stimson and Frankfurter accepted the probability of defeat soon after the party's statewide convention, when rank-and-file politicians and Taft's followers indicated little enthusiasm for Roosevelt's man. They continued the race, however, consoled by the traditional illusion of all reformers that their efforts would educate the public and keep the levers of power temporarily beyond the grasp of corrupt opponents. On balance, Roosevelt's gigantic ego proved to be a more formidable opponent than Stimson's rival, John A. Dix, a dull-witted paper manufacturer. Roosevelt stumped the entire state for his friend and candidate, but he used these occasions to call attention to his own programs and achievements. The self-praise reached the point where New York newspapers ran a daily tally of the colonel's use of the first person singular. When Frankfurter politely called Roosevelt's attention to the box score, he promised to mention Stimson's name more frequently in the final days of the campaign, but the damage had already been done.[29]

Frankfurter never again undertook the task of actually running the details of a major political campaign. In the future, he would do less leg work and more intellectual labor behind the scenes, but a different blend would not have salvaged Stimson's candidacy. With Frankfurter, Bird, and Joseph Cotton in charge, their effort did not lack brains, polish, enthusiasm, or money. Stimson's speeches, many of them written by Frankfurter, were packed with information, well delivered, and covered the usual range of state issues, including agriculture, utility regulation, water power, taxation, and urban housing. Far from gregarious, Stimson did his best to shed the image of a cold, machinelike lawyer from the big city. He traveled across the state in an automobile to meet the voters directly, but his impressive vehicle, named "Twilight," probably intensified the skepticism of many rural voters who regarded him as an aloof, high-toned New Yorker, remote from their problems and concerns.

On election day, Stimson lost by about 65,000 votes out of more than one million cast, less because of his own defects or those of his advisers than because of the growing divisions within the Republican Party, the spectre of Roosevelt pulling wires behind the curtain, and a nationwide resurgence of the Democratic Party that put Woodrow Wilson into the governor's chair in New Jersey and a Democratic majority in Congress for the first time in sixteen years. During his eight years in the White House, Teddy Roosevelt had unleashed a national progressive crusade, but now it rushed in a thousand new directions, tossed up fresh leadership, and threatened to engulf the colonel and his own party as well.

Adrift on a turbulent political sea with a mutinous crew, the harried Taft took on additional ballast. Six months after the 1910 debacle, he asked Stimson to become secretary of war, an appointment that he hoped would bring administrative competence, appease the party's progressive wing, and perhaps confound his potential enemies. Stimson joined the administration, after telling the president that he remained loyal to Roosevelt's ideas and informing Roosevelt that he would probably support Taft for reelection. Stimson quickly offered Frankfurter the position of legal adviser in the department's Bureau of Insular Affairs, with formal jurisdiction over legal issues that touched the nation's overseas possessions and territories, but with an informal understanding that he would also become the secretary's roving assistant and chief trouble shooter on all issues. Once again faced with the unpleasant alternative of private practice, Frankfurter accepted. After all, the salary was larger than had first been offered him in New York, and he sensed as others did that Washington had now become the center stage of the nation's unfolding political struggle.

CHAPTER 3

EMPIRE, ARMAGEDDON, AND HARVARD

NOT YET THIRTY, Frankfurter entered Washington in 1911 with the aplomb of a sophisticated political veteran. "I'm getting, I feel, an increasing sense of true worths," he told Buckner shortly after arriving. "I'm increasingly proof against counterfeits. More than ever have I a sense of the potentialities of places, of the call for accomplishment of office and less and less a hankering for the office, or a foolish awe for its holder. There is less of the blasé than ever in me but also less ambition for station or for power."[1] This piece of self-analysis was both true and false. He had developed an uncanny ability to take the measure of other people's strengths and weaknesses and to turn these perceptions to his own advantage through exhortation, flattery, and intimidation. He possessed as well a superb grasp of the mechanics of power and a desire to exercise it. As one sign of his growing self-confidence, he began to keep a diary that reflected both a shrewd historical sense and some intimation, no doubt, of his future immortality.

Frankfurter filled his diary with acute, humorous, and pungent observations on persons and events in the Taft administration, provided some analysis of major policy conflicts, and passed along an endless stream of gossip, the basic lubricant of politics. After lunching with Brandeis, he noted, for example, that the famous Boston reformer possessed Lincoln's fundamental sympathies, but "I wish he had his patience, his magnanimity, his humor." Taft displayed "the optimism of the near-sighted," while his attorney general, George Wickersham, had "a vivid, fresh, agile, prehensile mind . . . pretty much as superficial as my own." Major General Clarence Edwards, the chief of the Bureau of Insular Affairs, seemed to be "an inordinate, childishly conceited person . . . and totally ignorant of the big forces that are at work in the country."[2] As Frankfurter grew older, the gay detachment and self-mockery vanished from the diary and he poured into it more of the frustrations, recriminations, and self-pity generated by years of political conflict in Washington. Even with these flaws, it might have become one of the great historical documents of the twentieth century had he found the time to maintain the entries regularly, but even in 1911, diary writing remained among the lowest of his priorities. "Felix is getting on here with his usual speed," his roommate Winfred Denison reported to Emma. "The only trouble with him is that he wants to sit up all night and sleep all day. . . . Why in the world did you fail to teach him that black air means night and time to sleep and that white air means day and time to be awake?"[3]

Despite Frankfurter's boundless energy, Washington in 1911 remained an indolent Southern village with little automobile traffic where the Taft administration drifted slowly toward disaster. In three years, the president had managed to antagonize all of the major factions within his own party. Taft had strengthened the powers of the ICC and placed Charles Evans Hughes on the Supreme Court, but liberal Republicans still regarded him as a reactionary who had become a coward during the struggle to unseat the autocratic speaker of the House, "Uncle Joe" Cannon. Taft, moreover, had defended Richard Ballinger against the saintly Pinchot and attempted to purge the party's progressives in the 1910 primary elections. Powerful farm groups resented Taft's tariff policies. Even the titans of industry and banking, heavy contributors to his 1908 campaign, became unnerved by the president's ringing endorsement of the antitrust laws. Pilloried by opponents on the left and the right, pampered by sycophantic advisers, trapped by his wife's illness and his own lassitude, Taft at times awaited the end with stoicism, but also thrashed around like a proud, cornered animal. "He is indeed," Frankfurter wrote in his diary, "the tragedy of opportunities of greatness unrealized."[4] The president's speeches, he complained to Buckner, "left me with a moral and mental bellyache. He seems now bent on attaining greatness through scolding and invoking the horrific dread of a French Revolution."[5] Bored by his job and resenting Roosevelt more each day, Taft never rose above the level of mediocrity described by Justice Holmes: "I doubt if he can go higher than the first rate second rate."[6]

The War Department that Frankfurter entered epitomized the regime's difficulties, although the problems that afflicted this particular executive department had been accumulated over a generation and had escaped from even Roosevelt's reform impulses. Charged with manifold tasks—raising and training the Army, undertaking public works, and running the country's new colonial empire—the War Department remained in fact a loose collection of independent fiefdoms, bereft of centralized direction. Cabinet secretaries came and left with the regularity of presidential elections, while the bureau chiefs, closely tied to key committees in the Congress, endured and prospered within their separate bailiwicks. The results were both ludicrous and tragic. The Army, for example, consisted of roughly 75,000 men, without reserves, adequate equipment, common purpose, discipline, or tactics, scattered at forty-nine posts in twenty-four states and territories. No American general had ever commanded a unit larger than a regiment in decades. Reluctantly, Congress had created the position of chief of staff in order to provide greater strategic coordination, but neither the present occupant of that post, General Leonard Wood, nor the secretary of war had been able to subdue the Congress or the bureau chiefs led by Major General Fred Ainsworth, custodian of records and pensions since the Cleveland administration. The United States Army was not a modern fighting force, but a ramshackle mechanism for pumping federal money into local economies and congressional districts.[7]

A similar lack of vision characterized the department's public works effort. The Army Corps of Engineers had broad jurisdiction over the nation's navigable streams and rivers, but it had narrowed this writ to include only flood control, the construction of endless levees, and harbor improvements—all conducted on a pork-barrel principle that dispersed money widely throughout many states and made systematic resource management nearly impossible. On the frontiers of empire in the Philippines, Puerto Rico, Panama, and Cuba, where Americans had taken up the white man's burden, isolated departmental bureaucrats promoted capitalism and social order without much direction from Washington or a great deal of concern for the welfare of their native subjects. With its decentralized structure of authority, glaring inefficiency, petty corruption, and political intrigue, the War Department seemed ripe for a large dose of progressive moralism and management provided by Frankfurter and Stimson.

Frankfurter concentrated his energies upon insular affairs and water power issues, while the secretary attempted to bring a measure of order to the Army's untidy affairs. With lukewarm support from the president, Stimson put forth an ambitious program of military reforms that included short-term enlistments, the creation of a reserve force, consolidation of the domestic posts, and increased authority for the chief of staff. These proposals for greater centralization encountered stiff resistance from congressmen and General Ainsworth and when the latter became embroiled with General Wood in a struggle over custody of the muster rolls, Stimson presented this wily bureaucratic opponent with the choice of a court martial or resignation. Despite Taft's irresolution, Ainsworth stepped down. "You can little realize what clear-thinking courage H.L.S. exhibited in this," Frankfurter told Buckner after the dust had settled. "Through long years of immunity, supported by a powerful Congressional backing, the native brusqueness and intolerant force of Ainsworth . . . acquired an over-powering dominance that no one dreamt of challenging. . . . The whole situation gives one a new sense of worth and stimulus of the rectitude, the rare courage of Stimson."[8]

In the Ainsworth affair, Stimson and Frankfurter struck a blow for civilian direction of the military bureaucracy, but the defeat of the General proved to be a pyrrhic victory. Ainsworth's friends in the Congress retaliated by curtailing Stimson's reform program, and they nearly succeeded in driving the fatuous Wood from office as well. The chief of staff, whom Frankfurter described as an "intensely ambitious, aggrandizing man," also proved to be an incompetent leader. On the whole, Stimson's campaign to centralize strategic planning and improve the Army's military preparedness did not prove very successful, a fact born out by the chaos that plagued American military efforts during the early months of World War I.[9]

Frankfurter came to Washington at the high tide of diplomacy by the big stick and the dollar. He seldom questioned the task of the Bureau of Insular Affairs or the morality of the new American empire that stretched from the Caribbean into Asia. He found his immediate superior, Major General Edwards, to be "extremely superficial," deplored the narrow political vision of imperial bureaucrats, but believed in the white man's burden with a greater emphasis upon efficiency. Returning from an inspection tour of Cuba in 1912, he informed Buckner that military intervention by the United States would probably decline in the future because local leaders had been made aware of America's determination to enforce the Platt Amendment. "If we go down there again," he noted, "we are likely not to leave until the whole governmental framework is overhauled, so that we can leave behind us a firm foundation of stability." Should the Cubans again prove rebellious, he hoped Stimson would pick Buckner for the job of restoring order. "I can conceive of few things that would appeal more strongly to your professional appetite," he concluded, "your sense of service, and sheer good fun."[10] On the other hand, he showed some awareness of America's cultural chauvinism by noting that the United States had been foolish to attempt a complete revision of the Cuban legal system, because "I think the tendency to impose bodily our own codes and laws upon our Latin relations is only one of the manifestations of Anglo-Saxon insularity and the untested assumption of superiority."[11]

Certain aspects of the military command structure appealed to Frankfurter's passion for order, efficiency, and quick, decisive action. He remained in awe of American efforts in the Panama Canal Zone and of its resident autocrat, General George W. Goethals, who ran his local empire through executive orders of the president without resorting to Congress for what Frankfurter called "procrustean legislation." By means of presidential fiat, Goethals had been able to adopt many progressive reforms, including workmen's compensation. That these arrangements contained the seeds of potential abuse did not disturb the bureau's young legal officer. "The need is for a definite centralized government," he wrote, "subordinating everything to running the Canal—the problem is the management of the great public work not the government of a republic."[12] In his opinion, there was no fundamental conflict between vigorous, centralized authority and democratic government, either in the United States or the colonies. The largest hope for Puerto Rico, he wrote in 1911, "lies in the increasing participation of its natives in the administration of their affairs. . . . Wherever possible, government should come from themselves instead of being handed down to them." Yet he disliked the local Puerto Rican practice of electing all of the marshals and secretaries in the municipal courts. "The assumption that all our officers ought to be elective is one of the greatest fallacies, as it is one of the worst banes of our democracy," he wrote, echoing the views of Roosevelt. "The tendency in this country, and especially in states where the democratic movement is the strongest, is to diminish the number of elective officers and centralize responsibility upon a few important officials directly elected by the people."[13]

He shared, of course, Roosevelt's nationalism and belief that only a powerful government could successfully resist the forces of private greed and social disintegration. As the bureau's chief legal representative, he became a resourceful defender of executive authority and the prerogatives of imperial administration. In his first appearance before the Supreme Court of the United States, for example, he successfully defended the government of Puerto Rico in a suit brought by disgruntled land owners attempting to recover rents and profits on old property claims. In order to provide a governmental framework for the former Spanish colony, Congress had, in 1900, adopted the Organic Act, which granted the island a qualified independence, including the traditional power to sue and be sued. Although the island and its government remained wholly at the mercy of American economic and military power, Frankfurter argued that Puerto Rico was in fact completely sovereign and could not therefore be sued without its own consent. The provisions of the Organic Act, he told the justices, only confirmed Puerto Rico's sovereignty and recognized a limited liability to be sued in cases where consent had been given by the sovereign. Speaking through the tortured prose of Chief Justice Edward White, the justices agreed with Frankfurter's dubious interpretation of the Organic Act and noted that allowing the suits to proceed would "denature the government created by the . . . act." This legal proposition must have seemed rather disingenuous to Puerto Rican nationalists.[14]

Frankfurter scored another notable triumph for the empire by defending W. Cameron Forbes, the grandson of Ralph Waldo Emerson and the Governor General of the Philippines, against charges that he had illegally detained and deported resident Chinese aliens from the islands. Emerson "passed through him without stopping," Frankfurter noted of Forbes, but before the Supreme Court he claimed that the governor general possessed inherent executive authority to deport aliens, even though no act of Congress, presidential order, or local Philippine statute authorized these summary proceedings. Holmes and the other justices upheld his sweeping claims as "incident of the self-determination, however limited, given by the United States." Holmes also noted approvingly that the local Philippine legislature had ratified the deportations *after* they took place and also prohibited local courts from interfering with the governor general's repressive tactics.[15]

On behalf of Cameron Forbes and the empire, Frankfurter became a faithful defender of the general strategy promoted by the secretary of war, who noted on one occasion that the United States should not be "overafraid of paternalism" when seeking to "encourage good business methods and the development of merchandising and production." Because they were new to the business of empire, Stimson believed, the Americans had a "tremendous amount to learn, for instance from the Germans" in this area of business-government cooperation abroad.[16] At the same time, a large measure of the progressives' concern for extending democracy and popular government filtered into Frankfurter's own thinking about the empire, especially where participation could be harmonized with strong executive leadership. He believed, for instance, that the Puerto Ricans should be granted American citizenship and more autonomy in running their own affairs, but not statehood, because "I don't believe you could muster a corporal's guard in favor of it here."[17]

Before leaving the War Department, moreover, Frankfurter drafted a proposal for expanded Filipino participation in the island's government, including majority control in both the legislature and the executive council, where the appointment of Americans had prevailed in the past. He also warned the department about the dangers of fostering a local Filipino oligarchy under American supervision. "In the name of self-government," he wrote, "we cannot allow government to fall into the hands of a small, masterful, highly-educated, wealth minority, who have on the whole, but little community of interest and little sympathy with the great masses who are slowly emerging out of centuries-old conditions of indifference and peonage."[18]

By the end of his years in the War Department, Frankfurter's maturing views on the Philippines resembled the liberal attutide of his close friend Denison, who joined the governor general's staff as secretary of the interior for the Philippines. The Americans had accomplished much good in the islands, Denison noted, but "it was done, as might have been expected, in a Hand-me-down way. Benevolent, but patronizing, like a first-class Roman pro-counsul." He resented the "unsympathetic and autocratic point of view" of the resident Americans toward the Filipinos and vowed to bring about a larger measure of native participation in the formation of local policy. "It's the same old question that split the Republican Party, " he told Frankfurter, "and makes you and me Bull Moosers . . . the struggle . . . between those who believe in government coming from the top down and those who believe in government coming from the bottom up."[19] Frankfurter deplored the fact that Wilson and the Democrats failed to implement their promise of early independence for the islands, but the Jones Act of 1916 granted to the Filipinos a larger share in their nation's government along the lines outlined earlier by Frankfurter. Even then, however, the prospects of avoiding the domination by a local oligarchy seemed remote.[20]

⫸⫸⫸⫸

Even more than the Philippines, the social miseries of Puerto Rico attracted Frankfurter's attention from the beginning of his tenure in the bureau, because that colonial outpost of a million inhabitants reflected the progressive struggle between entrenched economic privilege and grinding poverty. In the wake of America's military triumph over Spain, Yankee entrepreneurs and colonial managers had replaced Hispanic feudalism with the more dynamic exploitation of modern capitalism. Backed with the financial resources of large American corporations, a tiny clique of Spanish and American landowners seized control of the best sugar-growing properties, brought ruin to the small farmers, and displaced much of the rural population with machinery on the large plantations.

The human consequences of America's "economic development" program were shocking: high unemployment, especially during slack months after the sugar harvest; an illiteracy rate that approached 80 percent of the adult population; growing urban slums in San Juan, where desperate people from the countryside came in search of work. One BIA report summarized the grim reality of Puerto Rico in 1917: the annual sugar crop had increased from 43,000 tons in 1898 to 483,500 tons two decades later; the price of sugar had never been higher on world markets, and "yet the majority of the Puerto Ricans are today not only starving but are living in filth and wretchedness. Each year since the American occupation fewer Puero Ricans own farms or live on them, and rapidly all the best lands are being controlled by the large sugar centrals."[21]

In 1911, this island empire of unbridled rapaciousness faced the growing militancy of rural laborers and the desire of the American governor, George Colton, to counter social unrest with a program of economic diversification and educational reforms. Colton, backed by a small faction of enlightened businessmen, hoped to solve the island's mounting unemployment problems by encouraging industrial development and service occupations, attracting new foreign investments, and transforming the educational system. He wished to place greater emphasis upon vocational training, but here he met the opposition of his own secretary of education, E. G. Dexter, who believed in a classical, liberal arts curriculum that catered to the needs of the island's tiny social elite. Colton's reform programs also faced the hostility of a planter oligarchy that wished to maintain a large pool of cheap, rural laborers, hated taxation, and ran the country's school system through their influence in the local legislature. The governor's efforts encountered too the suspicions of Puerto Rican schoolteachers, many of them socialists, who distrusted their Yankee overlords and who believed that their nation's problems could be solved best through strikes, political agitation, and cultural nationalism.[22]

Trapped in a crossfire of local greed, indifference, and social tension, Colton turned to the War Department for assistance, and Stimson delegated the explosive problem to Frankfurter, who immediately sought the advice of A. Lincoln Filene, the progressive reformer and Boston department store tycoon. Frankfurter knew that Filene served on the executive board of the Boston Vocational Bureau, a corporate-sponsored research organization headed by Meyer Bloomfield which had pioneered in the development of vocational guidance and training for the city's public schools. Although organized labor viewed these efforts with considerable suspicion as another capitalist plot to steal the workers' skills and dilute the strength of trade unions, Bloomfield's agency enjoyed wide support in Massachusetts among businessmen and professionals who saw the programs as one way to raise the industrial skills and opportunities of the urban poor. Frankfurter wanted Bloomfield to do for Puerto Rico what he had done for Boston: formulate "a permanent and farsighted educational policy" that would focus upon the needs of the island's working class. "Inasmuch as a radical change in educational theory is contemplated," Frankfurter boldly informed General Edwards, "the time is opportune to have an expert study made into the conditions prevailing. . . . In other words, the idea is to get detailed facts as a sure basis of effective action."[23]

Once Bloomfield accepted the task, Frankfurter oiled the administrative machinery. With the assistance of Edwards and Colton, he even convinced Dexter to invite the Bostonians to the island, although he knew that they would probably write a report critical of the existing regime. He took great delight in this small bureaucratic triumph.

Dexter's "feelings and dignity will thus be preserved," he wrote, "and I feel the better that the public object was accomplished without private hurt of a very faithful official. It seems to me in most cases some thoughts of others and a little capacity for adjustment will go far to . . . further reforms [by] preventing friction and even enlisting the support or at least avoiding opposition of possible victims of reform." Both Stimson and he had already decided that Dexter would have to be replaced in order "to promote a change in the method of education and of increasing the amount of industrial education."[24]

Frankfurter expected more from Bloomfield than a dry inventory of educational problems. He hoped to use the educational report as a Trojan horse for the investigation of other social and economic problems on the island. "I think there is a real chance of doing a big piece of work," he told Filene. He urged Bloomfield to paint his report on a broad canvas: "I hope you will have an opportunity to scratch the surface into the general economic and industrial conditions. . . . This, of course, involves an investigation into the labor situation, the socially advisable system of taxation . . . and the general industrial and economic problems that will suggest themselves."[25] Bloomfield did not disappoint him. Within three months, he and A. L. Ratner, Assistant Superintendent of the Boston public schools, had compiled a devastating analysis of conditions in Puerto Rico.

Echoing old complaints, including those from Dexter, Ratner deplored the stingy appropriations made by the local legislature to the island's educational system that resulted, for example, in the rental of all school buildings, even in the city of San Juan, where these structures remained "dark, dingy, and shocking." The vast majority of teachers, Ratner observed, seemed very dedicated, but most of them had graduated from the normal department of the University of Puerto Rico, where only a ninth-grade diploma gained admission. Only ten agricultural instructors had been hired for the entire island and what vocational training existed struck him as generally useless. Students made baskets and displayed them at the insular fair in San Juan, but these objects were "but of little use either in the home or as a commercial product." In the case of woodworking, the students made tiny machetes, models of ancient ploughs, and miniature chairs that appealed to tourists, but none of them had much practical function. In order to correct this deplorable situation, Ratner urged the addition of at least ten new industrial schools, where students could receive competent instruction in carpentry, printing, plumbing, electrical work, pattern drafting, dress making, and millinery.[26]

The Puerto Rican schools attempted to make good citizens, Bloomfield wrote, but they had failed to produce "homemakers, producers, skilled workers, self-reliant, and efficient breadwinners." The children of the more prosperous classes in the cities thrived on a curriculum devoted to academic subjects that prepared them for elite careers in commerce and the professions, but little effort had been made to train other, poor children for skilled trades. "The children in the rural districts," Bloomfield said, "might well forego some of the book-learning and classroom instruction and learn road building, planting, yard ornamentation, and simple industrial work of both educational and marketable value." In addition to more vocational courses, the schools should instill in the population modern habits of business management in order "to encourage children how to keep track of the economic aspects of their work."[27]

Bloomfield also singled out for criticism the island's one-crop economy and polarized class structure that prevented the development of intermediate and competing social interests. The basic aim of education, he suggested, "must be to develop that backbone of any population—an elevated and progressive working class, self-supporting, independent, adventurous, and ambitious." Vocational education and economic diversification could promote social stability, but Bloomfield feared a future of rising social violence owing to poor housing, low wages, chronic inflation, and the absence of any organized method for airing grievances among the workers. "The patent fact in Puerto Rico," he concluded, "is the rapid and enormous wealth of a few, the wretched poverty of the many, and the relatively insignificant return made by large capital to the public welfare. . . . Without any stretch of the imagination one can see developing class hatred and a menacing unrest."[28]

Like many other grandiose plans of the progressive era, Frankfurter's "big piece of work" in Puerto Rican education proved to be more rhetoric than substance. Initially, he attempted to secure a post for Bloomfield as treasurer of the insular government, but this scheme had to be aborted when it turned out that the educational reformer had "little equipment or experience for a position involving financial or business judgment."[29] Undaunted, Frankfurter offered Bloomfield the education position vacated by Dexter but the Boston reformer declined this invitation to put his ideas into action. Frankfurter himself soon became preoccupied with a host of other bureau problems—"stopping rat holes or most often undoing the rat's mischief"—and with the presidential campaign of 1912. Like Stimson and Governor

Colton, he too underestimated the hostility of groups in Puerto Rico, especially the wealthy planters who dominated educational finances and who were not in the least interested in Bloomfield's program to create "an elevated and progressive working class, self-supporting, independent, adventurous, and ambitious."

In retrospect, the Frankfurter-Bloomfield educational strategy for the island contained many defects. Their emphasis upon vocational education, a staple preoccupation of many progressive era reformers, tended to reinforce existing class distinctions, whatever the disclaimer of educational prophets such as Bloomfield and John Dewey. Their strategy did anticipate a distant Puerto Rican future, when the one-crop sugar monopoly had been broken and the economy diversified through the development of light manufacturing and tourism. Their program represented a more sophisticated alternative to the crude imperialism of the time, one appropriate to the needs of a complex, urbanized economy, but Puerto Rico did not make this transition until after World War II. Despite these inherent weaknesses, the Frankfurter-Bloomfield perspective represented a vast improvement upon the orthodoxies of the war department's imperial managers.

When, true to Bloomfield's predictions, sugar workers, teachers, and students went on strike throughout the island in 1915, the new governor could only recommend that he receive discretionary power to call upon Army troops to quell the disorders. As for educational reforms, the island's military commander suggested that the basic goal should be the eradication of socialism and other radical ideas through "an increase in the number of English teachers in the schools, the retention of an American at the head of the Insular School system and the abolition of the use of the Spanish language whenever possible."[30] In contrast to these dreary recommendations, Frankfurter had advanced a noble program.

<hr />

As Stimson's steady companion and principal adviser on domestic issues, Frankfurter caught regular glimpses of Taft's executive abilities. What he saw, especially of the president's casual approach to insular affairs, confirmed his impression that the rotund, jovial Ohioan represented the nadir of progressive efforts and a positive obstacle to further reforms. When, for example, he and Stimson arrived one morning at the White House to present their program for new labor regulations in the Panama Canal Zone, Taft turned up an hour late for the meeting and could not recall the reasons for holding it. They had to use all of their persuasion to convince the president that the federal government should lease rather than sell valuable water-power sites to private companies, charge them for the privilege of generating electricity on the public lands, and recapture the lease when the companies failed to carry out their contract to develop the property.[31] "Stimson," he noted in his diary, "says Taft is an enigma to him—he doesn't seem to be able to get up drive, doesn't think thoroughly and is stubborn. . . . Taft doesn't care, he has no abiding convictions about the things that are the vital issues of the day."[32] Taft's vaunted judicial mindedness and machinelike mentality, he told Buckner, seemed to be largely myths invented by the president's supporters: "He has all of Hamlet's indecision, but not a particle of his deep meditation, his painful truth-searching. Inertia, not intellect, has him in the grip."[33]

As Taft's stock plummeted, Frankfurter looked to Roosevelt to salvage the progressive cause. He wished that he had been in Washington "while the surging, pervasive, dynamic personality of T.R. gave impetus and tone and passion to the government, and when he gathered about him the stout loyal band of able men."[34] This desire to be a part of Roosevelt's "stout loyal band of able men" was powerfully reinforced by his living arrangements in the capitol and by his expanding network of friendships that centered around the brilliant Robert Grosvenor Valentine, then nearly forty, a graduate of Harvard, who had taught Coleridge to MIT students, sold bonds on Wall Street, and become a leading proponent of scientific management and industrial democracy after studying with Frederick W. Taylor. But unlike Taylor, who deplored labor unions, the aristocratic Valentine believed that workers could play a positive role in advancing industrial efficiency if they were given an opportunity to participate more fully in the production decisions that shaped their lives. Fatally attracted to New England Brahmins, Frankfurter could not resist Valentine.

Destined to become even more famous as an industrial relations adviser, Valentine had been appointed Commissioner of Indian Affairs by Taft, four years after joining the Federal Indian Service in 1905. He and the president quarreled constantly, however, over national Indian policies, especially over Taft's insistence that schoolteachers wear clerical garb on the reservations. Along with Pinchot and other Roosevelt loyalists, Valentine became a center of sedition within the administration, and many of the rebels gathered at his home on Nineteenth Street, where Frankfurter and Denison became permanent residents. They dubbed it "the House of Truth" and in-

vited other young men to join them: Loring Christie, a Canadian, one
of Denison's pals from the Justice Department, plus another genuine
aristocrat, Lord Eustace Percy, seventh son of the seventh duke of
Northumberland, then on the staff of the British ambassador.[35]

"The House of Truth" bubbled with heated political debates and
endless discussions about the law, art, journalism, European diplomacy, and the relative merits of socialism versus liberalism. Its good
wine, pretty girls, and intense conversations attracted an eclectic band
of politicians, bureaucrats, judges, writers, and philosophers, many of
them already celebrated in their fields and those who aspired to be so.
Gutzon Borglum, the sculptor, came and drew a sketch of his proposed monument in the Black Hills, much to the delight of Justice and
Mrs. Oliver Wendell Holmes. Arthur Willert, the Washington corres-
pondent for the London *Times*, became a regular dinner guest, in addition to lawyers such as Stanley King, the future president of Amherst
College, and the courtly John Lord O'Brian. They also entertained
Justice Horace Lurton, who politely told Frankfurter that he mixed
drinks better than he argued cases. From New York, Learned Hand
sent his friend, Herbert Croly, an architect turned political theorist,
whose 1909 book, *The Promise of American Life*, formed the basis of
Roosevelt's New Nationalism and raised the ideals of many young
men and women with its blistering attack upon America's aimless
commercialism. With Croly came a younger man, Walter Lippmann,
a Harvard graduate with a gifted pen, who had absorbed both Marx
and Freud, and who was then writing two of the most remarkable
books of the era — *Preface to Politics* and *Drift and Mastery* — the latter a
ringing affirmation of Roosevelt's policies and a plea for expanding the
role of experts in American society.

Brandeis also came regularly. The Jewish Brahmin, then at the
peak of his career as a reformer, had begun to assume truly heroic
stature in Frankfurter's eyes. He had recently defended Louis Glavis
and Pinchot in their conflict with Taft and Richard Ballinger over
Alaskan coal lands, and this effort had been so brilliant that he made
the President of the United States appear to be either a liar or an
incompetent administrator who could not manage the business of his
own administration. A foe of monopoly and of the great Wall Street
banking syndicates, Brandeis then also waged a titanic battle with
Charles S. Mellen, a satellite of the Morgans, who conceived it to be
his duty to combine all of New England's railroad lines into a single
transportation company. Brandeis believed Mellen to be a tyrant and
a fool — perceptions soon verified by the ICC and several bankruptcy
courts.[36]

Most of the permanent residents and guests at "the House of Truth" shared a similar contempt for Taft and, with the exception of Brandeis, a deep conviction that only Roosevelt and the New Nationalism could save the nation from industrial despotism or class warfare. Brandeis remained deeply skeptical of Roosevelt's motives and hostile to his program of economic and governmental centralization. He attempted to wean Frankfurter away from his infatuation with the colonel's ideas. "Successes are rarely one man's work, or the work of a number of men consciously cooperating," he lectured Frankfurter. "I should have little faith, therefore, in a small group of men evolving a social system or important elements of such a system. We must rely upon all America (and the rest of the world) for our social inventions and discoveries."[37] Frankfurter, then a devoted New Nationalist, remained unconvinced, but both he and Brandeis sensed that 1912 would be a turning point in the nation's political life and that the central issue of the presidential campaign would be the future relationship between the giant corporations and the federal government.

That relationship had been thrown into appalling confusion by two decisions of the Supreme Court in 1911, when the justices upheld the convictions of the American Tobacco Company and Standard Oil Company for restraining trade and attempting to create monopolies banned by the Sherman Act. Although the Court sustained the government's indictment of the two corporate behemoths, a majority of the justices took the occasion to overrule more than a decade of precedent by declaring that the antitrust law prohibited only "unreasonable" restraints of trade and that they would determine the scope of wrongdoing in the future on a case-by-case basis.[38] This decision infuriated many progressives, who saw the new "rule of reason" as a gaping judicial loophole through which the Court would allow many corporations to escape just retribution for their economic sins. In addition, the judicial remedy adopted by the Court in these two cases required the dissolution of parent holding companies, but permitted large stockholders to retain indirect control of the smaller corporate units.

Frankfurter and Stimson attempted to convince Taft that the Court's posture required additional clarifying legislation and perhaps the creation of a new federal regulatory agency to assist the Justice Department's campaign against monopolies, but the president flatly rejected this advice. Instead, Taft praised the Court's decision, maintained that the judicial branch alone should have jurisdiction over questions that touched property rights, and suggested that all criticism of the Court bordered upon communist propaganda. Despite

Taft's hostility, a group of progressive Republicans, led by Senator La Follette, introduced new legislation to revise the antitrust law by carefully defining many "unreasonable" trade practices. La Follette's bill, which had been crafted by Brandeis, also permitted injured parties to recover civil damages on the basis of the government's evidence and outlawed the type of interlocking stock ownership approved by the Court in its recent decisions. Brandeis's measure resembled the plan put before Taft by Stimson and Frankfurter, except that they also suggested the creation of a regulatory commission modeled after the ICC. Taft, however, rejected any alterations in antitrust enforcement, a position that struck Frankfurter as both administratively unwise and politically stupid.[39]

"Here he [Taft] floats around the country talking on the industrial situation," he wrote, "without having the thing at all thought out, without having formulated a definite policy."[40] In fact, Taft's position on corporate regulation grew more precise and rigid as the opposition intensified from both left-wing progressives and the business community. He and Wickersham began to apply the law with a vengeance by indicting the United States Steel Corporation and they added allegations that Roosevelt himself had furthered the company's monopolistic grip on the industry.[41] With that indictment, Roosevelt's Bull Moose revolt began in earnest, gathered momentum once he defeated Taft in several primary elections, and once the president, controlling the machinery of the national convention, denied Roosevelt the party's nomination.

Frankfurter hoped to join the fray. "The air I breath here—outside of home—is fetid," he complained to Buckner in the summer of 1912. "I feel myself cramped, of dubious fitness in the current of things. I chafe that I am not where I long to be. I have the sniff of the fight and find myself—a cog in bureaucracy. I want to be out of here, even or perhaps because the third party fight is a folly—to me it's real, the odds are challenging, the regenerative power of ideas and ideals as political ammunition too stirring a fancy of mine to sit remotely by."[42] He shared the sentiments of millions—trade unionists, professionals, intellectuals, social workers, dirt farmers, idealists, and scoundrels— who wished to stand with Roosevelt at Armageddon and battle for the Lord. "I feel we have broken through the crust of complacency," he noted after Roosevelt bolted from the Republicans. "The upheaval has been wholesome, despite all the claptrap, the rancor, the mouthings, and the vacuities. . . . We are in for government as the biggest responsible agency for organized social reform."[43]

The issues of this campaign, depreciated in the currency of later historians, were genuine and divisive for the participants. With the exception of Eugene Deb's socialist platform, Roosevelt's third party advocated the most far-reaching social welfare program prior to the 1930s, including a ban on child labor, an eight-hour day, and social insurance. On the question of business regulation, Roosevelt's party rejected antitrust litigation as the *only* effective method of corporate control. The colonel believed that existing firms should not be broken up, unless their dominant positions had been gained through unfair methods of competition, such as the vicious price cutting waged by Standard Oil and American Tobacco. Purged of these offensive tactics, Roosevelt believed, the American people should accept giant corporations as a necessary part of modern life, permit additional mergers, and place their faith in strict regulation by the federal government. The only way to meet a billion-dollar corporation, he was fond of saying, "is by invoking the protection of a hundred-billion dollar government" The Progressive platform called for the creation of a federal agency to control all interstate corporations and promised that "under such a system . . . legitimate business, freed from confusion, uncertainty and fruitless litigation, will develop normally."[44]

Taft and the Republicans, attempting to meet Roosevelt's challenge, finally advocated unspecified revisions of the antitrust law, even though the president himself continued to insist that the Supreme Court had applied the law correctly and would do so again. The most serious challenge to Roosevelt came from Woodrow Wilson and his new intellectual mentor, Brandeis, who scorned the big business — big government paternalism of the Bull Moosers. "I do not want to live under a philanthropy," Wilson declared. "I do not want to be taken care of by the government. . . . If the government is to tell big businessmen how to run their business, then don't you see that big businessmen have to get closer to the government even than they are now?"[45]

Brandeis advised Wilson that existing firms should be dissolved where they had gained monopolistic control, regardless of how that control had been acquired. He believed that most of the giant companies had been formed for the purpose of enriching bankers and eliminating competition. Not monuments to efficiency, their size alone represented a moral and political incubus upon the nation's social life. "Roosevelt does not say 'I want to substitute monopoly for competition,'" Brandeis wrote, "but he says that private monopoly in industry is permissible. If you say that, you give away the whole case; because monopoly is the path of least effort. . . . Roosevelt with his good trusts and bad trusts has always stood for monopoly."[46] He and Wilson placed their faith in competition, which they believed could be restored and maintained once the federal government dismantled the offending companies and insisted upon fair play in the future. "For my part," Wilson wrote, "I want the pigmy to have a chance to come out," an idea that also appealed to Brandeis, but that led Walter Lippmann to remark that the New Freedom endorsed liberty for the little profiteers.

Several times during the course of the 1912 campaign, Frankfurter thought seriously about leaving the War Department in order to fight openly for Roosevelt, but the combined pressure of Stimson, Brandeis, and Roosevelt himself convinced him that he should remain on duty to battle for progressive causes within the administration, especially in the field of water-power regulation. Unlike Valentine, Pinchot, Brandeis, Croly, and Perkins, he did not have a large private fortune or even a source of income apart from the government. "After much and dubious searching of heart," he told Hand, "I have decided it's my bigger job to stay and I can only hope that it won't come up to plague me in the years to come."[47] Observing from the sidelines, Frankfurter still managed to pump regular suggestions into Roosevelt's inner circle of advisers through his frequent meetings with Valentine, Croly, and Hand, all of whom took an active role in the Bull Moose campaign.

Frankfurter worked frantically to maintain the enthusiasm of Hand, a congenital pessimist, whose cynicism about politicians usually overwhelmed his devotion to the new party. "I wish he [Roosevelt] could be chloroformed for eight months and then elected," the judge lamented. "I am weary to death of the Rule of the People and a millennium created by constant elections and never-ending suspicion of authority." Nearly all of the declarations of the candidates, he confessed, "fill me with sadness and even with contempt."[48] By late summer, even Frankfurter accepted the inevitability of Wilson's victory, but he remained skeptical of both the New Jersey governor and his party. "The Democratic party in its traditional ideals of government as to states rights, separation of powers, strict construction, etc., is not a fit instrument for working out the social and economic problems of the day," he wrote. Worst of all, he told Hand, "has been Wilson's sneer against government by experts." His campaign statements in this respect had been "vicious, because we are singularly in need in this country of the deliberateness and truthfulness of really scientific expertness."[49]

In the course of the heated campaign, Frankfurter also expressed considerable irritation about Brandeis, who he knew provided Wilson with powerful ammunition against the Progressive Party on the issues of business regulation. Brandeis, he alleged, gave "a very unfair slant to the Progressive position. One would think that the Progressive position is in favor of creating monopolies instead of recognizing inevitable industrial expansion and controlling these forces. Brandeis's dictum . . . that big business should be allowed to grow, but not to be made strikes me as a not very helpful generality."[50] Had the "people's lawyer" spent some time in the Justice Department enforcing the antitrust laws, he concluded, "a few years . . . would convince him of the utter hopelessness of making the dividing line by law suits, and would reveal ihe need of a permanent administrative tribunal."[51]

In the final analysis, of course, the division within the Republican Party contributed more to Wilson's victory than all the rhetorical battles over the virtues of "regulated monopoly" as opposed to "regulated competition." Domestically, at least, Armageddon had been postponed, thanks to Taft's stubbornness, Roosevelt's vanity, and the simple desire of the voters to change parties after more than two decades. The electorate, noted Elihu Root "is like a man in bed. He wants to roll over. He doesn't know why he wants to roll over, but he just does; and he'll do it." For the first time since 1892, the Democrats had captured the White House with a candidate who, despite the barnacles of party and platform, seemed moderately progressive, an intellectual, and perhaps a person of destiny.[52]

❊❊❊

Wilson's victory presented Frankfurter with a pressing career crisis. He had backed the wrong horse. He was not certain whether the new regime would permit him to stay in the War Department and he was not certain that he would stay if asked. The new administration, he suspected, would cramp his freewheeling style and no doubt limit his influence, because Stimson would leave the War Department. "I'm afraid the period of saturation may be setting in for me here," he wrote. "They do want Democrats, for one thing. Then W. W. doesn't tap his resources. He is singularly self-dependent, and even secretive."[53] On the other hand, the mere thought of returning to private practice in New York or elsewhere filled him with loathing. "I have none of Sam's [Rosensohn's] fire and flame for the mere intellectual problems of the profession," he confessed to Buckner. "I can't quite become a crusader for the rule in Shelley's case or shipwreck a friendship . . . through disagreement on a picayune point of pleading. Nor does the conflict of the courtroom call the ego's all-consuming ardor, which lifts you to the pitch of intensity. . . . The jury is wine to your lips; for me they are twelve torturing nuisances."[54]

Private practice, he told another friend, "means putting one's time in to put money in other people's pockets." Briefly, he flirted with the idea of joining Valentine's industrial relations firm or even going abroad "to fuss a little at the Universities" in England and Germany, but his heart remained closest to the law because "in a legalistic country like ours, industrial questions and social problems have to be dealt with by a lawyer, and for such things I feel a fitness."[55] The social struggles of the immediate future, he believed, could be resolved peacefully through law, but the dominant training of most lawyers placed them on the side of the status quo and made them hostile to reform. "How steeped we lawyers are in legalism," he complained to Hand, "and how much education among the well disposed is the essential pre-requisite to a greater realization of social democracy."[56] Narrow legal training, moreover, plagued society in the form of lawyers who became judges and who from these positions of authority vetoed the will of the people. "They regard private property as the cornerstone of existence," Hand fumed, "but they have no confidence that they can justify it before the people at large. . . . They want to put the whole weight of government on nine elderly gentlemen at Washington."[57]

Frankfurter carried these subversive ideas about law and the judiciary back to the Harvard Law School in 1912, when he addressed the twenty-fifth anniversary dinner of the *Law Review*. News of his influential friends and many administrative battles had already filtered back to Cambridge, where younger law students perceived him to be one of Washington's social lions, who roomed with titled Englishmen and rode around Rock Creek Park with assorted princesses and duchesses. When Herbert Ehrmann asked Max Lowenthal about a speaker for the Harvard Menorah Society, the latter recommended Frankfurter. "Who," asked Ehrmann, "is Felix Frankfurter?" "Felix Frankfurter," Lowenthal, the older and wiser student, quipped, "is the greatest man in the world." So it must have seemed to many of the aspiring young lawyers, who listened to his alumni address. "If facts are changing," he told them, "law cannot be static. So called immutable principles must accommodate themselves to facts of life, for facts are stubborn and will not yield." American society was riddled with social inequality, he noted, but lawyers and judges often failed to take

account of this fact when deciding the fate of social legislation. Whatever seemed reasonable on economic or social grounds, he urged,
ought to be constitutional, "whether or not it accords with our individual notions of economics." Of course, legislatures might make mis-
takes, but legislation had to be empirical and experimental and "the
Constitution was not intended to limit this field of experimentation."[58]

These remarks pleased the more progressive-minded students, but
not many of the alumni, judging by Frankfurter's immediate lament
to Hand: "The more I talk with lawyers—even the kind that were at
the dinner—the more I realize how much the profession is still in the
grip of conventional thinking." The one ray of hope at the school
seemed to be "the younger crowd," who were "thinking along the
lines that we, in our smugness, regard as the right lines."[59] He was
especially impressed by one of the school's newest faculty members,
Roscoe Pound, a botanist turned legal historian and philosopher who
had arrived in Cambridge in 1909. Pound, too, believed that lawyers
had been narrowly trained through the conventional law school curriculum that emphasized the case method and the study of common-
law rules. In several articles, the most famous of which denounced
judicial clichés about "liberty of contract," he urged judges and lawyers to become more familiar with the disciplines of economics, political science, sociology, and psychology. Exposure to the social sciences, Pound believed, would better equip the profession to meet the
social conflicts of the era that could not be intelligently resolved
through stale legal doctrine alone. "I have talked much with [Stimson]
about your writings and he is always 'at' the President to awaken his
mind to the situation," Frankfurter told Pound. "He is going to ask
the President to read your articles. . . . I want to get . . . them into
the President's mind and feeling."[60] Pound's ideas did not dent Taft's
thinking about the law or the courts, but Frankfurter believed that the
Nebraskan's influence would incline the law school "more and more
in favor of a sociological conception of jurisprudence" that would be
compatible with social reform.[61]

By 1913, Pound and other Harvard insurgents hoped to add
Frankfurter to their ranks. The initial prompting came from Denison,
who wrote to his old friend, Ned Warren: "If you see any reasonable
opening in your faculty for Frankfurter, I wish you would let me
know about it." The new administration in Washington might retain
him, Denison noted, but Harvard should not let the opportunity pass
to recruit someone who "has made a tremendous impression with the

Supreme Court." Denison was quick to add that his roommate knew nothing about this inquiry and might decline an offer from Cambridge, "but I thought I would sound the land."[62] After a hastily called faculty meeting, Warren reported back: "To a man, we want Frankfurter." He pointed out to Denison, however, that the school did not have money for a new position and that efforts would have to be made to raise an endowment through private sources.[63]

Encouraged by Warren's response, Denison secured Frankfurter's assent, while the law school's dean, Ezra Thayer, approached Stimson with the plan to raise "new money" in order to hire his young protégé. "It seems to me," Thayer told him, "that with the spirit which is abroad nowadays it ought to be possible to find someone who is enough interested in the things that Frankfurter stands for to meet this difficulty." "Pound has seen Brandeis," he added, "who is very much interested, and who, I understand, will try to interest Mr. [Jacob] Schiff."[64]

Stimson, however, remained unenthusiastic about the Harvard post until Brandeis finally convinced him that the law school needed Frankfurter and that the latter had a great desire to go there. Stimson looked upon academic life as too remote from the real world and a waste of Frankfurter's enormous talent "for keeping in touch with the center of things—for knowing sympathetically men who are doing and thinking." Washington, he told Frankfurter bluntly, remained "the big uncomfortable caldron in which American problems are brewing, and you must not lose touch with it."[65] At last, Brandeis overcame this resistance, and even persuaded Stimson to bring "the matter to the attention of men in New York, who would recognize the great opportunity for public service that was offered." His own recent battles with the great financiers, Brandeis told Stimson, "seem to disqualify me for that task."[66]

Years later, reflecting upon his Harvard appointment, Frankfurter recalled: "if I had received a letter from an Indian princess asking me to marry her, I wouldn't have been more surprised."[67] As proof of this surprise, he drafted a long, detailed memorandum that outlined the pros and cons of going to Cambridge as against staying in Washington, and he consulted for days with Hand, Croly, Roosevelt, Holmes, Stimson, and Brandeis. Seldom had an academic birth been attended by such distinguished midwives, many of whom advised him to remain in Washington. "That you will end there [Harvard] is evidently likely and desirable," Hand remarked, "but not now. . . . Besides, the fight is now just on and you can actively help, particularly in conservation. Your place for awhile is just where you are."[68] Croly believed that going to Harvard was a very bad idea, Frankfurter reported, because "he is afraid I'd become a pillar of society. Me—a pillar!"[69]

Frankfurter agonized, too, about the motives of some of his new financial sponsors, because Stimson had raised money from wealthy German Jews, who represented both the forces of economic conservatism, and the subtle ties of ethnic obligation. "I should feel uncomfortable to have any part of the money given by people who feel a generous impulse towards me," he told Walter Meyer, a New York railroad attorney. "I would wear uneasily the subtle collar of a benefactor." He did not hesitate to pass moral judgment upon some potential contributors, by rejecting money from Henry Morgenthau, Sr., a notorious real estate promoter and free-spending Democrat, but accepting the benevolence of Otto Kahn's partner, Schiff. "There is no reason why Mr. Schiff should not feel a legitimate pride in a Jew filling a certain position in any sphere of life," he wrote. "My whole feeling is only that my personality and my symbolic significance are subordinate to the job that is to be done up there [at Harvard]. And, so far as my own feelings go, I should want the donors to be touched with what should and can be done at Cambridge rather than with the indirect significance of the person who does it."[70]

Despite Frankfurter's caveats, Schiff and others probably contributed for the wrong reasons. They had little interest in promoting Frankfurter's brand of legal progressivism or in "the job that is to be done up there," but they favored the idea of a Jew breaking into the gentile stronghold of the Harvard Law School. The alliance of the great banker and the young progressive seemed somewhat perverse, but it returned Frankfurter to Cambridge and he, at least, knew what he would do there. "I am not a scholar," he told Hand bluntly. "But, with Pound there, I see this as an opportunity for somebody to help fashion a jurisprudence adequate to our industrial and economic needs. . . . It tempts me as an opportunity to ride in the Trojan horse of our heresies."[71]

CHAPTER 4

LEGAL PROGRESSIVE

THE SUMMER OF 1914 brought Frankfurter to Harvard and war to Europe, ending a decade of fragile peace and shattering the optimism of many American reformers about the upward spiral of human progress. Returning to Boston on July 29 after visiting Frederick Taylor in Maine, he and Valentine learned that Archduke Ferdinand of Austria had been assassinated at Sarajevo. Within a week, Russia, Austria, Germany, France, and England were locked in a murderous struggle. "It obsesses my mind to think that where ten days ago there were millions of men engaged in peaceful and profitable pursuits," Hand lamented, "now apparently they are all to begin killing each other as rapidly as possible."[1] A year earlier, Frankfurter and Eustace Percy had discussed at "the House of Truth" the desirability of adopting the "Wisconsin idea," through which American and British politics could be guided by the intelligence and rationality of university-trained experts. Such idealistic schemes now appeared ludicrous in a world where the social and intellectual elites of five nations—poets, philosophers, lawyers, and professors—attempted to kill each other in the name of nationalism.

"We are fighting now, not because we believe our cause to be a just one," Percy confessed to him from England, "but because the State has a claim on our lives. I hope we are learning after all that obedience is the prime necessity of life. You can't question the State because the only way you know you are a man at all is by measuring yourself against the State." Without the state, Percy argued, "one might become a monkey without knowing it. . . . That may sound a German idea of the State, but as a matter of fact—it is simply a Greek one. There is all the difference in the world between the two."[2] On the basis of this reasoning, thousands of Englishmen, Frenchmen, and Germans marched to their doom at the Marne and the Somme in "a world of dead fathers and crippled brothers and crazy screaming sons."[3]

In addition to Europe, the contagion of international violence spread to the western hemisphere as well in 1914, where the Wilson administration attempted to guide the course of the Mexican Revolution in a manner consistent with the president's vision of constitutionalism, morality, and America's economic interests. When Mexico's temporary dictator, General Victoriano Huerta, refused to tolerate Wilson's interference, the president seized upon the arrest of a Navy paymaster and his crew in Tampico as a pretext for toppling the regime. Without waiting for Congress to act, he sent the Marines into Vera Cruz, where they took over the port city at the cost of 126 Mexican and 19 American lives. The invasion, however, outraged even Huerta's bitterest enemies, united all Mexican factions against the United States, and encouraged Wilson to believe that he could manipulate the revolution at will. His bullying of the Mexicans and spread-eagle oratory disgusted Frankfurter, who believed that progressives should set their own house in order before venturing to correct political abuses south of the border. "Gosh it is a mess," he complained to Hand. "To that boy [Wilson] words are things. He talks about the Mexicans as they used to talk about the 'economic man' and there never was a more closed-minded man than W. W. . . . How the thing has smashed. The honeymoon is over—Brandeis is hopeless about him, [Raymond] Stevens & [William] Kent say the jig is up and to hear talk Teddy might start on his Cabinet tomorrow. . . . And the domestic program is smashed—trusts, water power, all, all is gone."[4]

This pessimism proved somewhat premature. Despite the Mexican debacle and the brief derangement of the economy following the outbreak of the war in Europe, Wilson had earlier pushed through Congress a vigorous reform program that lowered tariff duties, overhauled the nation's commercial banking system, closed loopholes in the antitrust laws as Brandeis had recommended, and created a new Federal Trade Commission. Within a month, even Frankfurter rejoiced that "Tommy's [Federal] Reserve Board is very *fine*."[5] Over these progressive efforts in the United States, however, now hung the shadow of Europe's collective madness, the probability that America's precarious neutrality could not long survive, and a waning belief in the perfectability of human societies. "From this nightmare of a month," Percy wrote to Frankfurter a year later, "I bring you at least this message—Never believe again, as we have believed in the past, that this world is ours to shape. . . . Oh! This philosophy of 'evolution' which has blinded the sight of a generation of which the judgment for the sins of their fathers and their fathers' fathers, as well as their own, was about to fall."[6]

Because he was an American, removed from the scent of gunpowder and the stench of Europe's rotting flesh, and because he remained throughout his life something of an optimist, Frankfurter did not experience during these years the nightmares and cynicism that gripped his aristocratic friend in England. Even when tragedy struck close to home, he refused to become fatalistic about the human condition in a seemingly irrational universe. In 1915, for example, Ezra Thayer, suffering from insomnia, a chronic bladder illness, and a "morbid New England conscience," took his own life by jumping into the Charles River. Frankfurter believed that the dean committed suicide during "one of those stray, disheartened moments with no dissuading influences about. He was left rudderless and went." Had a "good buoyant friend" taken Thayer away from Cambridge for the summer, he added, the tragedy could have been avoided, which seemed "cruelly wasteful—because avoidable."[7] In an effort to banish Thayer's death and the European calamity from his mind and hoping to silence his own doubts about the future, Frankfurter plunged furiously into the routine of teaching law. "This war has made us all realize how thin the veneer of reason is, or perhaps better, how controlling instincts are," he told Buckner. "It has made me feel therefore more than ever, the thing to do is catch them young so that their instincts will be illumined; or, at least, that they will not confound instinct, desires, with impersonal reason." He remained confident that "one can plant in them 'seminal suggestions' and by gradual infiltration of personality, make them realize that they were born neither for comfort nor for stagnation."[8]

Frankfurter attempted to instill several "seminal suggestions" in the minds of Harvard students, in particular the idea that the acquisition of legal rules, without an adequate understanding of the social and economic consequences of those rules, produced narrow-minded lawyers and socially dangerous judges. Along with Pound, he wished to supplement the traditional case method of instruction with large doses of history, economics, political science, and sociology in order to demonstrate the importance of the law's social context. "My unscholarliness may help to save me and the students from Langdellian sterilization," he told Holmes. "I do appreciate his [Langdell's] work as a pedagogic innovator, but it strikes me the school has to do a bigger job than high technique."[9] In a curriculum largely dominated by the study of the common law, Frankfurter intended in addition to focus his students' attention upon the legislative process and the emerging field of administrative law. Students should discover that "the law" constituted more than judge-made rules and that legislation could become a positive force in the resolution of social problems. "Practically no organized thought is available in this country as to the scope of legislative law," he complained to Holmes, "except . . . the common lawyer's implicit distrust of legislation, law students leave the Law Schools ignorant and indifferent to legislation."[10]

Above all, he wished to promote the ideal of judicial restraint in the tradition of Thayer and Holmes. Judges, he believed, should not substitute their own policy choices for those of the popular branches of government in the mistaken idea that they possessed infallible insight into the Constitution. Or, as Holmes reminded him, "A law should be called good if it reflects the will of the dominant forces of the community even if it will take us to hell."[11] Through his own life and work, Frankfurter hoped to provide a counterexample to the profession's dominant mentality of private practice, corporate law, and money making, because he represented a newer model of professional opportunity that bridged the growing sector of public law and the old, aristocratic ideal of government service.

During these years, he taught a first-year course in criminal law and what became one of the school's most famous offerings: Public Utilities. "You learn no law in Public U," wrote the student-poet, Francis Plimpton,

> That is its fascination
> But Felix gives a point of view
> And pleasant conversation.

Less charitably, some students recalled that the course seemed to be "loose-jointed and rather haphazard," with the principle emphasis upon the legislative and administrative history of the Interstate Commerce Commission. The discussion of some cases dragged on for weeks, peppered with bits of information and anecdotes about judges, senators, presidents, philosophers, and historians. "We were not learning law," one student confessed later, "that was not our business. We were gaining some measure of understanding of law that both reflected and shaped a nation's growth—some understanding of its method and some appreciation of its content." Faced with thorny legal problems later, he recalled, the most fruitful ideas for solving them often came "from the recollection of something that had been said, something that had been done, in the course in Public Utilities."[12]

Harold Laski, the brilliant young political theorist then studying at Harvard, noted that Frankfurter and Austin Scott, another assistant professor, generated much enthusiasm among the students, but Scott held the edge because he was more organized and systematic in his presentations. "Frankfurter's always giving you Holmes," one student complained. "They don't make much of Holmes in Minnesota."[13] Whatever the students' response to his efforts, Frankfurter loved his work. "Those boys," he exclaimed to Sofy Buckner. "I'm thrilled and awed and humbled when I think of the job ahead of me. I wish I had time—oh, loads of time—the amount of preparation is so enormous."[14] Experience in the classroom confirmed his belief in "catching them young . . . before habits and bills and babies absorb the 24 hour day."[15] Even after two years, he could not quite believe that he was a Harvard professor and at times he doubted whether he belonged among the intellectual giants of the profession. "I'm all too conscious of my own inadequacy for the job I have," he told Pound, "but I leave that to the Lord and go ahead with the equipment I have. . . . While tilling my small patch, I have the strength of your constant encouragement and friendship."[16]

Tilling his small patch of academic ground at Harvard did not begin to deplete Frankfurter's energies. "I'm not a cloistered scholar," he reminded Holmes, "and not even Cambridge, I think, can spoil my zest of life and my need of steering my boat through the currents of its rigorous realities."[17] Before leaving Washington, he had helped Croly to found a new magazine of social and political criticism, whose purpose was "to give a more vigorous, consistent, comprehensive, and enlightened expression to the Progressive principle than . . . it receives from any existing publication." Their journal must, he told Croly, "criticize uncompromisingly half-hearted performance, narrow ideas and cheap personalities, and it would try to embody a single-minded, whole-hearted and well-balanced liberalism." As for readership, they should attempt to attract, in addition to intellectuals and professionals, many enlightened businessmen, by preaching "voluntary cooperation, both among producers and between employers and their employees." The journal's own management, moreover, ought to reflect progressive ideals, by recruiting women for editorial positions, spurning the desire to make money from the publication, and practicing "those cooperative methods and . . . humanizing ideals which we . . . recommend to other people."[18]

Only the Harvard appointment prevented him from joining Croly as the founding editor of *The New Republic*, once they secured financial backing from the wealthy liberal philanthropist, Willard Dickerman Straight. Frankfurter's decision to go to Harvard bitterly disappointed Croly. "You are the only man I have ever met who really understands Progressivism as I understand it," the latter told him. "I know of nobody else at present to whom I would be willing to turn over the conduct of the paper."[19] Despite Frankfurter's defection, Croly recruited a brilliant cast of editors and contributors for the new journal, including Lippmann, Walter Weyl, and Francis Hackett, former book editor of the *Chicago Daily News*.

In order to mollify his old friends and satisfy his own taste for polemical writing, Frankfurter became a regular contributor on issues relating to law and the judiciary; in addition, he frequently raced to New York for editorial conferences. "Felix of course is a world in himself," Laski remarked, but he worried a great deal about his friend's hectic, whirlwind pace. "He is always nervously restless, dashing here and there in a kind of creative fertility that drives me to despair," he told Holmes. "I don't find him able to sit down solidly to a single thing. . . . I wish he were a little more concentrated. . . . To New York three times in one week is a drain I wonder whether even he can stand."[20]

Holmes, nearly seventy-five, relished the ferment, the energy, the kaleidoscopic activities of his youthful friend, but he remained wholly unmoved by all efforts to remake the social universe, including Frankfurter's efforts at *The New Republic*. "I don't believe some of the things deeply implied in the writings of Croly and Lippmann," he confided to Frankfurter, "much as I delight in them—and I almost need your encouragement not to think that I am an old hulk on the sands. But as I still take a hand in the actual I try not to be too much bullied by clever remarks from the cloister."[21] *The New Republic*, the justice informed his friend Lewis Einstein, "is rather solemn for my taste; but the young men who write in it are, some of them, friends of mine, which doesn't prevent an occasional, flattering reference to this old man, and I get great pleasure from our occasional talks."[22]

~~~~~

In addition to running his law school classes and guiding *The New Republic* through its first years, Frankfurter's "creative fertility" focused as well upon efforts to reshape the judicial interpretation of the Constitution. By the time of Wilson's presidency, the Supreme Court had somewhat moderated its opposition to both state and federal reform programs, without, however, capitulating entirely to Holmes's latitudinarian attitude about the fundamental law or judicial review. Pilloried by the bar for decisions such as *Lochner* and *Adair*, harassed by his own dissenting members, and rocked by Roosevelt's attacks, the justices bent with the progressive storm. In 1911, for example, the Court upheld a state law that prohibited railroad companies from limiting their liability to injured employees by means of individual contracts, and they also sustained the power of Congress to fix the working hours of the carriers' interstate employees.[23] "There is no absolute freedom to do as one wills or to contract as one chooses," Charles Evans Hughes wrote for the majority, sharply curtailing the extreme "liberty of contract" doctrine put forth in *Lochner* and *Adair*. "The guaranty [sic] of liberty does not withdraw from legislative supervision that wide department of activity which consists of the making of contracts, or deny to government the power to provide restrictive safeguards."[24]

The Court's temporary burst of toleration gave progressives new hope. "I think for the next ten years there'll be little cause for complaint," Frankfurter told Hand, shortly after the *McGuire* decision. "The recent batch of . . . decisions seems to me to indicate a real desire to pull in the reins. A very wide conception of the police power and a restrictive meaning of 'liberty' and 'due process' will allow practically every piece of legislation, at all defensible . . . to pass muster."[25] But on this occasion as on others, Frankfurter proved to be a poor forecaster of the Court's actual behavior, largely because he underestimated the impact of Taft's efforts to fill the bench with men who believed it their duty to defend property rights, resist the growth of organized labor, and fight socialistic legislation. As a sop to the progressives, the president placed Hughes on the Court, but followed this appointment with four reactionaries: Horace Lurton, Willis Van

Devanter, Joseph Lamar, and Mahlon Pitney. In addition, Taft elevated Edward White, the conservative Louisianan, to the chief justiceship. Pitney, for example, had gained a well-deserved reputation in New Jersey for harassing unions and breaking strikes through sweeping injunctions, while Lurton, who had served with Taft on the Circuit Court of Appeals, believed that the justices should never yield to what he called "the clamor of a temporary majority upon the pretense that otherwise popular government is prevented."[26]

Taft's appointments quickly returned the Court to a conservative course. In 1915, with only Holmes, Hughes, and William Day in dissent, the justices struck down a Kansas law that had made it a misdemeanor for employers "to coerce, require, demand, or influence" any person to enter into a contract not to join or become or remain "a member of any labor organization." This statute, Pitney wrote, interfered with the freedom of both employers and employees to fix the terms of their own bargains and therefore constituted "a substantial impairment of liberty in the long established constitutional sense." This precious constitutional right, Pitney concluded, remained "as essential to the laborer as to the capitalist, to the poor as to the rich," although as Holmes noted in dissent, a worker might believe that he could only secure a fair contract by means of a labor union.[27] Pitney's resurrection of *Lochner* stunned Frankfurter and confirmed Hand's estimate that "their work is pitiable. . . . most of it would disgrace any capable boy of 20 who had been trained by you and your colleagues. . . . I should honestly have much more respect for a trained pupil of St. Thomas, than for most of those worthy mastiffs."[28] Frankfurter characterized the *Coppage* decision as "unbelievable," the product of "arterial sclerosis" in judges "who move in their own small narrow groove which gradually makes for comfort and gradually makes the rest of the world unknown and therefore unnatural."[29]

Perhaps the most distressing aspect of the *Coppage* case was the fact that Wilson's first Court appointee, former Attorney General James McReynolds, joined Pitney's opinion, a result that encouraged Frankfurter and others to fight for a progressive appointee when the next vacancy on the Court occurred in 1916. Faced with a worsening diplomatic situation abroad and the prospect of a difficult reelection campaign, Wilson fulfilled their wildest hopes by nominating Brandeis. "He is a man who cares nothing for money," wrote the new attorney general, "and for the last twenty years his lifework has been standing up for personal liberty as against property rights." Brandeis, he continued, "is a radical, but one radical in nine is not a bad thing on the Supreme Bench." The prospect of one radical in nine, however, horrified conservatives and precipitated a bitter, six-month struggle over Brandeis's confirmation in the Senate.[30]

Frankfurter soon found himself in the thick of the battle. "The fight is now on and I'm not at all sad about the outcome no matter what," he told Katherine Ludington, the militant feminist and suffragette. "Brandeis is simply paying the price for the rest of us. Only we must be insistent and drive home the big significance of it all."[31] "The rest of us" it turned out, included both those who fought for progressive causes and American Jews, because the Brandeis nomination called down the wrath of those who wished to preserve the Court's doctrinal and ethnic purity. Seldom had a nominee stimulated more venemous opposition. Taft, Elihu Root, and six former presidents of the American Bar Association condemned Wilson's choice as unfit to hold judicial office. They were joined by spokesmen of the Boston legal, business, and cultural elite, including the President of Harvard, A. Lawrence Lowell, Moorfield Storey, Austen George Fox, Sidney Winslow, and Clarence Walker Barron.

The conservative Brahmins denounced Brandeis's "general reputation" and his lack of "judicial temperament" because he had taken sides on controversial issues of the day, such as the trusts and minimum wage laws. Lawyers, politicians and businessmen who had crossed swords with Brandeis branded him as "untrustworthy," "devious," and "ruthless in the attainment of his objects." "Mr. Brandeis has been a rebellious and troublesome member of the most homogenous, self-centered, and self-complacent community in the United States," Lippmann wrote in *The New Republic*. "They undertook to destroy the reputation of a man, to prevent a public servant from using his great abilities to the best public advantage."[32]

Brandeis did not lack devoted and resourceful supporters, especially his law partner, Edward McClennen, and Frankfurter, who compiled evidence to refute most of the charges and organized a letter-writing campaign on behalf of their nominee. "Isn't the Brandeis thing fine," Frankfurter told Hand, "if only to hear them howl and to drag into the aerated open all this bunk of sterilized removal of the Court from the issues of life on which they pass."[33] The opposition of Root, one of Stimson's closest friends and a pillar of the national bar, galled Frankfurter, because he admired the former secretary of state and believed that Root acted out of blind partisanship. "Are you familiar with the details of Mr. Brandeis' life, with his aims and his purposes and his motives?" he asked Root. "Are you familiar with his approach to public questions . . .? And is your judgment of his 'professional career' apart from the Ballinger case founded on a study or knowledge such as you would want made of your career before judgment of it is ventured?"[34] In the end, however, it required more than indignation and sarcasm to save the nominee. Wilson refused to compromise on the appointment and by turning the struggle into a party issue, he secured enough votes in the Judiciary Committee and the full Senate to gain a narrow victory.[35]

Frankfurter, who had fought harder than anyone, was under no illusion that the appointment would by itself transform the Court's jurisprudence. Brandeis represented only a single vote and the *Coppage* case, for example, had been decided by a majority of six. On the other hand, the appointment clearly demonstrated Wilson's growing commitment to progressivism, including many of the social welfare measures advocated by the Bull Moose insurgents in 1912. Symbolically as well as substantively, the Brandeis victory ranked among the most impressive triumphs of Wilson's first term, because it brought to the nation's highest court a devoted spokesman for those who believed in the affirmative powers of government and that the law should promote social and economic justice. Although overshadowed by the drama in Washington, an equally important struggle over the future of America's legal institutions raged that same year in Cambridge, where the law school attempted to fill the deanship left vacant by Thayer's death.

The significance of the Harvard battle was certainly not lost upon Frankfurter, who supported the candidacy of Pound in Cambridge while battling in Washington for Brandeis. In Frankfurter's pantheon of heroes, Pound hardly ranked with Brandeis, Stimson, or Holmes, but he stood head and shoulders above the candidates endorsed by other faculty members and by President Lowell, who backed the appointment of several Wall Street lawyers with impeccable social credentials, including Learned Hand's cousin, Augustus. Candidly, Frankfurter criticized Pound's "provincialisms, his unjudicial mindedness, his hasty, inadequate thinking when he isn't technically thinking." He and the Nebraskan shared different "hopes and faiths," especially with respect to Pound's distaste for public affairs and his plodding historical method that sometimes confused exhaustive details with profundity. On the other hand, Frankfurter preferred Pound to Joe Cotton, who "never paid for anything, but expected things to be brought to him on a gold platter," and to Hand, who was "too completely the lawyer for my taste, [and] too rigid at that."[36]

Pound also appealed to Frankfurter, because he, too, represented the social outsider, the "unmannered alien" from Lowell's perspective, who did not quite fit the model of law school gentility. In addition, Pound valued legal research and possessed a generous attitude toward the social sciences. "Scholarship is such a new thing in this country," Frankfurter told Pound, "and the recognition of its need still newer. . . . Your deanship will come as a spur to these men all over the country, it will make for standards of rigorous discipline and fruitful scholarship."[37] Reluctantly, Lowell finally accepted Pound, but only, Frankfurter believed, "with boorish ungraciousness that indicated he didn't want him to take it."[38] Pound's rising national reputation, although tinged with radicalism, forced the Harvard leadership to ignore Lowell's objections as well as the tepid support from key faculty members such as Williston and Beale, who represented the entrenched common-law tradition. "The trick is done," Frankfurter informed Buckner. "Roscoe from 'the short grass country' has attained to the scholastic peerage. Maybe they'll now consider him their social equal even when they ask him to dinner. . . . Hurrah for Nebraska! Hurrah for the Lord who is no respecter of geography."[39]

❧❧❧

The appointments of Brandeis and Pound represented important victories for the cause of legal progressivism, but changing the content of reigning legal doctrine proved to be more difficult than infiltrating the Supreme Court and the Harvard Law School. Frankfurter learned how difficult in 1916, when the nation's highest court decided the fate of two controversial Oregon laws, one limiting the hours of all workers in the state to ten per day and the other permitting the state's Industrial Welfare Commission to fix minimum wages for women and children. Representing the National Consumers' League, Brandeis had defended the minimum wage statute before the Supreme Court in 1914, but the death of Justice Lurton and bitter divisions on the Court prevented a final decision. Instead, the justices rescheduled arguments on both the minimum-wage law and the ten-hour statute for early January 1917, and with Brandeis now on the bench, Frankfurter took up his unfinished task on behalf of the Consumers' League and its redoubtable executive secretary, Florence Kelley. Over summer vacation, he honed the league's briefs and plotted their strategy with Josephine Goldmark, the organization's chief researcher and Brandeis's sister-in-law.[40]

All of Frankfurter's careful preparation nearly broke down when

Oregon's attorney general consented to dispense with oral arguments, despite objections from the league and other interested parties that such a course of action would only help the legislation's foes. With the Oregon laws and his own place in the history books at stake, Frankfurter took the unorthodox step of personally urging the necessity of oral arguments upon Chief Justice White, who finally accepted the professor's advice while clad in his bathrobe and slippers. "I always regarded that as my single most successful professional achievement," Frankfurter recalled, years later. "That's what is called *ex parte* practice."[41] On January 18 and 19, he made his appearance before all of the justices, who, according to one reporter, listened "intently to the plea of a small, dark, smooth-faced lawyer, mostly head, eyes and glasses, who looked as if he had stepped out of the sophomore classroom of a neighboring college. He lectured the Court quietly, but with a due sense of its indebtedness to him for setting it right where it has been wrong."[42]

In the case of maximum-hours laws and other restraints upon contractual freedom, the Court needed all the help it could get in order to extricate constitutional doctrine from the logical morass that had ensued once the justices began to weigh the constitutionality of social welfare laws against the vague language of the Fourteenth Amendment's due process clause. By the time of Frankfurter's appearance in 1917, a majority of the Court had held that the states could in certain circumstances regulate contractual agreements between private parties without depriving them of "life, liberty, or property, without due process of law." For example, the states could fix the hours to be worked by employees on public projects,[43] fix the hours of labor in "dangerous" or "unhealthy" occupations,[44] and generally limit the hours of women employed in sundry occupations.[45] These regulations the Court found to be legitimate exercises of the state's police power, designed to protect the community's health, welfare, and morals. On the other hand, a majority of justices had struck down efforts to eliminate the "yellow dog contract" or limit the hours of bakery workers. These regulations, according to Justice Harlan and others, constituted "an arbitrary interference with the liberty of contract which no government can legally justify in a free land."[46]

In brief, the Court had developed two competing lines of precedent that transformed constitutional litigation into a game of Russian roulette for the state legislatures, because the social and economic prejudices of one or two justices might determine the outcome of important social policy. "Judicial opinion," complained the Oregon Su-

preme Court, "has not reached any settled or stable basis upon which
to rest."[47] In this situation, Brandies argued, wise judges should leave
the line drawing to the legislatures, unless their decision lacked any
rational basis. "The question is merely whether . . . you can see that
the legislators had no ground on which they could, as reasonable men,
deem this legislation appropriate to abolish or mitigate the evils believed to exist or apprehended. If you cannot find that, the law must
stand."[48]

Frankfurter shared Brandeis's point of view. Despite his intellectual and social snobbery, he did not endorse government by the judiciary, but placed his faith instead in the judgments of experts, vindicated by legislative majorities. Unlike Holmes, moreover, he believed
that human beings remained masters of their destiny and that they
could shape a better future through social experimentation and the
trial-and-error methods of democratic politics. He brought the full
measure of these convictions to bear upon the Oregon statutes, which,
he told the justices, represented a valid exercise of that state's police
power, intended to protect the whole community from a host of social
evils that resulted from long hours of deleterious labor and inadequate
wages.

The Court's conservatives, led by Justice McReynolds, remained
unmoved by Frankfurter's legal arguments or by the dense factual
brief that attempted to document actual working conditions throughout the state. In their opinion, the Court should pay more attention to
the Constitution and far less to the reports of sociologists and economists. "Ten hours! Ten hours! Ten hours!" McReynolds snapped
from the bench. "If ten, why not four?" Calmly, Frankfurter replied
over his spectacles: "Your honor, if by chance . . . your physician
should find that you're eating too much meat, it isn't necessary for
him to urge you to become a vegetarian." This retort delighted
Holmes, who muttered very loudly, "Good for you!"[49] Despite
McReynold's hectoring, Frankfurter's arguments carried the day. On
April 9, one week after the United States declared war on Germany,
the justices upheld the ten-hour law, including its overtime pay provisions that required offending employers to pay time and one-half for
all work in excess of the statutory limit. Even with Brandeis not voting, five justices endorsed Frankfurter's views.[50] On the other hand,
the minimum wage law survived, but only because the Court remained equally divided, a result that allowed the Oregon decision to
stand, but established no binding federal precedent. Had Brandeis

participated, there can be little doubt that a major constitutional watershed would have been crossed in 1917, sparing the nation another decade of legal frustration in the area of minimum-wage legislation.[51]

The Brandeis appointment, Pound's elevation to the deanship, and the *Bunting* decision raised Frankfurter's hopes that progressivism had established a permanent foothold in the nation's legal order, and these hopes gained new life two months later when five justices again upheld the authority of Congress to fix an eight-hour day for railroad workers, including a temporary provision for maintaining existing rates of pay based on a standard ten-hour day.[52] His euphoria collapsed, however, when the Court handed down its judgment in *Hitchman Coal & Coke Company* v. *Mitchell* at the end of the 1917 term. Speaking through Justice Pitney, six members of the Court upheld a sweeping injunction against officials and organizers of the United Mine Workers, who had attempted to recruit members at the West Virginia mine, where the workers had signed "yellow dog" contracts agreeing not to join a union while employed by the company. Although no miner had yet taken out a membership in the union, Pitney declared that the organizing efforts alone constituted an unlawful invasion of contractual rights.[53] Brandeis's eloquent dissent, which pointed out that Pitney's reasoning actually did great violence to traditional theories of contractual liability as well as unnecessarily limiting the freedom of choice available to workers, attracted only two supporters, Holmes and John Clarke, the last of Wilson's appointees.

The *Hitchman* decision, probably the most antilabor opinion since the notorious *Debs* case, indicated that Taft's appointees still commanded influence on the nation's highest court and that the road ahead, especially in the area of social legislation and the rights of labor, would be stony indeed. "Judges continue to indulge 'the illusion of mathematical certainty' and to think they are, like silkworms, unfolding 'law' from the legal cocoon," Frankfurter lamented to Holmes. "In fact they are but translating their own unconscious economic prejudices or assumptions. The *Hitchman* case is a striking demonstration of the truth of this observation."[54] While *Bunting* and *Wilson* v. *New* marked the high tide of legal progressivism, *Hitchman* recaptured for conservatives much of the ground lost since *Lochner* and *Adair*. In Cambridge, sociological jurisprudence had secured a tiny beachhead; its grip upon the thinking of the United States Supreme Court, however, seemed very frail in the summer of 1917 as Americans went off to war.

Private grief and psychological turmoil often blighted Frankfurter's moments of public triumph in 1916 and 1917. One year after Thayer's suicide, his own father died in New York, having fulfilled few of his own grandiose material ambitions and leaving his sons to find other, more powerful role models. "My father loved *life*," Frankfurter emphasized, several years later. "He thought we were here for joy; Joy was his emphasis."[55] Leopold's death left him sad, somewhat guilty, and not a little relieved. Several months later, he sustained a devastating blow when Robert Valentine suddenly dropped dead in a New York restaurant. A man of wit, social polish, and social conscience, Valentine represented Frankfurter's ideal of civic virtue and gracious living. He poured out his grief to Holmes: "No one I know lived with completer courage, with gayer sincerity and fine honesty. He was gay and gallant and concerned about others. . . . How Valentine's life—its wonderful pluck and struggle and joy—refutes those who would alter the wisdom of all ages that struggle is the law of life—its law and its salt."[56] Valentine's death left a gap in Frankfurter's life that neither Stimson nor Brandeis, Buckner nor Pound could quite fill.

Shadowed by death, he had not been very successful at love either, despite a constant parade of attractive young women who regularly caught his attention and provoked endless teasing from Buckner and Laski, two connoisseurs of pulchritude. Neither he nor they had been prepared for the devastating impact of Marion Denman. He had met this beautiful but frail daughter of a Congregational minister from Longmeadow, Massachusetts, during the spring of 1913, before he left Washington for Harvard. Except for money, Marion Denman seemed to be a carbon copy of Valentine—well bred, genteel, and concerned about social problems. She had graduated with honors from Smith College and briefly attended the New York School of Social Work. With her shimmering auburn hair and hazel eyes, she reminded Laski of a portrait by Luini and he and Justice Holmes called her Luina. Sharp-tongued, intelligent, coquettish, and a trifle vain, she easily won Frankfurter's heart.

During the next four years, in person and by means of amorous letters filled with poetry and politics, he courted her in New York City, Washington, and Springfield. "You know," her mother remarked with considerable alarm after his first visit to their home, "I think he wants to marry Marion."[57] The heat of his pursuit became too intense for the young woman on several occasions. His passions and jealousies collided with her quest for independence, worldly experience, and self-expression. With considerable irritation, for example, she declined to advise him about going to Harvard, sensing perhaps a veiled invitation to share in a decision and a life about which she knew little. "My personal freedom is being interfered with," she told him bluntly, but then softened the blow by adding that this feeling also struggled against her love for him. "And then I think back and remember," she concluded, "that there never was a time when I didn't struggle against the domination of you."[58]

Their relationship blew hot and cold, plagued by Frankfurter's obsessive attention and by her indecision about whether to accept it or reject it. At times, he found her to be stubborn and unrelenting. "You threaten the securities of a person whose securities are only in the making, and will never be better than slow . . . and painful," she told him. "I must make my own life after my own pattern, even if it is less than it would be if I let myself follow you."[59] At other times, she succumbed to his obvious charm, devotion, and wild romanticism. "You give me more space for my vagaries," she wrote, "the days when I'm old and the days when I'm young. . . . I need somebody to look after the very young, little girl, and I don't know any man who could get as much out of the job as you."[60]

After the thrill of the chase, it must have come as something of a shock when Frankfurter announced in the summer of 1917 that he could not marry her because of uncertainty about the war and the emotional condition of his mother in the aftermath of Leopold's death. "I suppose it resolved itself into a choice between you and my mother," he wrote to Marion:

> Mother loved the only sight she had of you. . . . But alas! You in yourself were also a symbol—the symbol of difference in "race" and "faith" and all the other separating institutions born of the past. The thing goes deep, down to the very source of life, if it goes as it goes in those elders. I could not destroy what was left of zest and strength in her—most was expected of me, and there you are. For your understanding I know I've said more than was necessary. For your swiftness of mind and heart a hint suffices to reveal the depths. Well—thus it was not to have been, but I think of the glory that was.[61]

Temporarily breaking off this relationship proved to be a wrenching experience for Frankfurter, the young man from the fringes of the ghetto who had managed to dine regularly with members of the Yankee elite and who normally scorned the mystical ties of "race" and "faith" in favor of the progressive belief in science, reason, and the meritocracy. Briefly, he sacrificed his own desires before the claims of family duty "and all the other separating institutions born of the past." To his own amazement, perhaps, he was less of a Brahmin and more of a Jew than he had imagined for some time.

※-※-※

For Frankfurter as for other Americans during these years, the likelihood of war with Germany intruded upon even the most intimate moments of personal despair. By the spring of 1915, the rhetoric of neutrality could no longer disguise the flow of American food, munitions, and credit that sustained the Allied cause against the Kaiser's armies. However divided his own nation might be over the causes and nature of the European butchery, Wilson and most of his advisers displayed a marked preference for Great Britain. In a perfunctory manner, the president protested the illegal British blockade that threatened to choke off the economic boom in America, but he became choleric when the Germans responded to the trade imbalance by engaging in unrestricted submarine warfare against Allied shipping. Wilson then asserted a version of neutrality law that included the right of American citizens to travel safely on all belligerent vessels, a position that almost guaranteed conflict with the Germans. Increasingly, Wilson came to believe that the United States represented the only sane, disinterested nation in a world wracked by unreason and violence, and that this benign influence could be exercised only through armed intervention into the struggle. Many other progressives, unfortunately, shared this illusion.[62]

Frankfurter despised the shrill, chest-thumping preparedness speeches of Roosevelt and Leonard Wood, but he was certainly no pacifist. When Bryan resigned from the cabinet over Wilson's refusal to compromise on the right of Americans to travel on belligerent ships, Frankfurter denounced his gesture as "the sincerity of an ignorant man." Bryan's action, he told Katherine Ludington, "has helped to precipitate the very war he has so ardently sought to avert," because the Germans would exploit this appearance of division in the American government. Bryan, he noted, sarcastically, "thinks mere goodness of heart is enough."[63] On the other hand, he hoped that Wilson would not demand "the whole cessation of the submarine campaign," because, as he told Hand, "war on that issue seems less and less sensible and wise to me. And after seeing the West and South it sure wouldn't be a 'people's war.' "[64]

The campaigns for preparedness and Americanization, fueled by Roosevelt and financed by big business, soon filled him with despair, because they were guided by "sinister, ignorant forces" and seemed intent upon crushing the progressive movement. "No thought of labor, no imaginative effort to bring it into the counsels of the nation. . . . The preparedness views of a Leonard Wood make me wholly impatient—he has no vision about this country that goes beyond a German General's," he remarked to Ludington.[65] As the diplomatic crisis with Germany deepened, Frankfurter drew back for a moment from the horror of American intervention. War, he wrote, echoing the views of Wilson, "loosens forces that are so devastating, so unknown, so uncontrollable. . . . I cannot see war for us as the beckoning solution."[66]

His doubts and underlying pugnacity mirrored the wavering feelings of most Americans. He welcomed the respite of the "Arabic pledge," when the German government vowed not to attack unarmed passenger ships without warning, but at the same time he feared Germany's ambitions on the continent and in the years between 1915 and 1917, this fear became all-consuming, finally drowning his lingering skepticism about American belligerency. "Prussianism," he believed, probably could not be eradicated without American intervention. "Their demand for mastery, their intoxication about *das Deutsch* must be stamped out of the world," he wrote in early 1916. "Only German jingoism is the prevailing danger."[67]

In the presidential campaign of 1916, he remained undecided for months, but finally cast his vote for Wilson rather than for Hughes, although the president's grandiloquent foreign policy speeches did not arouse his confidence about the future. Wilson, he complained to Ludington, "was just words, however sincere in the ultimate search to give meaning to those vague words 'humanity,' and 'liberty' and 'America.' . . . He does make words do service for things and expects aspirations to be self-achieving."[68] Wilson's robust support of Brandeis and his assorted social welfare measures, including a federal ban on child labor, at last overcame Frankfurter's doubts. In addition, he feared that Hughes, once elected, might appoint his old *bête noir*, Taft, to the Supreme Court.[69]

In the wake of his narrow electoral victory, Wilson's diplomatic options grew narrower in 1917, once both sides rejected his mediation efforts and once Germany, reneging on its earlier promises, commenced unrestricted submarine warfare. The president delivered his famous "peace without victory" speech on January 22, which called for the creation of democratic governments throughout Europe, self-determination for each nation, freedom of the seas, and limitations upon armaments. Two weeks later he severed diplomatic relations with Germany. "Now we go in with deeper unity, stronger capacity and strength of a clear conscience," Frankfurter wrote, after attending a "war" meeting at *The New Republic* offices in New York. He, Croly, Lippmann, and others agreed that the nation had no choice but to fight in view of the fact that fanatics now held the upper hand in Germany. "Partisanship within the country must disappear," he told Ludington, "and every bit of effort and mind concentrated on clarifying American purpose and making it effective."[70]

For Frankfurter and many other progressives, the American declaration of war on April 4 brought a sense of relief and even exhiliration. They had become dedicated Wilsonians, whatever their previous allegiance in 1912, who like the president now believed that truth, justice, and democracy would prevail through the force of American arms. The right, Wilson had told the Congress, was more precious than peace. In the spring of 1917, Frankfurter shared that belief as well as the president's optimism about the shape of the future. "When this terrible battle will have been over," he wrote, "the democratic forces will break out anew. . . . I'm clearer than ever that democracy—the effective guidance of the minds and spirit of peoples—and force are the two halves of the scissors, and the two must cut together and in unison."[71] Like his colleague John Dewey, who set forth similar views in *The New Republic* to justify the war, Frankfurter believed that a war fought for progressive goals could be a beneficial war and that it was possible to reconcile violence with justice, force with democracy. In the heady spring of 1917, when words often did service for things, such results indeed seemed possible.[72]

CHAPTER 5

BISBEE AND MOONEY

DURING THE LAST YEARS of his life, bed-ridden and partially paralyzed from a stroke, Frankfurter often relived moments from his own past. He constantly sent his secretary Elsie Douglas on errands to his files, where she retrieved envelopes of correspondence with old colleagues and pages of faded yellow legal paper on which he had once made notations of conversations and drafts of memoranda. "The Justice grows weaker, spends little time out of bed, and lives in the past," she reported. "I am forever digging out earlier writings—Bisbee deportation, Philippine government, etc., etc."[1] In the twilight of his years, the springtime of his progressivism—the period immediately before, during, and after World War I—became one of Frankfurter's chief preoccupations, and in focusing upon these years he displayed a keen perception of the crucial events that helped to forge his public reputation. For during the war years, unquestionably, Frankfurter entered the nation's consciousness as an influential and oftentimes shadowy adviser in the fields of labor relations, foreign policy, and economic planning. He emerged from the tutelage of Stimson, Roosevelt, and Brandeis, became a political celebrity on his own, and a lightning rod for criticism as well because of his controversial stand on divisive public issues.

During the war years, the basic outlines of a durable Frankfurter legend took shape, rooted in the fevered imagination of his many enemies, the uncritical praise of admirers, and sometimes in the tangled record of events themselves. He was portrayed as an abrasive, cunning, brilliant, ruthless, and imperious administrator, who meddled in everyone's business and who perpetually attempted to extend the orbit of his own influence. "Mr. Wilson has charge of foreign policy and Felix seems to sponsor the rest of the government," Laski reported to Holmes. "To my certain knowledge he directs the War Department; Mr. [Newton] Baker is the pale wraith that Felix casts before him in his progress. I saw that he has almost annexed the Shipping Board; there are similar rumors from the Department of Justice."[2] Laski, however, often remained an uncritical admirer, one prone to hyperbolic observations. More to the point was the remark of an irritated William Howard Taft: "Mr. Frankfurter is like a good Chancellor, he wants to amplify his jurisdiction."[3]

Frankfurter found himself denounced alternately as a conservative masquerading as a radical and as a radical pretending to be a conservative. Militant labor leaders accused him of "conspiring with unfair employers to rob workers of the fruits of their organizations," but powerful industrialists branded him as a subversive who undermined American institutions by pampering strikers, bomb-throwing anarchists, and the Industrial Workers of the World. In the minds of those who crossed swords with him, Frankfurter played both roles, depending upon the particular issue and the extent to which they believed he had frustrated their noble objectives. In fact, he remained throughout this period a prowar progressive, who shared with many of his friends on *The New Republic* an exaggerated belief in the possibilities of social reform through national mobilization made possible by the state of emergency. And like these other prowar progressives, Frankfurter sometimes confused the requirements of mobilization with the demands of justice and sacrificed the immediate interests of ordinary citizens to the enticing vision of a world made safe for democracy.

"I'm at rest that we are in it," he told Hand, soon after the declaration of war. "No other way, I believe, could we have had a responsible opportunity for a hand in European, and therefore, world ordering. That's the objective of all my dreaming."[4] These hopes that the progressive ideals of order and progress could be extended beyond America's borders echoed the sentiments of Wilson, many of his advisers, large sections of the Republican Party, and Eastern intellectuals. But neither Frankfurter nor the president spoke for a majority of the American people, most of whom probably endorsed the views of Senator George Norris of Nebraska: "To whom does war bring prosperity?" he asked his colleagues. "Not to the soldier who for the munificent compensation of $16 per month shoulders his musket . . . not to the broken-hearted widow who waits for the return of the mangled body of her husband. . . . By our act we will make millions of our countrymen suffer . . . and all because we want to preserve the commercial right of American citizens to deliver munitions of war to belligerent nations."[5] On the farms, in the factories, mines, machine shops, and small businesses of the nation, opposition to the war ran deep, not only among pacifists, German Americans, socialists, Irishmen, and progressives like Norris, but also among countless citizens who either regarded the conflict as none of America's business or as a diabolical plot hatched by the money kings of Wall Street.

By the late spring and early summer of 1917, the Wilson administration faced a popular rebellion against American intervention, punctuated by draft resistance, strikes, torchlight parades, virulent press criticism, and the rising strength of the Socialist Party's antiwar candidates in state and local elections. Wilson and the prowar progressives fought back. The president branded liberals, socialists, and many labor leaders who opposed the war as stooges of the German government. "Woe be to the man or group of men that seeks to stand in our way in this day of high resolution," he warned. Attorney General Thomas Gregory asked for the Lord's mercy upon all war protestors, who "need expect none from an outraged people and an avenging government."[6] Congress, meanwhile, gave the president and his subordinates unprecedented authority over the nation's material and intellectual resources, which encouraged the administration to throttle dissent, educate the public, and prosecute the war, even in the face of considerable opposition. In so doing, they fashioned powerful instruments of official coercion and sanctioned a brutal display of popular lawlessness against groups and persons who did not endorse the Wilsonian crusade. By the end of the summer of 1917, war protest had become synonymous in many communities with treason.[7]

If these early manifestations of wartime hysteria troubled Frankfurter, he kept such doubts to himself. He had, after all, endorsed the proposition of Dewey and other progressives that democracy and force represented "two halves of the scissors, and the two must cut together and in unison." He had defined democracy as the "effective guidance of the mind and spirit of the people," a definition that suggested a large measure of manipulation of the masses by the political elite. Even before the declaration of war, he urged Newton Baker to appoint his friend Lippmann as chief of censorship, which he euphemistically described as "an instrument of intelligence between Washington and the country." Lippmann could handle the job, he informed the secretary of war, because he possessed "deep sympathy with the purposes of the Administration, insight into the ways of newspaper men, and personal persuasiveness in dealing with them so that right relations and confidence may be established."[8]

While sponsoring others, he soon found himself drawn into the wartime bureaucracy by the grim prospect of disintegrating labor standards, created by the procurement boom in federal contracts for training camps, munitions, and clothing. Shortly after April 6, Baker negotiated an agreement with Samuel Gompers, president of the American Federation of Labor, that provided for the adoption of union standards with respect to both wages and hours in the construction of cantonments for the Army. A far different situation developed in the clothing industry, where the War Department began to issue contracts without safeguards for the workers. Army quartermasters subordinated all questions of cost and labor conditions to the speed of delivery, which produced what one report described as "grave injury, loss, and disturbance" in the industry, benefiting those contractors who "resort to discredited sweating practices." After passing through two or three hands, government contracts were finally filled at far less than the government's price "by labor which is paid one-half or less of the usual wages." Furthermore, fly-by-night shops had been set up in remote districts "where they escape . . . from the state factory inspection and other measures of control."[9]

Canvassing the situation in Massachusetts, Frankfurter informed Baker, an old ally from the National Consumers' League, that the state's textile and woolen industries, swamped by heavy war orders, planned a "wholesale letting down of the bars as to hours, Sunday work, and night work for women." Unless the federal government improved its contracting procedures and enforcement machinery, he warned, labor's hard-won gains would be wiped out, the clothing industry would be thrown into chaos, and the worst suffering would fall upon the most vulnerable workers. He urged Baker to create a small committee in the secretary's office to take charge of this issue and he dismissed the existing war-labor program, controlled by Gompers and the Advisory Committee to the Council of National Defense, as "too slow of motion and too scattered in its thinking."[10] Well meaning, but extremely cautious, burdened with an antiquated bureaucracy and his own confusion, Baker pleaded with Frankfurter to come down to Washington for a weekend and straighten out the clothing industry. "I packed my suitcase," he recalled later, "and the weekend didn't terminate until the fall of 1919."[11]

Baker attempted to give his new recruit a major's commission, but Frankfurter refused on the grounds that "every pipsqueak Colonel would feel that he was more important." Instead, he joined Lippmann and Stanley King, another one of Brandeis's protégés, as Baker's principal civilian adviser, with a roving mandate to handle any problem that touched upon prosecution of the war. By late August, he had restored on paper at least a measure of decency in the clothing industry by drafting a model set of contracts that required manufacturers to adopt the eight-hour day, pay equal wages for equal work in the case of women and minorities, accept collective bargaining with their employees, and stop the employment of children under the age of sixteen. Consistent with the policies already adopted by Baker and Gompers, these recommendations did not require the closed shop or demand that employers bargain only with union representatives, but Frankfurter made certain that Baker expanded the number of inspectors available to police the clothing industry's new labor code.[12] Once the textile companies had been whipped into line, Baker encouraged Frankfurter to try his hand in the broader fields of wartime diplomacy with the ill-fated Morgenthau mission.

Much against his own wishes, Frankfurter found himself in Spain at the end of the summer, as a babysitter for Henry Morgenthau Sr., the rich and pompous former ambassador to Turkey, who had managed to convince the nation's chief military planners—including the president—that he could single-handedly detach the Turks from the Central Powers because of his personal friendship with Enver Pasha. Morgenthau, however, did not have the faintest idea about how to reach Turkey during the war or where to locate its rulers, and the mission became stranded in Spain. Undaunted, he moved his traveling circus, including Frankfurter, to Paris, where he attempted to convince General Pershing that Turkey could be knocked out of the war through a single, daring stroke that he had devised. When the general asked for maps, Morgenthau went to Brentano's bookstore for the items!

From Frankfurter's perspective, Morgenthau symbolized the vulgarity, stupidity, and myopia of the newly rich, who flaunted their money and attempted to influence politics through wealth alone. The

ambassador's lack of style also offended Frankfurter, who believed
that his antics confirmed the worst stereotypes of anti-Semites. "I assumed that was just the froth of the man," he recalled. "I didn't realize
that the froth was the man." For the rest of his life, Frankfurter looked
upon the hapless Morgenthau mission as one of the supreme examples
of the corrosive impact of money upon political life and of the absolute
necessity of entrusting diplomatic negotiations to skilled professionals.[13]

Morgenthau's *opera bouffe* was saved from complete disaster because Frankfurter used his time in Paris wisely, picked up important
gossip about the state of French politics, and wrote a penetrating report for Baker, the secretary of state, Robert Lansing, and Wilson's
eminence gris, Colonel House. Unless substantial numbers of American
troops reached Europe by the end of the year, he warned, "the defeat-
ist elements" in French politics, led by the unpredictable Joseph Caillaux, would gain greater support in the Chamber of Deputies. The
French army remained mutinous, Caillaux and his followers detested
the British, and they might seek a separate peace with Germany.
Equally menacing was his discovery of no trace in France of "the larger aim which brought the United States into the war" and that "very
little impetus can be expected to come out of France itself for . . . the
war purposes of the United States." Finally, he warned Baker and
House that the French had already begun to plan for the peace conference by creating special committees of experts in various areas and
"we should equip ourselves with like knowledge."[14]

Frankfurter's grim assessment spurred greater efforts on the military front and, more crucially, his report prompted House to recruit a
nucleus of American experts to advise the president on the full range
of issues that might emerge at the peace conference. For recommendations about personnel for this top-secret project, House turned again
to Frankfurter, who recommended that Lippmann take charge of the
informal planning group that became known as "The Inquiry."
"Frankfurter has been here," House told Wilson in early September,
"and many others interested in the subject, and there will be no difficulty in bringing together a group . . . to get the data and information
you desire." House adopted many of Frankfurter's suggestions, but
took umbrage at the latter's intimacy with many reporters as well as
his efforts to insinuate more of his friends into the enterprise. House,
a genteel anti-Semite, told the president that "the objection to Lippmann is that he is a Jew, but unlike other Jews he is a silent one. . . .
Thanks to Frankfurter, quite a number of people know that you have

this work in mind for me to do." A month later, he still complained to Wilson that "the Jews from every tribe have descended in force, and they seem determined to break in with a jimmy if they are not let in."[15]

Morgenthau's escapade, the travail of the French, and even House's venom paled in comparison with the labor turmoil that greeted Frankfurter upon his return from Europe. In the meat-packing plants of Chicago, in the cool, lush forests of the Pacific Northwest, and in the deserts of Arizona, the Wilson administration reaped a bitter harvest of years of corporate arrogance and neglect by trade unionism when tens of thousands of workers, the majority of them unskilled, struck against pay checks that failed to keep pace with inflation and working conditions that sometimes resembled serfdom. Vital war materials—meat, lumber, and copper—were at stake in these disputes that threatened to derail the nation's war machine before Colonel House could convene his corps of experts. In the summer of 1917, Arizona above all became the symbol of wartime labor struggles that pitted employers against workers and workers against each other, with the government of the United States seemingly unable to provide a coherent program that guaranteed both industrial production and industrial justice.

❧❧❧

Much of Frankfurter' subsequent frame as a wartime labor mediator rested upon his efforts on behalf of the President's Mediation Commission, created by Wilson in September 1917 with the hope that it could resolve major strikes, principally in Arizona's violence-plagued copper industry. Ironically, Frankfurter resisted the formation of the very commission that soon incurred the wrath of conservatives and radicals alike. "I was opposed to the whole idea," he told Marion Denman, "but Woody had gone too far to retrace his steps, and if there was to be such a commission it's as well that he sent me with them."[16] Gradually, his reluctance turned to enthusiasm as he discovered that Arizona's copper industry contained the difficulties of the entire war-labor program and would test the administration's ability to match the rhetoric of democracy with the realities of industrial life in America. "As I get deeper and deeper into these marooned outposts of the country," he told Katherine Ludington, "far from the intimacies of my own life, it all seems, it all is, part of the whole. The war, the economic and racial conflicts and cross currents that produced it, the industrial anarchies, our American striving to realize the democratic faith—here."[17]

Without question, in the summer of 1917 Arizona's copper camps exhibited most of the unresolved problems of the nation's industrial order that had remained virtually untouched by progressive reforms. In the searing heat of this frontier state, workers hoped to shape their job conditions and employers refused to tolerate these aspirations. The labor force, moreover, was torn by ethnic divisions and by bitter strife between conservative, prowar trade unionists—led by Gompers and the AFL—and radical, antiwar groups, who looked to the socialist Party or the Industrial Workers of the World for inspiration. In addition, the industry's paralysis symbolized the bureaucratic and political chaos that characterized the administration's initial efforts to cope with nationwide labor disorders. Arizona also tested the values and sympathies of middle-class progressives like Frankfurter, who had worked for a decade or more to advance labor's economic and legal rights. Now, he and others had to reconcile their peacetime enthusiasms with the demands of total war and attempt to implement their ideals in a new setting against both the authoritarian mentality of corporate managers and the passions of a working class that remained often indifferent to the liberal rhetoric of efficiency and reform.

Faced with rising food prices, low wages, and soaring copper profits that sprang from the war boom, Arizona's miners became increasingly militant after 1914. The rebellion began among the boilermakers in the Globe-Miami region, who successfully struck for a restoration of wage cuts in 1915. It gained new dynamism from the Mexicans in the Ray and Clifton districts, who struck in order to secure the right to organize unions in self-defense against production arrangements that functioned on the basis of racial discrimination, intimidation, and petty despotism, or as one Clifton miner described the camps of Phelps Dodge, Jackling, and Guggenheim: "One continued sickening mess of extortion, fraud, graft, and . . . shameless, unblushing robbery."[18] By the summer of 1916, close to 4,000 miners and craft workers, the vast majority Mexicans, Slavs, and Italians, had walked off the job in half a dozen other copper camps, where Arizona's reform-minded governor, George Hunt, found conditions bordering upon "inhuman injustice."[19]

Labor shortages in the state, plus the insatiable demand for copper, forced the companies to grant wage increases that temporarily quelled these strikes, but the operators refused to bow to the workers' major demands, especially nondiscrimination against union members. During the strikes, nonetheless, many of the immigrant miners had formed local unions chartered by the Arizona State Federation of Labor, which much to the displeasure of Gompers had fallen under the influence of socialists and militant industrial unionists who opposed the AFL's conservative, craft-oriented philosophy. The AFL's principal metal-mining affiliate, the International Union of Mine, Mill, and Smelter Workers (IUMMSW), led by Charles Moyer, had provided little aid to the strikers, who now looked either to the Arizona federation or to the IWW for support. The copper barons opposed all labor organizations, regardless of their ideological hue, thus setting the stage for an industrial conflict of enormous social complexity and appalling violence.[20]

By the middle of June 1917, the secretary of labor, William B. Wilson, optimistically told Baker that "the situation in Arizona is very well in hand," but a few days later, seventy five miners had been driven at gunpoint from the town of Jerome, and strikes had erupted again at Clifton, Globe-Miami, and Bisbee, near the Mexican border. Moyer, who had once been a member of the IWW but had become increasingly preoccupied with maintaining control of the moribund IUMMSW, repudiated the strikes and confessed that his local organizers could not influence the miners. "I have done everything in my power to hold the men," he told Gompers, "but they will go out . . . unless the operators agree to conference."[21]

Moyer and Gompers relied upon business leaders, above all the redoubtable Bernard Baruch, to make the companies more reasonable, but Baruch, who headed the government's raw materials program and who had large copper investments himself, could not sway the operators. "The owners . . . say they cannot concede," he told the secretary of labor. "While I am in favor of making every possible concession, at the same time we certainly should preserve the status quo and not permit anything to be used as leverage to change conditions from the standpoint of the employer or the employee." The companies, however, anxious to use the leverage of the war to destroy the workers' organizations, clamored for military assistance, encouraged the formation of citizens' loyalty leagues in the various camps, and pushed for the adoption of local laws that banned all picketing and public assemblies.[22]

Labor Department mediators had little success getting the parties to negotiate, and representatives from the Justice and War Departments improvised their responses from one strike to the next, usually acting on the basis of distaste for the miners. One United States Attorney, for example, urged the detention of all aliens, strikers, and protestors, even before passage of the Espionage Act provided a legal basis for indictments. "The Mexican element . . . is a most dangerous one." reported Thomas Flynn, "and amenable only to the discipline of force if they . . . start trouble."[23]

Military commanders improvised their own policies in the face of vague and confusing instructions from the secretary of war. Some officers refused local pleas for federal troops, but Major General William Bundel sent 400 soldiers to Globe, where they intimidated picketing workers and escorted strike breakers back to work, much to the chagrin of the Labor Department's mediators. From the town of Ray, Lieutenant J. E. Lewis proudly announced that his cavalry unit had rescued the citizens from what he called a "threatened IWW strike among the Spanish and Mexican miners." This industrial relations expert reported, moreover, that owing to excellent living conditions and high wages, "there is no reason for labor trouble here . . . barring the uncertainty of the Mexican temperament."[24]

The copper barons also took matters into their own hands, when state and federal assistance did not materialize. The worst vigilante activity took place in Bisbee, where Walter Douglas, the head of Phelps Dodge, persuaded the town's merchants and Sheriff Harry Wheeler to solve the strike by deporting over one thousand workers and their sympathizers. Led by Wheeler and one of Theodore Roosevelt's old friends, Jack Greenway, the posse loaded the strikers into cattle cars and dumped them in the deserts of New Mexico without food or water.[25] Following the deportation, Phelps Dodge organized a local kangaroo court to rid the town of remaining union members, suspected IWWs, and all protesting citizens. Even Governor William Campbell, who had not been timid about requesting federal troops, expressed shock at the ugly turn of events in Bisbee. "You folks," he told Bisbee officials, "are breaking the law down there everyday—every minute."[26]

Only the opposition of the railway unions prevented a similar deportation of strikers from the town of Globe, and when that solution failed, the companies, loyalty leaguers, and the local sheriff filled the jail with pickets arrested on charges of vagrancy and "rioting" on the public highway. "Arizona," the state's assistant attorney general informed the President of the United States, "is in a deplorable condition."[27]

From his station in the War Department, Frankfurter watched the Arizona debacle with disgust and horror. In early September he wrote Baker a long memorandum that contained a scathing attack upon

Gompers, the AFL, and the administration's labor policy in general. "It will be fatal to the handling of the labor situation," he told Baker, "to assume that Mr. Gompers controls all labor or even all organized labor with which the Government should deal, or to assume that all those who are not for Mr. Gompers are for the I. W. W." The administration should open communications with "constructive and responsible radicals" in the labor movement, even if they opposed Gompers's leadership. He told Baker to fight the creation of a commission Gompers had urged upon Wilson, because it would be "too much identified with the authorities and the employing interests which have . . . shown only negative hostility towards this radical but non-IWW element."[28]

Frankfurter wrote a brash document, especially the denunciation of Gompers, because the latter had received from Wilson a virtually impregnable position in the bureaucracy as a result of his support for the war that he once characterized as "the most wonderful crusade ever entered upon by man in the whole history of the world."[29] Given the hostility of other labor leaders and workers, Wilson could ill afford to do anything to undermine Gompers's authority. Nor did it seem likely that the president would accept Frankfurter's key proposal to send an informal group of mediators to Arizona, headed by Sidney Hillman of the clothing workers, who had ties with labor radicals and anti-Gompers forces in the AFL.[30] Frankfurter's recommendations, moreover, contained a vulgar caricature of the Wobblies, who did not usually instigate violence, and he underestimated Gompers, who hoped to resolve the Arizona impasse on terms that would strengthen the AFL and punish his enemies in the labor movement.

The AFL president gave Wilson an ultimatum on August 10: either the government and the copper companies would deal with "bona fide organized constructive labor . . . or they will have . . . to take the consequences of the so-called IWW with all that it implies." He pushed a resolution through the Council of National Defense that asked the president to name a special mediation commission, and despite objections from Baker, Frankfurter, and others, he secured all of his immediate objectives. The President's Mediation Commission, packed with AFL stalwarts, included the secretary of labor, the president of the United Mine Workers in Illinois, John H. Walker, and the chairman of the Washington State Federation of Labor, Ernest P. March. A Pennsylvania coal operator, Jackson Spangler, and Verner Reed, a well-to-do rancher and mining entrepreneur, represented business.[31]

Vanity, fondness for Baker, and a quick reassessment of Gompers's influence forced Frankfurter to accept a position as secretary and legal counsel to the commission whose creation he had opposed. Outside the commission, he risked banishment to the periphery of labor policy, a role he seldom relished. Inside the commission, he could advance his own fortunes and attempt to enlighten those who wielded more power. In addition, his presence might soften criticism of Baker and the military, who had not acted with intelligence or prudence in the Arizona conflict. He invited Max Lowenthal to join the expedition, even though Lowenthal, a former Harvard student and clerk to Judge Julian Mack, professed little knowledge of economics, copper mining, or labor relations. "Neither does anybody else," Frankfurter quipped, "Come along."[32]

For nearly two months the Mediation Commission remained in Arizona, sleeping and eating in railroad cars, endlessly listening to and negotiating with managers, workers, public officials, and ordinary citizens, who filled stenographers' notebooks with testimony that exhibited their hatred, fear, and ignorance. Frankfurter found some respite from this grueling routine in long, twilight walks with Reed's spiritual adviser, a Catholic priest named O'Dwyer, with whom he discussed the mysteries of the universe, the perversity of human nature, and the frustrations they encountered in their attempts to mediate a settlement to the strikes. "I'm . . . sort of a dry nurse for various pets of this administration," he told Marion with some irritation, comparing Secretary Wilson to Henry Morgenthau. Wilson, he confided to Hand, was "a dear old soul—shrewd and wise, but with all the limitations of a narrow intellectual experience." He struggled to make the members of the commission understand the principles of scientific management and to make them "forget that I am young, that I am a lawyer and a professor."[33]

Despite his subordinate position, Frankfurter quickly took charge of the commission's more thorny political problems and promptly won the hatred of the copper companies, who resented federal interference with their labor relations and balked at negotiations. The general manager of the Arizona Copper Company, for example, did not yield until Lord Percy, responding to Frankfurter's urgent cables, put pressure on stockholders in Scotland.[34] Likewise, Frankfurter engineered an elaborate bluff with Stanley King in the War Department that led Anaconda officials to believe the government was about to take over the Inspiration mine and operate it under receivership. Although both Frankfurter and King knew the administration had no such authority, Anaconda officials in New York backed down and sent their local manager to the negotiating table.[35]

The attitude of the copper producers, who blamed the miners' lack of patriotism for the disorders, infuriated Frankfurter. "The thing is so shallow and so pathetic, as well as brutal," he told Hand. "These old bags, who have fought labor, and unions as poison for decades, now wrap themselves in the flag and are confirmed in their old biases and . . . obscurantism by a passionate patriotism. Gee—but it's awful and then they wonder at the fecundity of the IWW."[36] The Wobblies recruited followers, he told Brandeis, because of the stupidity and selfishness of "the national government, various state governments, capital *and* the old line trade unionism of the AFL."[37]

Frankfurter dealt harshly with those managers who he believed obstructed the commission's efforts and endangered the entire war production program. He could be equally ruthless when faced with recalcitrant miners. In the Clifton district, for example, he persuaded the workers to return to the mines on the promise that wage increases would be forthcoming if the cost of the increase could be passed on through higher copper prices, a method that required approval from the War Industries Board. He characterized this tactic as "a neat solution of a very knotty problem," but when the War Industries Board balked at selective price increases for the mines in the Clifton area, he told Eugene Meyer flatly: "If . . . the War Industries Board doesn't feel like making any changes . . . it doesn't need to make any. Everybody understands it and nobody will be affected. In other words, forget about it."[38]

Despite the concern he expressed to Baker about opening up communication with "constructive and responsible radicals," Frankfurter quietly accepted the commission's desire to crack down on those strikers who opposed Gompers and the IUMMSW. On paper the settlements negotiated by the commission seemed generous toward the miners. Strikers were to be reemployed, discrimination against union members was forbidden, and elected grievance committees were to meet regularly with management. The settlements, however, did not compel the companies to bargain with union representatives, and banned strikes for the duration of the war. The fine print of the reemployment agreements, however, excluded many workers from protection, especially "those who since the beginning of the strike have been guilty of utterances disloyal to the United States, or who are members of any organization that refuses to recognize the obligation of contracts."[39] The managers as well as the AFL representatives insisted upon these "anti-Wobbly" provisions, in addition to clauses that discriminated against foreign-born miners by giving preference in rehiring to married men "and those with dependents over single men."

Ironically, the miners in Bisbee, where the worst examples of employer repression had occurred, received the least protection from the commission, which condemned the deportation as "wholly illegal" and urged the prosecution of those responsible. Frankfurter, who wrote the Bisbee report, had considerable difficulty persuading the commissioners to keep his blunt language in the document. "I don't know whether Wilson will stand for it," he reported. "Its only defect is its colorless mildness and understated accuracy."[40] Having slapped the operators on the wrist, the commissioners next commended the nonstrikers for their patriotism and instructed the local managers not to establish an elected grievance committee immediately, because, as Secretary Wilson explained, "it might be throwing into their minds the suggestion that grievance committees ought to be organized."[41] Within a month after the commission left Bisbee, one miner reported to his brother that the companies were still "hunting out union men now and when they find one . . . [Phelps Dodge] sends in an order to fire him."[42]

By the end of November, the state produced copper again, skilled workers had gained some protection, Gompers had punished his radical opponents, but the miners in most camps continued to live under the crude domination of the companies and hostile local authorities. "Conditions in the [Globe] district," one miner lamented, are "two hundred percent worse by reason of the settlements."[43] A year later, the Rev. William Scarlett reported to Frankfurter that "the companies have succeeded in killing unionism. It has fallen away to a pathetic shadow of its former self. . . . And the outlook unless . . . the unions [are] strengthened before the War ends, is discouraging."[44] Even Secretary Wilson confessed "that when an investigation is made, you will find that the situation isn't well in hand at Globe-Miami . . . and that it is absolutely out of hand in the Bisbee-Warren District."[45]

Despite his failure to carry through on ideas outlined in the memorandum to Baker and his willingness to go along with harsh treatment of the Wobblies, Frankfurter felt the anguish of the miners and sensed the underlying issues of the brutal conflict better than any member of the commission. "These Mexicans are supposed to be all that is bad," he wrote, "when the truth of the matter is that they are merely different than the whites who boss them." The managers, he noted, remained "blind to what's going on in the world," especially to the democratic impulses unleashed by Wilson's soaring rhetoric. "They control a quarry," he wrote, "and forget it's also a community." The miners, on the other hand, "feel they were not treated as men, were without a share in determining the conditions of their labor, and their labor is their life. . . . In a word, there is no fellowship for them in the great industrial enterprise which absorbs them." The workers' basic complaint, he told Brandeis, "is as to their position as wage-earners. It's . . . a fight for the status of free manhood."[46]

Unfortunately, his sympathetic understanding of the miners' plight did not decisively influence the commission's procedures or final recommendations, which focused more narrowly upon the protection of AFL loyalists, attempted to purge the camps of radicals, and guaranteed a dependable supply of copper. Even if Frankfurter had objected strenuously to the results, which he did not, the Gompers faction on the commission would have proceeded in much the same fashion. His influence became even slighter once the commission departed from Arizona, and left enforcement of the settlements in the hands of the companies and two mediators from the Labor Department, who proved wholly inadequate to the task.

The operators continued to discriminate against union members, actually reduced production in order to deny reemployment to many strikers, ignored the grievance procedures, and deported individual workers who protested.[47] Required to patrol the entire state of Arizona, the mediators remained overworked and tended to adopt the companies' point of view on most issues, a policy that led the legal rights committee of the Arizona Federation of Labor to remark that the commission's work would remain "very much of a farce as long as the Government permits these [copper] men . . . to virtually enforce the findings . . . according to their own ideas, and impose such additional requirements and conditions as they see fit."[48] Arizona, Frankfurter assured the Reverend Scarlett, required "education and execution," but these ingredients seemed sadly lacking after the Mediation Commission retired from the field.[49]

❧❧❧

Not all of the commission's efforts proved as barren for the workers as those in Arizona. In highly organized industries with fewer ethnic divisions and in urban areas where the unions had considerable political influence, labor fared better. In both the Pacific coast telephone industry and the Chicago meat-packing plants, for instance, the commission ended protracted strikes with settlements that included wage increases, greater protection for union members during the war, and limited collective bargaining, although in neither case did it require employers to recognize unions or to accept a closed shop.[50] On the other hand, the commission experienced little success in the lumber industry of the Pacific Northwest, where, because of the neglect of the AFL and intolerable working conditions, the Wobblies had gained a strong following among the lumberjacks and the saw-mill workers. "The labor situation in these parts is ugly," Frankfurter told Brandeis. "There is no other word to describe it."[51]

Before the commission brought the two sides to the negotiating table, Baker ordered federal troops into the region under the command of General Brice P. Disque and gave him instructions to begin spruce production through the formation of a new labor organization composed of soldiers and nonstriking lumberjacks. Baker acted largely on his own, without notifying the commission, a development that Frankfurter ridiculed as another example of the "criminal methods of administration" that plagued the War Department's handling of all labor problems. With considerable bitterness, he poured out his frustrations to Brandeis: "While we were sent out here to settle matters, Baker, Gompers and [Louis] Post make arrangements largely confusing the issue, by providing for the use of soldiers in the camps." Baker and Gompers even commenced independent negotiations with the producers. "Having sent us out to settle matters," he fumed, "they unsettle it behind our backs."[52]

The Mediation Commission experienced less success than Frankfurter and others later recalled in their memories, but given its domination by the AFL, the brief period of its existence, and the limited resources available, this outcome is hardly surprising. From the point of view of the workers involved, the commission's presence in Arizona, California, Chicago, and Washington brought a temporary respite from employer abuses, but did little to reverse the historic patterns of discrimination against unions or hostility to collective bargaining. By advocating the adoption of the eight-hour day and providing elected grievance committees in some industries, the commission outraged many employers, who loathed all federal interference with the prerogatives of management. They were hardly mollified by the commission's attack on the IWW and other radicals, a device that Frankfurter condemned privately but accepted passively in the course of his assignment.

Neither the Mediation Commission nor any other government

agency had a mandate in 1917 to advance the cause of unionization among American workers, an objective that frightened most businessmen and would have disrupted the war effort had it been attempted. Patriotic zeal and widespread distrust of all strikers became epidemic in American communities during these years, a process which turned an already conservative public even more violently toward the right. The administration's own jingoism fueled much of the hysteria directed against Wobblies, German Americans, socialists, and conscientious objectors, but local vigilante groups and public officials did not lag far behind the federal government. Frankfurter discovered these sober facts when he became enbroiled in the case of Thomas J. Mooney.

※〉※〉※〉

Mooney, a sometime iron moulder, part-time IWW, and full-time labor organizer, and Warren Billings, a shoe-lining cutter and migratory radical, had been tried and convicted of murder in San Francisco for their alleged role in that city's Preparedness Day bombing of July 22, 1916, which claimed the lives of ten people and wounded forty others. Their trial took place against a background of a nationwide "anarchist scare" and a series of festering strikes in San Francisco that demonstrated the desire of the city's employers to crush organized labor and create an open-shop environment.

Both men went to trial under several handicaps in a city polarized by labor unrest, the war, and whipped into a patriotic frenzy by William Randolph Hearst's *Examiner*. They had participated in recent strikes, associated with known anarchists, spoken out against the war, and been brought to trial and acquitted earlier in Oakland on the charge of bombing the power lines of the Pacific Gas and Electric Company. Charles Marron Fickert, a former Stanford football hero and leader of the local preparedness forces, led the prosecution team. As the city's district attorney, he presented the case as the final confrontation between middle-class law and order and the revolutionary tendencies of San Francisco's proletariat. "The exploiters of labor on the Pacific coast," wrote the progressive lawyer, Frank Walsh, "seized upon . . . labor's best and purest leaders for sacrifice. . . . A vicious and obsolete jury system, a corrupt press, and millions of dollars in the hands of conscienceless men are . . . aiming at their destruction."[53]

Mooney and Billings may not have exemplified "labor's best and purest leaders," but Fickert and the city's business establishment

spared no effort to convict them. Sentenced to hang by Judge Franklin
Griffin after a speedy jury verdict, Mooney might have been executed
without much controversy, had it not been for the tireless efforts of
American anarchists, led by Emma Goldman and Alexander
Berkman, and the greed of one Edward Ringall, who attempted to
blackmail the prosecution's chief witness, Frank Oxman. The anarchists raised money for legal appeals and organized huge protests
abroad, including one before the American embassy in Russia, where
the faltering Kerensky government urged the Wilson administration
to examine the case. Labor leaders in Illinois, meanwhile, had come
into possession of two letters written by Oxman to Ringall before the
trial, in which the Oregon rancher had urged his friend to come to San
Francisco in order to support his claim to being an eyewitness to the
bombing.

In these letters, Oxman told Ringall, "you will only haf [*sic*] to
answer 3 and 4 questions and I will post you on them. . . . I need a
witness." Ringall was also told "you will only haf [*sic*] to say you seen
me on July 22 in San Frisco and that will be Easey dun [*sic*]." Oxman's
letters cast serious doubt upon the veracity of the prosecution's chief
witness and the state's entire case against Mooney, who remained on
death row pending the outcome of his appeal to the California Supreme Court. "Anybody taking a look at these letters," remarked the
city's assistant district attorney, "not understanding all the facts . . .
certainly . . . might get the wrong idea about the letters." Oxman
survived a perjury trial and Fickert turned back a turbulent recall election based upon suggestions that he had railroaded Mooney, but even
the trial judge believed that the defendants deserved a new trial in
light of the Oxman-Rigall correspondence.[54]

Frankfurter had never heard of Tom Mooney until Wilson asked
him to investigate the tangled issues during the Mediation Commission's trip to the West. Like the president, who responded to pressure
from the Kerensky government and who hoped to keep the Russians
in the war, Frankfurter initially regarded the case as a problem in
diplomacy. He soon discovered otherwise, after studying the evidence
gathered by George Arnold, the son-in-law of California's progressive
congressman, William Kent. Arnold also arranged interviews for
Frankfurter with Mooney, Fickert, Judge Griffin, and the defense
lawyers. In addition, he talked with other California attorneys who
convinced him that the state's case against Mooney was scandalously
defective and he chatted with the condemned man's priest, Archbishop Hanna of San Francisco, who assured him that Tom was a very
bad boy, "but he didn't do this."[55]

Choosing his words carefully and pitching his arguments to conform to Wilson's idealism, Frankfurter wrote a report that the president released at the end of January 1918. On the advice of California attorneys who were close to the case, he anticipated a negative decision from the state's highest court; he urged a pardon for Mooney and his retrial on one of the remaining, open indictments. Nowhere did he argue Mooney's guilt or innocence, but the hint of injustice could hardly be disguised. "War is fought with moral as well as material resources," he wrote. "We are in this war to vindicate the moral claims of unstained processes of law, however slow, at times, such processes may be. These claims must be tempered by the fire of our own devotion to them at home."[56]

The report smelled of treason to conservatives, many of whom still smarted over Frankfurter's report on the Bisbee deportation. Fickert accused him of listening only to Mooney's friends and of refusing to permit the prosecution to file a brief. In fact, Fickert and his staff had attempted to sabotage the report. They had been given adequate time to respond to the defense lawyers' claims, but apparently hoped to drag out the proceedings until after the state supreme court had acted or Mooney had been executed.[57] Other critics denounced Frankfurter for subverting American federalism by commenting upon the criminal proceedings of a sovereign state while employed by the national government.[58]

The most hysterical salvo came from the old Rough Rider himself, who accused Frankfurter of besmirching the reputation of God-fearing, patriotic Americans (Jack Greenway in Bisbee and Fickert in San Francisco), destroying respect for law and order, and coddling anarchists, bomb throwers, and cowards. "You are engaged in excusing men precisely like the Bolsheviki in Russia," Roosevelt roared, "who are murderers and encouragers of murder, who are traitors to their allies, to democracy, and to civilization, as well as to the United States."[59] Roosevelt' attack pained Frankfurter, although he knew it came from a mind sadly disoriented by the war and by the loss of a son in combat. He stood his ground, however, and reminded the former president that in this time of crisis, it was important "to prevent ignorance or selfishness or prejudice from using the disguise of patriotism for ends alien to the national interest."[60]

Surely, he told Roosevelt, "it is not a law of necessity that whatever Jack Greenway does is right." American workers demanded a larger voice in the industrial process, he added, and unless the nation corrected "grave and accumulating evils we shall find the disintegrating forces in our country gaining ground."[61] He preached good conservative doctrine that Roosevelt himself had used to justify social reforms, but the former president now remained immune to reason. "I cannot agree with you in your assumption that the IWW is patriotic and is devoted to the purposes of the war and its prosecution," he told Frankfurter, oblivious to the fact that neither the latter nor the Mediation Commission had ever spoken well of the Wobblies or done anything to further their cause.[62]

Despite the furor raised by his Mooney report, it had little immediate impact upon the fate of the convicted labor leader. Two months after its publication, as Frankfurter had predicted, the highest court in California affirmed Mooney's conviction and death sentence on the narrow grounds that it could not take cognizance of evidence introduced after the trial, although at least one of the justices criticized the decision and confessed privately that he did not believe Mooney "guilty of the crime of which he was convicted."[63] President Wilson, who had quickly lost interest in the case once Lenin and the Bolsheviks took Russia out of the war, nonetheless urged California's governor, William D. Stephens, to commute the condemned man's sentence. Further pressure was put on the governor by Judge Griffin and the Hearst papers, who urged a new trial.

"Those assassins out there seem determined to murder these people brazenly," Walsh complained, when the governor failed to act. "They seemed to be shut off from the rest of the world."[64] Finally, several weeks after the Armistice and in the wake of new revelations made by John Densmore of the Labor Department that suggested even worse misconduct in Fickert's office, the governor commuted Mooney's sentence to life imprisonment, a decision that made little sense from the point of view of justice or even from the perspective of Stephens himself, who continued to insist that Mooney was "a vicious and heartless murderer," who had participated in "one of the most atrocious crimes . . . ever perpetrated in the history of our country."[65] Understandably, Mooney's supporters complained bitterly about this craven decision, which prevented a new trial, protected Ficker's tarnished reputation from further inquiry, and salvaged the governor's own political career. "Of all the crimes committed against you in the name of justice," Walsh told Mooney, "this last is the worst. . . . The great mass of the American people believe in your innocence."[66] In the winter of 1918, unfortunately, most Americans remained preoccupied with other matters and despite the efforts of Frankfurter, Walsh, and Densmore, they remained ignorant of Mooney's fate. He remained in prison for another twenty years, until he was finally pardoned by Governor Olson toward the end of the Great Depression.

The Mooney case and his efforts with the Mediation Commission taught Frankfurter several painful lessons about the war effort, the bureaucracy, and the problems of justice. He learned, for example, the terrible power of wartime hysteria and the difficulty in the federal system of correcting local miscarriages of justice, where entrenched public officials remained hostile to outside critics. In the beginning he regarded Tom Mooney as a diplomatic problem, related to "the most effective prosecution of war aims," because the case generated negative publicity among America's allies and potential allies. Gradually, the arguments and passion of Mooney's supporters convinced him of the necessity for a new trial. Shocked by Stephens's unprincipled decision, he actively joined efforts to reopen the case over the next two decades.

The commission's attempt to resolve bitter industrial disputes and the lack of effective coordination among agencies of the federal government convinced him, too, that the nation's wartime labor efforts required more vigorous, centralized direction apart from the tradition-laden departments of a peacetime executive branch. Nearly eight months after the declaration of war, he realized, the United States continued to improvise its response to strikes and lockouts on an ad hoc basis. In terms of wages, hours, working conditions, and grievance procedures, the domestic labor situation in many regions and industries bordered upon anarchy. "The confusion of authority, its haphazardness, the multiplicity of agencies without a central direction," he complained to Brandeis, "cannot go on much longer."[67] In this crisis of labor relations, he sensed an opportunity to organize power on a grand scale, to promote social reform, and incidentally, to swell his own influence.

CHAPTER 6

THE CZAR OF LABOR

"THIS WAR," declared Newton D. Baker, "is being fought in every factory, every workshop, every home in the country by those marvelously subtle processes of modern scientific achievement by which are all co-ordinated."[1] Most Americans and many of the secretary's own assistants, unable to discern "those marvelously subtle processes," did not share his optimism about the nation's mobilization effort. They saw instead only hesitation, confusion, and rampant ad hoc decision making that seemed to produce more recriminations than war materials. The enunciation of noble objectives and the raising of an army proved easier than providing the industrial resources to sustain them.

The American economy staggered under the simultaneous demands of war and civilian production. It lacked direction, not energy. In a universe of "cost-plus" contracts, where procurement officers from the government and private capitalists scrambled over one another for men, machines, raw materials, credit, and transportation, each priority met an equally compelling priority, and few priorities were filled except by means of bureaucratic cunning and blind chance. Fearful of civilian experts, many of whom where recruited from big business, Baker sided with his procurement officers and bureau chiefs, who stoutly resisted a more centralized system of resource allocation. In the case of fuel and food production, a primitive structure of price controls and allocation had been established under a single administrator, but elsewhere chaos reigned. The fierce winter of 1917–1918 nearly brought the vaunted war machine to a standstill.[2]

Strikes and lockouts, most of them unresolved by the President's Mediation Commission, created numerous production bottlenecks and aggravated labor shortages produced by military conscription and competitive bidding among war contractors. Without cargo ships, finished goods accumulated in the Eastern ports, clogging the arteries of production and transportation across the continent. In France obsolete docking facilities and shrinking warehouse space choked off more Atlantic commerce than German U-boats. Snow storms, ingrained habits of competition, and years of financial mismanagement left the nation's railroads strangling in a maze of lost freight cars, missed connections, and rotting equipment, while in the hastily constructed cantonments, American soldiers suffered from epidemics of disease and the lack of basic equipment. Some of them used broomsticks for training rifles.

Neither Baker nor the War Department bore sole responsibility for these problems, but the secretary had not helped matters with his stubborn refusal to curb the power of his procurement officers or his inability to delegate authority to others. Suspicious of the generals, businessmen, and labor leaders who contended for his favor, Baker attempted to solve this problem by monopolizing all the levers of power, and by attempting to play the roles of military strategist, captain of industry, and labor mediator all at the same time. He played none of them very well and became increasingly paranoid as criticism of his department mounted in the press and in Congress. "Dear good Baker is swamped," Frankfurter told Brandeis. "He has no time to think out the real things—and makes all the blunders of fatigue and shallowness."[3]

The crisis of production and the War Department's internal disarray galvanized Frankfurter into action. Although he admired Baker, he hated inefficiency more. When the secretary asked him for a frank appraisal of the department's problems in preparation for congressional hearings, Frankfurter prepared a scathing report. "Baker," Colonel House noted, "was rather dumbfounded at the audacity of it."[4] The department's administrative difficulties had ancient roots, Frankfurter wrote, attempting to soften the blow somewhat, but nine months of war had compounded these problems to the point where the department had now become a major obstacle to victory. "We have failed just because this impossible task has been placed upon the shoulders of a single individual. . . . It is a responsibility which no mortal can discharge."[5]

The secretary of war, Frankfurter argued, should concentrate exclusively upon military training and strategy. Industrial production should be guided by a single expert, similar to the food administrator or the railroad administrator, who would absorb "all the existing supply committees and boards . . . [the] War Industries Board, and the committees of the Council of National Defense." The situation also required "a singleheaded labor administrator," who could bring some degree of order to the "numerous, fragmentary, independent, concurrent and conflicting agencies" that now functioned in this area, but produced "unnecessary unrest . . . wasteful competition for skilled workers . . . lack of attainable efficiency, and . . . the dislocation of the labor supply." He feared that the Labor Department could not accomplish these goals, because of the longstanding resentment of employers against the agency, but he still believed Secretary Wilson might play a useful role "without the handicap . . . of bringing the Department with him."[6]

Frankfurter's plan envisioned nothing less than the dismemberment of the War Department's improvised empire, a strategy that did not please Baker or his generals, who distrusted greater civilian control over production. But Frankfurter, able to recruit powerful allies, had laid his plans carefully. Two days later, Brandeis urged an identical reorganization plan upon Colonel House, including the idea for a "small council of . . . men freed from the details of administration . . . to consider the broad questions of policy in internal and external affairs."[7] The justice's views carried extraordinary weight with the president, who received similar advice from William McAdoo, Baruch, and other business leaders. They argued bitterly over the question of who would get the new bureaucratic plum, but they united behind Frankfurter's desire for greater centralization over war production. When Wilson finally named Baruch to head a reorganized War Industries Board in March, the financier received less authority than Frankfurter had proposed, but more than Baker or the military chiefs thought desirable.[8]

Frankfurter had less success implementing his plea for "a singleheaded labor administrator." This idea generated fierce opposition from the many "fragmentary, independent, concurrent and conflicting agencies" that had already been created to adjust labor disputes in particular sectors of the economy. The Railroad Wage Commission and the Shipbuilding Labor Adjustment Board, for example, refused to surrender any of their independence, as did the mediation boards for cantonment construction, the arsenals, and the harness and saddlery industry. Gompers looked with suspicion upon dilution of the Labor Department's jurisdiction or his own influence within the bureaucracy. And most businessmen disliked the idea of any federal interference with wages, hours, or recruiting practices. Secretary Wilson skillfully wove these forces into a coalition to defeat Frankfurter's cherished idea.

He secured the president's blessing for a two-month study of the Frankfurter proposal, packed this War Labor Conference Board with conservative businessmen and AFL loyalists, and saw to it that their report generally endorsed the status quo. Wilson's group urged the creation of yet another adjustment agency—the War Labor Board—but with its authority limited to those cases not already covered by present boards "to make clear . . . there is no intention to substitute this Board for the . . . other agencies already established."[9] The president quickly named Frank Walsh and William Howard Taft as co-chairmen of the new adjustment board, which performed notable service in the settlement of major urban transit strikes, but the Walsh-Taft board did not begin to grapple with war labor problems from a comprehensive point of view. Its settlements displayed the same parochialism and opportunism that plagued the activities of the other adjustment boards.[10]

As a sop to Frankfurter, who urged greater national standardization with respect to labor relations, the conference board adopted a set of broad guidelines to assist the various adjustment boards, but these principles largely codified existing practices. Workers could not be fired for "legitimate trade union activities," but they could not seek a union shop where they had failed to win recognition before the war. The basic eight-hour day was to be enforced, but only in those situations where "existing law requires it." When fixing wages, hours, and working conditions, the various boards were instructed to pay close attention to local standards, but also to guarantee "the subsistence of the worker and his family in health and reasonable comfort."[11] Within these broad guidelines, the adjustment boards retained broad discretion to resolve labor conflicts as best they could and to continue the furious competition for able-bodied workers in their respective industries and geographic regions.

As Frankfurter predicted, the creation of another adjustment board and the articulation of general principles did little to improve the nation's chaotic labor situation. Government contractors and private industry continued to fight one another for labor, and the separate adjustment boards failed to coordinate their efforts with respect to wages, hours, overtime pay, or conditions. In order to lure more workers, for example, the Shipbuilding Adjustment Board insisted upon fixing a wage scale above that paid by other government contractors or private industry, but this practice generated similar wage demands from unions in the Navy yards. Employees in the arsenals also demanded the shipyard rates, and the discontent soon spread to the private munitions plants as well.

The National Adjustment Commission set longshoremen's rates in San Diego at 65 cents per hour, but the Navy fixed its rate at 70 cents in the same location. The Railway Adjustment Board adopted machine-shop rates without consulting the War or Navy departments, while the War and Navy departments fixed their scales without consulting either the shipbuilding or railroad boards. No national or industrywide standards prevailed with respect to overtime pay or enforcement of the eight-hour day. In one ordnance shop, workers who made rifle parts were on the basic eight-hour day, but those who made the tools and jigs worked longer hours. When the Labor Department dispatched a recruiter to the Hampton Roads region to hire 300 common laborers for the Army and Navy, the men vanished from the train depot with another government contractor who offered higher wages. "Competitive bidding for labor . . . is flagrant and on the increase," reported Robert Woolley of the ICC. "Government boards establish diverse standards, officers of labor unions confess to finding it increasingly difficult, and frequently impossible, to hold their men. At certain points serious shortages of skilled labor are offset by a similar surplus at other points."[12]

Frankfurter had been stymied initially by Wilson in his efforts to centralize the administration of the war-labor program. Now, as the crisis deepened, he adopted a new strategy. Instead of recommending a particular plan of reorganization, he would recommend a particular person—Brandeis—whom neither the president nor the secretary of labor could easily reject. This suggestion, which apparently carried the justice's own approval, indicates how desperate the progressive forces had become in the face of escalating labor turmoil and the inability of the administration to manage these conflicts. Woolley, one of Brandeis's old friends, urged the president to draft the justice as his chief labor administrator on April 19, and he followed up this initial suggestion a week later with the hint that the chief justice and "his fellow conservatives" would probably consent to the appointment because they, too, hoped "to do something big to help win the war." According to Woolley, Frankfurter stood ready to deliver the endorsement of Holmes.[13]

Neither Woolley nor Frankfurter would have made these suggestions without consulting Brandeis, who apparently believed that some arrangement could be worked out for a temporary leave of absence from the Court. Frankfurter put intense pressure on Baker to join the draft-Brandeis movement. "The man can be secured," he told the secretary, "if the President is convinced of his indispensability. The earnestness of your conviction will materially influence the President's decision. . . . Brandeis is needed to help assure the 'illusions' that are at stake in this war."[14]

Wilson had once remarked that he needed Brandeis everywhere in the administration, but now, despite Frankfurter's furious lobbying, he remained cool to the idea of recruiting the Court's most liberal justice. "Go slow, please," he told Woolley. "I admire and trust him [Brandeis] as much as you do, but I am not convinced that it would be wise to choose a member of the Supreme Court just at this juncture."[15] In his caution, the president displayed more wisdom than Franfurter, who believed that the emergency required perhaps even the sacrifice of long-range progressive goals with respect to the judiciary.

But even Wilson could not ignore much longer the chaos that plagued the administration's efforts with respect to labor standards. Responding to complaints from Frankfurter and others, he created the War Labor Policies Board on May 7, composed of all representatives from government agencies concerned with war production. And he named Frankfurter as chairman. The advocate of centralization had become, almost by default, the potential czar of labor, but at a time and under circumstances that did not offer much hope of dazzling success.

❦❦❦

As one of many improvised agencies created during the war, the War Labor Policies Board occupied run-down, temporary quarters on H Street in an old school building. Its furniture consisted of used chairs and desks from the War and Labor Departments, which symbolized the board's status among the major bureaucratic satraps of wartime Washington. It had no formal authority over these other government departments or private industry, apart from the power of necessity and the persuasive voice of its chairman. That was more

than enough for Frankfurter, who soon won the grudging respect, if
not always the cooperation, of representatives from the Navy, the
Army, the War Production Board, the Railroad Administration, and
the Shipping Board. His command of labor statistics, his administrative finesse, and his charm quickly won the confidence of the dashing
assistant secretary of the Navy, Franklin D. Roosevelt, who brought
the Harvard professor home to lunch regularly, much to his wife's
annoyance. "An interesting little man but very jew," Eleanor
Roosevelt confided to her mother-in-law.[16]

Without a powerful mandate, Frankfurter realized that he would
have to influence the decision-making process more informally,
through contacts with officials like Roosevelt. He also began to operate a one-man employment agency for a government that was in dire
need of competent lawyers to staff its burgeoning network of temporary agencies. This project also served his purposes, because most of
the recruits bore the imprimature of the Harvard Law School and he
placed them where they could advance the objectives of the policies
board on questions relating to labor. "Gerry Henderson and Stephen-
son have made good with a bang with the Shipping Board," he reported to Pound. "They increased the salary of the former to $3,000 and
the latter to $2,000—that's pretty big for such youngsters. All the
other boys . . . are doing nicely."[17] Very shortly other officials began
to complain about Frankfurter's "boys," who formed a network of
intelligence and intrigue that stretched from the Justice Department
to the Emergency Fleet Corporation.

The grumbling about Frankfurter did not stop with other government officials. Despite his well-intentioned efforts on behalf of the
Bisbee miners and Tom Mooney, many labor leaders did not greet his
appointment with enthusiasm. They distrusted the new board and its
chairman, who had acquired a reputation for patriotic intensity and
rough tactics at the bargaining table. Worse yet, he seemed to have
friends on both sides of the labor-management fence. "I am worried
and troubled about this Frankfurter board," the head of the machinists' union complained. He believed that the War Labor Policies
Board represented the interests of big business, would attempt to impose maximum wages, and thereby deny to workers their just share of
the expanding economic pie. "The worst labor baiters in the country
are behind this board," Sam Lavit told Frank Walsh, and "if this thing
is not stopped it may lead to real trouble for the workers will not stand
for a maximum wage."[18]

These fears became epidemic among the well-organized, prosperous craft unions in the AFL such as the machinists, who benefited from the system of decentralized wage adjustments that encouraged both private industry and the government to boost wages and overtime pay for skilled metal workers, boilermakers, iron moulders, and plumbers. Without enforceable, nationwide standards, for example, the machinists' union had been able to secure sizable wage increases from the Shipping Board, the Railway Adjustment Board, and private employers, all of whom competed for these skilled laborers. A similar pattern of bargaining became characteristic for the building trades, where it produced intense wage competition that benefited some unions in the short run but aggravated an inflationary spiral that injured the poorest workers who lacked the bargaining leverage of the machinists and other skilled trades. Unbridled wage competition also encouraged workers to move rapidly from one region of the country to another, intensified the problem of the labor turnover, and disrupted production in many vital war industries.

Not surprisingly, Frankfurter regarded this situation as wasteful, unjust, and unpatriotic. He bluntly defined production as the key to victory and the efficient allocation of manpower as the key to production. Without more uniform standards, especially with respect to wages, he believed, the economic machine could not operate at peak levels. "The need of the hour is production," he said, shortly after taking office, "the fullest munitioning, equipment, and feeding of the forces at the front. . . . There is much to be done, but it will be done because it must be done."[19] These efforts at standardization, however, stirred up the wrath of many groups—other government officials who did not wish to abandon their competitive advantage with respect to certain groups of workers, union leaders who equated their members' welfare with the national interest, and industrialists who measured social progress according to the backward practices of their own companies. It was a task certain to generate heated rhetoric and numerous enemies.

Frankfurter, for example, actively supported the efforts of the United States Employment Service, which attempted to channel skilled workers through its offices and to impose sanctions upon both employers and unions who defied this allocation system or the settlements proposed by the various wage boards. Employers, of course, resented this program and Frankfurter's support for the employment service because the agency made it more difficult to recruit new workers during a lockout. The unions complained that the employment service, the policies board, and its chairman sanctioned strike breaking, because they continued to provide workers to companies where the unions rebelled against decisions reached by the adjustment boards.[20]

Frankfurter's quest for wage stabilization failed, a casualty of the policies board's brief existence, the hostility of other government agencies, and the stupendous complexity of the undertaking itself. Nonetheless, he had succeeded in organizing joint employer-employee boards for both the metal and building trades before the Armistice, and these boards had begun to fix regional wage standards for both the government and private industry.[21] The policies board also required that "all wage adjusting agencies should be governed by the same standards for the same trades in the same localities . . . and should keep informed regarding zones fixed by other boards and conform to them."[22] One month before the end of the war, he finally brought together all the national labor adjustment boards into a single conference that promised greater uniformity in the immediate future. This effort died, however, with the November Armistice and the sudden disintegration of the boards themselves.[23]

The policies board never achieved the complete harmony and cooperation among the splintered labor agencies that Frankfurter desired, but under his leadership it displayed a broad and sympathetic concern for the welfare of American workers. Energetic, patriotic, and reform-minded like its own chairman, the policies board surveyed dozens of issues that ranged from the reliability of industrial statistics to life insurance for government employees. The sublime at times competed with the ridiculous. The board adopted, for instance, a detailed sanitary code for the explosives industry, which specified the size of windows in all toilet facilities: not less than one foot wide, with an area not less than six feet square. For each additional toilet, the windows were to be enlarged by one square foot.[24] At the chairman's urging, the board also recommended the creation of a United States War Badge Commission to provide medals to civilian workers in industries that had accepted the government's policies. In order to qualify, the worker had to perform four consecutive months of meritorious service and swear "that he will at all times consider the interests and needs of the United States Government as paramount to any and all other interests." The medal was to be worn on the left breast and "wherever possible . . . conferred personally by a Government official."[25]

While civil libertarians cringed over the war badge oath, employers who held government contracts in states without workmen's compensation laws denounced the board's recommendation that they join the federal program for the duration of the war. Likewise, the board's reports on life insurance, night work by women, enforcement of state labor codes, and profiteering remained models of progressive compassion and expertise that offended the sensibilities of conservative businessmen. The board's committee on living conditions, for instance, urged new legislation to give the president broad authority to impose rent controls in key industrial areas, a proposal hardly endorsed by "the worst labor baiters in the country." Nor did Frankfurter win many business allies on the issue of the eight-hour day, which became the most controversial battle of all.

Every group—workers, employers, government bureaucrats—accepted the necessity for working longer hours during the war and paying overtime, but if the eight-hour day became the general standard, employees would generally earn more money. In 1918, however, the eight-hour day was far from universal in American industry. Federal law required it on all government contracts, except for the purchase of items normally available on the open market without particular specifications. This distinction began to make little sense once the government's demand for war materials expanded to include a wide range of civilian goods, and it generated considerable discontent among workers who received different overtime rates depending upon technical contractual language that bore little relationship to the actual production process. Where firms manufactured one product both for the government and the private market, the workers who produced this commodity often received different amounts of overtime, although they performed the same tasks.

Gompers and the AFL leadership demanded the immediate, blanket adoption of the eight-hour day for all employees. With equal vehemence, employers resisted any modification in federal law, feared the extension of the eight-hour day to private industry, and resented any reduction in their profit margins. The issue might have been resolved early in the mobilization effort, had Wilson adopted the recommendation of the Mediation Commission, but instead, matters drifted until the spring of 1918, when the War Labor Conference Board urged the maintenance of the status quo. Gompers immediately set about to overturn this policy, by bringing pressure upon all of the individual adjustment boards to adopt the eight-hour day. This strategy brought him into sharp conflict with Frankfurter, who sympathized with the objective but believed that it should have been accomplished earlier. Now, with the war hanging in the balance, he feared a major confrontation with industry over the issue.

In view of the recommendations by the War Labor Conference Board, he noted, a sudden shift to the eight-hour day would strike many manufacturers as arbitrary and encourage some to decline government contracts. What then could the government do—take over the plants? He pointed out to the secretary of labor that the administration had been forced to that extreme in the cases of the Western Union and Smith and Wesson companies, where the employers refused to submit to the jurisdiction of wage adjustment boards, but the results had not been pleasant for either labor or the war effort.[26] Instead of the wholesale adoption of the eight-hour day, Frankfurter proposed a compromise: the policies board would proceed case by case and "such extension should be made where the conditions of any specific industry or a given industrial center call for it."[27]

Frankfurter's compromise was not enough for the AFL, and it also drew a strong dissent from Frank Walsh, the darling of the labor radicals, who attempted to mobilize his friends against the policies board and its chairman. "It is my effort, as Joint-Chairman of the War Labor Board," he announced, "to immediately apply it to all industries, on the theory that it does not hamper or limit in any way production of military necessities, but, on the contrary, accelerates the same and makes for speedy, high-grade production."[28]

On this issue, however, Walsh played to the grandstands. He did not have the votes on the War Labor Board to extend the eight-hour day nationwide, although two of the board's umpires had made the recommendation in particular disputes. Moreover, Walsh had been a member of the War Labor Conference Board that had voted without dissent to maintain the status quo. His behavior therefore irritated Frankfurter, who lost no opportunity to denounce it, even to Walsh's newspaper friends, with "a little speech to the effect that he [Frankfurter] was doing his job and no one could stop him."[29] Walsh, he complained to Hand, "persistently seeds to arid partisanship. Even the partisanship of the proletariat where his dominant feelings lie."[30]

Despite a "real fight" with Walsh and the latter's massive propaganda campaign against the policies board, Frankfurter made a vigorous effort to extend the eight-hour day to the steel industry, long a bastion of antiunion settlement. In Judge Elbert H. Gary, the doyen of United States Steel and the American Steel and Iron Institute, he faced a more formidable enemy than Walsh. Wealthy, well manicured, pompous, and unscrupulous, he epitomized the primitive era of capitalist accumulation. Present at the birth of the giant steel company, Gary prided himself on running the enterprise without interference from competitors, consumers, employees, or the government. He reminded Frankfurter of those stiff-necked entrepreneurs whom John Walker described as resembling the girl in Scotland "who wouldn't dance with a man because she thought that if a man put his arms around her she'd have a baby." Gary felt that way about meeting with labor representatives or even discussing his company's employee relations.

He responded coolly to Frankfurter's invitation to come to Washington for a discussion about these issues. "We have experienced little difficulty in our own labor matters during a good many years," he wrote, "and we dislike very much to see any agitation which is calculated to disturb our relations. I have been hoping you, or someone representing you, would be in New York in the near future."[31] Gary did not appear in Washington for two months.

When he did show up, the meeting became more acrimonious than the correspondence. Gary claimed that Frankfurter had already made up his mind about the eight-hour day and that the conference could serve no useful purpose. The steel industry, Frankfurter shot back, represented "the great isolated exception to the onward movement of the basic eight-hour day," and he rattled off the names of other companies that had adopted the program voluntarily. These companies had bowed only to government coercion, Gary retorted, and the eight-hour day would be a "calamity" for his company, the steel industry, and the entire war effort.

What would happen, Frankfurter inquired, when employees at U.S. Steel raised this matter as a grievance before the War Labor Board? Why not avoid a nasty confrontation? "A small number of employees . . . might make complaints," Gary confessed, "but we would have to see that that portion . . . who did not make the complaint were protected." On that sour note, the meeting ended, with Gary daring Frankfurter or anyone else in the government to impose the standard on his company. After leaving the meeting he began to spread false rumors throughout the business community that the chairman of the War Labor Policies Board had attempted to blackmail him with the threat of a federal take over of the steel industry. Nothing could have been further from Frankfurter's mind.[32]

Gary's conduct struck him as arrogant and foolish, but what Frankfurter might have done about the steel industry became wholly academic during the first two weeks of November. In rapid succession, the Kaiser abdicated, the Germans proclaimed a republic, and General Foch signed an armistice agreement. Suddenly, the far-reaching plans of the War Labor Policies Board and his battles with Walsh and Gary paled in comparison with the issues of peace making abroad and postwar reconstruction at home.

❊❊❊

The Great War destroyed four empires, shook the social and economic foundations of all the belligerents, and left in its wake millions of dead, maimed, and homeless people. From the perspective of many Europeans, there were no victors, only survivors. Unscathed, prosperous, and eternally optimistic, the people of the United States remained an island of relative security in a world otherwise gripped by fear, social chaos, and a thirst for vengeance. Woodrow Wilson's utopian peace formula—including the removal of trade barriers, a reduction in armaments, self-determination for the nationalities of Central Europe, and a "general association of nations"—stirred the enthusiasm of a great many progressives in the United States, but this vision soon fell victim to the Allies' own more sordid desires, Wilson's zeal to eradicate the Bolshevik regime in Russia, and a devastating political defeat inflicted by the Republicans in the November elections. A hero in Paris, Wilson found himself rejected in Kansas.

Nearly a year before the Versailles Peace Conference formally began, Colonel House sent Frankfurter abroad once again, this time to survey the attitudes of European labor and socialist groups about the Fourteen Points. Frankfurter quickly learned that Wilson would have enormous difficulty when he attempted to shape European realities to his own ideals. "The fact is," he told House, "that neither the French nor English Governments are enthusiastic (to put it mildly) over Mr. Wilson's principles and the people, the masses, more and more realize it." The president's ideals appealed to left-wing trade unionists, socialists, and intellectuals and his grip on the English and French masses "is one of the most inspiring manifestations of faith that history records." Unfortunately, Frankfurter reported, these groups lacked organization and distrusted their own governments. They looked to the Americans for assistance in purging their own regimes of "imperialist war aims" and implementing a truly democratic peace.[33]

Arthur Henderson, the leader of the Labour Party who had been driven out of the war cabinet for his alleged pacifism, represented for

Frankfurter the potential basis of a pro-Wilson coalition on the continent. Henderson hoped to form an Inter-Allied Labor Mission, composed of radical unions and socialists, which he intended to send to the United States as a demonstration of support for Wilson and the Fourteen Points. These efforts, Frankfurter told House, should be welcomed. "If wisely managed it will be easy to make them do whatever the President thinks it wise they should do," he informed the colonel. "If the Allies could be gotten to scrap all their treaties and stand on Mr. Wilson's general principles, the whole tone of English and French labor and liberal feeling . . . would be tremendously lifted."[34]

Frankfurter proposed that Wilson attempt to mobilize "the great labor organizations of the allied countries" behind the Fourteen Points, but instead of adopting this bold strategy, Wilson pursued a more cautious program that left him ultimately at the mercy of Europe's most reactionary political forces. In deference to Lloyd George, he vetoed the Henderson visit. Next, he dispatched Gompers and a delegation of AFL regulars to England and France where they were told to boost the morale of European workers and explain Wilson's peace plan. Instead, they shocked their hosts with their jingoism, denunciations of socialism, and appalling ignorance of the European situation. "They probably rendered not a little mischief," Frankfurter told House," . . . the resulting atmosphere is rather disturbed."[35] Even more bluntly, Ramsay MacDonald noted that the American Federation of Labor was "hopelessly out of date," and had "no grasp of the realities of European politics."[36]

Frankfurter's disillusionment with Wilsonian peace making began with the rejection of Henderson's mission and the Gompers fiasco. After spurning the Republican leadership at home, Wilson also seemed to be cutting himself off from potential allies abroad. He proposed to slay the dragons of the old order single-handedly, through the force of his noble ideals and soaring rhetoric. This, Frankfurter knew, was a prescription for disaster. The principles of the League of Nations, he told Manley Hudson, "are too new, too vast to enlist the understanding and the faith of the American people, in view of our traditional isolation."[37] The president and many of his advisers, he told Lippmann sadly, "were the naivest children in the world."[38] On the other hand, Frankfurter probably expected too much from Wilson. How was it possible for a president who had jailed dissenters in his own country and dispatched troops to Siberia to make common cause with the European left?

The debacle of peace making mirrored the administration's hapless efforts to manage the domestic transition from war to peace. On the day of the Armistice, Frankfurter urged the secretary of labor to seek united action by all the government agencies concerned with production to avoid "needless unemployment and misery and inevitable lowering of labor standards." He feared that "reactionary groups" who "still regard labor as a commodity" would take advantage of the decline in war contracts and the demobilization of soldiers to destroy whatever gains workers had made in various industries. Labor should not bear the brunt of efforts to cut production costs, he urged, until a corresponding decline took place in the high cost of living. Unless the federal government guided the reconversion process, he warned, the country would be rocked by unemployment, strikes, and social disorder.[39]

Wilson's senior advisers, many of whom regarded the wartime government regulations as a great aberration, did not share Frankfurter's anxiety. Baker stated the prevailing orthodoxy after a meeting with Baruch and Russell Leffingwell from the treasury department: "There is no necessity for governmental action. . . . The resumption of American industry and commerce is a matter of removing from the enterprise of America those restrictions, temporary in character, which it was found necessary to impose during the period of the war."[40] Without leadership from the president or the cabinet, many of the labor adjustment boards crumbled in the face of opposition from the business community. By early December, Walsh complained that the War Labor Board had "come to the point where it cannot be anything but a disappointing mirage to the working people of the country."[41] A spokesman for the Railroad Adjustment Board predicted "chaos in industrial relations as soon as the railways were returned to private control," and Major Tully of the War Department blamed the government for "throwing up its hands and turning everything to the two remaining parties to handle the best way they can . . . all courts of appeal are disintegrating.[42]

Frankfurter, who had been the most consistent advocate of strong federal controls over labor-management relations during the war, watched helplessly as the adjustment boards languished, the Army released soldiers indiscriminately into a swollen labor market, price controls broke down, and Congress abolished the employment service. The great progressive crusade had turned into a rout by the spring of 1919. "Now the starch is out of the administration," he told Hand. "Cold feet prevail on a wide area. . . . 'Tommy' has given up—pro tem—the U.S. to make a world . . . and his paralyzed subordinates are meek and timid. They have practically announced bankruptcy and have invited the Republicans as receivers. God help us!"[43] America, he told Lippmann in disgust, was now "the most reactionary country in the world."[44] Within a month, he had resigned from the administration and returned to Cambridge. The worst was yet to come.

CHAPTER 7

THE RED SCARE

FRANKFURTER QUICKLY DISCOVERED that even the Harvard Law School offered little shelter from the storms that battered the nation's economic, political, and constitutional foundations in 1919 and 1920. Determined to maintain their wartime gains but largely abandoned by the Wilson administration, millions of American workers took matters into their own hands by going out on strike to secure recognition for their new unions, higher wages, and assorted political demands. Within the AFL, long a bastion of conservative trade unionism and laissez-faire ideology, some leaders called for the nationalization of basic industries and the formation of a separate labor party. With equal militancy, employers resolved to resist their workers' demands and, where possible, to restore conditions to a prewar level.

Beginning with the Seattle general strike in February and reaching a climax in the great steel walkout in September, four million workers marched on picket lines in 1919 in 3,600 separate confrontations with their employers, a record never matched in American history. Few industries or regions of the country escaped from the strife, which even touched the Boston police force and took the form of ugly racial riots in half a dozen cities where companies attempted to open their plants with black strike breakers. Although bread-and-butter economic issues generated the most discontent, frightened businessmen and public officials portrayed the disorders as a nationwide revolutionary conspiracy to overthrow the government.

With its Siberian invasion and anti-Bolshevik propaganda, the Wilson administration did little to combat the antiradical paranoia that was fueled by a series of bombings in the late spring and early summer. Instead, the secretary of labor affirmed that the Seattle strike and other disturbances sprang from an attempt to "establish the Soviet form of government in the U.S. and put into effect the economic theories of the Bolsheviki of Russia." According to the attorney general, A. Mitchell Palmer, "the blaze of revolution" threatened to devour American institutions, "licking the alters of churches, leaping into the belfry of the school bell, crawling into the sacred corners of American homes, seeking to replace marriage vows with libertine laws, burning up the foundations of society." A young graduate of the Georgetown University Law School, J. Edgar Hoover, chief of the Justice Department's intelligence division, blamed racial violence upon black leaders who displayed "an outspoken advocacy of the Bolsheviki or Soviet doctrines."[1]

The nation soon found itself in the grip of a full-blown antiradical crusade, which fell indiscriminately upon members of the Communist Party, socialists, strikers, and outspoken critics of the economic status quo. State governments passed criminal anarchism laws and so-called "red flag" statutes that punished the teaching of revolution or the advocacy of industrial change through force or violence. The Wilson administration crushed the steel strike with federal troops and likewise intimidated the coal miners. Where official action proved ineffective or vacillating, employers could count upon private detectives, the American Legion, and a posse comitatus of patriots to stem the red tide of revolution. In Centralia, Washington, for example, organizers from the IWW and representatives of the legion exchanged gunfire, mobs assaulted the workers' strike headquarters, arrested over a thousand alleged conspirators, and lynched a local union leader. When the Seattle *Union Record* demanded an investigation of the carnage, federal agents seized the newspaper's presses, banned the publication from the mails, and indicted its editors for sedition.

The brutal climax came on January 2, 1920, when Palmer and Hoover directed the arrest of between five and ten thousand persons—mostly aliens—in federal raids upon Communist Party offices, pool halls, union headquarters, bars, and cafés in over thirty cities.

The federal agents and immigration officials who carried out this operation seldom troubled themselves with the formality of search or arrest warrants. Those who were held in custody endured terrible conditions in local prisons such as Detroit's, where "eight hundred persons were detained for up to six days in a dark, windowless, narrow corridor. . . . they had access to one toilet and were denied food for twenty-four hours."[2] Those who survived the ordeals of arrest and detention faced the equally harrowing experience of administrative deportation hearings, through which the government intended to purge the nation of undesirable subversives.[3]

In the tense political atmosphere of 1919, when members of the United States Senate solemnly labeled Jane Addams, Lillian Wald, and Oswald Villard as "dangerous radicals," Frankfurter's return to Cambridge generated near panic among proper Bostonians because of his identification with labor and the Mooney case. Conservatives initially took aim, however, not at Frankfurter but at one of his former students, Gerry Henderson, who became a candidate for a teaching position at the law school after wartime service with the Shipping Board. When the Harvard Corporation vetoed the appointment, Pound blamed wild rumors about Henderson's alleged Bolshevism and threatened to resign from the deanship if the corporation rejected the faculty's advice again. In a grim mood, Pound predicted worse times ahead for the law school. "They are gunning hard for Felix," Brandeis reported to his wife after a meeting with the dean. "Old Boston is unregenerate and I am not sorry to have escaped a struggle there that would have been as nasty as it is unending. F. F. is evidently considered by the elect as 'dangerous' as I was; and it looks as if some whom F. considered his friends are as unrelenting as were some who were called mine."[4]

Although he did not relish a fight with Boston's establishment, neither did Frankfurter believe that the law school could tolerate another Henderson episode. If future confrontations developed with the corporation, he told Pound, they should not hesitate to rally the faculty, the students, and influential alumni. "Above all don't worry about me," he reassured the dean. "Of course it won't be 'comfortable' for a time, but there is no illusion about American affairs in my mind and why should anyone just now expect 'comfort.' But I feel like a race horse—and I shall feel even more so, when I get back."[5]

His own rendezvous with the red scare came soon enough, and when it did, the circumstances fulfilled the worst suspicions of Boston conservatives. On Armistice Day, 1919, he presided at a huge rally in Faneuil Hall that was called for the purpose of urging the Wilson administration to extend diplomatic recognition to the Soviet Union. Radicals turned out in force for the meeting, but the principal organizers were several members of Boston's social elite, including one of the city's most prominent bankers, John T. Moors, and Harvard historian, Samuel Eliot Morison. Frankfurter politely declined their initial offer to chair the meeting on the grounds that his presence would only inflame conservatives, but when the organizers could not find a respectable Beacon Hill Yankee to open the session, he reluctantly accepted the task.

In his speech, Frankfurter deplored both American intervention into the Russian civil war and Wilson's policy of nonrecognition of the Bolshevik regime, but these sentiments hardly stamped him as a radical in 1919. Similar pleas had been made by Jan Smuts, Lord Asquith, and other conservatives, a point that Frankfurter did not fail to mention. "I dare say I shall be called a Bolsheviki," he told the crowd, "in fact, I am sure of it. I have no patience for the Bolshevik form of government, so far as I understand it. . . . But I know as little or even less of what is supposed to be the substitute for it." Military intervention by the United States, he told the cheering mob, violated the principles for which the country had entered the war, above all the ideal of self-determination for each nation. The fate of Russia, he concluded, "is purely for the decision of the Russian people."[6]

Within days of the meeting, he received a telephone call from Thomas Nelson Perkins, legal counsel to the Harvard Corporation and a member of the venerable Boston law firm of Ropes, Gray, and Gorham, who opened their conversation by saying: "What's this Communist meeting you presided over?" Before Frankfurter could explain, Perkins began reading an angry letter from a Harvard alumnus, "a man of influence and large property," who, he reported, objected to the university's red professors and had been "after Laski and you and the rest of you."[7] Perkins followed up this call with more letters and a luncheon meeting at which he attempted to instill in Frankfurter a proper concern for the difficult situation in which his conduct had placed the law school and the university. "You are one of the people that have tended to arouse extreme views on the part of people on the other side of questions," Perkins told him. "In normal times it may well be that the world needs the stimulus that comes from a real disagreement. At the present time it seems to me that it is important not to rock the boat."[8] Frankfurter's behavior, he added, would probably make it impossible for the school to raise money from sensitive alumni.

Nothing so stirred Frankfurter's anger as the whiff of intimidation. He had met Perkins in Washington during the war and come away with the impression of an arrogant, second-rate legal mind with little sensitivity to the problems of economic reform and social justice. Now Perkins's remarks confirmed this impression, and he proceeded to lecture the university's chief legal officer on the dangers of political repression and moral cowardice. "You know as well as I do," he told Perkins, "that at present there is raging a form of lynch law in the North, much more ominous, because less crude, than the well-known brand of the South. I should feel like a poltroon if I suppressed my convictions . . . because . . . some people would shy off from contributing money." Attacks against him and other faculty members should be resisted by the university's highest officials, because "arrogance, intolerance, force are the same enemies to civilization whether indulged in by Lenine [sic] or Ledyard, by Trotzky [sic] or Gary."[9] If he and other moderates kept silent because of the ignorance of extremists, he predicted, revolution and orthodoxy would be left alone to fight it out. "Sanity and goodwill do not just happen in this world," he reminded Perkins. "They must be fought for and won."[10]

In this verbal joust with Perkins, Frankfurter received little encouragement from his friends once rumors of the battle leaked out to Harvard alumni. "I think you are too level-headed to be looking for martyrdom," Holmes cautioned him. "Martyrs I suspect generally are damned fools. . . . Of course, I believe in academic freedom, but on the other hand it is to be remembered that a professor's conduct may affect the goodwill of the institution to which he belongs."[11] The usually pugnacious Hand reminded him that the country needed "cement" not "explosives" in its current travail, and that no purpose would be served "in nailing your colors to the mast in a cyclone."[12] That remark brought a blunt response from Frankfurter, who invited the judge up to Cambridge in order to witness at first hand "the cowed atmosphere that so many of the teaching staff are living in." As a lawyer he could find other employment, "but the teachers of mathematics and philosophy and history have no alternative. . . . 'Freedom' is a subtle thing and I could convince you on the spot that a very corrosive force has been set loose here by the attitude behind Perkins' letters."[13]

Perkins and his allies, Frankfurter warned Hand, wanted nothing

Emma Frankfurter, 1898.
(Library of Congress)

Felix Frankfurter, age 12.
(Harvard Law School)

Clionia Debating Society, City College of New York, 1900. Frankfurter, third row, fourth from the right, wearing bow tie. (*Harvard Law School*)

Henry L. Stimson, United States Attorney, 1907. (*Library of Congress*)

Louis D. Brandeis, 1910.
(Library of Congress)

Justice Oliver Wendell
Holmes, Jr., 1924.
(Library of Congress)

Harvard Law School Faculty, 1927. Frankfurter, back row, second from right; James Landis, back row, third from right; Dean Roscoe Pound, front row, left. (*Harvard Law School*)

Frankfurter, left, and Governor Al Smith of New York at the Union Club, New York, 1928. *(Library of Congress)*

Frankfurter, right, and James Landis off to law school classes, 1933. *(Library of Congress; ACME Photo)*

Frankfurter at Oxford, 1934. *(Library of Congress)*

Felix and Marion Frankfurter leave Back Bay Station, Boston, January 18, 1939, after his appointment to the Supreme Court. *(Library of Congress)*

Mr. Justice Frankfurter. (New York Times *photo*, *1957*)

less than his complete surrender or transformation into "a quiet, well-behaved, boot-licking harmless teacher, who doesn't defend 'communists' and generally shuts his mouth about things that involve the prejudices of his crowd." He would not bow to their threats. The most disgusting thing about the whole affair, he added, was the fact that Perkins had pedigree, money, power, prestige, "everything that should make for freedom," yet he capitulated to the antiradical hysteria. "What's the use of all of Nelson's 'red bloodedness' and 'bowels,'" he asked Hand, "if they don't move."[14] Even in a cyclone, he preferred to nail his colors to the mast.

While the leaders of State Street howled about Harvard's growing Soviet menace, Frankfurter and Marion Denman made December wedding plans. "I suppose between the death of the League and its resurrection," he told Manley Hudson, "it's open season for private alliances. At all events, with or without your approval, I'm going off during the Christmas recess to get married. I'll see whether there is anything in their distinction between 'law in books' and 'law in action.' Her name is Marion Denman—and beyond that Petrarch and Dante and Shakespeare have said all and more that is to be said."[15]

For a professor at the Harvard Law School, he handled the legal arrangements very badly, by asking first Holmes and then Hand to officiate at the ceremony. But neither federal judge had proper jurisdiction and they settled upon Benjamin Cardozo from the New York Court of Appeals, who followed their instructions to perform the act "with the minimum number of words that your sense of the significant ones and the law allows."[16] At the last moment, Hand also found it necessary to remind the groom to bring a valid marriage license. "Having got this butterfly chloroformed for the nonce," he told his friend, "we don't propose to have him wake up till he is well skewered in a vital spot."[17]

Conspicuously, Emma Frankfurter did not join the small wedding party of seven persons, because she felt offended by the absence of religious sanctions and the fact that Felix had chosen a *shicksa* for his bride. But five years had now passed since his father's death, and the war had brought independence in many forms. "The girl was positively radiant—bubbling over with a gentle, suffused happiness which made me feel how right all was," Laski reported to Holmes. "The general result on Felix goes straight to my heart."[18] After a brief honeymoon in North Carolina, the "two cooing doves" returned to Cambridge. "To see their anxiety for each other's proper protection against the snow etc. is charming," Laski observed. "The boy is very happy. The girl is still rather reticent and shy . . . but she makes him sing an unceasing song."[19]

They moved into a large, comfortable home on Brattle Street, a fashionable Cambridge neighborhood that was more renowned for its architecturally distinguished houses than for its radical politics. She filled it with her good taste, charm, and wit; he with countless friends and endless conversations. The new groom now spent more time at home than in his law school office, a fact that greatly amused Brandeis. "Felix is not at the Law School as much . . . and has not as much hold on the individual students as formerly," he reported to his wife. "Harold [Laski] says Pound stands first in their affection—easily—then comes Chaffee [*sic*] and Felix is hardly an easy third. Thus does matrimony mar!!"[20]

Their marriage fused opposites. Her cool reserve set off his ebullience. Her practical nature balanced his romanticism. His tastes ran to the law, history, and politics; hers to novels and poetry. Marion was a formidable woman—sharp-tongued, intuitively shrewd about people and situations—who took great pleasure in puncturing his usually hyperbolic observations about life. "Oh, Felix," she would say, "there you go running off again." Her husband, she often remarked, had only two basic faults: first, he always got off the subject during a heated conversation; second, he usually got back on it again. It was a relationship built upon passion, friendship, and intellectual respect, but one also doomed to considerable emotional strain, symbolized by his hasty departure to rescue a labor union and imprisoned radicals even before their luggage had been unpacked on Brattle Street. "Do you know what it's like," she confided to a friend, "to be married to a man who is never tired?"[21]

❧❧❧

The first plea for help had come from Sidney Hillman, the embattled leader of the Amalgamated Clothing Workers, whose union was under siege in Rochester, New York, where the Michael Stern Company had secured a temporary injunction against continuation of a strike. Stern's lawyers hoped to make the injunction permanent, bankrupt the union with a large suit for damages, and have the Amalgamated declared illegal. "I'm in this typically colorless American city . . . on a very interesting labor litigation," Frankfurter told Holmes, "having a grand time defending an injunction suit along industrial and economic lines and away from the arid 'legal rights' assumptions of a Pitney in the Hitchman case."[22]

In his defense of the union's tactics, Frankfurter relied upon Holmes's famous essay on tort liability, where the latter suggested that the law did not seek to indemnify persons for all harm. A merchant, for example, could not legally complain that his business had been injured by the mere opening of another, competing business down the street. "There are certain things which the law allows a man to do," Holmes wrote, "notwithstanding the fact that he foresees that harm will follow from them."[23] Striking employees, who sought to improve their own economic situation by means of a strike, Frankfurter argued in Rochester, fell into this category of exceptions, although their activities clearly injured Stern's business. To buttress these contentions, he presented the court with substantial economic data on wages and living conditions among industrial workers in the Rochester area.

Adolph J. Rodenbeck, the "incredibly wooden" trial judge, did not view legal doctrine from a Holmesian point of view, nor did he greatly appreciate Frankfurter's long sociological discourse on economic conditions in Rochester. The law, Rodenbeck implied, should control the case, not fancy statistical tables or high-toned theory. He granted the permanent injunction and awarded the company damages with the caustic observation that "the Amalgamated Clothing Workers, instead of endeavoring to secure recognition by an example of an enlightened and reasonable administration in other factories, chose to force their way into plaintiff's factories by secrecy, and by a strike backed by its powerful influence and supported by acts that the law condemns."[24] This decision dealt a severe blow to a union that Frankfurter believed to be among the most progressive in the country. Given the antilabor mood of both the bench and the bar, he advised Hillman not to appeal the decision, but to work out a compromise with the Stern company in exchange for ending the strike and reemploying some of the Amalgamated's workers. The employers drove a tough bargain, but finally agreed to drop their action for damages.[25]

The second call to action came from the federal district court in Boston, where Judge George W. Anderson, a courageous civil libertarian, invited Frankfurter and Zechariah Chafee to participate amici curiae on behalf of William T. Colyer and nineteen other aliens arrested during the Palmer raids and held for deportation. Frankfurter and Chafee filed writs of habeas corpus and concentrated their legal attack on the methods of arrest, detention, and interrogation employed by the government against these members of the Communist Party and the Communist Labor Party. The federal immigration laws, they pointed out, vested administrative authority in the Department of Labor, not in agents of the Justice Department, who carried out the arrests and ran the deportation hearings. In addition, immigration officials had revised their regulations prior to the arrests in order to deny the aliens legal representation during the hearings. Evidence introduced at the hearings to prove the defendants' subversive intentions had been secured through illegal searches and seizures. These procedural defects alone, Frankfurter believed, doomed the government's case and made it unnecessary for the court to rule on the constitutionality of the immigration law or other statutory issues.

Anderson accepted these arguments and freed nine of the aliens on procedural grounds, but then proceeded to release all nineteen with a much broader ruling that shocked conservatives and probably surprised even Frankfurter. The Immigration Act of 1918 permitted the deportation of aliens who advocated the overthrow of the government by force of violence, Anderson wrote, but this ban did not include those who urged a general strike, the only form of "force" or "violence" preached by the communists and the CLP. By itself, membership in these organizations could not become grounds for deportation. In one of the harshest indictments of government misconduct ever made by an American jurist, Anderson condemned the warrantless arrests, the barbaric detention methods used at Deer Island, and the attempts by officials from the Immigration Service and the Department of Justice to cover up their wrongdoing.[26]

The Frankfurter-Chafee brief, Anderson's decision in *Colver*, and the heroic efforts of the assistant secretary of labor, Louis Post, who cancelled thousands of deportation warrants, dampened the fires of the red scare and helped to destroy the presidential ambitions of Palmer. So, too, did a *Report upon the Illegal Practices of the United States Department of Justice* signed by Frankfurter, Chafee, Pound, and nine other prominent lawyers. This document, according to Charles Evans Hughes, catalogued violations of personal rights "that savor of the worst practices of tyranny."[27] From the point of view of Palmer and his red-hunting allies, however, Frankfurter displayed a dangerous sympathy for "alien anarchists . . . in preference to the testimony of sworn officers of the Government."[28]

The Faneuil Hall gathering, Frankfurter's defense of Hillman and alien communists, and his blast against Palmer generated one last conservative assault upon the law school and its faculty. Their target was not Frankfurter this time but his young colleague, Chafee, the scion of a wealthy Rhode Island family, who had written a series of articles in the *Harvard Law Review* criticizing the Supreme Court's decision in the famous *Abrams* case and endorsing the dissenting views of Holmes and Brandeis. To make matters even worse, Chafee and Frankfurter had petitioned President Wilson asking clemency for Abrams and for others convicted under the espionage and sedition laws.[29]

In the spring of 1921, Austen G. Fox, a prominent New York lawyer who had led the attack on Brandeis's nomination, and twenty other alumni of the law school asked the Board of Overseers to investigate Chafee's "fitness to teach" on the grounds that his *Abrams* articles contained "intentional falsehoods" and "reckless indifference to the truth." Instead of dismissing these absurd charges, the overseers charged their Committee to Visit the Law School (which included Cardozo, Augustus Hand, Julian Mack, and Stimson) to investigate the accusations and this august body proceeded to do so.

> In Boston's Harvard Club they met,
>   with awful portent dire;
> In righteous wrath each face was set—
>   They said to Zechariah:
>
> Young man, if students hear you air
>   Opinions any broader,
> Just think what will become of their
>   Respect for Law and Order!
>
> Now Zach gave way before the strength
>   Of those irate grandmommas,
> In fact apologized at length—
>   For several misplaced commas.[30]

Despite the levity of poets, the Chafee inquiry represented a serious attack upon academic freedom, and the outcome was not certain until the final vote, when the committee "acquitted" him by a vote of six to five. Cardozo, according to rumors, cast the decisive ballot in a case that shed little credit upon either the Board of Overseers or the members of the visiting committee. Frankfurter pumped Hand for information about the decision, but the latter remained mute. "The heretics will have to be content with an acquittal by silence," he said. "I think nothing will come out. . . . The good thing about old Gus is, that however much to me he may rave and curse, you will always find him in the end on the right side."[31] Frankfurter, perhaps, had his doubts.

Frankfurter's record during the war and the red scare was not as radical as most conservatives claimed, nor was it as glorious as his own memoirs later suggested. Contemporary critics blamed him for de-

stroying the Wobblies and adopting a reactionary posture with respect
to organized labor.[32] His views on the IWW remained less sympathetic than those of Frank Walsh and others, but still in advance of the
AFL and the majority of government officials. At the same time, he
condemned the Justice Department's brutal repression of the Wobblies and deplored the use of military force in the lumber industry.
The destruction of the left by the government would have taken place
in 1917 and 1918 with or without Frankfurter's endorsement.

As the head of the War Labor Policies Board, his efforts focused
chiefly upon increased production and industrial efficiency, yet he
remained alert to the interests of labor as well. He battled Judge Gary,
endorsed the basic eight-hour day, and supported collective bargaining. It was no conservative who spoke out against the Bisbee deportation, Mooney's conviction, and the Palmer raids. It took courage to
stand with William Colyer and communist aliens in a Boston courtroom in 1920. Thomas Nelson Perkins and Austin Fox knew he was
not in their camp.

In common with many other progressives, Frankfurter lost a great
many illusions during the Great Crusade and its painful aftermath.
He now doubted the wisdom of centralizing authority in the federal
government. The once devoted New Nationlist, who endorsed the
ideas of Croly, Lippmann, and Roosevelt, became less sanguine about
running the entire country from Washington. He now saw more value
in Brandeis's emphasis upon local and state efforts to cope with many
social problems. Decent, progressive reforms had flowed from the nation's capitol between 1917 and 1920, but so, too, had the forces of
reaction and repression.

The character of individuals, he now believed, determined the
quality of political life more than specific programs or tidy administrative structures. Wilson's peace-making efforts collapsed not because of
poor advice, defects in the Versailles Treaty, or flaws in the league
covenant, but because the president possessed a narrow, intolerant
mind and an inflated ego that rejected other points of view. In a world
made somewhat less safe for democracy, there was much to be pessimistic about, but Frankfurter remained ever the optimist, much to the
amazement of his friends. "You see," he told Hand, "I can't help
believing it's the one assurance we've got—to peg away, genially and
generously, along the road of reason. The odds are all against her, I
know, but that's all the more cause for pegging away."[33]

✦ CHAPTER 8 ✦

ZIONIST

ON THE JEWISH HIGH HOLY DAY of Rosh Hashanah in 1917, Frankfurter remarked to Katherine Ludington that he had been to New York City where "we had another ceremony . . . I dreaded. . . . But somehow it came off very fittingly and on the right early Fall day. I'm rather happy that I can go through these symbolic religious events without a sense of discord or disrespect (by my mere presence) to the believers, tho the significance for me is not creedal."[1] At about the same time, his friend Walter Lippmann asked him: "What is a 'Jew' anyway?" And he responded: "A Jew is a person whom non-Jews regard as a Jew."[2] These casual observations epitomized the religious and cultural agnosticism of many assimilated German Jews in the progressive era, who, if they thought of themselves as Jewish, did so only in a narrow religious sense. In Frankfurter's case, even the bonds of religion had become attenuated, leaving only the negative identification supplied by some gentiles.[3]

Yet during these years Frankfurter became an active Zionist who labored with Brandeis, Julian Mack, and others to create a Jewish homeland in Palestine. His own conversion to Zionism and the growth of nationalistic sentiments among middle- and upper-class Jews came as something of a surprise to close friends like Max Lowenthal: "Your turning to it [Zionism] hit me, but mostly in the myself sense of me. . . . Some of us must tail your kite; and some of us will be all the slower about coming to Zionism, because we'll want to be sure that it isn't to Brandeis and yourself that we're really being impelled."[4] In retrospect, however, Frankfurter's support for Zionism sprang logically from his own progress within American society, the social conditions faced by middle-class Jews at the time, and the manner in which Brandeis transformed the European-inspired movement into another progressive crusade.

Modern Zionism may have flourished among poor peasants and ghetto dwellers, but its chief propagandist had been a sophisticated, cosmopolitan Viennese Jew from the middle class, Theodore Herzl, who became disillusioned with the liberal ideals of assimilation in the wake of the Dreyfus case and other manifestations of anti-Semitism in Austria and Germany. In *Der Judenstaat*, written in 1896, Herzl argued that Jews would never escape from prejudice and oppression even in the most enlightened European societies until they had created their own nation-state. Almost single-handedly, he organized the first Zionist Congress at Basle in 1897, where 204 delegates adopted a program that urged the creation of "a home in Palestine secured by public law," Jewish colonization of Palestine, then controlled by the Ottoman Turks, and the organization of all Jews throughout the world to support this project through the "strengthening and fostering of Jewish national sentiment and consciousness."[5]

In America, Herzl's seeds fell initially upon barren soil. The vast majority of Jewish professionals and businessmen, scrambling up the ladders of opportunity in a land seemingly without prejudice, remained aloof or openly antagonistic to a set of ideas that had little relevance to their own social condition, and that might, they believed, provoke charges of disloyalty. Reform rabbis, who ministered to these wealthy, assimilated congregations and who prided themselves on doctrinal modernity, ridiculed the Zionists' dream of Palestine. On the other hand, orthodox Jews looked upon the scheme as blasphemous. "Young man, you are going against God's will," an elderly New York Jew told a young Zionist. "If He wanted us to have Zion again, He would restore it without the help of the so-called Zionists. God doesn't need apprentices, believe me. Please go *schnorr* [beg money] somewhere else and let us lament in peace, like good Jews." Nor did Herzl's vision find favor with the rulers of Turkey or the powerful statesmen of Western Europe. By 1914, the Jewish population in Palestine numbered only 85,000 in fifty-nine tiny settlements.[6]

Except among a handful of Russian Jews in the sweatshops, tenements, and coffeehouses of New York's Lower East Side, Zionism in America remained without a large constituency, and poorly organized. Herzl and his personal secretary, Jacob deHaas, had chartered various groups—Poale Zion, Mizrachi, and the knights of Zion—that all presumed to speak on behalf of the Americans, but these groups remained hopelessly divided over religious and political doctrine. Out of 1.5 million Jews, perhaps 20,000 paid their *shekel* to one local Zionist organization or another, but Chaim Weizmann's description of the problems that plagued Zionist efforts in England held true for the United States as well: "A handful of devotees to the cause among the lower middle classes, indifference or hostility among the upper classes."[7]

Prior to 1914, Frankfurter had not been among the devotees of Zionism in America. Quite the opposite. Agnostic, assimilated, and successful within the gentile power structure, his only participation within Jewish affairs came through his membership in the American Jewish Committee. This elite organization, formed in 1906 under the leadership of the nation's wealthiest and most influential German Jews, protested pogroms in Russia, fought immigration restriction in the United States, and hoped to Americanize the Eastern Europeans. Dominated by the money and prestige of Jacob Schiff, Louis Marshall, Oscar Straus, and others, the AJC remained anti-Zionist, oligarchical, and very patronizing in its attitude toward the Yiddish-speaking Jews on the Lower East Side. When Marshall, an attorney with clients among the East Side's thriving business community, proposed to expand the group's leadership and recruitment policies, this idea came under sharp attack. "Is it necessary that this Committee represent the riff raff and everybody?" asked Adolph Kraus. "If the Committee represents the representative and high class Jews of America, that is enough."[8]

Brandeis, who had negotiated a protocol of peace for the strife-torn garment industry, had begun to forge social alliances with the Eastern European Jews. He had even taken out a membership in the American Zionist Federation in 1912 after an emotional meeting with deHaas. Frankfurter, on the other hand, knew few of the Eastern Europeans personally, except for Morris Cohen, the precocious young philosopher with whom he had roomed at Harvard. Socially and intellectually, he lived among the Brahmins, where their desire to accept him sometimes lagged behind his desire for acceptance. Neither he nor Brandeis had gained access to the social circle of the Jewish elite, where their advanced ideas about labor unions and political reform were greeted with considerable skepticism. When Brandeis began to recast Zionist ideals in conformity with the American situation after 1914, he offered Frankfurter and other professional, secular, middle-class Jews a new progressive campaign and a fresh psychological relationship to other Jews and gentiles.

In addition to the inspiration provided by Brandeis, the journey of Frankfurter and other American Jews to Zionism was hastened by an awareness of the deplorable conditions faced by Jews in Palestine and Europe during the war and by a resurgence of anti-Semitism in their own society. Without respect to social class or nation, world Jewry faced a hostile environment after 1914. As conscripts and civilians, they encountered death, disease, and starvation on the battlefields of Eastern Europe. In Palestine, they faced extinction at the hands of the Turkish government, allied with the Germans, which prevented the export of cash crops and cut off the Zionist settlements from all credit facilities. The Turks also expelled nearly 4,000 Jews from the country when they refused to become naturalized citizens. With its own organization and finances disrupted by the war, the European-led World Zionist Organization could do little to aid the Jews in Palestine.

In America, the proponents of immigration restriction, many of them anti-Semites, pushed a literacy test through Congress in 1913 and 1915, in the hope that this measure would stem the tide of Eastern Europeans and others. Although both Taft and Wilson vetoed these laws, the ranks of restrictionists continued to grow in a world of closing frontiers and bitter ethnic tensions, which left many Jews to doubt that America would long remain hospitable to Europe's refugees. American Jews on every socioeconomic level felt the stings of anti-Semitism in these years. The rich found themselves and their children barred from posh resorts, fashionable clubs, and the best private schools. Middle-class and professional Jews met similar rejection. The Century Club in New York closed its doors to the famed scientist Jacques Loeb. Princeton fired Horace Kallen, a Harvard graduate who had trained with William James and George Santayana, when other faculty members learned of his religion. "No sooner did they discover I was a Jew than they decided that I must be cut off and shut out," he wrote. "In those days, such a frame of mind was anything but unusual."[9]

In urban, working-class neighborhoods, "Jew baiting" became a favorite sport among other ethnic groups who resented the intrustion of newcomers. New York's police commissioner, Theodore Bingham, alleged that Jews committed half of the city's crime, a charge he later confessed included counting all the Jewish "criminals" who peddled their goods in the streets without a license. Bingham's charges nonetheless became front-page news in New York, along with other lurid stories that linked the city's Jewish community to prostitution rings and the spread of gangland violence.[10]

The height of American anti-Semitism came with the Leo Frank case in 1913. A Brooklyn-born Jew, Cornell graduate, and manager of his uncle's pencil factory in Atlanta, Frank came to trial in Georgia for the torture slaying of Mary Phagan, a young company employee who, some witnesses alleged, had been in his company hours before her death. Frank's guilt or innocence soon became irrelevant as Georgia newspapers reminded readers of "the lust of the licentious Jew for the Gentile," and mobs outside the courtroom screamed "hang the Jew or we will hang you." In this environment of hysteria and intimidation, the jury convicted Frank and sentenced him to death, a judgment later upheld by both the state's highest court and by the United States Supreme Court over vigorous dissents by Holmes and Hughes.[11]

Georgia's governor commuted Frank's sentence to life imprisonment, but on August 16, 1915, while recuperating in a hospital from an attack by another inmate, he was seized by a mob and murdered. The lynching of Leo Frank sent shock waves of anger, fear, and despair throughout the American Jewish community, especially among the prosperous and secure Jews who had contributed time and money to the young man's defense fund. It became their Dreyfus affair, shattering the optimistic belief in assimilation, equal justice, and American exceptionalism. As never before in the nation's history, a large portion of the society seemed actively hostile to Jews as a group and determined to portray them as grasping social climbers, political subversives, murderous hoodlums, and crazed sex fiends. Many American Jews now sought a new definition of their relationship to the society, and Brandeis provided it.[12]

His vision of Zionism challenged anti-Semitic stereotypes by emphasizing positive aspects of Jewish character and culture and by dramatizing the perfect compatibility between America's political traditions, progressive reforms, and Herzl's ideas. Drawing upon the writings of Kallen and others, Brandeis sought to inspire in American Jews a fresh pride in their unique heritage, a militant faith in ethnic pluralism rather than assimilation, and the desire for solidarity in the face of rising anti-Semitism. All of these goals could be realized, he believed, through Zionism. "To be good Americans," he told an audience in 1914, shortly after assuming direction of the Provisional Executive Committee for General Zionist Affairs, "we must be better Jews, and to be better Jews, we must become Zionists."[13]

Against the old charge that Zionism fostered a dual loyalty among American Jews, Brandeis argued that "multiple loyalties are objectionable only if they are inconsistent." Americans could be loyal to the United States as well as to their state, city, family, profession, and fraternal order without being unpatriotic. Every Irish American who supported home rule for Ireland "was a better man and a better American for the sacrifice he made," and likewise, every American Jew who aided in securing the Jewish homeland in Palestine "will . . . be a better man and a better American for doing so."[14]

Devotion to the Zionist cause, Brandeis believed, would promote a new feeling of unity among American Jews of all classes and restore social and ethical values lost as a consequence of urbanization, industrialization, and assimilation. Zionists could not expect "wholly to eradicate the belief in the policy of assimilation," he wrote, but "assimilation is national suicide . . . [that] can be prevented only by preserving national characteristics and life." In order to accomplish this objective, Jews required "a land where the Jewish life may be naturally led, the Jewish language spoken, and the Jewish spirit prevail . . . and that land is our fathers' land; it is Palestine."[15] From Brandeis's point of view, Zionism promised to reaffirm basic American values, strengthen Jewish moral fiber against the many temptations of modern life, and produce supermen such as Aaron Aaronsohn, the pioneer, scientist, and warrior, who became a Jewish version of Davey Crockett in Palestine.[16]

By contributing to the settlement of Palestine, Brandeis concluded, American Zionists could extend the progressive crusade for social justice abroad because of the opportunities for economic planning in a new land. They could build a society as yet untouched by giant corporations, predatory wealth, and class conflict. In Palestine, he believed, community interests might prevail over egotistical individualism because much of the land, water, natural resources, and public utilities would be owned collectively by the people. The Jews of Palestine would scorn idleness, waste, and conspicuous consumption. They would lead a simple, austere life that Brandeis admired, one liberated from the ceaseless striving for economic advantage and social display. "Our main task must be to make fine men and women in Palestine," he wrote, "and it will be desirable to correct there, so far as possible, those distortions of character and mind which too much commercialism, enforced by separation from the land many centuries, has entailed."[17] At a time of horrible suffering for Jews in Europe and considerable self-doubt for many others in the United States, these romantic, altruistic, and heroic ideas found a responsive constituency.

☙☙☙

Not even Brandeis's eloquence compensated for the immediate weaknesses of the Zionist organization in the United States. When he assumed leadership of the Provisional Executive Committee for General Zionist Affairs in the summer of 1914, the treasury contained only $15,000 and total membership stood at 12,000. Four years later, at the time of the Paris Peace Conference, the Zionist Organization of America had recruited 175,000 members and managed an annual budget in excess of three million dollars. Brandeis may have hated bigness, but Zionism became an exception. He welded together the old-time Zionist leaders such as deHaas, Louis Lipsky, and Richard Gottheil with the new converts such as Frankfurter and Mack into an efficient instrument for raising money and recruiting members. "Organize, Organize, Organize," he commanded, "until every Jew in America must stand up and be counted, counted with us, or prove himself, wittingly or unwittingly, of the few who are against their own people."[18]

In addition to forging an effective group of leaders, Brandeis and his allies faced the vehement opposition of other Jews. Led by David Philipson, the former president of the Central Conference of American Rabbis, the reform wing of Judaism resisted efforts to redirect the thinking and financial resources of their synagogues in the direction of Palestine. "The United States is our Palestine," Philipson declared, "and Washington our Jerusalem."[19] If they hoped to expand their base of support beyond the urban working class and a handful of intellectuals, Brandeis and Frankfurter had to capture the middle-class citadels of reform Judaism in the cities and suburbs of Cincinnati, San Francisco, Minneapolis, and Boston. This became Frankfurter's principle project during the westward journey of the President's Mediation Commission.

The issue of divided loyalty had to be faced squarely with the prosperous, middle-class Jews in places such as San Francisco, he told deHaas, "in view of the happy state of their condition," but hostility to Zionism could be overcome by using recruiters who were also lawyers, doctors, and "men of unquestioned position in their community."[20] Frankfurter urged a similar strategy for Seattle where, he reported, the Jewish community seemed to be controlled by a "slavish disciple of Philipson," but where he had begun to build a rebellion around a group of younger Jews, including "a very intelligent Harvard Law School man" with growing local influence.[21] The Balfour Declaration of 1917, with its promise of British support for a Jewish homeland in Palestine, gave an enormous lift to these organizational efforts but the work remained long, tedious, and often frustrating. "No doubt about Philipson's power," Brandeis told his brother, "nor that he is a son of a gun."[22]

Opposition also came from the very wealthy Jews—Schiff, Sulzberger, Marshall, and Warburg—who believed that Brandeis's efforts would rekindle accusations of Jewish disloyalty and intensify anti-Semitism in the United States. In addition, they looked upon Brandeis and Frankfurter as the Jewish Jacobins, who intended to subvert the fixed structure of leadership in the community by uniting the Eastern European hoi polloi and the middle-class professionals against the aristocracy. The Zionists, fumed Schiff, hoped to "segregate Jews into a separate class" and their agitation bordered upon "treason to the principle of American citizenship and to the love and gratitude we should feel to this country."[23] Schiff and his friends successfully blocked the Zionists' access to large donors by organizing the American Jewish Relief Committee and they fought against efforts to organize a national Jewish congress which the Zionists hoped to use as a forum for discussing both the social condition of Jews in the United States and the settlement of Palestine.

Brandeis and Frankfurter wanted the congress to be democratically elected from a broad spectrum of Jewish organizations, without a fixed number of delegates from older, established groups such as the American Jewish Committee. This formula infuriated the elite, who predicted that the congress would divide the nation's Jews, fall under the domination of radicals, and elevate what Henry Moskowitz called "unwise and unworthy leadership," by which he meant the Yiddish-speaking masses and their middle-class friends. "There is no room in the United States for any other Congress upon national lines," Schiff said, "except the American Congress."[24]

Brandeis needed the Russians in order to establish his credibility with the leaders of the American Jewish Committee, but he also needed the money and influence of Schiff and the AJC in order to conduct expensive relief programs in Palestine. Faced with this dilemma, he compromised, much to the dismay of the Eastern Europeans who regarded the congress fight as a mortal struggle between democracy and despotism, a description once used by Brandeis himself. In exchange for a larger Zionist voice in the distribution of Jewish relief funds, Brandeis agreed that the AJC would receive one-quarter of the delegates to any congress, that the agenda would avoid all discussion of "group rights" for Jews in existing countries, and that Palestine would be referred to as "a Jewish National Home" rather than "the Jewish National Home." A year later, Brandeis agreed to delay the congress entirely until after the war, another compromise that dismayed the Russians.

Although they, too, wished to compromise, the members of the elite also hoped to destroy Brandeis's effectiveness as a leader of the Zionist forces. They lured him to a so-called "peace conference" at the Hotel Astor two weeks after his confirmation by the Senate and turned the session into an ugly verbal free-for-all. The entire affair was spread across the pages of the *New York Times*, complete with a sanctimonious editorial that questioned the propriety of such nonjudicial behavior. Within two months, Brandeis had resigned from all official positions within the Zionist organization, although he continued to dominate the executive committee through his surrogates. The militant Eastern European Zionists felt betrayed by Brandeis's sudden alliance with the AJC and by his decision to remain on the Court rather than devote all his time to the cause.[25]

Rhetorically, Brandeis and Frankfurter had portrayed the congress battle as a fight for democracy within the American Jewish community. They had used the issue to swell the Zionists' claim to leadership. On the other hand, both Brandeis and Frankfurter wished to centralize authority within the Zionist organization and believed that leadership should come from what the latter called "men of unquestioned position in their communities." Ideally, they hoped that this leadership would come from the practical, reform-minded professionals rather than from the wealthy bankers and businessmen who dominated the AJC, but they preferred even that old elite to the volatile workers, intellectuals, and journalists from the Lower East Side.

When Brandeis, Frankfurter, and Mack reorganized the Federation of American Zionists in 1917–1918, they made certain that members paid dues directly to the national organization rather than to the many local Zionist groups who had dominated the movement in the past. By controlling the purse strings, they hoped to increase the authority of the executive committee under Mack and deHaas and reduce the influence of the socialists and religious fundamentalists, who had large followings among the Eastern Europeans. "We shall be so strong," Brandeis remarked, "that both Poali [*sic*] Zion and Mizrachi severally and in conspiracy will be relatively insignificant and unable to hamper our progress. We can never have unity of action, if we take them into our organization as factions."[26] Within the Zionist movement, Brandeis and Frankfurter rose to power on a platform of democracy and opposition to the old elite, but once in power, they abandoned populist rhetoric and made common cause with the established Jewish leaders. The road to Zion, they believed, could be travelled only with substantial funds provided by the latter in concert with the disciplined, managerial leadership of middle-class professionals. Zionism's more emotional, ideological factions, they feared, threatened to disrupt the journey.

❧❧❧

Although he gave many speeches on behalf of Zionism, organized new cadres in the West, and joined Brandeis in protracted negotiations with the American Jewish Committee, Frankfurter did not play a steady role in the movement until after his resignation from the government in early 1919. Even with Brandeis's formal withdrawal from the leadership, he remained far less prominent than Mack or deHaas, but stood ever in the wings as the chief emergency fireman who could be called upon to put out political brush fires that threatened Jewish interests in Palestine. One such issue, of course, was the Balfour Declaration of 1917 that expressed British support for "the establishment in Palestine of a national home for the Jewish people."

During the negotiations between Whitehall and Washington over the precise wording of the document, Frankfurter orchestrated the response of American Zionists, most of whom wished to bring immediate pressure upon Wilson to endorse the British proposal. He cautioned delay. "The President temperamentally is unwilling to create occasions," he noted. "He only takes advantage of opportunities. . . . We ought to make argument by action these days and not by demands. In all kinds of ways we should stimulate and contribute to the military and civil service. Those will make the strongest arguments for us and will furnish the basis for the more formative arguments of our war aims."[27] Frankfurter had read Wilson perfectly. The president informed Brandeis and Rabbi Wise that he supported the Balfour Declaration, but he refused to endorse the document openly until

1918, when British and Arab forces had gained the upper hand militarily against the Turks.[28]

Zionist ambitions, Frankfurter believed, complemented the strategic interests of the United States and the Wilsonian rhetoric of self-determination. "Zionism is one of those durable dreams which is moving the thought, the feelings and will of the world," he wrote, "in the realization that it is a concrete application of the principle of small nationalities."[29] At the same time, he was not naïve enough to believe that the Wilson administration shared his views. Colonel House did not regard the Balfour Declaration with much enthusiasm. The State Department, led by Secretary Robert Lansing, expressed open hostility, and the president himself remained somewhat perplexed about how to reconcile the ideals of self-determination with the conflicting aspirations of Jews and Arabs. Wilson and House wanted no part of a joint Anglo-American mandate over the conquered Turkish lands, yet they distrusted British and French designs upon the area and believed that the European powers manipulated Zionism and Arab nationalism for their own imperial purposes.

The attitude of many European Zionists such as Weizmann, who openly acknowledged the clear relationship between England's imperial security and a new Jewish homeland in Palestine, aroused anxiety both in the Wilson administration and among American Zionists, who feared negative diplomatic reactions from Washington and eventual betrayal by Whitehall. "Britain appears now to be reaching out after all of Syria to the north," Robert Szold cautioned Frankfurter. "She acts on every hand as if she were in Palestine to stay, now building trunk highways, large headquarters at Haifa and making preparations for the large public concessions. The tendency is clear. Apparent encouragement of Arab demands . . . repression of Jewish activity and . . . Britain left in unfettered control, politically and economically."[30]

Arab nationalism, kindled by the British promise of independence and the leadership of King Feisal and T. E. Lawrence, presented another dilemma for the Zionists, since non-Jews constituted the vast majority of the Palestine population. In the first flush of victory after the Balfour Declaration, many Zionist leaders believed that Jewish, Arab, and British interests could be easily reconciled. "I am convinced that the more the Arab movement, as represented by Feisal, develops, and the more successful it is in the field, the less conflict there will be between this movement and Zionism," wrote Weizmann. "The so-called Arab question in Palestine would assume only a purely local character."[31] Brandeis and Frankfurter did not share this optimistic assessment because they doubted that Feisal could speak for all of the Arabs. They cautioned Zionist leaders to downplay the idea of a Jewish state for fear of undermining Arab moderates like Feisal and inflaming the extreme nationalists. The phrase "homeland in Palestine," Brandeis remarked, "sits well."[32]

In the treacherous rip tides of big power ambitions and rivalry among the Arabs, Frankfurter knew that Zionist hopes depended less upon neat verbal formulas and more upon building up Jewish institutions in Palestine. Despite the skepticism of Szold and others, he believed that the eventual success of Zionism depended upon securing a British mandate over the area at the peace conference with strong guarantees for future Jewish immigration and self-government. When the British named Weizmann to a commission to investigate conditions in Palestine and when the latter suggested building a Hebrew university on Mt. Scopus, Frankfurter seized upon the idea as a perfect opportunity to increase American influence within the Zionist movement, build up Jewish resources in Palestine, and cement Zionist friendship with the British.

"The most effective way of asserting American power for the present," he told deHaas from England, "is through money. Money is needed intrinsically, money is needed still more for purposes of prestige—as to the source and symbol of power of Zionism in this country. . . . The imperative need is money, money, money. With that all the other things will come to us."[33] The Hebrew university, he reported to Mack, had fired the imagination of Balfour and Lloyd George "as a dramatic way of showing the kind of thing Zionism signifies in the very throes of a terrific warfare." The Americans, he argued, should at least match the funds of Baron Edmund James deRothschild, who alone had pledged $25,000. When Mack expressed some skepticism about raising large sums of money quickly, Frankfurter fumed: "If those rich friends of yours cannot see beyond a real estate block in the Bronx . . . then I cannot possibly appeal to them."[34]

Under Frankfurter's constant hectoring, the money began to flow across the Atlantic to London and to Palestine. Within three months, Weizmann laid the university's cornerstone. Through his network of friends in the State Department, Frankfurter also secured the safe, regular delivery of Zionist funds to Palestine, despite a lack of enthusiasm among the agency's top officials. He gained diplomatic approval as well for a medical unit that the Americans sent to the area as another symbol of their growing commitment. Tirelessly, he attempted to persuade lower-level bureaucrats of the reasonableness of Zionist efforts, especially the assistant secretary, William Phillips, who "does not keep alert to the actual facts . . . and needs fresh saturation into our point of view. He shall have it."[35]

Frankfurter's most decisive contribution came in the spring and summer of 1919 at Versailles. To the peace conference of Wilsonian idealism, seething nationalism, and petty intrigues, the Zionists sent an impressive delegation: Weizmann, Mack, Wise, Marshall, the brilliant young lawyer, Benjamin Cohen, and Aaronsohn, agronomist, secret agent, and pioneer, who it was said knew every acre of ground, stream, and plant species in Palestine. Even among this dazzling cast, Frankfurter stood out as a spokesman because of his negotiating skills, legal craftsmanship, and swift access to the key figures in the American and British delegations who ultimately determined the fate of Palestine: House, Philip Kerr (secretary to Lloyd George), Eustace Percy, and Loring Christie, his old roommates from the House of Truth. No one enjoyed more fully the complete confidence of the absent prophet, Brandeis. Largely because of Frankfurter's advice, the justice agreed to travel to Palestine via London and Paris in the summer of 1919 when Zionist fortunes at Versailles hung in the balance. While other advisers urged caution or cancellation of the trip, Frankfurter knew that the publicity generated by the Palestine tour could prove decisive in Paris. He was right.[36]

At Paris, he struggled to secure the British mandate over Palestine, generous boundaries for the new territory against French claims in Syria, and guarantees for future Jewish immigration and economic development. Although the final boundaries remained unclear until the San Remo Conference a year later, Frankfurter laid the foundations. He appeared everywhere at Versailles, not only with the foreign ministers and presidential confidants such as Balfour and House, but also with the lowly technical experts who fed these leaders basic information. Frankfurter knew where real power lay. "The draft [of the mandate] is now in the hands of the English who are at work on the mandates and also the Americans," he told Brandeis. "We are working with both of them quite easily. . . . David Miller [counsellor to the American delegation] will probably be the ultimate blue pencil."[37] Shortly, he reported that "the essentials are secured, namely, that Palestine will be set aside as the foundation for the Jewish homeland and that Great Britain will be named mandatory."[38]

In addition to directing Zionist strategy with respect to the mandate, Frankfurter became the tireless peace maker among clashing Jewish factions in Paris and operated an extensive propaganda campaign against the movement's chief opponents. Among the latter were many British and French Jews, led by Lucian Wolf, and Frankfurter's old nemesis, Henry Morgenthau, who turned up in Paris bearing an anti-Zionist petition signed by most of his friends. "The man is without character, except concentrated self-seeking," Frankfurter exploded, "and he is incapacitated from analysing or understanding a simple political difficulty. . . . Take base metal, stamp on it the seal of government, call it an ambassador and you can never drive it out of circulation."[39] He became more than irate when other Zionists suggested sending Morgenthau on a mission to Poland in order to investigate conditions there among Jews. They apparently hoped to purchase the ambassador's support with this form of flattery.

Frankfurter's objections to Morgenthau encountered opposition from Marshall and other leaders, who insisted that he join the Polish expedition, a proposition that evoked for Frankfurter terrible memories of his last mission with Uncle Henry. Poland also presented the Zionists with a horrible dilemma. The government of Ignace Jan Paderewski, the pianist-politician, encouraged anti-Semitism among the peasantry and landed gentry, while many Polish Jews sympathized with communism, an idea without broad appeal to the British, already terrified by the spectre of Bolshevism in Russia, Hungary, and Germany. In his dealings with British leaders over Poland, therefore, Frankfurter walked a tightrope. He described the vicious pogroms condoned by the present regime, but at the same time he recommended support for Paderewski's government. This policy comported well with London's prejudices but did not promise much relief for Poland's Jews. On the other hand, probably no government wholly sympathetic to the Jews could have long survived in Poland; and even Paderewski's collapsed within a year.[40]

Even for someone with Frankfurter's guile, Polish politics remained largely unfathomable and beyond control. He experienced greater success in maintaining the shaky coalition at Paris between the wealthy Western Jews such as Baron Rothschild and the fiery Eastern Europeans, who demanded a larger voice in Zionist affairs. The baron looked upon Palestine as "one of his art collections," Frankfurter reported, and "he is very distrustful of Weizmann; like all Frenchmen, fearful of Russian Bolshevism."[41] For this reason, Frankfurter advised, the Americans should expand their role within the world organization and also within Palestine. "We cannot talk as well nor are we as cultured as the Eastern Europeans," he confessed, "but circumstances have made us better workers, given us a stronger sense of reality. Moreover, Americans serve the added purpose of allaying fears of Bolshevism."[42] With Frankfurter as the principal mediator, the two European factions maintained chilly cooperation.

His greatest victory took place at a villa in the Bois de Boulogne, where against the backdrop of rising Arab protests in Palestine, he sat down to discuss peace with King Feisal and his boyish, charismatic ally, Lawrence. Frankfurter showed Feisal the proposed Zionist borders for Palestine, which included plans for an extensive hydroelectric project and irrigation system on lands claimed by France for the Syrians. He told Feisal of his hope that Jews and Arabs could develop the land together without fighting and without bloodshed. Several days later, Feisal sent a remarkable reply. Jews and Arabs were "cousins in race," the king affirmed, who had suffered "similar oppressions at the hands of the powers" and should now stand together. He regarded the Zionists' demands as "moderate and proper" and vowed "we will do our best in so far as we are concerned to help them through."[43]

Feisel and the Arab delegation at Paris proved far less menacing to Zionism than fundamentalist Christians led by Charles R. Crane, a wealthy industrialist, and Henry C. King, the president of Oberlin College and a leader of the American Missionary Association. Echoing the concerns of other Protestant missionary groups that were active in the Middle East, Crane and King convinced President Wilson that they should survey local attitudes in the region with specific reference to the Balfour Declaration. Although he had already endorsed the declaration, Wilson agreed to the mission.

Frankfurter first attempted to kill the project, but when that failed, he sought to limit the scope of the Crane-King inquiry "to take Palestine out of the field of controversy."[44] Colonel House, the president, and Crane at first agreed to this limitation, but then reneged on the bargain in the face of other Protestant demands to include Palestine. Not even Brandeis's hasty visit to the area could stop the inquiry or alter the contents of the final report. In this document, King and Crane argued that Moslems and Christian Arabs favored an enlarged, united Syria that included Palestine. Their survey showed, they claimed, widespread opposition to the Zionist program. Had it been made public at the time, the King-Crane report would have delighted the French, alienated the British, and gravely disappointed the Zionists, but the administration quietly buried the document shortly after Wilson's illness.[45]

Despite its pro-Arab and anti-Semitic overtones, the Crane-King report contained a large measure of truth that even the most passion-

ate Zionists could not ignore. Arab hostility to Jewish designs on
Palestine continued to grow, some of it encouraged by local British
officials, but much of it arising without their support. Whatever the
Zionists' historic claims, the Arabs feared the loss of their present
majority and many prepared to fight to keep it. "Whether there is
more anti-Jewish feeling than before is difficult to determine," Henry
Freidenwald reported to Frankfurter. "Some of the better Arabs realize that there is no incompatibility between the development of Hebrew and Arabic culture side by side and that there is room for both.
Probably, however, the opposition is more intense. . . . Some of the
English officers think that large Jewish immigration would have to be
supported by the bayonet and that neither Britain nor any other country is willing to undertake the job."[46]

The next three decades confirmed this tragic observation. Feisal
and Lawrence did not speak for the Palestinian Arabs or for the many
local British administrators, who remained determined to prevent im-
plementation of the Balfour Declaration, regardless of the paper
promises made at Versailles or San Remo. Nor, despite the façade of
Zionist unity at Paris, could Frankfurter prevent the movement from
splitting apart over future strategy once the initial diplomatic victories
had been gained. The Americans had taken financial and political control of the movement during the chaotic days of war. Now, the old
European leaders wanted it back.

﷽

As newcomers to the Zionist struggle, Americans such as Frankfurter acknowledged their huge debt to the Europeans who had kept
Herzl's dream alive in the lean years before World War I and who had
played a crucial role in securing the Balfour Declaration. At the same
time, however, the Americans knew that only their superb organizational skills and deep pocketbooks had kept the Palestine colonies sol-
vent during the war. The Americans, in brief, now expected to play a
larger role, comparable to that played at Versailles, in Zionism's future.

Influenced by deHaas's lingering distrust of Weizman, many of
the American Zionists harbored negative and frequently patronizing
attitudes about their European allies. "You should keep your mind
quite open," Frankfurter reported to Brandeis, "in regard to Weizmann's future usefulness," a point of view that clearly suggested the
superiority of the Americans.[47] Following a meeting of the Greater

Actions Comite, Brandeis expressed grave doubts about Weizmann and the Eastern Europeans. "The spirit is willing, and the flesh strong enough," he wrote, "but the East Europeans have much to learn in practical affairs. The Russians are fine in spirit, but not housebroken."[48]

From the perspective of Brandeis and Frankfurter, the movement should now focus all of its energies upon Palestine and deemphasize political agitation and propaganda among Jewish communities in the West, except for fund-raising purposes. Palestine must be prepared for massive Jewish immigration, a task that demanded the skills of scientific experts and technicians who could drain swamps, fight disease, build dams and irrigation systems, purchase land, and wisely invest capital. Political orators and religious prophets, Brandeis believed, ought to take a back seat now to practical men of affairs. Although he favored collective ownership of key natural resources and public utilities, Brandeis also hoped to create for Palestine a series of limited-dividend, joint-stock companies to facilitate the raising of capital from Jews in America and Europe. He believed that all Zionist projects should be managed on a strict businesslike basis and that all Jews, Zionists as well as non-Zionists, should participate in these economic efforts.

Given Brandeis's priorities, a collision with the Eastern Europeans, who wished to expand political agitation and cultural programs in the West, was almost inevitable. The first skirmish came over Brandeis's campaign to eradicate malaria in Palestine and to eliminate the administrative chaos that had plagued the American medical unit there. Members of the Zionist Commission in Palestine insisted that the unit conduct all of its business in Hebrew, an arrangement which the Americans regarded as grossly inefficient because all of their official correspondence had to be routed through Jerusalem, translated from English into Hebrew, and then translated back into English once it reached London. For Brandeis and his followers, the medical unit's problems symbolized the obstacles that would confront Zionism if cultural and religious fanatics gained the upper hand.

From the point of view of Weizmann and many of the Russian Jews, however, the battle over the medical unit symbolized the Americans' indifference and insensitivity to the desires for a Jewish cultural renaissance in Palestine and elsewhere. The Americans seemed to be philistine bookkeepers and social engineers, Zionists of the head rather than of the heart, who wished to concentrate upon the petty details of economic development to the neglect of spiritual and cultural values. Weizmann and his followers hoped to devote a substantial portion of the movement's resources to *gegenwartsarbeit*, the propagation of Hebrew and Jewish culture in Europe and the United States as well as in Palestine. For Brandeis and the assimilated Jews of America, England, and France, however, this program appeared to be a waste of time and money that could be better spent on Palestine.

"I am definitely opposed to any *gegenwartsarbeit*, domestic or foreign, for the Zionist Organization," Brandeis told deHaas. "We are specialists on Palestine."[49] Weizmann resented this opposition to his program and also the fact that the rich Americans seemed eager to control the world movement, but unwilling to give up their current occupations and devote themselves forever to Zionism. Privately, he regarded Brandeis's journey to Palestine as a form of glorified tourism that had not deepened the justice's understanding of the country or its problems.[50]

A deep schism opened up between Weizmann and the Brandeisians at the meeting of the Actions Comite in 1919. With the assistance of Sylvain Levi, who represented the interests of Baron deRothschild, Brandeis and Frankfurter secured enough votes to defeat Weizmann's plans, but the latter vowed to carry the battle to the next full meeting of international leaders scheduled for 1920. Because he had helped to engineer Weizmann's defeat, Frankfurter came in for sharp attack from the Russian chemist. "We shall never forget this vote," Weizmann told him, nor the fact that the Americans seemed to have a limited understanding of true Zionist ideals. The Americans, Weizmann fumed, wished "to reduce Zionist activities to a chartered company without profits, but not to lift it to a great movement capable of shaking the . . . external slavery [of Jews] to pieces." The Americans, moreover, "have job positions to lose in contradistinction to the sans-culottes who have nothing to lose." Brandeis, he lectured Frankfurter, "could have been a prophet in Israel—you have in you the makings of a Lasalle. Instead, you are choosing to be only a professor at Harvard and Brandeis only a judge in the Supreme Court."[51]

The wounds of 1919 did not heal. A second confrontation between the two factions took place over the financial structure of a new agency—the Keren Hayesod or Endowment Fund—designed to collect money throughout the world for Palestine development. Weizmann and his followers wanted to lump all the monies together, with no distinction between investment funds for specific Palestine projects and regular donations that could be used for other Zionist purposes. In addition, they wished to centralize financial control within the

World Zionist Organization and reduce the autonomy of various national bodies. Not surprisingly, these features of the Keren Hayesod repelled Brandeis, who deplored the sloppy accounting procedures and any dilution of American independence in fund raising. He returned to the United States in 1920 determined to pursue his own dreams of economic development for Palestine and to prevent the virus of *gegenwartsarbeit* and Keren Hayesod from infecting American Zionism.[52]

Some of Brandeis's closest advisers, notably deHaas, relished the growing schism, which they blamed solely upon Weizmann's egotism and duplicity, an interpretation encouraged by the justice. Frankfurter, initially, did not support the militants. He endorsed Brandeis's rejection of the Keren Hayesod and doubted the value of cultural work in the Diaspora, but he hoped that the two sides could find common ground through the exercise of mutual patience and tact. His perception of the Russian leader had undergone considerable revision since their first meetings, when he had advised Brandeis that "collaborative effort, even docility, could be imposed upon Weizmann without difficulty."[53] He soon discovered that he had underestimated the latter's competence and tenacity.

Even during their moments of conflict in 1919 and 1920, moreover, Frankfurter grew to like Weizmann and many of his disciples. More romantic than Brandeis, blessed with a softer personality, and tolerant of human frailties, Frankfurter seldom attributed the growing strife to the Europeans' defective morality or weak character. "You must permit us to discuss things with you . . . be patient enough to show us we are wrong," he told Weizmann. "It's a simple thing we want—that we be allowed to cooperate with you, in thought and action. And less—on sober thought—you would not want."[54] In turn, the Europeans warmed up to Frankfurter, who, even Brandeis conceded, "of all Americans, is I believe the closest friend of Dr. Weizmann." The Europeans felt "more at home" talking with either Frankfurter or Judge Mack, recalled Ben Cohen, and had Brandeis not been involved, the tragic division "would not have arisen in the form it did."[55]

Once Brandeis turned his back on Weizmann and resolved to maintain American independence, however, Frankfurter had to make a painful choice. He sided with Brandeis and became one of the justice's most hawkish supporters. At the annual Zionist Organization of America convention in 1920, for example, he helped to write the Brandeisians' platform and pushed it through the assembly over the

sullen opposition of Weizmann's allies. He and Brandeis began to increase the executive committee's control over all activities in America,
and to urge the expulsion of dissenters from the organization. "The
proper place for such opposition," Brandeis declared, "is among the
outs."[56]

Once a proponent of compromise, Frankfurter believed that a state
of war now existed between the two factions. They should resist the
diversion of more talk and give no quarter to the enemy. He became
increasingly impatient with those critics of Brandeis who deplored the
new regime of centralization and ideological conformity in the Zionist
Organization. Angrily, he urged even greater authority for Judge
Mack and the executive committee against what he called "this abstract miasma about 'participation' and 'unity' etc., etc., etc.,—the
metaphysics of small businessmen and journalists and weak lawyers."[57]

In his single-minded effort to impose Brandeis's ideals upon
American Zionism, Frankfurter ignored one basic contradiction.
Their cries for centralization and unity came at the very time when
they fought Weizmann and the world organization on the issues of
national autonomy and the necessity for diversity in Zionist beliefs.
"Unity does not necessarily imply uniformity," Brandeis said. "Nor
does it necessarily imply concentration of power. . . . We must
among other things define for the World Organization and the Federation the proper spheres of initiative and of other action."[58] Within the
American organization, however, neither Brandeis nor Frankfurter
tolerated much dissent, and their behavior gave rise to growing
charges of "tyranny" and "dictatorship" that Weizmann and his followers shrewdly exploited.

The Eastern Europeans within the American organization, most
of whom had joined Brandeis and Frankfurter in the earlier battle
against the Jewish elite, now turned the rhetoric of democracy against
their new leaders. The "small businessmen and journalists and weak
lawyers" who formed the Zionist shock troops on the Lower East Side
rallied to the idea of *gegenwarsarbeit* and Keren Hayesod. They came
to believe that Weizmann and the Russians were correct: Brandeis,
Frankfurter, Mack and Wise, those exemplary models of assimilation
and progressivism, lacked *Yiddishkeit* and the true spirit of Zionism.

At the tumultuous 1921 Zionist convention in Cleveland, with
Weizmann in attendance and the question of Keren Hayesod before
the delegates, "the small businessmen and journalists and weak lawyers" took the organization away from the Brandeisians, most of

whom, including the justice and Frankfurter, resigned in disgust from all official positions. "I'm glad it has come, the way it did," Frankfurter told Brandeis on the eve of their anticipated defeat. "Mack and some of the others . . . will now see things in a way they otherwise never would. Sad one is, but not tragic about it. The movement may be hurt by it, but not in the long run."[59]

Before the decade ended, the Cleveland victors and Weizmann came to appreciate the wisdom of Brandeis's program for Palestine, but neither the justice nor Frankfurter again played a formal role in Zionist affairs comparable to the years between 1917 and 1921. Both men shared the bitter disappointment in British policy under the mandate, which during the 1920s and 1930s usually discouraged Jewish immigration, tolerated Arab violence, and undermined the spirit of the Balfour Declaration. Throughout the twists and turns of British policy, however, Frankfurter remained a devout Anglophile as he had remained a devout American even during the most emotional moments of the Zionist crusade.

Despite Weizmann's criticism, Frankfurter had been a Zionist of the heart as well as of the head. Along with other assimilated American Jews of his generation, Frankfurter felt attracted to Zionism because it appealed to his pride in being Jewish, afforded a collective response to the rising fury of anti-Semitism, and offered prosperous middle-class professionals the opportunity to employ their expertise on behalf of something other than self-aggrandizement. But he could never become a full-time Zionist leader, he told Brandeis, because "dependence is my most sensitive spot and I just would be a deadened and ineffective paid employee of the organization."[60] But at other moments he perhaps wondered what it would have been like to be a Zionist Lasalle, instead of only a professor at Harvard.

CHAPTER 9

SCHOOL AND SCHOLAR

IN THE DECADE after Versailles, America seldom nourished the dreams of progressives who joined the Bull Moose revolt, rallied to Wilson's New Freedom, or joined the wartime bureaucracy in the expectation of making the world safe for democracy. If the nation's political consciousness did not regress to the era of Cleveland and McKinley, neither did it display the social compassion, intellectual ferment, and moral outrage that distinguished the careers of Jane Addams, Louis Brandeis, Max Eastman, Florence Kelley, and Walter Lippmann. The basic structure of many progressive reforms remained in place—consumer protection laws, utility commissions, the Federal Trade Commission, the ICC—but the fires of reform burned low in many regulatory agencies, the result of mediocre appointments, slashed budgets, and outright capitulation to narrow interest groups. Other areas of progressive striving, especially collective bargaining for labor, minimum-wage laws, and the elimination of child labor, did not survive the war years. Personal gain, not public service, dominated the decade's political ethics, symbolized by the peculations of Albert B. Fall and by a president who proclaimed that business was the nation's business.

Many progressives, disillusioned by the continental bloodbath, the Red Scare, Wilson's failures as a peace maker, and the severity of the final treaties, flatly rejected internationalism and turned inward upon America. Frankfurter briefly joined them. "The whole discussion about the League," he told the pacifist Alice Hamilton in 1924, "must be turned from abstract idealizations such as 'duty to humanity,' . . . 'moral responsibility,' etc., etc., to concrete realities such as having this country assume political responsibilities for the various conflicts that are bound to rise." But he doubted that the United States should become involved in "all European conflicts and controversies."[1] A year later he chided Herbert Feis for the latter's "world stuff talk" and suggested that America could best serve humanity by concentrating upon its own internal social problems. "Nor do I care," he snapped, "if you call me 'isolationist' and 'little American' and what not."[2]

In a decade of rapid demographic movement, blatant materialism, soaring crime rates, and mounting ethnic tensions, the country faced many social problems, and few regions of the country or institutions remained isolated from the shock of change, including the august Harvard Law School. "Law School affairs are first-rate," Frankfurter remarked to a colleague early in the decade. "Pound and I are very happy—and even [President] Lowell and I speak at the same dinners."[3] His euphoria soon collapsed during bitter conflicts over institutional growth, admissions standards, the curriculum, and faculty recruitment.

Like many of the decade's notable business tycoons, Roscoe Pound believed that more was better. Scholarly, short-tempered, and querulous, he wanted the law school to grow larger and seldom tolerated opposition to these dreams of expansion. By means of increasing its endowment, raising money from the great foundations, building more classrooms, admitting new students, and hiring more permanent faculty, the dean believed that Harvard could become the General Motors of American law schools—the biggest and the best in all fields of legal education. In Pound's judgment, the intellectual quality of the school could not be maintained without numerical growth, because the small size of the existing faculty limited competent instruction in many areas of public and private law.

Pound also believed that the faculty's research productivity suffered because of their excessive teaching load, and he hoped to end the practice of hiring visiting professors on a year-by-year basis to cover many basic courses. "I have gone on now for twelve years switching men about in the curriculum and giving them no real chance to master any one subject and write upon it as they should," he complained to Frankfurter. "After fifteen years of filibustering in curriculum I am absolutely through. This matter of taking up a new subject every once in a while is a tremendous waste of one's energies." He thought it preposterous that Frankfurter, who had been hired to teach administrative law, should volunteer to teach a section of criminal law. "You ought not to be wasting your energies by scattering them over the whole curriculum any longer," he fumed. "I insist that that policy must be abandoned."[4]

Although he did not object to improvements in the school's physical plant and foundation support for faculty research, Frankfurter rejected Pound's strategy of growth. He wished to keep the size of both the student body and the faculty closer to prewar levels in order to maintain the school's elite status, intimate methods of instruction, and academic quality. He equated large enrollments and huge faculty with the evils of commercialism, the curse of bigness, and the deterioration of academic standards, a point of view also held by Justice Brandeis, who argued that instead of building a bigger Harvard the faculty should attempt to create twenty Harvards scattered across the country. When student enrollment soared to one thousand early in the decade, Frankfurter gloomily remarked to Holmes that "the school will soon be a fit subject for restraint under the Sherman Law if size be the test."[5]

An avowed elitist on the subject of legal education, Frankfurter wished to maintain the handicraft model of instruction, where professors taught a small number of very bright students and where, because of their own intellectual versatility, the faculty taught a variety of courses. The fact that some courses might not be offered at Harvard did not disturb him in the least, and he liked the idea of hiring young instructors on a short-term basis in order to meet the school's annual teaching deficit. The younger men brought fresh ideas and vitality to the classrooms; the best of them might be invited to remain as permanent faculty if they survived the grueling competition.

Pound, on the other hand, hoped to institute a factory model of legal education, based upon the ideas of specialization, breadth, and a division of labor. Not all of the school's instructors might be intellectual giants, he reasoned, but more courses could be offered to more students on a regular basis. In Frankfurter's opinion, this program surrendered quality to quantity and represented a capitulation to the worst values in American society. "The numbers problem will have to be faced . . . and Pound is in no temper I'm sorry to say, to face [it]," he told Chafee. "Mass production has even the best minds in its grip."[6] The law school, he told Hand, "to me means the qualities of Ames, Thayer, Gray, Sam Williston. . . . I know the dangers of giving the past a golden hue, but I feel smugly safeguarded against that danger." He feared "a terrible deterioration in quality on our faculty" and singled out as the cause "this assumption that if you have money then you will find great men. . . . a snare and a delusion—and worse."[7]

Their battle came to a head in the fall of 1925 when the dean proposed the addition of three new faculty members—Crane, Goodrich, and Thurston—to teach courses on municipal corporations, advanced equity, quasicontract, and restraint of trade. All of these courses, Frankfurter believed, were marginal to the school's mission, and furthermore, the three candidates did not impress him. He was unsparing in his criticism, especially of Crane, "a good mediocrity, a good plodder," and Thurston, who had led a career of "unrelieved sterility." Of course, he told Joe Warren, sarcastically, "large organizations have general drayhorses to do drayhorse work; but there's no room, if this is to be the premier law school of the country . . . for drayhorses here."[8] Pound had his way on this issue, but Frankfurter's opposition irritated him greatly, and be began to fill his diary with regular complaints about his colleague, who he noted, "as last year, opposed everything."[9]

Frankfurter, of course, did not fight all additions to the faculty. He worked diligently to recruit established scholars such as Thomas Reed Powell and Edmund Morgan, as well as talented young professors such as James Landis and Calvert Magruder. These men impressed him as worthy successors to Ames, Thayer, and Gray; moreover, they generally shared his social liberalism and commitment to reform. Many of Pound's appointments, on the contrary, seemed motivated solely by the exigencies of an expanding curriculum, without much regard for intellectual quality. "I think it is up to us to cut the coat of courses according to the available cloth of fit teachers," he told Pound bluntly. "If we cannot get men of real distinction, let's cut courses and quite mercilessly."[10] He despaired, however, of blunting the dean's devotion to growth and his ability to carry a majority of the faculty with him. "There is not the slightest chance of that limitation of numbers which you and I so deeply care about," he told Chafee. The expansion, he feared, would "go on forever like an industrial plant."[11]

The trends in American legal education during the decade did not inspire Frankfurter's confidence, because at Harvard and elsewhere they seemed designed to satisfy the vulgar spirit of commercialism. The students who came to Harvard, he told Hand, seemed dominated by "a pretty crass materialism." They hoped to become "big money-making lawyers in New York and Chicago" and neither the law school nor the profession at large provided them with alternative models of success. Throughout the decade, he condemned those law professors who earned fat incomes from the American Law Institute by perfecting the rules of commercial law, and those leaders of the bar who glorified corporate practice.

He voted for Robert La Follette and not John W. Davis in the 1924 presidential election because, as he told Hand, the latter "from the time public office gave him prestige . . . capitalized it in terms of big money-making for himself and of service to the powerful." Davis could have remained a "free lawyer" in the tradition of Brandeis, but instead he became part of "the financial-legal complex which gave him an income . . . of not less than two hundred thousand dollars." That was no example for young lawyers who needed "the discouragement of material ambitions and the instilling of spiritual concerns."[12]

With equal vehemence, he chastized Charles Evans Hughes for his active defense of the Interborough Railway Company. The former Supreme Court justice, governor, and presidential candidate, he argued, "ought by now to be free from the need of making money and ought to serve as an example to younger men by not taking every case in which there is a big retainer." Hughes, he complained, "wrapped himself in a cloak of self-righteousness," but in his own legal practice did not set "very inspiring standards for the youth of this country."[13]

As a teacher, despite his complaints about rising enrollments, declining academic standards, commercialism, and moral decay, Frankfurter did not retreat into a vanishing world of Victorian legal education. His methods of instruction, which emphasized original student research in the third year of study, attempted to provide a fresh experience for many students who did not earn a coveted position on the *Harvard Law Review*. These students, he believed, deserved something better than another year of studying cases "merely as a method of . . . finding out what cases hold, what the doctrines are." Frankfurter's seminars promoted self-discipline, discouraged intellectual passivity, and brought forth a bountiful harvest of impressive student essays, including studies of diversity jurisdiction in the federal courts, the administrative control of aliens, workmen's compensation programs, zoning reforms in New York State, and public utility regulation in Minnesota.[14]

He saw his small seminars and the intellectual intimacy they fostered as essential to combatting the emotional problems of institutional size. He preferred being close to a few students instead of entertaining a huge throng in the lecture hall. "The dominant note of the place is impersonal," he lamented in 1930. "The vastness of the reading room, the great mass of students who are necessarily total strangers to each other, the lack of any common life not only of the School as a whole but of individual classes—all make against having that feeling of at-homeness without which there can be no inner peace and satisfaction."[15] He developed a fierce loyalty to many students and he expected loyalty in return, a demand that often brought charges of paternalism and favoritism, especially from those students who remained outside the charmed circle. "He loved his proteges," Mrs. Mark De Wolfe Howe remarked, "but he also owned them." Frankfurter, of course, believed that he sustained a community within an institution that more and more resembled a mechanical assembly line, and that he had lost the battle in the face of burgeoning enrollments and rapid physical growth.[16]

Harvard could not escape from the alienating forces of mass education during the 1920s, nor could it avoid the social strife generated by increased mobility and the struggle for economic opportunity that pitted old Yankees against many newcomers, especially the Jews, the Irish, and the Italians. He deplored the growth ethic that opened up more classrooms to these minorities, but Frankfurter insisted that the institution remain open to all students and scholars on the basis of academic merit alone. President Lowell and some faculty members had very different ideas. While encouraging institutional expansion, they hoped to curb the admission of those groups who threatened Yankee hegemony at Harvard.

Beginning in 1922, several years before Congress adopted a national quota system with respect to all foreign immigration, Lowell raised the idea of a *numerus clauses* or "Jewish quota" with Judge Mack, the only Jew on the Harvard Board of Overseers. The quota, Lowell assured him, would apply only to transfer students, not to freshmen who could still gain places through competitive examinations. Harvard's Jews should get behind this plan, Lowell argued, because it would protect their stake in the institution and prevent an outburst of anti-Semitism. Lowell prevailed upon the board to appoint a faculty committee to "consider principles and methods for more effectively sifting candidates for admission," but he successfully resisted Mack's request that Frankfurter serve on the committee. Lowell told Mack that his candidate did not have an open mind on the subject, and had earned a reputation for being obstreperous and unreasonable.[17]

Superficially, the faculty's report constituted a victory for the forces of toleration, because it specifically rejected "discrimination on grounds of race or religion" as a basis for limiting admissions to Harvard. On the other hand, it advocated increased admissions for students from small towns and rural areas in order to promote greater geographical balance and cultural diversity, an indirect quota system that discriminated against the largest Eastern cities and their foreign-born populations. This veiled quota system, masquerading under the banner of geographical balance, did not fool Frankfurter or other Jews. "That's a hellovah 'compromise' Lowell has worked out," he told Pound angrily. "I should certainly be shocked if that slimy talk affects anyone that matters in Cambridge."[18]

Lowell's bigotry, however, had many imitators among those who mattered in Cambridge. After meeting with other deans to discuss academic scholarships, Pound noted in his diary that they rejected his advice to base financial awards upon grades and seemed "determined to cut off Jews wherever possible." In the law school, he remarked a year later, certain members of the faculty, led by Warren and Richard Ames, had become "very intolerant" about "orthodox Jews who can't take examinations on Saturday."[19] Warren, in fact, supported an "Americanization" campaign for the law school that would have reduced both the number of Jewish students and the financial aid available to them by giving preference to factors other than academic ability. This suggestion especially drew Frankfurter's fire because it threatened his vision of the law school as a meritocracy where brains counted for more than social background, race, or religion. "The great thing about the School when I was a student," he told Pound, "was that Skull & Bones, Hasty Pudding, an H, family fortune, skin, creed—nothing particularly mattered, except scholarship and character objectively ascertained."[20]

Frankfurter himself, according to critics and admirers, lavished special attention upon talented non-Jews—James Landis, Dean Acheson, Alger Hiss—but placed extraordinary academic demands upon many Jewish students who, he knew, faced many obstacles in the law school and the profession. That he may have done so out of a paternalistic desire to prepare Jewish students for the worst of all possible worlds and to toughen their resolve to succeed can hardly excuse the double standard, but it does provide a sad commentary upon the psychological wounds inflicted by anti-Semitism. Whatever the actual truth of Frankfurter's own behavior (and there is considerable evidence to suggest that he treated Henry J. Friendly or Paul Freund as generously as he did Landis or Hiss), it remained far removed from the crude ethnic stereotypes that plagued the thinking of the profession's Anglo-Saxon elite.

When, for instance, the dean of Michigan's law school told Pound about the "tough-fibered and tremendously ambitious" students "one generation away from Southeastern Europe," who withstood academic pressures better than "finer-minded and finer-fibered men of different ancestral experience," the latter responded that at Harvard "Jews and Italians furnished nine tenths of the cases of stage fright" in the classrooms. It was very rare, Pound added, for "your Simon pure Yankee or your man from Dixie [to be] affected in that fashion." The students from the ghetto, he concluded "furnish nearly all our cases of nervous breakdown."[21]

When he attempted to find employment for Jewish graduates during these years, Frankfurter met open anti-Semitism among lawyers in New York City and Boston. In a world of shrinking public service jobs, corporate hostility, and academic prejudice, Jews even from the Harvard Law School faced bleak futures. "None of the so-called desirable firms will take a Jew," he complained bitterly, and wondered "whether this School shouldn't tell Jewish students that they go through . . . at their own risk of ever having an opportunity of entering the best law offices."[22] Jews who hoped to enter academic life met similar obstacles. Frankfurter attempted to add another Jew to the law school faculty, but this effort encountered fierce opposition from Lowell, timidity from other colleagues, and something less than wholehearted support from Pound, who by the end of the decade had grown weary of battling the administration over issues of academic freedom and faculty self-government.

In 1928, with only two dissenting votes, the law school faculty recommended to the Harvard administration a five-year assistant professorship in criminal law for Nathan Margold. One of Frankfurter's protégés, Margold had already taught for one year at the school and received laudatory reviews from students and colleagues alike. Lowell, however, refused to submit the nomination to the Board of Overseers. Instead, he attempted to persuade Margold to leave, and when that failed, he offered the young man another one-year instructorship with vague promises about renewal for an additional three years. The president's conduct outraged Margold's allies, led by Frankfurter, Powell, and Morgan. They rejected the compromise as an insult to the faculty's academic judgment and demanded that Lowell set forth in writing his reasons for turning down the five-year appointment.

Frankfurter, for one, believed that Lowell objected to Margold because the latter was Jewish, inclined to social liberalism, and another potential source of radicalism in the law school. He also believed that several of his colleagues shared these prejudices, but allowed Lowell to do their dirty work for them. During a bitter faculty meeting at the end of February, a majority of the professors endorsed Pound's position that they should not fight Lowell over Margold, but, in the words of Williston, "keep in mind the utility of the law school." Even Chafee sided with the Pound forces, because he believed it to be pointless to send the Margold nomination back to Lowell. His vote drew a sharp rebuke from Frankfurter. "You can have no more doubt than did Maguire, Morgan, Bohlen, Powell, Magruder, Landis, Foster, and Redlich," he said, "that he [Margold] was not rejected on the merits, that the rule of reason did not operate."[23]

By the end of the decade, conflicts over institutional growth, the curriculum, and appointments had brought the Frankfurter-Pound relationship, once filled with mutual warmth and friendship, to the point of complete rupture. The final split came over the question of the directorship for the new research institute of public law and Frankfurter's belief that the dean had conspired to fail one of his brightest graduate students during an oral examination.

Although Frankfurter had little interest in becoming director of the institute, he had strong feelings about other potential candidates. Pound took offense at his blunt comments and blamed him for stirring up opposition to many of the nominees. Powell, Landis, and other firebrands, he complained, "won't play, except under F.F." President Lowell, of course, would have nothing to do with Frankfurter as director of this or any other institute, and even refused to increase the latter's regular salary in 1929 at a time when other law faculty received a raise. Predictably, Frankfurter blamed Pound for his sagging financial condition, a feeling shared by other faculty members as well, who blamed the dean for not standing up to the parsimonious administration.[24]

The graduate student was Nathan Nathanson, who had been flunked by Pound and by William McCurdy, another faculty member, who, even Lowell conceded, did not like Jews. Nathanson survived the ordeal to become a distinguished scholar in his own right, but he received his degree only after Frankfurter made what Pound described as a "great row" in the faculty meeting, denounced McCurdy for prejudice, and scolded the dean for asking "technical and unfair" questions designed to trap an unwary student.[25]

Once allied in the struggle for a new jurisprudence, Frankfurter and Pound had become implacable enemies by the end of the decade. The former accused the latter of moral cowardice and of condoning bigotry; Pound blamed Frankfurter for drawing the law school into perpetual controversy, placing his own interests and ego ahead of the institution's, and sabotaging needed changes. The dean's pending marriage, Frankfurter told Chafee in 1932, would not help matters, because "through marriage corruption doth not take on incorruption." Pound, he complained, had "tried to blacken my character by down right lies, [spread] widely over the country, from the Supreme Court Justices down."[26]

Professionally, these were not the happiest years for Frankfurter, although he delighted in the colleagueship of Powell, Morgan, Landis, and Chafee, enjoyed a steady stream of bright, adoring students, and shared unusual intimacy with two members of the Supreme Court. In addition, he now had more time than ever before to explore the problems of justice and of judicial power in a democratic society.

❧❧❧

No one worried more about Frankfurter's academic productivity than Harold Laski. A prolific writer, the young Englishman noted that the professor had a vexing habit of scattering his energies across too many worthy causes. "I think he badly needs some kind of settling influence," Laski reported to Holmes. "He wastes the time that ought to be given to the permanent work that is in him in writing fine letters to antiquated New York lawyers with doubts about the Constitution."[27] If their friend ever allowed himself "to sit down and think over what he has seen," Laski added, "his immense intellectual agility ought to turn it to good account."[28]

Laski hoped that following Frankfurter's return to Harvard, marriage, and withdrawal from Zionist activities, his "creative fertility" would at last be focused upon solid academic pursuits. "Felix is going to write a book," he told Holmes, enthusiastically. "He'll write on the 14th Amendment and that's the realization of one of my most eager hopes. . . . I feel as happy as a frog in a pond with an abundance of flies."[29]

Laski's dreams soon faded. During the next nineteen years of his

life at Harvard, Frankfurter wrote many things about the Fourteenth
Amendment, but never a single, focused book on that subject, although he sketched outlines of chapters from time to time and summarized most of his ideas in a series of 1938 lectures on Holmes.[30] In fact,
Frankfurter's publication record was not dazzling in quantity. He became James Bryne Professor of Administrative Law in 1921 on the
basis of four published articles, two of which could be charitably described as mediocre.[31] This slender output grew significantly over the
next ten years in a series of notable law review articles, books, and
unsigned editorials in *The New Republic* that focused upon a host of
historical and contemporary topics. In terms of sheer erudition, he
never equaled Pound or Williston, but they, in turn, lacked his ra-
pierlike prose style and failed to influence as broad an audience of
informed lay opinion.

With respect to his abilities in the classroom, students confirmed
the observations of Brandeis and others: they ranked him below the
school's great lecturers, but many of the ablest scrambled for the limited seats in his third-year seminars on administrative law, federal
jurisdiction, or public utilities. "There were no neutrals about Felix,"
one recalled. "You either thought the sun rose and set down his neck;
or you despised him. My guess is that the vote would have gone about
two-to-one in his favor."[32] Those young men who cast positive votes
were an impressive group—Landis, Friendly, Freund, Acheson, John
Dickinson, Robert Patterson, Thomas Corcoran, the Hiss brothers,
and Erwin Griswold.

After one rigorous summer of research, picnics, good wine, and
growing friendship, Landis confessed: "I suppose I'm nearing more
and more each day the brink of pure idolotry."[33] From the point of
view of many young law students who thirsted after heroes in a time
of intellectual disillusionment and uncertainty, Frankfurter held forth
the ideals of disinterested public service. He seemed to be a figure of
both destiny and boundless influence. "He is a man whose writings
and point of view I consider very important to one, who like myself,
hopes to use his legal training in the industrial field," wrote an idealistic first-year student, David Lilienthal. "I plan to take his course in
Public Utilitites . . . and thus come to know him better."[34]

Those students who did not immediately lust for well-paying jobs
in New York or Boston also knew that Frankfurter each year dispensed clerkships with Holmes and Brandeis. His friendship with
both justices flourished in these years, rooted in mutual affection, a
shared perspective upon the role of the federal judiciary, a near mysti-

cal attachment to the traditions of the Harvard Law School, and a parade of eager young men who came from Cambridge bearing Felix's imprimatur. "Make the choice of the man & I shall obey," Brandeis told him. "Acheson is doing much better work this year, no doubt mainly because of his greater experience; partly, perhaps, because I talked the situation over with him frankly."[35] Alger Hiss seemed to be a nice lad, Holmes reported, but "of course he must understand that I reserve liberty to die or resign."[36]

Although the intellectual rewards and social connections proved invaluable, the clerks received little pay and labored under Spartan conditions, especially with Brandeis. He kept the heat very low, refused to own an automobile, served bland meals, and became outraged when one clerk turned up for his assignment with a new wife in tow. Brandeis wanted his clerks to live simple, monastic lives, devoting themselves to legal research without any distractions.[37]

The law clerks, in turn, provided Frankfurter with an endless flow of information and gossip about the Court and its members. They became experts about various justices and did not hesitate after a few months to challenge their old professor. "I think that you rather do Pitney an injustice," Acheson lectured him. "The common idea tends to identify Pitney and Van Devanter, but nothing is more mistaken. Pitney is a splendid lawyer in the strict sense. That is he has not the philosophical attitude of Holmes; he could never say that the life of the law was not logic; but taking the law as he knows it he will accept the traditional method of legal reasoning and the end to which it brings him no matter whether he likes it or not."[38] Although their observations could be witty, shrewd, and tantalizing, even the smartest clerks were no substitute for Holmes and Brandeis, who freely confided in Frankfurter about the Court's business, their own frustrations, and occasional triumphs.

Of the two men, Holmes remained the more sardonic and pungent. "The years have no more effect upon his mind than machine gun bullets on a tank," Acheson reported. Now in his eighties, Holmes's opinions about human nature or the absurd possibilities of human progress had not been mellowed by the war. Life for Holmes would always be somewhat nasty, brutish, and cruel; and rich would exploit the poor; reformers railed pointlessly against the inevitable forces of greed, stupidity, and inertia. He felt some kinship with the Court's blackest conservatives, but because he looked upon all social life as basically an amoral contest of strength and believed, too, in governmental power to maintain order—Holmes granted legislative majorities broad authority to regulate property rights and personal liberties.[39]

He scorned Frankfurter's social liberalism, but delighted in the younger man's companionship, frequent letters, and entourage of able students. "I think that perhaps you have a bias on the labor side," he warned Frankfurter, "and may not show quite so clearly the terrors of a mob let loose as the wrongs to the union."[40]

To Frankfurter he regularly complained about the misguided zeal of reformers who "damned Rockefeller when he embodied the inevitables," and also about slow-witted colleagues who lamented that the Court overruled too many cases. "We overrule nothing but talk," he quipped. He sent the professor limericks and shared with him the discomfort his opinions sometimes caused among other justices. "I have a little case," he reported, "whether it will go or not I don't know. As originally written it had a tiny pair of testicles—but the scruples of my brethren have caused their removal and it sings in a very soft voice now."[41]

They shared together the excitement of rereading *Moby Dick* and Benet's stirring poem, "John Brown's Body," although the former appealed more to Holmes than the latter, because it "realizes the terrors of the world . . . the abysses of the human spirit."[42] Eagerly, the old man waited for Frankfurter's letters (usually filled with praise for recent opinions) and the opportunity to "jaw" in person about the Court, politics, and people. "I am an empty bottle," Holmes told him on one occasion, "and suppose I need washing out. . . . hope I may see you before long."[43]

Brandeis came in these years to regard Frankfurter as a son, who would tend the fires of reform that judicial duty now made it impossible for him to maintain. He paid the latter's emergency medical bills and regularly supplemented his Harvard salary with checks to "defray the disbursements of our joint adventure."[44] These activities included everything from researching an article for *The New Republic* to preparing legal briefs for the Consumers League. Frankfurter, once the ardent New Nationalist, moved closer in these years to Brandeis's social philosophy that emphasized the values of decentralization, smaller economic units, and competition. "The most potent cause of our failures," Brandeis told Laski, "has been our unbounded faith in the efficacy of machinery and our worship of the false god Bigness."[45] To Frankfurter he reiterated his belief that "bigness is the greatest curse. . . . Our futile attempts to curb them [giant corporations] result simply in bringing the law into greater contempt."[46]

For Brandeis, the ideal societies would be no larger than Denmark and Palestine in the age of windmills and bicycles. He thoroughly distrusted centralized authority, whether exercized by the supermen of business, impatient national reformers, or autocratic federal judges. Fearful of power, he remained more sensitive than Holmes to legislative invasions of civil liberties, yet tolerated what most of his colleagues regarded as extreme regulations of property and contractual relationships.[47] Apart from their shared belief in a posture of judicial restraint, Brandeis and Holmes made a curious pair—one a profane agnostic who regarded law as essentially organized force, barren of any transcendent purpose; the other a prophet of moral uplift and reform who perceived law to be the instrument of moral regeneration through the educative processes of self-government. Together, they left a deep impression upon Frankfurter's own views of the law, which not surprisingly vascillated between the absolutism of Brandeis and the relativism of Holmes.

With the exception of his own wife, Brandeis confided in Frankfurter about the Court's inner workings as he did with no one else. In order to manage the aging Justice McKenna, he reported, the Court should "appoint guardians for him." Unfortunately, Van Devanter, McReynolds, and Chief Justice Taft had all failed in that task and McKenna continued to do "mischief" by "sending up a balloon just to show that he is there. . . . His opinions are often suppressed . . . held up and held up and he gets mad and throws up the opinion and it's given to someone else." Holmes, he lamented, should read more economics and less ancient philosophy. The chief justice struck him as a "benevolent, good-natured distillery drummer. . . . His face has nothing in it—it's so vapid." McReynolds would have given Balzac great pleasure, Brandeis believed, because "I watch his face closely and at times, with his good features, he has a look of manly beauty, of intellectual beauty, and at other times he looks like an infantile moron." The latter's boorishness, he added, "gives Holmes pain, much pain."[48]

Van Devanter, he reported, remained the real power behind the throne. He manuevered in the style of a "Jesuit general . . . always helpful to everybody, always ready for the C.J. . . . and then he is 'in' with all the Republican politicians." Pitney seemed cursed by his rigid Presbyterian upbringing, had "no imagination whatever," but had been "much influenced by his experience and he had had mighty little." McReynold's opinions were "simply dreadful." Holmes believed he possessed "the irrational impulses of a savage," and Wilson's former attorney general remained the Court's biggest headache because of his rudeness, laziness, and constant inattention to oral arguments that necessitated frequent rehearings. Surprisingly, Brandeis noted that because of Taft's administrative skills in the conference, "the judges go home less tired emotionally and less weary physically than in White's day."[49]

These scalding observations did not find their way into Frankfurter's courses at Harvard or his published writings about the Court during the 1920s. He continued to discuss the Court's divisions publicly in terms of clashing economic, social, and moral values, but seldom in terms of dark, irrational impulses alluded to by Holmes and Brandeis. Privately, he knew that Van Devanter's solicitude disguised a writing block that bordered upon complete impotence and that McReynold's "savage" conduct arose from both feelings of insecurity and rabid anti-Semitism. The seamier aspects of the Court's collective life, nonetheless, colored his growing skepticism about the entire enterprise of judicial review. In addition, he could draw upon his own experience before the Taft Court during the decade when judicial decisions fell with stunning regularity against the lingering forces of social reform.

Beginning with the 1921 decision in *Duplex Printing Co.* v. *Deering*, the Taft Court dealt organized labor a series of heavy legal blows by means of cramped statutory construction and an expansive definition of the due process clauses that harkened back to the days of *Lochner* and *Adair*. In *Duplex*, over a powerful dissent by Brandeis, five justices emasculated section 20 of the Clayton Anti-Trust Act which had been intended by Congress to curtail the use of injunctions in labor disputes.[50] Having stripped labor of Federal protection, the Taft Court also denied workers the benefits of state legislation by striking down Arizona's antiinjunction statute on the grounds that it deprived employers of "property" without due process of law as well as equal protection of the laws.[51]

Duplex and *Truax* did not exhaust the Court's repertoire. Invoking the due process clause, they struck down a standard-weight bread law intended to protect consumers from fraud; voided a New York statute that fixed the resale price of theater tickets sold by scalpers; and overturned a state law that regulated the fees of private employment agencies.[52] A rate award that guaranteed Baltimore's street railways a 6.26 percent return (calculated on the inflated reproduction of their property) they held to violate the due process clause, as well as a Kansas statute that required compulsory arbitration in situations where employers and employees had been unable to reach voluntary agreements.[53]

Finally, in an opinion tht drove even Taft into dissent, Justice Sutherland and four of his brethren held that the due process clause prevented Congress from fixing minimum wages for women workers in the District of Columbia. It was, he intoned, "a naked, arbitrary exercise" of legislative power that trampled upon the freedom of workers and forced employers to make forced contributions to their employees' welfare without regard to the amount of labor expended. "To sustain the individual freedom of action contemplated by the Constitution," he concluded, "is not to strike down the common good but to exalt it; for surely the good of society as a whole cannot be better served than by the preservation against arbitrary restraint of the liberties of its constituent members."[54]

The *Adkins* decision especially displeased Frankfurter because he had prepared the briefs and argued the case. On the basis of earlier decisions in *Muller* and *Bunting*, he and others believed that the Court had overruled *sub silentio* the odious doctrines of "liberty of contract." More than any single judgment of the postwar period, *Adkins* led him to question judicial review and the due process clause. "The whole thing we thought gained in 1912 is now thrown overboard and we are just where we were," he lamented to Hand. "I confess I did not expect it again. . . . I can't see anything we get out of the 5th and 14th Amendments in the least commensurate with that danger. . . . It seems to me that the place to hit is the Amendments themselves."[55]

A year later, Frankfurter adopted a more radical posture in the pages of *The New Republic*. "We have had fifty years of experiment with the Fourteenth Amendment," he wrote, "and the centralizing authority lodged with the Supreme Court over the domestic affairs of forty-eight widely different States is an authority which it simply cannot discharge with safety either to itself or to the States." The due process clause, he concluded, "ought to go."[56]

He did not soften these views when the Taft Court invoked the due process clause to strike down illiberal legislation such as a Nebraska law that prohibited public and private school instruction in languages other than English. Nebraska's law offended against the Fourteenth Amendment, wrote Justice McReynolds for a majority that included Brandeis, because it violated both the liberty of language teachers to earn a living and of parents to control the education of their children.[57] This opinion drew a dissent from Holmes, who argued that since the state could prohibit the teaching of some subjects, the choice ought to be left to the legislature, unless its decision "passes the bounds of reason and assumes the character of a merely arbitrary fiat."[58]

Frankfurter, the graduate from PS 25 and Miss Hogan's star pupil, agreed with Holmes. He did so both because of patriotic enthusiasm for the nation's common schools and also because of his mounting distrust of all forms of judicial absolutism under the due process clause. "Of course, I regard such know-nothing legislation as uncivilized," he assured Hand, "but for the life of me I can't see how it meets the condemnation of want of 'due process' unless we frankly recognize that the Supreme Court of the United States is the revisory legislative body."[59]

The Court's due process veto, he believed, stunted the democratic process in many ways. It thwarted the popular will in areas of social reform such as *Adkins*, but, in addition, it encouraged people to believe that the judiciary would always save them from foolish legislation and potential tyranny. Such blind faith in judicial guardians, he believed, generated cynicism and irresponsibility in the legislatures and among the voters. During times of public hysteria, moreover, the Court had proven itself to be a frail bulwark against conservative efforts to eradicate dissent and dissenters.

He returned to these themes several years later when the Court again used the due process clause to enjoin the operation of an Oregon law that would have abolished private schools.[60] Although even Holmes now joined McReynold's opinion that overturned the statute, Frankfurter cautioned liberals not to rejoice. The same judicial reasoning used in *Meyers* and *Pierce*, he noted, had also doomed antiinjunction statutes and minimum-wage laws. "For ourselves," he wrote, "we regard the cost of this power of the Supreme Court on the whole as greater than its gains." After all, the hysteria that produced illiberal laws like those in Nebraska and Oregon might subside, "but when the Supreme Court strikes down legislation directed against trade unions, or enshrines the labor injunction into the Constitution, or denies to women in industry the meager protection of minimum wage legislation, we are faced with action more far-reaching, because ever so much more durable and authoritative than even the most mischievous of repealable state legislation."[61]

In his writings throughout the decade, Frankfurter remained more of a latitudinarian on the issue of legislative power and the Fourteenth Amendment than either Holmes or Brandeis. Although he endorsed the latter's dissent in *Meyers*, for example, Frankfurter sided with Brandeis in *Pennsylvania Coal Co.* v. *Mahon*. In this celebrated case, Holmes and the other justices overturned an injunction against the company that had prevented it from mining on property in violation of the state's Kohler Act, a statute designed to protect dwellings from cave-ins resulting from such excavations.[62] Agreeing with Brandeis, Frankfurter saw nothing objectionable in the Pennsylvania law, which "merely prevents the owner from making a use which interferes with paramount rights of the public."[63]

Unlike both Holmes and Brandeis, he found nothing constitutionally defective in an industrial relations court created by Kansas that permitted compulsory arbitration and price fixing by the state.[64] "Thus fails another social experiment," he wrote, "not because it has been tried and found wanting, but because it has been tried and found unconstitutional." Compulsory arbitration seemed to him ineffective and probably unfair in view of the weakness of trade unions, but he did not believe that the Fourteenth Amendment prevented the legislation. "This obstruction is again found in the 'due process' clause," he noted. "The plain fact is that the Court puts this meaning into the phrase 'due process' and then finds it there. . . . It was for the legislature of Kansas, and not for the Supreme Court, to kill it."[65]

A Supreme Court composed entirely of Brandeis, Holmes, Cardozo, and Hand, he told the latter, might be trusted with the Fourteenth Amendment, "but one has no business to assume in the run of life our Court will have dominantly such a membership and the question then becomes a balancing of gains and costs. And I must say I increasingly have me doots. . . . We expect our Courts to do it all."[66]

A decade before he took Holmes's seat on the Court, Frankfurter's views on the proper scope of judicial review under the due process clauses had taken very rigid form as a result of the constitutional struggles of the Taft years. As the *Meyers*, *Mahon*, and *Wolff* cases suggest, he was prepared to grant the legislature sweeping discretion in areas that touched both property rights and personal liberty.

The Constitution, he believed, permitted vigorous, effective government and social experimentation. It contained two broad categories of limitations upon governmental authority, but judicial discretion remained different with respect to each category. There were, for instance, very specific prohibitions such as the Fourth Amendment, a provision rooted in the history of a particular grievance, and also specific limitations of power such as the requirement that no state "shall enter into any treaty, alliance, or confederation." On the other hand, the Constitution also contained general standards requiring fair play and broad divisions of power between states and the nation—"undefined clauses" such as "due process of law" or "commerce among the states." Here, Frankfurter believed, the scope of judicial interpretation remained much greater because "application is largely unrestricted and the room for play of individual judgment as to policy is correspondingly wide." But this breadth of application, he reasoned, called for extreme judicial modesty and restraint, not open-ended revision of legislative choices.[67]

In the case of the due process clauses, he believed, too many American judges since the Civil War had poured their own conceptions of desirable public policy into the words, "confounding personal convictions upon ephemeral policies with enduring principles of right and wrong."[68] The correct judicial posture, he concluded, ought to be one of deference to the legislature's judgment, unless that choice "passes the bounds of reason and assumes the character of a merely arbitrary fiat."

Of course, even Holmes admitted that a state might "pass the bounds of reason" when adopting a general statute or when applying the law in a particular situation.[69] But generally speaking, he did not believe that the Court had the duty under the due process clauses to defend natural rights or so-called "fundamental rights" against regulation by a legislative majority. Holmes remained a constitutional relativist who usually bowed to the will of the majority, even when it spoke in harsh, repressive terms. With respect to the due process clauses, Frankfurter shared Holmes's perspective upon the judicial role, not the emerging activism of Brandeis, who wished to hold legislatures to higher standards of necessity in situations that touched upon freedom of speech, press, religion, and political association.[70]

"Law is revealed more and more as the comprehension of contradictories," Frankfurter wrote at the end of the decade, "the art of mediating between antitheses. Precedent and justice, stability and progress, the individual and society, liberty and authority—these are life's antinomies and they are the burdens of the law."[71] Judicial intolerance and absolutism could not flourish alongside such sentiments, but the question remained whether such artful balancing did not also lead to the complete abdication of judicial responsibility under the Constitution. Without standards, without agreement on the boundaries of reason, how could judges mediate between antitheses?

❊❊❊

During the decade, both Frankfurter's scholarly writings and polemical editorials for *The New Republic* reflected his central preoccupations with the role of federal courts, the relationship between law and

social science research, and the problems of criminal justice. Of these
three areas, the issues of federal jurisdiction and federal judicial activism received the most sustained attention because they involved questions that remained closest to his concerns as a reformer: the proper
role of the Supreme Court and other federal courts, the continued
vitality of American federalism, and the labor injunction.

The Supreme Court's aggressive utilization of the due process
clause to destroy social experimentation in the states dramatized for
him the grave dangers of centralization that lurked in every exercise of
federal judicial power. The votes of five men could potentially control
the destinies of forty-eight states. Brandeis's robust defense of decentralization and localism made more sense to Frankfurter as the federal
judicial veto continued to thwart the goals of social reformers throughout the decade. "If we are to attain our national ideals," Brandeis told
him, "It must be via the States, etc. I am convinced that the century of
national expansion in governmental function as well as in territory
should now be followed by intense high-minded work in the communities and for that it does not need supermen."[72]

Writing in the *Yale Law Journal* a few years later, Frankfurter and
his young colleague, Landis, argued that reformers had failed to utilize the compact clause of the Constitution which permitted two or
more states to enter into agreements about common social and economic problems. The nation's legal resources should not be limited to
an exclusive duality between state and federal power, they noted, because the compact clause made it possible for several states, with the
consent of Congress, to develop regional solutions in such areas as soil
conservation, water resources, and the regulation of electric power.
Legislation by means of the compact clause also held out the additional benefit of reduced judicial intervention. "The judicial instrument is
too static and too sporadic for adjusting a social-economic issue con-
tinuously alive in an area embracing more than a half a dozen States,"
they concluded, pointing to the example of the Colorado River Compact and other attempts at water apportionment where "continuous
and creative administration is needed; not litigation, necessarily a sporadic process, securing at best merely episodic and mutilated settlements."[73]

In addition to replacing "the occasional explosions of law suits"
with creative administrative solutions, they argued, interstate com-
pacts promised as well to strengthen "regional interests, regional cul-
tures and regional interdependencies" against the "depressing forces
of standardization." Echoing Brandeis, they noted that the social

problems of modern America ought not to be left at the mercy of "false antithesis embodied in the shibboleths 'States Rights' and 'National Supremacy.' . . . Our regions are realities. Political thinking must respond to these realities. Instead of leading to parochialism, it will bring a fresh ferment of political thought whereby national aims may be achieved through various forms of political adjustment."[74]

Devotion to federalism and a preoccupation with local autonomy became even more pronounced in Frankfurter's and Landis's historic 1927 collaboration, *The Business of the Supreme Court*, which traced the distribution of judicial power between state and federal courts from 1789 to the Taft era.[75] Wholly apart from substantive doctrines of constitutional law, they wrote, federal jurisdiction had continued to grow at the expense of state tribunals since the late eighteenth century and showed few signs of immediate limitation. This expansion of federal jurisdiction arose from deep-rooted fears of local resistance to national authority, the growth of federal criminal statutes, powerful commercial interests who sought protection in national courts, and the Supreme Court's own desire to aggrandize influence by means of tortured statutory interpretations. This centralizing trend, however, threatened to weaken American federalism by undermining the independence of state courts and by placing an intolerable burden of litigation upon the federal bench.

Their work contained both a descriptive analysis and a plea for change. Although Congress had revised the structure of the nation's courts many times since the original Judiciary Act of 1978—including the addition of intermediate circuit courts and the landmark certiorari statute of 1925—Frankfurter and Landis noted that the legislature had not attempted to revise the two main sources of all federal jurisdiction: cases that arose under the Constitution, laws, and treaties of the United States; and litigation arising solely because of the diverse state citizenship of the parties. In both of these areas, they believed, Congress should increase the role of state courts, reduce the flow of litigants into the federal courts, and return the interpretation of local law to local tribunals.

The topsylike growth of federal penal law into such areas as drug addiction, automobile thefts, and simple fraud seemed to Frankfurter both unwise and potentially dangerous, because these cases clogged the lower federal dockets and represented an unnecessary expansion of national authority over essentially local crimes.[76] In addition, he reserved some of his harshest criticism for the exercise of diversity jurisdiction by federal courts in situations where the only justification for utilizing national tribunals was the fact that the litigants resided in different states. Business corporations had reaped the largest benefits from this jurisdiction and the Supreme Court's decision in *Swift* v. *Tyson* that permitted federal courts to apply their own "general jurisprudence" in such cases rather than the common law of the states.[77]

Although many giant corporations did the bulk of their business in states other than the one of their incorporation, these noncharter states could not resolve disputes between that corporation and local residents in local courts without the firm's consent. Such corporations reserved the option to begin the litigation in federal courts under a different set of substantive rules. "This jurisdiction has been consciously abused," Frankfurter and Landis wrote. "Men incorporate in a foreign state solely to avoid subjection to the laws of the state in which they carry on business and to obtain the advantages of federal jurisdiction." They denounced *Swift* v. *Tyson* as "mischievous . . . baffling in its application, untenable in theory, and . . . a perversion of the purposes of the framers of the First Judiciary Act." True federalism suffered. The corporations prospered because they could select the tribunal most sympathetic to their interests.[78]

In addition to the due process clause, diversity jurisdiction, and *Swift* v. *Tyson*, Frankfurter singled out the labor injunction and the contempt powers of federal judges as a spreading judicial cancer that undermined respect for law and inhibited needed social reforms. Judges not only granted this remedy in ex parte proceedings on flimsy evidence, but ultimately determined the scope of their own order by holding parties in contempt without jury trials. Moreover, the courts had sabotaged all legislative efforts to curb this abuse by means of ingenious statutory interpretation and constitutional rulings that "generated the growing conviction that the powers of the government are perverted by and in the aid of employers."[79]

He pilloried the Taft Court for decisions such as *Duplex* and *Truax* and strongly condemned the sweeping injunction issued by Judge James H. Wilkerson against the railroad shopmen's union. Wilkerson's decree, which even the *Journal of Commerce* denounced as too extreme, restrained union officials from "in any manner by letters . . . words of mouth . . . oral persuasion or suggestion . . . or otherwise in any manner whatsoever . . . encouraging any person . . . to abandon the employment of said railway companies." Frankfurter doubted that even Congress could place these limitations upon speech, but, he noted, ironically, "what's the Constitution between friends!—even though one of them happens to be the Attorney General of the United States and the other a federal judge."[80]

Near the end of the decade, Frankfurter and Nathan Greene published *The Labor Injunction*, a comprehensive and devastating critique of judicial abuses in this field. In addition to providing a thorough historical account of the labor injunction, they called for new legislation to limit the enforcement of "yellow dog" contracts in federal courts, to modify the Supreme Court's interpretation of the Clayton Act, and to require jury trials in criminal contempt cases arising under that statute.[81]

Federal judges who abused their contempt powers in nonlabor cases also drew Frankfurter's fire, especially Julius M. Mayer, who sentenced the New York City comptroller to jail for six months after he criticized the judge's conduct in the appointment of receivers for financially troubled traction companies. Although the litigation had not begun and although federal law limited a judge's contempt power to "misbehavior of any person in their presence, or so near thereto as to obstruct the administration of justice," Mayer jailed the comptroller for writing a letter in which he refused to join a conference with the companies unless granted prior access to their financial records.[82]

Judge Mayer's egregious conduct led Frankfurter to write an article one year later reminding the judiciary of Judge Peck's impeachment in 1831 and the origins of the federal contempt statute that had been designed to protect persons from such judicial tyranny. He praised efforts in Congress to require jury trials in a limited category of "indirect" contempts and blasted judicial rhetoric that extolled the "inherent powers" of judges in this field: "At least let us not import into the Constitution of the United States," he concluded, "discredited practices of Stuart England."[83]

Frankfurter expected little from the judicial branch in terms of immediate social improvement but he continued to believe that the bench and the bar could be influenced for the better through exposure to social science research and methodology. For one whose skepticism about absolute values mirrored the relativism of Holmes, Frankfurter at times displayed a curiously naive faith in the capacity of academic investigators to discover "the truth" or "the facts" about various social problems. This faith sprang, in part, from the initial success of the Brandeis-type legal brief, where courts seemed willing to modify received legal values in the face of powerful sociological and economic evidence to the contrary. "As science has demonstrated that there is no sharp difference in kind as to the effect of labor on men and women," Frankfurter wrote in 1916, "courts recently have followed the guidance of science and refused to be controlled by outworn ignorance. . . . 'Common understanding' has ceased to be the reliance in matters calling for essentially scientific determination."[84]

Cases such as *Duplex* and *Adkins*, however, suggested that the Supreme Court had not yet capitulated to "essentially scientific determination." A majority of the justices continued to practice their own legal science without much reference to the wisdom of other disciplines. Frankfurter, nonetheless, did not abandon hope. "The stuff of these contests are facts, and judgment upon facts," he wrote in 1924. "Every tendency to deal with them abstractly, to formulate them in terms of sterile legal questions, is bound to result in sterile conclusions unrelated to actualities. The reports are strewn with wrecks of legislation considered in vacuo and torn out of the context of life which evoked the legislation and alone made it intelligible."[85]

These convictions led him to participate actively in two of the era's largest research projects concerned with the administration of criminal justice in Cleveland and Boston. The Cleveland report, initially stimulated by local outrage over the involvement of a municipal judge in an underworld assassination plot, addressed itself to the problem of how the existing legal machinery of one city functioned with respect to criminal activity. From the police precinct through the stage of final legal appeals, the investigators' conclusions were not reassuring in terms of efficiency, public safety, or fairness to the accused.

Cleveland's criminal justice system presented the dreary spectacle of nineteenth-century institutions attempting to cope with the staggering social and legal problems of a twentieth-century city. Methods of crime detection remained so primitive that the sophistication of the police force seldom matched that of professional criminals. Administrative delay, political favoritism, and simple incompetence plagued the prosecutors' offices. But even these defects paled in comparison with the daily nightmare of confusion and injustice in the city's courtrooms. Less brutal than inept, less oppressive than venal, Cleveland's courts ground out a heavy toll of crimes punished too severely and crimes that escaped punishment altogether. Justice in Cleveland was not swift, certain, or impartial.

Frankfurter and Pound wrote a series of brilliant recommendations at the end of the report, which called for improved police work, a reorganization of the prosecutors' office, streamlined court procedures, and an upgrading of legal education. These proposals made eminently good sense to the Harvard experts and to the middle-class professionals who began the Cleveland inquiry but, unfortunately, they remained hopelessly beyond the city's immediate political capacity to implement.[86]

Frankfurter hoped that the Boston inquiry would focus less upon the criminal justice system and more upon the roots of criminal behavior. "Our work proceeds on the conviction shared by those who have most widely thought about the problem of crime," he wrote, "that what we most need is a body of scientific knowledge about the criminal. Not *a priori* assumptions, nor mass generalizations based on a few instances, but a steady accumulation of intensive knowledge in regard to the social and individual life of the criminal."[87] He assembled an impressive group of experts, including Raymond Fosdick, Albert Bettman, and Herman Adler, veterans of the Cleveland report, as well as Lippmann, who agreed to study the relationship between the press and crime. Although the Boston survey never brought forth a single volume comparable to the Cleveland report, Frankfurter's preliminary findings echoed the orthodox progressive view on crime and criminal justice in America.

He called for improved administrative controls, more research data, and greater professionalism. Americans, he lamented, did not approach crime with the same scientific spirit that they lavished upon issues of public health or engineering, where trained specialists devoted a lifetime to the diagnosis and solution of concrete problems. In the area of crime, Americans still functioned on the basis of impulse, antiquated moral notions, and superstitions. "The equipment of the man in the street is a wholly inadequate resource. . . . In the United States there is no body of highly trained, richly endowed people who are drawn to the problems of crime."[88] If these recommendations seemed to emphasize the technical management of crime rather than its social and economic origins, Frankfurter also made a striking plea for the individualization of treatment, instead of what he called the "more or less fixed tariffs of punishment for abstractly similar criminal conduct. What is needed is to discard this bankrupt major premise."[89]

As a scholar, teacher, journalist, and lawyer, Frankfurter developed over the course of the decade a profound skepticism about the integrity of the judicial process. Despite pungent criticism from the bench, the bar, and the legal intelligensia, most of the nation's legal institutions seemed anxious, as Brandeis once remarked, "to endow property with active, militant power which would make it dominant over men."[90] The setbacks of this era left an indelible impression upon his perception of the correct judicial role in American society. But nothing—not even the *Adkins* defeat, the Cleveland survey, or the behavior of judges such as Mayer and Wilkerson—quite prepared him for the ordeal of the Sacco-Vanzetti case. "I am not as confident as in the old district attorney days," he remarked to Hand in 1923, "that 'the ghost of the innocent man convicted is an unreal dream.' . . . But the worst of it is that protection for the accused does the least good where it is most needed,—namely where the passion of the community is aroused, and conviction comes not from the evidence but from the atmosphere."[91] This proved to be a prescient observation.

❊❊ CHAPTER 10 ❊❊

THE TWO
ITALIANS

SHORTLY AFTER MIDNIGHT on August 23, 1927, the Commonwealth of Massachusetts electrocuted two Italian immigrants, Nicola Sacco and Bartolomeo Vanzetti, for the crimes of robbery and murder. Wherever crowds of men, women, and children gathered on that night to await news from Charleston State Prison, the first reports of their execution stirred every human emotion. In New York's Union Square people cried, screamed, fainted, and ripped at their clothing. In Paris angry mobs poured onto the Boulevard Sebastapol, smashed windows, and uprooted street lights. Huge demonstrations rocked Berlin, London, Madrid, Mexico City, Moscow, Tokyo, and even Johannesburg, where protestors put the torch to an American flag on the steps of the city hall. "No one of age would ever forget the night," wrote one historian recently; "it was one of those events by which people mark their lives."[1]

It marked Frankfurter's life forever. "I remember seeing him the day after the men were executed," Hand recalled, "and he was like a madman. He was really beside himself. I wouldn't have thought of trying to talk with him."[2] He would not forget where he had been on that night. With Marion and a friend, he walked the humid, dark streets of Beacon Hill until a radio bulletin announced that the executions were in progress: "Sacco gone, Vanzetti going." Emotionally drained, Marion collapsed and nearly fell to the pavement. In the months ahead she recovered sufficiently to help a young newspaperman, Gardner Jackson, edit the deathhouse letters of Sacco and Vanzetti, but her mental depression increased and she began regular visits to a psychiatrist to whom she poured out her frustrations, especially "the difficulties she had encountered in having married a Jew . . . the social pressures to which she was subjected, and her inner struggle against this complex of circumstances."[3] Childless and plagued by Marion's physical ailments, which baffled doctors and resisted treatment, their marriage had sustained a near-fatal blow from a seven-year ordeal that one reporter dismissed initially as "just a couple of wops in a jam."[4]

Nor did Frankfurter's public life remain unscathed. For the next three decades, the Sacco-Vanzetti case left an indelible mark upon his political and legal career. Conservatives denounced Frankfurter for his 1927 essay in the *Atlantic Monthly* which criticized the trial and the sentence.[5] The Chief Justice of the United States Supreme Court labeled him "an expert in attempting to save murderous anarchists from the gallows or the electric chair."[6] His article, according to Francis Russell, "was like a lighted fuse leading to a power magazine," because it gave the case an international audience and "made it in its last few months intellectually chic."[7] And it may have been Frankfurter, among others, whom William F. Buckley had in mind when he excoriated those who used the Sacco-Vanzetti case "to indict the existing order, condemn our institutions . . . scrape away at the Puritan ethic, tear and wrench the nation and cause it to bleed across the pages of history."[8] With equal vehemence, liberals later inquired: how could Frankfurter, defender of Sacco and Vanzetti, become a judge who displayed so little sensitivity to the plight of left-wing dissenters? In brief, the case became one symbolic yardstick by which others measured and evaluated the rest of his life.

This yardstick seems inappropriate, however, insofar as it suggests that Frankfurter agreed with the Left's analysis of the case, altered his own views on American society as a result of the ordeal, or later cast off the radical baggage collected in these years. Quite the contrary. The Sacco-Vanzetti case reinforced many of his negative opinions about the legal system—especially the awesome power of judges and prosecutors—but it did not lead him to a fresh analysis of these issues or to a wholesale repudiation of the legal order.

The novelist John Dos Passos, for example, could write about the Sacco-Vanzetti case that "our nation has been beaten by strangers who have bought the law and fenced off the meadows and cut down the woods for pulp and turned our pleasant cities into slums and sweated the wealth out of our people and when they want to they hire the executioner to throw the switch."[9] Frankfurter wrote that he knew of "no better issue on which to meet the forces of intolerance, suppression and materialism than the Sacco-Vanzetti case," but for him the basic question always remained "the moral foundations of our profession" and whether "we, as law-teachers, are merely going to deal with antiquarian law or are going to recognize our responsibility as . . . the guardians of law and justice in action."[10] A vast intellectual and emotional chasm separated those two perspectives.

He entered the case rather late, nearly five years after it had become a *cause célèbre* among Italian Americans, the Left, intellectuals, and a handful of Boston's Brahmins—all of whom considered Sacco and Vanzetti to be hapless victims of the Red Scare hysteria against radicals and foreigners. Preoccupied with his recent marriage, the legal defense of Hillman's battered union, and the deportation cases, Frankfurter paid little attention to a series of holdups and shootouts that wracked the railroads, textile mills, and shoe factories of Massachusetts and Rhode Island during the winter and spring of 1919–20.

On Christmas eve 1919, four men—one armed with a shotgun—attempted to rob the payroll truck of the L.Q. White Shoe Company in Bridgewater. Four months later on April 15, 1920, a similar gang stopped a paymaster and guard outside the factory of the Slater Morrill Shoe Company in South Braintree. They shot to death both men and drove away with more than $15,000 in cash. In May, pursuing a hunch of the Bridgewater police chief, who believed that the crime wave had been masterminded by Italian "Bolsheviki" or anarchists, officers arrested Sacco, shoemaker, and Vanzetti, a fishpeddler, on the Bridgewater-to-Brockton trolley, after they and friends had attempted to retrieve an automobile from a local garage.

At the time of their arrest, both men were armed: Sacco with a .32 Colt automatic and assorted ammunition; Vanzetti with a Harrington Richardson .38 revolver. The latter also carried several shotgun shells in his pocket. By the middle of the summer of 1920, Vanzetti had been tried and convicted of the attempted robbery in Bridgewater, and both had been found guilty of robbery and homicide in connection with the South Braintree holdup. For the next seven years, the question of their guilt or innocence as well as the fairness of their trials shook the political and legal foundations of the commonwealth.[11]

Sacco and Vanzetti's supporters had a simple explanation for the guilty verdicts: they had been convicted by a bigoted judge and jury because they were Italians and anarchists at a time when public sentiment ran high against foreigners and radicals. They had been condemned for their ethnicity and extreme political opinions, not because of convincing proof relating to participation in armed robbery and murder. Unquestionably, the evidence of prejudice on the part of the trial judge, Webster Thayer, the chief prosecutor, Frederick Katzmann, and at least one of the jurors, was considerable.

In order to believe the pair guilty, the jury had to dismiss the sworn testimony of nearly a dozen witnesses — most of them other Italians — who placed Sacco and Vanzetti elsewhere when the crimes took place.[12] Katzmann ridiculed the credibility of these witnesses with the suggestion that "some of those Italians up there told you what to say."[13] A friend of more than twenty years testified that the foreman of the jury, Walter Ripley — a former police chief whose views probably carried great weight with the others — believed that the accused men should be punished even before the trial began. When this friend expressed doubt about their guilt, Ripley replied, "Damn them, they ought to hang them anyway!"[14]

Throughout his cross-examination of both Sacco and Vanzetti, the prosecutor highlighted their unorthodox political behavior and opinions, including the fact that they had fled the country to avoid the draft and believed in the necessity of overthrowing capitalism.[15] Thayer, a short, cadaverous Yankee, Dartmouth College graduate, and Odd Fellow who was noted for his fierce temper and stupendous vanity, abetted the prosecution's efforts by tolerating a broad range of political questions and by mocking the defendants' ideas.[16] At the conclusion of an ealier trial, Thayer had denounced a jury for acquitting a person charged with criminal anarchy, and during the Sacco-Vanzetti case he referred to their lawyer, Fred Moore, as "that long-haired anarchist from the West."[17] In his final instructions to the jurors, Thayer compared each of them to "the true soldier" who responded to the call to duty "in the spirit of supreme American loyalty" — an obvious contrast to the defendants whom the prosecution had labeled as draft dodgers.[18] After rejecting several defense motions for a new trial, Thayer remarked to a Dartmouth faculty member "Did you see what I did with those anarchistic bastards the other day? I guess that will hold them for a while."[19] According to Professor James Richardson, who reported Thayer's boast in a later affidavit, "it was very evident that Judge Thayer regarded these men with a feeling which can only fairly be described as abhorrence."[20]

On the other hand, as Justice Holmes later remarked, "I doubt if anyone would say that there was no evidence warranting a conviction."[21] Indeed, the evidence of guilt, although vigorously disputed by the defense, was not trivial. Katzmann and his associates produced eye witnesses who placed both men at the South Braintree robbery and several who identified Sacco as one of the gunmen shooting bullets into the guard and paymaster.[22] At least one ballistics expert for the commonwealth believed that Sacco's .32 Colt automatic had fired one of the six bullets recovered from the bodies, and other testimony suggested that Vanzetti's revolver was the one carried by the payroll guard and stolen during the shootout.[23] In addition, the prosecutors noted that Sacco and Vanzetti displayed "consciousness of guilt" by lying repeatedly about their friends and activities after the arrest.[24] The trial lasted thirty days but the jury reached a verdict in five hours after Katzmann exhorted them "to stand together, you men of Norfolk."[25]

Katzmann, Thayer, and other patriots regarded the Dedham trial as a struggle between Americanism and alien invaders. The defendants and most of their initial supporters looked upon it as another episode in the long war between capital and labor that would further educate and radicalize the nation's working class. After Vanzetti's initial conviction for attempted robbery, his close friend Aldino Felicani, editor of Boston's largest Italian-language socialist newspaper, turned for assistance to the celebrated anarchist leader, Carlo Tresca. Although Sacco and Vanzetti belonged to a group of *antiorganizzatori* anarchists who had feuded with Tresca over many issues — including expropriation of the bourgeoisie — the latter devoted his considerable talents to raising money and publicizing the case among other Italians, anarchists, intellectuals, and trade unionists.[26] With Tresca came his girlfriend, Elizabeth Gurley Flynn, as well as other radicals who had survived the Red Scare. Tresca urged Felicani and the defense committee to hire Moore as chief counsel, and his presence in Dedham swelled the ranks of the Left even further.

The flamboyant Moore, house attorney for the Left, had defended Wobblies at Lawrence, Everett, and Chicago. With the possible exception of Clarence Darrow, he was reputed to be the most class-conscious lawyer of the day. In addition, he had earned a reputation for demagoguery, baiting judges, seducing women, and using dope. He wore sandals in Thayer's courtroom. Moore gave Sacco and Vanzetti an inspired but erratic defense which later led some of their supporters to blame him for their fate, but Eugene Lyons seems closer to the truth with his observation that Moore "sometimes subordinated the literal needs of legalistic procedure to the larger needs of the case as a symbol of the class struggle. If he had not done so, Sacco and Vanzetti would have died six years earlier, without the solace of martyrdom." His trenchant cross-examinations destroyed the credibility of several prosecution witnesses, yet inexplicably, it was he, not the prosecutors, who insisted upon the ballistics tests that proved to be very damaging to Sacco's case.[27]

Moore also raised a great deal of money for the defense and forged important bonds of sympathy with Boston's liberal community during the trial. He earned the support if not the admiration of John Codman of the New England Civil Liberties Committee, ace reporters Frank Sibley and Jackson, and Elizabeth Glendower Evans, pacifist, suffragette, and *grande dame* of genteel reform. The widow of one of Brandeis's classmates at Harvard, Auntie Bee sparked Frankfurter's interest in the case; Moore's ballistic evidence and testimony about it led him to read the complete trial record and to conclude that at the very least Sacco and Vanzetti deserved a new trial.[28]

◆➤➤➤➤➤

Fred Moore, bohemian, radical, legal spokesman for many social outcasts, became as controversial as his clients during the trial. Frankfurter, well tailored and liberal, who regarded Moore as "a blatherskite from the west," became equally controversial once he entered the case after 1927.[29] What finally drew him into battle, in addition to Auntie Bee's constant inquiries, was the fact that Sacco and Vanzetti acquired a new lawyer: William Goodrich Thompson, pillar of the Boston Bar and a close friend of Stimson's, who argued several motions for a new trial before Judge Thayer beginning in 1923.

In addition to Daly's allegations about the foreman of the jury, Thompson presented Thayer with an affidavit from the recently deceased Captain William H. Proctor, former head of the Massachusetts State Police, an important government witness. In this explosive document, signed one year before his death, Proctor swore that his true opinion about the ballistics evidence had not been given at the trial and that the prosecutors had been party to the deception:

> During the preparation for the trial, my attention was repeatedly called by the District Attorney and his assistants to the question: whether I could find any evidence which would justify the opinion that the particu-

lar bullet taken from the body of Berardelli, which came from a Colt automatic pistol, came from the particular Colt automatic pistol taken from Sacco. . . . At no time was I able to find any evidence whatever which tended to convince me . . . and I so informed the District Attorney. . . . At the trial, the District Attorney did not ask me whether I had found any evidence that the so-called mortal bullet which I have referred to . . . passed through Sacco's pistol, nor was I asked that question on cross-examination. The District Attorney desired to ask me that question, but I had repeatedly told him that if he did I should be obliged to answer in the negative; consequently, he put to me this question: Q. Have you an opinion as to whether bullet No. 3 was fired from the Colt automatic which is in evidence? To which I answered, "I have." He then proceeded. Q. And what is your opinion? A. My opinion is that it is consistent with being fired by that pistol. . . . That is still my opinion for the reason that bullet number 3, in my judgment, passed through some Colt automatic pistol, but I do not intend by that answer to imply that I had found any evidence that the so-called mortal bullet had passed through this particular Colt automatic pistol and the District Atorney well knew that I did not so intend and framed his question accordingly.[30]

In his summation to the jury, Katzmann argued that "we have proved to you beyond any reasonable doubt that the defendant Sacco fired a bullet from a Colt automatic that killed Alessandro Berardelli," and Thayer, in his charge to the jury, stressed the unanimity of government witnesses on this crucial issue.[31] In their affidavits, neither Katzmann nor his assistant specifically denied Proctor's accusations. Instead, they both denied that they had "repeatedly" asked Proctor about his opinion or that he had "repeatedly" answered in the negative about the so-called mortal bullet.[32]

Before his death, Proctor had often quarreled with Katzmann and other officials about various aspects of the case. A sixteen-year veteran of police investigations, who had headed the South Braintree inquiry from the beginning, Proctor had been taken off the case shortly before the trial. This fact heightened speculation that the captain believed the two men to be innocent. One defense attorney swore that Proctor had told him during the trial: "These are not the right men. Oh, no you haven't got the right men."[33] Even Katzmann admitted that he had "no recollection" of these doubts, but he could not deny that Proctor had expressed them.[34] In 1923, according to another Boston attorney, Proctor remarked: "I have been too long in the game, and I'm getting to be too old to want to see a couple of fellows go to the chair for something I don't think they did."[35]

In October 1924, however, Thayer turned down Thompson's motion for a new trial by rejecting the defense's interpretation of Proctor's affidavit. In Thayer's opinion, the former head of the state police had not "by prearrangement (which means intentional) compromised the truth with the District Attorney by . . . testifying knowingly to something that was false." He ridiculed Thompson's claim as "illogical, unreasonable, and unsound." It displayed the "absurdity and the length to which counsel, in their over-enthusiasm during heated discussion, will sometimes go," but he would prevent their "metaphysical argument" from tarnishing the reputation of Katzmann and his associates.[36]

The prosecution's guarded reply to Proctor's affidavit and Thayer's ruling outraged Frankfurter, who watched silently in the courtroom that day. Katzmann appeared to be a man bent upon securing a conviction at all costs. Thayer seemed to be more concerned with protecting the state's honor than with the pursuit of the truth. Frankfurter's disgust at their conduct intensified as he pored over the volumes of testimony during the next six months. His doubts about the defendants' guilt swelled even further in the wake of a startling confession by Celestino Madeiros and the investigations of one of his former students, Herbert Ehrmann, which suggested that the robbery had been carried out by professional bandits, not political anarchists.

Madeiros, a young Portuguese hoodlum who was under sentence of death for bank robbery and murder, confessed on November 18, 1925 that he had taken part in the holdup along with Italians (whom he refused to identify) from the Providence area and that neither Sacco nor Vanzetti had been members of the gang. Madeiros's reconstruction of the robbery did not fit the known facts perfectly, but his tale prompted further investigations by Thompson, who through Frankfurter and Pound secured the services of Ehrmann, a bright, indefatigable graduate of the law school and veteran of the Cleveland crime survey. After travelling to a dozen cities in four states and interviewing hundreds of police officials, convicts, and ex-convicts, Ehrmann and his wife came to the conclusion that Madeiros had told the truth: the crime had been carried out by a band of desperadoes from Providence, led by Frank and Joe Morelli, who had been arrested by federal agents for robbing freight cars in 1920, including shipments from Slater and Morrill at the South Braintree station. On the day of the holdup at the shoe factory, the Morellis had been free on bail and desperate for funds to pay their legal bills. They drove a shiny new Buick, similar to the one seen at the robbery. Joe Morelli, then serving a sentence in Leavenworth, bore a striking resemblance to Nick Sacco.[37]

Neither Madeiro's confession nor Ehrmann's speculations impressed Judge Thayer. Less that a year after the revelation, he again rejected Thompson's motion for a new trial with a scathing attack upon Madeiro's character as "a crook, a thief, a robber, a liar, a rum-runner, a 'bouncer' in a house of ill-fame, a smuggler, and a man who had been convicted and sentenced to death." Instead, he preferred to believe the counteraffidavits from the Morelli gang members, all of whom denied involvement in the South Braintree robbery, but whose character references were hardly superior to those of Madeiros. "Since the trial . . . of these cases," Thayer added, gratuitously, "a new type of disease would seem to have developed. It might be called 'lego-psychic neurosis' or hysteria which means: 'a belief in the existence of something which in fact and truth has no such existence.' "[38] Limited by statute to ruling upon contested points of law, the Supreme Judicial Court of Massachusetts affirmed Thayer's denial of the Madeiros motion as within the discretion of a trial judge. The same court had also spurned Thompson's earlier appeal on the Proctor motion with the tart observation that "the burden was on the defendants to establish wilful misconduct by the prosecuting officer . . . and the conclusion of the judge that this burden had not been sustained cannot as a matter of law be set aside by us."[39]

A month before the high court's second negative ruling, Frankfurter published his withering attack upon the commonwealth's case in the pages of the nation's premier literary magazine. An expanded version soon appeared in book form as well. He had written the piece originally at Thompson's urging and planned to publish it in *The New Republic*, which under Croly's influence had criticized the case since 1920.[40] When Ellery Sedgwick of the *Atlantic Monthly* expressed enthusiasm for the project, Frankfurter quickly changed the forum for his blast against Massachusetts justice. He could now influence more than the old progressives, liberals, and intellectuals who read Croly's magazine. He could reach "the best people," the solid middle-class lawyers, doctors, teachers, and businessmen who subscribed to Sedgwick's genteel journal.[41]

Frankfurter painted a grim portrait of Boston's collective hysteria during the Red Scare. He reviewed in detail the damaging Proctor affidavit, and the Madeiros-Morelli evidence, but he saved his harshest criticism for Katzmann, Thayer, and the Supreme Judicial Court of Massachusetts. "The prosecutor," he wrote, "systematically played on the feelings of the jury by exploiting the unpatriotic and despised beliefs of Sacco and Vanzetti, and the judge allowed him thus to divert and pervert the jury's mind."[42] He described Thayer's ruling on the Madeiros motion as "a farrago of misquotations, misrepresentations, suppressions, and mutilations . . . literally honeycombed with demonstrable errors, and infused by a spirit alien to judicial utterance."[43]

Katzmann's behavior as detailed in the Proctor affidavit, he argued, would not have been tolerated in Great Britain, violated the ethical canons of the American Bar Association, and should have been condemned by the state's highest court on the basis of its own prior decisions.[44] He found it impossible to reconcile that court's defense of Thayer's conduct with its recent ruling that proper judicial discretion required "the calmness of a cool mind, free from partiality, not swayed by sympathy nor warped by prejudice nor moved by any kind of influence save alone the overwhelming passion to do that which is just."[45]

Privately, he expressed even greater loathing for Thayer's behavior. "An accused is not entitled to a wise judge, or a learned judge, or a wholly calm judge," he told Arthur Hill, the able Boston attorney who argued many of the final appeals in the case. "But, surely the essence of an Anglo-American trial, particularly in a capital case, implies a judge. And a judge means a person capable of deciding free from the operation of a rooted hostility, amounting to abhorrence, for the very men who are before him for life." Because of this rooted hostility, Frankfurter believed, Thayer had been unable to perform as a judge, but he had been clever enough to disguise it during the trial "with appropriate forms, so as to clothe the exercise of his hostile discretion in the forms and appearances of a true exercise of discretion." From the beginning of the trial, he concluded, Thayer had been "possessed by his hatred of these 'anarchistic bastards' . . . even though he did not call them 'anarchistic bastards' in open court."[46]

His salvo in the *Atlantic* produced several important consequences. It provided more ammunition for all of those, including the *Boston Herald* and other newspapers, who demanded a new trial for the two men. It inspired a bitter counterattack by Thayer's defenders and polarized opinion about the case even more. In addition, it became a potent factor in the decision by Governor Alvan T. Fuller to appoint a special advisory committee to review all of the evidence in the case. Tresca and Moore had kept Sacco and Vanzetti alive for nearly seven years by generating outrage about the case among Italians, radicals, trade unionists, and a few liberals. Frankfurter's dissent reached deeper into the state's establishment. He stirred doubts among State Street lawyers and Beacon Hill bankers that had to be stilled before the commonwealth could carry out the death sentences.

Not even Frankfurter's report on the Bisbee deportation generated more bitterness from conservatives. In his diary entry for February 28, Pound noted that his entire day had been absorbed by "all sorts of people complaining about Frankfurter's article." It had been, he lamented, a "very annoying day."[47] Months after the executions, he still reported a "general outcry by graduates agst. FF."[48] Annoyed that Frankfurter had kept the article secret until publication, he told him that it might have been prudent to wait for a ruling by the Supreme Judicial Court on the Madeiros motion before printing criticism. Frankfurter exploded. He did not know when the court would finally hand down its opinion. The two men might be dead before the article went to press. In addition, he pointed out, nobody lifted an eyebrow when the members of the Worcester Bar Association formally endorsed Judge Thayer's handling of the case before his article appeared. "As to the impropriety of writing about a case while it is pending," he concluded, "the claim is utter tosh." Stung by the vehemence of Frankfurter's defense, Pound shortly relented. It had been necessary for him to write when he did, the dean admitted a few days later, "in the interests of justice."[49]

Influential Harvard alumni, such as Thomas Perkins of Ropes, Gray, Boyden and Perkins, again chided him for rushing into print, becoming too controversial, and hurting the university's fund-raising efforts. Frankfurter took great pleasure in pointing out to Perkins that Raymond B. Fosdick, representing the Rockefeller interests, gave nearly $100,000 to the law school fund after the article appeared. "What I had done in connection with the Sacco-Vanzetti case seems to have called forth commendation in quarters whose opinions you probably value highly," he told Perkins, dryly.[50] "The foulest and meanest slanders" had been inflicted upon him, he told Eustace Seligman, "even by people from whom one might expect responsibility." He was accused of being on the payroll of the Communist Party and of reaping large financial rewards from the article, when in fact Sedgwick had paid him a pittance and Frankfurter gave the book royalties to the defense fund.[51]

The most vitriolic attack came from John Henry Wigmore, the celebrated expert on the law of evidence, who had been dean of the Northwestern law school for over thirty years and who, in Frankfurter's opinion, had become "one of the casualties of the war . . . increasingly violent and recklessly indifferent to facts."[52] A friend of Judge Thayer's, who probably encouraged the effort, Wigmore received premium space and banner headlines in the *Boston Transcript* to answer Frankfurter, "the plausible pundit" and "contra-canonical critic."

Wigmore accused Frankfurter of disrupting the administration of justice, of suppressing certain facts about the case and distorting others, but his own letters betrayed a woefully inadequate reading of the trial record, ignorance of Massachusetts law, and manipulation of what law he did know. In the end, he took refuge in ethnic slurs and patriotic hyperbole: "The thugs of India, the Cammorra of Naples, the Black Hand of Sicily, the anarchists of czardom—when did their attempts to impose their will by violence ever equal in range of operations and vicious directness, the organized efficiency of this cabal to which Sacco and Vanzetti belong?"[53]

Calmly, Frankfurter replied in Frank Buxton's *Boston Herald*. Given Wigmore's intemperance and superficial knowledge of the case, it was like shooting fish in a barrel. "With your crushing reply . . . those responsible for his intercession should feel humiliated," Brandeis wrote, "if their prejudices have not made them proof against emotions as well as ideas."[54] Samuel Williston thought Frankfurter had "pulverized" his former classmate in the exchange, and President Lowell, according to Norman Hapgood, declared: "Wigmore is a fool! Wigmore is a fool! He should have known that Frankfurter would be shrewd enough to be accurate."[55]

❧❧❧

For both the condemned men and for Frankfurter, April became a turning point. The Supreme Judicial Court's decision moved them a step closer to death. He plunged deeper into the day-to-day strategy of the defense through an ad hoc citizens committee on Sacco and Vanzetti that met in the office of John F. Moors, a stockbroker in the venerable firm of Moors and Cabot. The committee was composed overwhelmingly of men and women from the liberal establishment of the Boston-Cambridge area, including Woodrow Wilson's son-in-law, Francis Sayre, Samuel Eliot Morison, Codman from the Civil Liberties Committee, Lois Rantoul of the Federated Churches of Greater Boston, Dr. Morton Prince, the distinguished psychiatrist, Mrs. Anna May Peabody, Thompson, Jackson, and Frankfurter. The only representatives from the more militant Sacco-Vanzetti Defense Committe were Jackson and Mary Donovan, the fiery socialist from the James Connolly Literary Society, although members from both groups trundled back and forth on many days between Moors's office and the Hanover Street headquarters of the defense committee.

Frankfurter played a crucial role in the group's fateful discussions on April 7. Their legal options had been narrowed radically by the Supreme Judicial Court's decision two days earlier. Neither Frankfurter nor Thompson, the two best lawyers present, now expected judicial relief from the state or federal courts although they had drawn up a motion for a new trial which directly attacked Thayer on the grounds of prejudice. But since this motion would have to be argued initially before Thayer and then, perhaps, before the Supreme Judicial Court again, they were not optimistic about the results. The United States Supreme Court, they noted, "has announced its decision not to interfere with a state court under the 'due process' clause, unless it is a very extreme case; and it would not regard this as such." They both feared the delay and the consequences of another negative ruling that would "engender the Philistine attitude that in addition to the highest court in Massachusetts 'finding Sacco and Vanzetti guilty,' the highest court in the land has decided likewise."[56]

Their best hope, Thompson suggested, was an appeal to Governor Fuller for clemency and this should be done in conjunction with a proposal made by Brandeis's former law partner, George Nutter, that Fuller "appoint some commission to investigate this whole thing." Thompson thought the death sentences would be commuted under those circumstances, "as he could not see how the Governor could allow the men to be executed in the face of the findings that would come out." Frankfurter buttressed this plea with the observation that similar machinery had been used effectively in England by the Home Secretary and that "such a commission composed of impartial, reliable citizens appointed by the Governor would be sufficient to enable them to get at the true facts." Thompson quickly tempered Frankfurter's optimism with the observation that "everything turns on the question of the personnel of the committee," but there was a general consensus that they had few choices left and that the strategy should be adopted, although both Sacco and Vanzetti had told their supporters they desired freedom, not commutation.

Thompson confessed that Sacco had nearly fired him the day before with the curt statement that "no capitalistic society would so organize its courts as to render justice, and that it was prefectly futile to appeal to the courts." For different reasons, Frankfurter and Thompson had also abandoned much hope in judicial remedies, but they wanted to pursue clemency efforts in order to frustrate the goals of "extreme radicals," who, in Thompson's opinion, "would be very glad to see them executed and made martyrs of, and this should be communicated to the Governor." He remained confident that Vanzetti, "a more intelligent man and more temperate," would go along with the appeal. When Mary Donovan objected to Thompson's remarks, a sharp argument followed, with Thompson and others denouncing "extreme radicals in New York and elsewhere who say that."[57]

Frankfurter and Thompson won the debate. Those present agreed that members of the committee, led by Moors, Prince, and Thompson, would see the Episcopal Bishop of Massachusetts, William Lawrence, later that afternoon and ask him to urge the inquiry upon Fuller.[58] Four days later, Lawrence, leader of the state's Protestant establishment and heir to one of its great textile fortunes, invited the governor to allay all doubts about the case and "call to your aid several citizens of well known character, experience, ability, and sense of justice to make a study of the trial and advise you." Fuller received identical requests from other clergymen, Roland Boyden of Ropes, Gray, Boyden and Perkins, the President Emeritus of Stanford University, David Starr Jordan, and Dean Pound. After examining the trial records himself for almost two months, Fuller announced the appointment of a special three-man advisory committee on June 1, headed by Bishop Lawrence's cousin, President Lowell, in addition to Samuel Stratton, the president of MIT and a retired probate judge, Robert Grant.[59]

In view of the fact that the Lowell committee finally sealed the fate of Sacco and Vanzetti, there was considerable irony in Fuller's acceptance of a plan blessed by strategists for the defense such as Frankfurter, who believed that this mechanism, "composed of impartial and reliable citizens . . . would . . . get at the true facts." Frankfurter had directed his *Atlantic Monthly* appeal to the hearts and minds of the nation's "best people." He intended that the governor's advisory committee, composed of similar, enlightened leaders, would vindicate the legal system by saving it from the extremists of the Right and the Left. While avoiding the suicidal tactics of radicals, an advisory committee of "impartial and reliable citizens" could correct the narrow prejudice of the grocer's son, Thayer, and educate the former Packard salesman in the governor's mansion. "I don't know Fuller," he told Norman Hapgood, "but I have a strong belief that he is independent but unimaginative and without background. He is one of these businessmen who has been inoculated with the belief in the wisdom of the courts." He advised Ehrmann on how to present the defense's case before the advisory committee. They should concentrate on influencing Lowell and Fuller. "I cannot believe that they are ruthlessly determined to have those men go to the chair, no matter what," he said. Fuller might be "an untutored mind . . . handicapped by a lack of critical faculties," but Ehrmann should accept this challenge instead of "bewailing the fact that he lacks trenchancy and intellectual penetration."[60]

But even Frankfurter, who had urged the creation of the advisory committee, had to admit that the future looked "very gloomy indeed" given Fuller's choice of advisers. The governor had selected three "reliable citizens" with impeccable reputations, but Lowell, Stratton, and Grant all came from what *The New Republic* called "the class in Boston most of whose members have sworn death to Sacco and Vanzetti."[61] They were not likely to be sympathetic to convicted Italian anarchists or especially eager to cast doubt upon the integrity of the state's judicial system. In addition to his efforts to create a Jewish quota system at Harvard, the aristocratic Lowell had been for many years vice president of the Immigration Restriction League. He had vigorously opposed Brandeis's appointment to the Supreme Court, and he nursed several grudges against Frankfurter. "The intensity of Lowell's animosity to Felix was a very large factor in what happened," Jackson believed. "Lowell was not able to surmount the depth of his feeling of hostility to Felix Frankfurter."[62] Grant, a second-rate local novelist and civil judge who had grown up with Lowell on Beacon Hill, once described Italy as a nation of thieves, and in a conversation with Holmes before his appointment he condemned Frankfurter's criticism of the trial.[63]

In addition to the composition of the advisory committee, the defense received other serious setbacks. In early June, the prosecution conducted new ballistics tests with the assistance of a New York expert, Major Calvin Goddard, and a comparison microscope. These tests convinced several people, including Dr. Augustus H. Gill, a former consultant to the defense, that the mortal bullet and one of the spent shells found near the scene of the robbery had been fired through Sacco's gun. Ehrmann and two reporters who viewed the same evidence were not persuaded by the demonstration, and the defense shortly attacked Goddard's findings with a new theory: between the arrest of Sacco and Vanzetti and the initial ballistics tests at Lowell, someone had manufactured the fatal bullet and the incriminating shell by firing them through Sacco's gun and substituting them for the real evidence. Thompson and others pointed an accusing finger at the deceased Captain Proctor.[64] Also to the dismay of the defense, the Lowell committee questioned many important witnesses in secret, including Judge Thayer and members of the jury, without permitting Thompson or Ehrmann to learn the substance of their testimony or to cross-examine them.

On the evening of August 3, seven days after receiving Lowell's final report, Fuller issued a terse five-page statement which concluded that the trial had been fair and that the two men were guilty. He would not grant clemency.[65] The Lowell report itself, issued four days later, reached the same conclusions. Judge Thayer had been "indiscreet in conversation with outsiders," but his conduct at the trial had been "scrupulously fair." Lowell and his associates found nothing remiss in Proctor's affidavit or in the prosecution's response. They dismissed the Madeiros confession, all of the alibi witnesses, and the accusations of manufactured evidence with the remark that "the defendants must be rather desperate on its merits when counsel feel it necessary to resort to a charge of this kind."[66] The committee found the commonwealth's ballistics testimony "more convincing" and added a new twist of its own: "the fatal bullet found in Berardelli's body was of a type no longer manufactured and so obsolete that the defendant's expert witness . . . was unable to find such bullets for purposes of experiment; yet the same obsolete type of cartridges was found in Sacco's pocket on his arrest."[67]

The sudden appearance in the report of the "obsolete bullet theory," an issue not raised during the trial or presented to the defense at the hearings, represented a flagrant example of the Lowell committee's bizarre procedures that usually handicapped Thompson and Ehrmann. Not content to establish the fairness of the trial, Lowell and his associates also attempted to prove Sacco and Vanzetti guilty again, but defense lawyers could not rebut potentially damaging evidence because it remained secret until the report appeared and their clients had been condemned. A lone juryman apparently created the "obsolete bullet theory" when he told the Lowell committee that he became convinced of Sacco's guilt after he discovered that the mortal bullet, manufactured by Winchester, was identical with six cartridges found in the denfendant's possession. The company had ceased producing them in 1917, and when one defense expert attempted to purchase some for the Lowell tests he had been unable to do so—hence the designation, "obsolete bullet." But the defense expert had canvassed only stores in the area between Dedham and Lawrence in 1921. This perfunctory search had no bearing upon the general availability of such ammunition at the time of the robbery. According to Ehrmann, other defense experts purchased identical Winchester cartridges in 1923 and as late as 1962.[68]

The conflicting ballistics evidence had not been decisive for the Lowell committee in any event. Norman Hapgood, who interviewed Lowell and Grant after the executions, reported that both men seemed to have placed little reliance upon either eye-witness testimony or the disputed bullets and shells. What impressed Grant "more than any other thing," according to Hapgood, "was the jury," two of whom voted to acquit the pair on the initial ballot. Grant also stressed the fact that Sacco and Vanzetti had lied and were "armed to the teeth" when arrested. He believed that the Supreme Judicial Court would have ordered a new trial if Thayer had been unfair.[69] Lowell's conclusion, Hapgood told Frankfurter, "rests fundamentally on circumstances of arrest of men . . . behavior of men when arrested, their lies, etc., etc., possession of firearms. That is the essence of the case."[70]

After reading Lowell's document, Frankfurter had no doubt that the committee had made up its mind before the inquiry began. "It proves to me," he told Thompson, heatedly, "the utter inaccessibility of their minds to fact and truth."[71] The President of Harvard, he wrote to Pound, "is part and parcel of the social forces which help to explain the conviction and forthcoming execution of two innocent men. . . . The Lowell report simply will not wash."[72]

※※-※※-※※

During the last frantic weeks before the executions, Boston became a magnet for liberals, radicals, poets, novelists, labor organizers, and intellectuals who arrived in the city to join protest demonstrations organized by the defense committee and the Communist Party. They carried placards, typed letters, made coffee, paraded before the state house, and often wound up in jail.[73] In the tiny seaside village of Duxbury near where the Pilgrims first landed, Frankfurter's summer home became a major command post that rivaled even the Hanover Street headquarters. Thanks to the efforts of the Massachusetts Attorney General, who authorized a wiretap on his telephone, we have an extensive record of his furious activities during these final days. The prosecutors gained valuable information about the defense's daily strategy from this surveillance as well as from informants planted at Hanover Street and the Bellevue Hotel where a Citizens National Committee for Sacco and Vanzetti operated.[74]

Consistent with his approach to the case from the beginning, Frankfurter made heroic efforts to mobilize liberals, moderates, and even conservatives against the executions and he worked to dilute the influence of the radicals. Nightly, he monitored Jackson's press releases and advised friendly reporters such as Waldo Cook of the *Springfield Republican* and F. Lauriston Bullard of the *Boston Herald* about defects in the Lowell report.[75] Largely at Frankfurter's urging, Paul Kellogg, the brilliant editor of the *Survey*, came to Boston to assist Jackson. "The whole burden of education—of informing the world . . . rests on the shoulders of Jackson," he told Kellogg. "He is a fine lad—young, but it is simply a crushing burden. Extremists from New York have come on here to capture the thing. Mike Gold and people like that said they are absolutely desperate. . . . He thought you could help him much better than anybody else."[76] Walter Lippmann's editorial attack on the commonwealth's case that appeared in the *New York World* sprang almost entirely from Frankfurter's efforts, and he made a similar but futile attempt to persuade the leaders of the *New York Times*.[77]

Drawing upon his extensive friendships with lawyers, old progressives, and Harvard Law School alumni in the New England and New York areas, he organized petition drives and letter-writing campaigns to bring pressure to bear upon Fuller and Lowell with the hope of securing commutation of the sentences. These efforts ought to focus, he told Katherine Ludington, upon going around "from conservative to conservative" in order to gather enough signatures and he proposed to begin with people like Julia Lathrop, the first head of the Children's Bureau, and C.C. Burlingham, the Nestor of the New York Bar.[78] With the aid of Ludington, and others, he raised money to pay Hill's legal expenses when the latter made final appeals for the condemned men and he helped to shape Hill's arguments before Thayer, the Supreme Judicial Court, Holmes, and Brandeis.[79]

While working day and night behind the scenes, he resisted every call to become more openly associated with the defense's final efforts. He would not join Hill in court or write a critique of the Lowell report. Concern for the defendants, not fear for his own reputation, dictated this prudence. The general public might be moved by his intervention, he told Ehrmann, but "the general public don't count" and those who did—above all the governor and his advisers—"are just violent on me." He told Thompson's law partner, George Mears, that most state officials considered him an "officious damned radical Jew who has meddled with this case" and that his appearance would make matters worse for the defense. "The feeling is intense on the part of the people who have to be moved and when I raise my voice it will be Frankfurter versus Lowell or Lowell versus Frankfurter and you will have the whole diversion of the issue." Friends in the executive branch had told him, he reported, that "it would be fatal for me just to raise my head above the surface."[80]

The defense's final maneuvers, guided by Frankfurter, Hill, and

Michael Musmanno, a dashing young Pittsburgh lawyer who had quit his practice to join the crusade, became a grim satire on the futility of the legal process. They filed a motion for a new trial on the grounds that Thayer's prejudice had denied Sacco and Vanzetti due process of law guaranteed by the Fourteenth Amendment. The problem with this approach, Frankfurter told Jackson, was the fact that "the incidents in the record are not very good. . . . He [Thayer] certainly was very careful. That cuss is cunning you know and he constantly was doing stuff which in itself is all right."[81] Their efforts to have Thayer disqualified from hearing their motion failed, and he finally refused to hear it on the grounds that a trial judge lacked jurisdiction once sentence had been passed. The Supreme Judicial Court also agreed that "a motion for a new trial in capital cases comes too late if made after sentence has been pronounced."[82]

Simultaneously, Thompson and Hill sought a writ of habeas corpus from three federal judges — Holmes, George Anderson, who had rescued aliens from illegal deportations in 1920, and James M. Morton of the district court — alleging that Thayer's prejudices had denied the two defendants due process of law. All three judges declined to intervene, Holmes with the observation: "I cannot think that prejudice on the part of a presiding judge however strong would deprive the Court of jurisdiction, that is of legal power to decide the case, and in my opinion nothing short of a want of legal power to decide the case authorizes me to interfere . . . with the proceedings of the State Court."[83] On August 20, Holmes also turned down an application for certiorari and a stay of execution based upon similar claims. "If the Constitution of Massachusetts had provided that a trial before a single Judge should be final, without appeal," he wrote, "it would have been consistent with the Constitution of the United States."[84]

Seldom one to criticize Holmes, Frankfurter attempted to put the best face upon his hero's conduct. Before denying the writ of habeas corpus, he reported, Holmes had told Thompson: "Those men could not have had a fair trial at that time in that setting. . . . I don't think I have to hear you on that — I know all about that."[85] The Supreme Court, however, had never reversed a state court on the grounds put forth by the defense, and, as Holmes told Laski, "I thought that the line must be drawn between external force, and prejudice — which could be alleged in every case."[86] Holmes may have been right on the law, but it is also true that he displayed little sympathy for the two condemned men. "Why this so much greater interest in red than black?" he asked Laski. "I think the row that has been made idiotical, if considered on its merits, but of course it is not on the merits that the row is made, but because it gives the extremists a chance to yell."[87]

Brandeis, on the contrary, evidenced great sympathy for Sacco and Vanzetti, but this proved to be the final irony: the one judge who shared most of Frankfurter's doubts about the case refused to hear Hill's arguments because of the intense participation in the controversy by his close friends and immediate family. "At first he [Brandeis] was not going to talk with us—he would not listen to us," one of Hill's associates told Frankfurter. "Mr. Hill insisted on telling his story, but he again repeated he would not do anything under any circumstances. . . . He refused the first minute he saw us. He knew what we were there for."[88] Shortly before the executions, Brandeis told Frankfurter: "You and Auntie B. have played noble parts," and later, he attempted to console his friend with the observation that "you have done all that was possible for you. And that all was more than would have [been] possible for any other person I know. But the end of S.V. is only the beginning. 'They know not what they do.' "[89]

By not acting like a judge, Thayer helped to convict Sacco and Vanzetti. Acting like a judge, Brandeis could not save them. This contradiction became too much for Jackson, who complained to Frankfurter about the "awful situation where your legal system will not insure moral demands; that is what leads to revolution." With mass demonstrations in the streets of Boston and rumors of a march on Charlestown State Prison, Frankfurter was enraged by Jackson's comment. "Now don't talk to me about that," he fumed, "because I have had to listen to my wife all day. I can shut you up but not her. All day long I have had to listen to it. I have tried to explain the situation but not defend it. She just won't take it in. I can tell you to shut up, but not her. Gardner, it is terribly important not to have the fight go over into unclean hands."[90]

Clearly, Jackson had touched a sensitive spot on the day when Frankfurter's grand strategy crumbled and all hope died for saving Sacco and Vanzetti. Neither rational editorials in the best newspapers, petitions from distinguished citizens, nor the Anglo-American legal system could stay the executioner's hand. But neither, given the heavily armed troops that ringed the prison, could mob violence have done so, whatever Frankfurter's fears about the struggle falling into "unclean hands."

He had begun only with doubts about the fairness of the trial and the misconduct of the district attorney. By August 23, he believed the two men to be innocent as well, a conviction he never abandoned, even in the face of evidence suggesting that Sacco might have been guilty.[91] Like many other critics of the case, he compared them to Jean Calas, Captain Dreyfus, and Tom Mooney; sentimentalized their "undeviatingly pure life," and tended to ignore the fact that both men had been dedicated, militant anarchocommunists, perhaps capable of robbery and murder in the interests of class struggle and assisting their comrades.[92] What Frankfurter carried away from the experience, above all, was not a commitment to revolution or radicalism, but a renewed devotion to the concepts of judicial restraint and law as the instrument of reason. If this were not so, he believed, then only blind prejudice and force would govern and in that struggle he had no doubt, the Thayers, the Katzmanns, and the Lowells probably outnumbered the Thompsons, Ehrmanns, and Frankfurters.

❧❧ CHAPTER 11 ❧❧

PROFESSOR
AND PRESIDENT

SELDOM DID FRANKFURTER'S LIFE reach the emotional trough of the months following the executions of Sacco and Vanzetti. "Yes," he told his colleague Thomas Reed Powell, "this has been a devastating summer," poisoned by "the systematic torturing of truth," and the judicial murder of two men who were "as gallant and fine a pair of humans as it has been my fortune to encounter in life."[1] Marion's illness and the sudden death of one of his favorite students at age thirty-six compounded the gloom. Then, two weeks into the new year, his mother died at the age of seventy-four. Together they had fulfilled the ancient dream of immigrant parent and child by wresting success from the sometimes unwilling hands of the establishment. To the consternation of those Massachusetts' officials who tapped his telephone, however, they conversed in German until the end. "To your good mother you have been a good son," Brandeis consoled him, "and a never-failing source of happiness."[2]

During the course of the next few years, his hopes for the law school hit bottom as well, buffeted by what he perceived to be the vindictiveness of Lowell, the sterile leadership of Pound, and the crude materialism that gripped the legal profession in the twilight of the Republican's New Era. Pound, he lamented, possessed much learning, "but not *Geist*." The dean had become a perfect illustration of Whitehead's warning about the curse of inert ideas in education. "He must know all the law that anybody knows or can possibly exist, and he naively believes that all his former students . . . are merely echoes of him," Frankfurter told Hand. "He is such a pathetically vain fellow."[3] He complained regularly to Hand about "the seduction of our youth by the New York law offices" that took place each year during Christmas vacation. "They want to be successful lawyers, and you and I know what that means. They want to be . . . counsel for Van Sweringens and the Appalachian Power Company and such like."[4] Only in the nation's shifting political mood, symbolized by the rising fortunes of Alfred E. Smith and Franklin Roosevelt, did he find cause for some optimism in addition to a new avenue for personal fulfillment.

"I am strong for Al," he told Chafee in the summer of 1928, one month after the Democratic Party had nominated the four-term New York governor, former subpoena server, alderman, and Tammany Hall sachem for the presidency.[5] Others shared his enthusiasm. "There is not in American life today," remarked the Kansas sage, William Allen White, "a clearer, stronger, more accurately working brain in any man's head than Al Smith's brain." Discounting White's hyperbole, Smith had compiled a strong record of progressivism in the Empire State during years otherwise saturated by governmental apathy and corruption. Eschewing complete identification with the old machine politics, the high school dropout surrounded himself with many bright, energetic social workers, civic reformers, and intellectuals, including Henry and Belle Moskowitz, Robert Moses, and Norman Hapgood. He streamlined a cumbersome state bureaucracy, built parks and recreation areas for the urban masses, pushed for tougher factory inspection laws, and saved water-power sites from the grasp of private utility companies.[6] Smith's programs and his pugnacious, freewheeling style of political combat brought Frankfurter back into the Democratic Party fold after the futile La Follette crusade and what he regarded as the moral misfortune of John W. Davis's candidacy in 1924.

"Al Smith in the White House would greatly add to the liveliness of life," he told Justice Holmes. "And snobs to the contrary, we'd even survive Mrs. Smith!"[7] He entered the campaign that fall with enthusiasm, urging Smith's virtues upon wavering liberals, advising the candidate on the subtleties of utility regulation, and firing an occasional blast against the Republican *wunderkind*, Herbert Hoover. "One thing is clear," he told the readers of *The New Republic*, "instead of Mr. Hoover educating the electrical industry, the power interests have educated Mr. Hoover." He identified Hoover with the vehement GOP opposition to federal development of Muscle Shoals and with the vulgar, probusiness mentality of the Harding-Coolidge era. "What we need now is not a mining engineer," he told Chafee, "but a social engineer."[8] The New Yorker's brown derby campaign rekindled the fire in other old progressives as well. "Al Smith's offensive is refreshingly Napoleonic," Brandeis remarked. "He is reminding us what a political opposition is for; and the gains now and hereafter should be great."[9]

Smith lost, but Brandeis's observation proved to be prophetic. Although Holmes dismissed the Democratic nominee as "a sort of fad among the New York highbrows (*New Republic*, Dewey, Cohen, F.F. *et al.*)," Smith's campaign did a great deal more than restore political morale among the progressives. Building upon the economic distress among industrial workers and farmers that La Follette had begun to exploit four years earlier, Smith ran up impressive majorities in the nation's largest metropolitan areas that prefigured the even larger Democratic gains of the next decade. A burst of anti-Catholic sentiment, Hoover's legendary reputation for efficiency, and the last warm rays of Republican prosperity combined to defeat Smith, but the ominous signs of pending economic calamity loomed on the horizon: a nervous stock market, sagging residential construction, and the faltering sale of consumer goods. "We were routed by 'the villainy of our fears,'" Brandeis remarked after the election, "the fears of the prosperous." Soon, those fears became epidemic.[10]

Even in the face of Smith's defeat, Frankfurter began to sense that the nation had now reached a decisive turning point, and Brandeis, for one, believed that his friend would play an important role in the transformation. "You have earned in the resuscitated Democratic Party a position as thinker," the justice told him, "which should enable you to exert much influence hereafter." Less than ten days after the election, Brandeis urged him to organize "from Smith's recent aids and others, a sort of general staff and expert body" that would supply "thought and research" for the "militant Democratic opposition."[11]

Within the resuscitated Democratic Party, Frankfurter soon began to concentrate his attention upon Smith's successor in New York, the former assistant secretary of the Navy and one-time vice-presidential candidate, Franklin Roosevelt, who carried the state by 25,000 votes

while Smith lost it by over 100,000. In 1928 Roosevelt hardly qualified as a member of the "militant Democratic opposition," but the
forty-six-year-old governor possessed many of the qualities that Smith
lacked. He was rich, charming, handsome, educated at Harvard, and
a polished if somewhat glib orator. Beginning his first term in Albany,
he was much in need of "thought and research" on issues about which
Frankfurter knew a great deal. "If, as I expect, Roosevelt is elected,"
Brandeis advised him, "I should like through you to put in early two
requests: (a) Far reaching attack on 'The Third Degree,' (b) Good
counsel in N.Y.'s cases before our Court."[12] Their combined advice
soon became much more extensive than the methods of police interrogation and the quality of the state's legal arguments in Washington.

In cultivating Roosevelt, Frankfurter reopened a relationship that
had first begun over lunch at the Harvard Club in 1906, flourished
briefly during the last years of the Wilson administration, and continued off and on in the postwar decade. In the history of political friendships, it was destined to become as important as Jackson's with Roger
Taney, Lincoln's with Billy Herndon, and Wilson's with Colonel
House. "Your victory is a great source of consolation and hope,"
Frankfurter told him, "For you have, as Smith has, the conception of
government which seems to me indispensable to the vitality of a democratic government, namely, the realization that the processes of government are essentially educational processes."[13] A heavy volume of
"Dear Frank" and "Dear Felix" letters began to flow between them as
well as increased telephone traffic from Albany to Cambridge and
frequent visits by Frankfurter to the Roosevelt home in Hyde Park on
the Hudson River.

Eagerly, he sent F.D.R. a copy of the Dodge Lectures he had
delivered at the Yale Law School, *The Public and Its Government*,
which emphasized many key ideas of his mature political philosophy—the indispensability of the administrative process in the management of contemporary economic life; the importance of nurturing
federalism and seeking state or regional solutions to social problems
that were not overwhelmingly national in scope; the adaptability of
the Constitution to the resolution of these conflicts; and the crucial
role that could be played in modern government by trained experts
recruited from the nation's universities and professional schools.
Above all, he hoped Roosevelt would absorb the final chapter, "Expert Administration and Democracy."

The burning political issues of the nineteenth century, Frankfurter wrote, "thrived in the main, on the levels of feeling and rhetoric." A

broadened franchise, popular elections, and the abolition of slavery were not questions that yielded to statistical analysis or social science research. "But feeling and rhetoric," he believed, "are blind guides for the understanding of contemporary political issues. They only distract and confuse." This was so, he reasoned, because the critical problems of the present—from corporate regulation to public health—remained "deeply enmeshed in intricate and technical facts" that had to be freed from "presupposition and partisanship." Such matters demanded a systematic effort "to contract the area of conflict and passion" and to widen "the area of accredited knowledge as the basis of action." The mission of reformers and the tasks of government remained the same: to expand the influence of specialists and the boundaries of professionalism.[14]

Frankfurter pointed out, however, that he did not advocate "a new type of oligarchy, namely, government by experts," but rather a system where specialists offered their best advice to the people's elected representatives, who retained the ultimate choice of action. The question of whether or not the federal government should itself operate Muscle Shoals or lease its water-power sites, he emphasized, "raises questions beyond the authority of engineer or economist. In the final analysis, we are in the realm of judgment regarding values as to which there is as yet no voice of science. . . . The expert should be on tap, but not on top."[15]

Despite his caveats about experts, Frankfurter's call for an expanded network of trained bureaucrats to solve the nation's problems betrayed considerable naïvete about the methods of intellectual inquiry in many academic disciplines, where even the most scrupulous investigator could not escape from the influence of "presupposition and partisanship" with respect to research interests, methods, and evidence. A certain insouciance also characterized his belief that these intellectual mandarins would remain subject to popular, democratic controls. In a decade that produced the first edition of the *Encyclopedia of the Social Sciences*, however, his confidence and myopia were hardly unusual. And in a country plagued historically by antiintellectualism and fear of expertise, where government had functioned usually on the basis of luck and greed, his manifesto remained a breath of fresh air. He hoped that its major premises would be fulfilled in his relationship with Roosevelt.

He peppered the governor with advice about utility regulation, public power, prison reform, and appointments in the executive and judicial branch. "It was grand to see you both last week," F.D.R.

wrote after the Frankfurters spent a day at the governor's mansion. "You stimulate me enormously. Repeat the dose again."[16] When Roosevelt needed suggestions about whom to select for a commission investigating the state's scandal-ridden Public Service Commission, Frankfurter came up with a list of names that included the most knowledgeable and progressive people in the field.[17] When he sought legal and political guidance on the explosive issue of removing the mayor of New York City from office, Frankfurter provided it. The facts uncovered about Jimmy Walker's debauched regime, he wrote, "ineluctably compel removal," a decision that infuriated Tammany Hall regulars, but boosted F.D.R.'s reputation among liberals and the good government wing of the Democratic Party. "Felix has more ideas per minute than any man of my acquaintance," Roosevelt marveled to an aid. "He has a brilliant mind but it clicks so fast it makes my head fairly spin. I find him tremendously interesting and stimulating."[18]

As the nation's economic woes intensified after the stock market crash and as Roosevelt became the party's front-runner for the 1932 nomination, Frankfurter also sang his praises to others, many of whom seriously doubted the latter's intellectual depth and seriousness of purpose. "Roosevelt is Roosevelt," complained Hand, who had voted for his Republican opponent in 1930. "Men with less ballast have carried more sail, and it is possible he will be President, though he has now so completely identified himself with the Hall that I should doubt it."[19] F.D.R., he added a few years later, seemed to be "vaguely well-meaning, without much capacity or willingness to make himself plain. So far as he does speak it is in the kind of talk that can mean anything or nothing."[20] Walter Lippmann likewise warned old progressives not to be taken in by this "pleasant man who, without any important qualifications for the office, would very much like to be President." Roosevelt, he declared, was "no crusader . . . no tribune of the people . . . no enemy of entrenched privilege."[21]

Frankfurter shared some of these doubts about the patrician from Hyde Park, although he voiced them with less cynicism and contempt than his friends. "I know his limitations," he told Lippman. "Most of them derive, I believe, from lack of an incisive intellect and a kind of optimism that sometimes makes him timid, as well as an ambition that leads to compromises with which we were familiar in Theodore Roosevelt and Wilson."[22] He worried about Roosevelt's "optimistic and naive limitations," but assured Herbert Feis, the State Department's young economic adviser, that "if he gets to the White House he

will exercise a talent for making politics interesting and talking to people about public affairs so that they won't seem like an Oppenheim
mystery tale."[23] Of course, he told Hand, he did not expect "the millennium from Roosevelt," but he suspected that "those 'soft' human
qualities in him which grated on so many people may turn out to be
one of the most important factors for a tolerably successful administration." Besides, he added, the most important quality in a democratic leader "is the capacity to mediate among the feelings and irra-
tionalities of his people," and Roosevelt seemed well equipped in that
respect.[24]

Whatever Roosevelt's defects, moreover, they seemed to grow less
when Frankfurter compared them to those of other contenders: the
once-defeated Smith, who turned increasingly conservative once the
economic crisis began; the incumbent Hoover, unable to cope with
the depression's spreading cancer; or his former boss, Newton D.
Baker, who had begun to resemble John W. Davis in the wealth of his
corporate clients. Frankfurter found it very awkward to break politically with the former governor, who had done so much to stimulate
progressive hopes in the Democratic Party. "My first choice, of
course, is Al," he told Ellery Sedgwick in early 1932, and as late as
October, after Smith had lost the nomination to Roosevelt, he attempted to soothe the former's ego with a reminder that "no one was
ever more ardent than I to have you in the White House."[25] But
Frankfurter, who carefully used the past tense in that letter, had already abandoned the Happy Warrior in the wake of his petulant attacks on Roosevelt and his call for a sales tax to promote national fiscal
solvency. Brandeis, too, thought Smith "lost totally."[26]

Shrewdly, Frankfurter diagnosed Hoover's weakness as a leader in
a time of mounting social confusion and conflict: the Great Engineer,
accustomed to giving orders, could not reconcile differences in the
political arena. "All of Hoover's achievements were at times of war,
famine and flood—where he had unlimited sentiments on his side," he
noted. "That's a very different thing from composing the needs of
contending groups in a democracy."[27] Baker, he noted sadly, had
done little since the end of the war except "to enlist on the side of the
powerful battalions in our society." His liberalism had evaporated and
he resembled "the tired radical" described by Walter Weyl.[28]

Frankfurter blamed the depression upon the greed and folly of the
financial community, the intolerable disparities in wealth and social
power that narrowed consumption and affronted democratic theory,
and the general addiction to money making that had constricted the

vision of a good society. "One does not have to be much of a radical in
the United States to satisfy the desire for greater fairness, for less
arrogant power in the hands of those who have the financial power,"
he told a skeptical Hand. "Why should you be surprised that the sons
of the wild jack-asses think what they think? I wonder at their moderation. If their minds were more penetrating, they would be less moderate." Approvingly, he quoted his friend John Maynard Keynes on
the necessity for "a revolution in our ways of thinking and feeling
about money," and the possibility that "perhaps . . . Russian Communism does represent the first confused stirrings of a great religion."[29]

At the same time, Frankfurter still considered himself to be an
"old-fashioned democrat crowded on the left by the discontented and
on the right by the too comfortable," in a situation where "impatience
and greed and/or snobbery swell the growing enemies of democracy."
Roosevelt, neither a radical, a snob, nor intoxicated with the spirit of
mammon, seemed to him the best candidate. "The general direction,
and not the specific program matters," he concluded, "and on the
basic general direction Frank Roosevelt has for me satisfied tests on
such tell-tale issues as taxation, unemployment and water power
which make me confident of the general direction in which he is going. I know all his limitations, and also value brains and culture. But I
don't see any use for brains and culture if they are not energized . . .
or if their weight is thrown in what seems to me the wrong direction."[30]

❧❧❧

Despite his wit, intelligence, and ardor, Frankfurter faced stiff
competition in the battle for Roosevelt's affections from other advisers
and courtiers, all of whom hoped to shape the direction of the 1932
presidential campaign and to influence the course of the new administration. For day-to-day wisdom, Roosevelt relied heavily upon his
wizened, astute press secretary, Louis M. Howe, the gum-chewing
Jim Farley and his ally, Ed Flynn from the Bronx, plus Samuel Rosenman, a gifted speech writer and legal adviser who, like Frankfurter, had been a devoted Smith partisan in 1928. But these men, basically political tacticians, focused their efforts on garnering votes,
building viable coalitions, and avoiding gaffes. None of them thought
systematically about the broad issues of political economy. For this
task, Rosenman suggested that they turn to the universities where

professors "wouldn't be afraid to strike out on new paths just because the paths are new." The result was the Brains Trust, a triumvirate of Columbia University academicians—Raymond Moley, Adolph A. Berle, Jr., and Rexford Guy Tugwell.[31]

In theory, Frankfurter had urged such an approach upon Roosevelt, but in practice he found it very annoying because these experts did not share his perception of the current crisis and became major rivals for intellectual leadership within the campaign. In addition to their faculty positions at Columbia, Moley, Berle, and Tugwell shared other things in common. They believed deeply in the necessity for increasing the federal government's management of the nation's economy, deplored the ideas of Brandeis and Wilson as nostalgic and unworkable, and two of them—Moley and Berle—had experienced abrasive personal conflicts with Frankfurter in the past. This last ingredient became perhaps the most decisive in fanning protracted guerrilla warfare between Frankfurter and the Brains Trust.

The taciturn, pipe-smoking Moley, a former mayor and superintendent of schools in Olmstead Falls, Ohio, had been a disciple of Tom Johnson and Newton D. Baker during the golden era of urban reform before World War I, taught political science at Western Reserve and Columbia, and earned a reputation as one of the country's leading criminologists because of his role in organizing crime surveys during the 1920s. On the basis of this experience, Roosevelt had tapped him to write a model parole law for New York before he became the unofficial leader of the Brains Trust.

Frankfurter, who had made a major contribution to the Cleveland crime survey, believed that Moley's reputation had been inflated, clashed with him often during the project, and regarded him as an academic entrepreneur who grabbed headlines but remained indifferent to real research. "At every chance Moley tried at once to 'knock' the Cleveland Survey and to claim credit for it as a pioneer job," Frankfurter complained. "I've never known such braying from such a third rater. He is unfit for the society of scholars."[32] Despite this harsh private judgment, he managed nonetheless to develop at least a working relationship with Moley, who enjoyed a close friendship with Roosevelt.

Such was not the case with Berle, the son of a Congregational minister who had graduated from Harvard with honors at the age of seventeen and from the Harvard Law School at twenty-one, "an infant prodigy who has irritated everybody by continuing to be a prodigy after he has ceased to be an infant." Aloof, sharp-tongued, and vain, Berle had worked briefly in Brandeis's law firm, served in military intelligence, taught law at Columbia, and coauthored a powerful book on the structure of the modern business corporation. There was a touch of Frankfurter in Berle that Frankfurter could not abide. They quarreled often in the classroom, Berle failed to bow down at the proper legal shrines, and he soon found himself barred from Frankfurter's inner circle of student favorites. Neither man got over the episode. Berle, according to Frankfurter, "was a boringly humorless creature with too much ego in his cosmos." He also suspected him of being a closet anti-Semite.[33]

Tugwell, with whom Frankfurter had not clashed before 1932, loomed as the most formidable rival of the three, because F.D.R. liked the young economist instantly. Urbane, humorous, with the sleek, chiseled features of a matinee idol, Tugwell had Moley's zest for reform without his ponderousness; he possessed Berle's brains but not his arrogance. And like Frankfurter, he could stimulate Roosevelt's thinking at all hours of the day or night.[34]

At the center of the Columbians' thinking about the Great Depression, its causes, and its cure stood the conundrum of the business corporation as analyzed by Berle and Gardner Means in their 1932 book, *The Modern Corporation and Private Property*. With far less levity but more statistics, Berle and Means focused upon what Thorstein Veblen had emphasized more than a generation earlier: the growing domination of a handful of corporate units over each major sector of the American economy. Immune to the frequent bursts of antitrust activity, this process of mergers and consolidations had sharply narrowed effective price competition, concentrated productive property into fewer and fewer hands, and created a new managerial elite isolated even from the control of stockholders. The nation's economic system had been brought to the threshold of private socialism, where the 200 largest firms controlled nearly one-half of all the corporate wealth.[35]

Big business worked technological miracles, reduced production costs, eliminated wasteful competition, and distributed an unprecedented quantity of material goods to the society. At the same time, it choked innovation, gouged consumers, and through a short-sighted wage policy contributed to the maldistribution of national income that triggered the economic collapse. In the interests of abundance, the members of the Brains Trust believed, giant enterprise seemed inevitable. In the interests of social peace and justice, they added, these behemoth organizations would have to be brought under centralized direction by public authorities in Washington. "Now the concentration has progressed so far," Berle told Brandeis, "that it seems unlikely to break up even in a period of stress. I can see nothing at the moment but to take this trend as it stands endeavoring to mold it so as to be useful."[36]

Moley, although somewhat more sensitive than Berle to the plight of small farmers, workers, and the nation's "forgotten man," nonetheless shared the latter's conviction that the era of business competition had ended and could not be restored. The task of Roosevelt's New Deal should be to direct the consolidated economic machine toward public ends. "We are no longer afraid of bigness," echoed Tugwell. "We are resolved to recognize openly that competition in most of its forms is wasteful and costly; that larger combinations must in any modern society prevail. . . . Unrestricted individual competition is the death, not the life of trade."[37]

These ideas reverberated throughout Roosevelt's campaign for the nomination and the presidency. Speaking at a Jefferson Day dinner in St. Paul on April 18 with a text crafted largely by Moley, he urged the creation of a "national community of interest" to fight the depression through "a large measure of cooperation . . . and what is most important, a more imaginative and purposeful planning." Although rejecting what he called "an economic life completely planned and regimented," F.D.R. declared his support for "economic planning, not for this period alone but for our needs for a long time to come."[38] A month later at Oglethorpe University, he deplored the haphazardness, waste, and "the thousands of dead-end trails" that scarred the nation's industrial development and that could have been prevented "by a larger measure of social planning." Only the national government, he suggested, could see to it that such control did not fall into the hands of "that small group of men whose chief outlook upon social welfare is tinctured by the fact . . . they can make huge profits from the lending of money and the marketing of securities."[39]

Neither the St. Paul nor the Ogelthorpe speech represented a wholehearted acceptance on Roosevelt's part of the Brains Trust's central gospel: the inevitability of giant enterprise and the desirability of centralized planning by the federal government. His calls for "more imaginative and purposeful planning" and "a larger measure of social planning" came in speeches that covered many other issues, including tariff reductions, the repeal of Prohibition, and the necessity for restoring purchasing power to farmers and industrial workers. The only concrete example of "more imaginative and purposeful planning" that

he offered in either speech focused upon government promotion of
electric power, hardly a startling suggestion.

The rhetoric of planning remained conspicuously absent from his
acceptance speech to the party in Chicago, and at the end of July he
argued that "the chief causes" of the nation's economic prostration
arose from Republican policies that had fostered "the merger of competitive business into monopolies." He pledged vigorous enforcement
of the antitrust laws, lower tariffs, currency stabilization, and a ban
on holding companies, and the use of commercial bank credit for speculative purposes. In short, Roosevelt offered a grab bag of proposals
that attempted to appeal to all of the diverse groups within the Democratic Party and the nation. "We would throw out pieces of theory,"
Tugwell recalled, "and perhaps they would find a place in his scheme.
. . . But the tapestry of the policy he was weaving was guided by an
artist's conception which was not made known to us."[40]

Despite the fuzziness of F.D.R.'s commitment to something called
economic planning, Frankfurter took alarm at the influence of the
Brains Trust, especially to the suggestion that big business was inevitable and that the nation's affairs could be efficiently managed by a
cadre of experts in Washington. In the ideas of Moley, Berle, and
Tugwell he sensed a faint odor of the benevolent despotism that per-
meated European fascism. Whether in business or government, he
told Lippmann, concentrated power usually brought disaster "because of the obfuscations and the arrogances which power almost in-
variably generates." He used as an example the defalcations and
abuses of New York bankers such as Charles Mitchell and Albert
Wiggin. "The crux of the business is not the wickedness of the Mitch-
ells but the power which is wielded by concentrated financial power,"
he noted. "Again I say the Lord hasn't created anybody competent to
rule wisely the kind of a thing the Chase bank was. . . . Brandeis saw
it all with a seer's discernment more than twenty years ago and everything that he prophesied since has been vindicated with an almost
tragic uncanniness."[41] Power, he believed, had to be dispersed, both
in the private and in the public sector.

Brandeis, who had become even more dedicated to the war against
bigness in American life, shared these sentiments. The present tendency "towards centralization must be arrested," he told his brother
before the stock market crash, "if we are to attain the American ideal,"
and the economic collapse only reinforced his desire for a rebirth of
localism, competition, and decentralized authority.[42] In the interests

of preserving small enterprises, he even sanctioned limitations upon cut-throat competition and graduated taxation that discouraged the spread of chain stores.[43] Nor did he look upon Washington, D.C., as the nation's savior. "I would rather have counterparts of Jim Curley as governors of several states," he told a shocked visitor, "than one heavily centralized national government under Harding."[44]

In a conversation with his former law clerk, Harry Shulman, the substance of which he repeated often to others during the 1930s, Brandeis outlined his program for economic recovery "to make men free" through the application of governmental restraints upon private economic power. First, he proposed to limit the power of bankers by expanding the postal savings system to include checking accounts and the underwriting of corporate securities. By means of heavy taxation, the private banking business should be broken up into commercial, savings, and investment units in order to "avoid the evils of great concentrations of financial power." Steep federal inheritance taxes should likewise limit the amount of property any person could acquire and pass down upon death to one million dollars, "although that may be too high," and excise taxes should also restrict the absolute size of corporations. "The federal government," he warned Shulman, "must not become too big just as corporations should not be permitted to become too big. You must remember that it is the littleness of man that limits the size of things we can undertake. Too much bigness may break the federal government as it has broken business." Finally, he endorsed a system of unemployment compensation that focused responsibility upon individual firms to guarantee regularity of employment and the maintenance of purchasing power.[45]

When Shulman suggested that critics would attack his proposals as an attempt to turn back the clock, Brandeis didn't flinch: why, he asked, shouldn't we turn the clock back in light of the failed policies of the present? Hadn't people repudiated other misguided programs, including Prohibition? "We must determine what it is desirable to do," he concluded, "and then we can find ways and means to do it." His depression remedies contained only one exception to the radical assault upon bigness and centralization. He urged the creation of a substantial federal public works program, financed initially through borrowing and later by means of heavy taxation upon the rich, as the most effective way to achieve full employment and create projects of lasting social importance in the areas of conservation, flood control, irrigation, electric power, and education. "We should avail [ourselves] of the present emergency," he told his daughter, "to get those public works which Americans would lack the insight and persistence to get for themselves in ordinary times."[46]

Frankfurter revered Brandeis as a substitute father, moral preceptor, and financial benefactor, but despite Laski's complaint that "Felix is clay in his hands," the younger man did not become simply a carbon copy of the justice. He did not share Brandeis's implacable hostility to bigness, for example, but he did endorse the latter's views on taxation and public works and remained deeply skeptical about the concentration of power in both corporate and governmental hands. He felt more comfortable with Brandeis's ideals than with those articulated by the Brains Trust. "Neither you nor I are doctrinaires either about the curse of bigness or the blessings of littleness," he confided to Moley. "Like most things that matter in this world, it's a question of more or less, of degree, of when is big too big, and when is little too little. In any event, what we most need is luminous and authentic experience."[47] On the other hand, he told William O. Douglas, who was then a Yale professor, that his thinking had changed a great deal since the days of the Bull Moose crusade. "I was a hot Hamiltonian when I went to Washington in 1911," he confessed, "but the years in the government service and all the rest of the years watching its operations intently have made me less jaunty about devices for running the whole continent from Washington." Powerful economic interests could more easily dominate a single regulatory institution, he warned, and progressives should be cautious about putting "all our eggs in one basket."[48]

Frankfurter began his counterattack against the Brains Trust in the summer of 1932. First, he turned down Governor Joseph Ely's surprise nomination to the Supreme Judicial Court of Massachusetts, with the observation that he owed a larger obligation to legal education and to the training of a more enlightened bar and judiciary. This decision was not wholly self-effacing or disinterested. By rejecting Ely, an ally of Al Smith who had made a series of bitter attacks on Roosevelt, he signaled loyalty to F.D.R. and a willingness to play a larger role in the campaign. He also avoided a bruising political struggle in Massachusetts, where former Governor Fuller vowed that he would sooner cut off his arm than see Frankfurter appointed. "With Ely pardoning murders and Frankfurter an open sympathizer with murders on the supreme bench," he remarked, "I see no reason why murder should not flourish in Massachusetts."[49] Frankfurter gave many reasons for declining the appointment, Berle told David Lilienthal, "but the real reason, I think, was that nasty opposition developed. I am sorry that he did not fight it out."[50]

Following the Democratic convention, Frankfurter met with Roosevelt, talked with him far into the night "as tho he might be one of my students," and laid out the entire Brandeis-Frankfurter plan for economic recovery and reform, including heavy spending for public works and drastic taxation to curb corporate bigness. In addition, he told Roosevelt that he needed someone "critical, skeptical, informed . . . at his side . . . one also with real knowledge of Washington . . . financial sense, shrewdness and caution . . . to supplement Moley, Tugwell and Berle." For this crucial position he recommended his old friend, Max Lowenthal, a strong ally of organized labor, then completing a trenchant analysis of the financial abuses connected with railroad receiverships. F.D.R. agreed that Lowenthal should attend the next session of the Brains Trust as Frankfurter's representative.[51]

The attempt at collaboration failed miserably. When Lowenthal walked into the next meeting of the Brains Trust, Moley and the others objected to his presence and a bitter argument erupted over the contents of a speech dealing with currency inflation. When Lowenthal criticized the material, written by Bernard Baruch's crony, General Hugh Johnson, Berle told him to shut up. "My impression was that his real motive was something else," Berle confided to a memorandum. "Either he was anxious for inflation (reflecting the views of the Amalgamated Clothing Workers' Union or some similar group), or he had been in touch with some of the Jewish financiers." Lowenthal, he added, was "the typical 'liberal on the make,' with some sincerity, some good ideas, considerably ability, and no loyalty — except to F.F. and the particular little group that revolves around him."[52] Berle then fired off an angry note to Frankfurter advising him to control his representative, which produced an explosion in Cambridge. "I am troubled that the judgment of a man so wise, . . . as is Lowenthal," he shot back, "should be deemed irrelevant simply because the issue had been previously discussed by your group."[53]

Within a few weeks, however, Roosevelt raised Frankfurter's hopes with a wide-ranging attack on economic concentration. At Columbus, Ohio, he blasted Hoover's programs and then declared: "I, too, believe in individualism. . . . I believe that our industrial and economic system is made for individual men and women, and not individual men and women for the benefit of the system. . . . We must go back to first principles; we must make American individualism what it was intended to be — equality of opportunity for all, the right of ex-

ploitation for none."[54] At the Commonwealth Club in San Francisco a
month later, he chided Theodore Roosevelt and the Supreme Court
for believing that concentrated industrial power was permissible as
long as the methods used to accumulate it had been reasonable. "Woodrow Wilson," he said, "saw the situation more clearly. . . . He saw,
in the highly centralized economic system, the despot of the twentieth
century," whose "irresponsibility and greed" threatened to reduce the
great mass of citizens to starvation and penury.[55]

Roosevelt's new rhetoric horrified members of the Brains Trust.
Tugwell referred to it as "the Columbus retreat," the "result of Brandeis's demands—his first show of force. . . . Collectivism was no
longer mentioned; Ogelthorpe was forgotten, and we were being
pushed aside."[56] He blamed "one old man in the shadows to whom the
awe and reverence of sonship went without reserve. This, of course,
was Brandeis. And Frankfurter was his prophet."[57] Berle complained
that "the Frankfurter group proposed to depend on ultra free markets
and a return to a small-scale production," both of which he looked
upon as anachronistic. He marveled at Frankfurter's influence and
expressed "an intense personal desire to see him shot."[58]

In the heat of their struggle to influence Roosevelt's thinking about
recovery and to secure places near the throne of power, both groups
tended to exaggerate the machinations of the other. Frankfurter and
Brandeis saw in impressionable Roosevelt, seduced by an all-powerful
Brains Trust devoted to fascist-style economic planning. Tugwell,
Berle, and Moley saw an equally pliant Roosevelt, led astray by the
cunning arguments of those who hoped to wage an "Indian war"
against the bankers and return America to the days of the horse and
buggy. But Roosevelt, a crafty politician, refused to become the cap-
tive of a single intellectual or political interest. As Frankfurter had
observed, F.D.R. knew how "to mediate among the feelings and irra-
tionalities of his people," whether they happened to be Southern
bourbons, Columbia economists, or Harvard lawyers.

In his Commonwealth Club address that praised Wilson, denounced economic giantism, and sang the praises of individualism, for
example, Roosevelt also pointed out that the country could not "turn
the clock back" on economic progress. He defeated Hoover with campaign promises that included the demand for a balanced federal budget, but also pledged sufficient appropriations to prevent "starvation
and dire need on the part of any of our citizens." One might expect
just about anything from such a president-elect and not surprisingly,
the battle to shape the New Deal began long before the inauguration.

Between the election and the inauguration, Frankfurter also came under fire from the Brains Trust for helping to arrange a series of meetings between F.D.R. and Hoover's outgoing secretary of state, Henry Stimson. Moley and Tugwell looked upon these contacts as part of a sinister conspiracy to weaken Roosevelt's resolve to pursue a program of economic nationalism in combating the depression and to tie the hands of the new administration before it had taken office. There can be little doubt that such ideas crossed the minds of Hoover and Stimson, both of whom expressed alarm over Roosevelt's wavering monetary beliefs, but Frankfurter did not share them. He had no interest in limiting Roosevelt's flexibility after March 4, but he remained far more sensitive than either Moley or Tugwell to the disintegration of Europe's economic and political order and its relationship to the United States. He hoped to sharpen F.D.R.'s perception of these relationships at a time when others attempted to deny or to obfuscate them.

The stock market panic and the ensuing liquidity crisis that choked off the flow of credit from American banks exposed the grotesque contradictions of America's postwar policies with respect to Europe and the rest of the world. On the one hand, the nation's major banks, flush with cash as a result of war-induced prosperity, followed a program of unabashed internationalism after 1918 by extending lavish short-term credits and long-term loans to the Europeans for the purposes of currency stabilization, economic recovery, and trade. American credit permitted Germany to pay the crushing reparations imposed by the Allies in the Versailles Treaty while stripped of her prime industrial facilities and merchant fleet but without reducing her own population to destitution. On the other hand, most American industrialists and politicians pursued a fiercely nationalistic program that insisted on the repayment of all war debts owed by the Allies to the United States government, raised tariff barriers to the point where the Europeans could not earn enough dollars to pay their bills, and rejected participation in any international organizations that might have moderated the ensuing chaos.

The official American attitude with respect to German reparations and Allied war debts symbolized this schizophrenic program. Reparations, according to every administration from Harding to Hoover, remained exclusively a European problem in which the Unites States had no interest since it did not receive them and had not ratified the

Versailles Treaty. How the Allies behaved toward Germany remained their business, not America's. Allied debts, on the contrary, were an American problem to be handled on a nation-by-nation basis, with each debtor paying its solemn obligations to Washington. Until the Wall Street crash and a worldwide credit squeeze made it painfully obvious, most American leaders ignored the fact that reparations, war debts, and trade had become intimately related and that the health of the Atlantic economy depended upon their wise management by the United States.

Economically, the United States had become deeply involved in Europe's destiny. Emotionally, morally, and diplomatically, she attempted to remain in splendid isolation. This contradiction, Frankfurter believed, the country had to face and resolve sooner or later. "We cannot keep out," he told Feis, "but we are going to keep free by letting the other side create situations for us which will inevitably demand action from us but under circumstances which impair our freedom because they have been allowed to create situations in which we have not had the say we should have had."[59] In the next ten years, no American offered a better summary of the terrible dilemma.

Cautiously, the Hoover administration attempted to face it before leaving office. In the summer of 1931, confronted with massive bank failures in Central Europe and spreading unemployment everywhere, Hoover called for a one-year moratorium on all intergovernmental debts. Meeting with French Premier Pierre Laval in October, the president also hinted broadly that if the Allies took the initiative with respect to a reduction in German reparations, the United States might scale down the war debts owed by England, France, and the others. These initiatives led ultimately to the Lausanne Conference of 1932, where the Allies offered such a package, but in the meantime Hoover refused to support openly any revision of war debts because he feared a backlash in the election. Although Congress approved the one-year moratorium, it overwhelmingly rejected any attempt to cancel or scale down the obligations. "The behavior of Congress . . . is precisely what was to be expected," Frankfurter lectured Feis, "in view of the total lack of education by the President of the 'folks back at home' and their representatives. . . . Having for years done everything to inculcate wrong views . . . the President should be the last person to be surprised at the present temper of Congress and public opinion generally."[60]

As Frankfurter feared, the moratorium and other short-term palliatives failed to stop Europe's slide into economic and political disaster. Driven by fear of extreme parties on the Right, sensing division among its old enemies, and buffeted by soaring unemployment, even conservative Weimar governments demanded the cancellation of all reparations. In France, governments fell like dominoes at the slightest hint of such concessions, unless linked to lower war debts and strong security guarantees from the Americans, neither of which came. England, eager to compromise with German moderates but also anxious to save her own economic skin, abandoned the gold standard and waged a trade war against her rivals through exchange restrictions, imperial quotas, and import prohibitions. By the bleak winter of 1932, extreme economic nationalism and militarism had become almost epidemic, symbolized by the crumbling Geneva disarmament talks, Japan's subjugation of Manchuria, the Ottawa agreements, the Hawley-Smoot tariff, and the long shadow cast by Adolph Hitler across the future of Germany.

"You have no greater duty," Frankfurter advised Feis, "than to put on record again and again . . . what the European situation means for our national economy, so that at least your superiors will not be without sober warning of what is ahead." He wondered how successful any "merely local national economic program" could be in the face of these rising national tensions and he urged Feis to advocate some bold diplomatic initiative, such as Robert Cecil's call for a 25 percent reduction in the armaments budgets of all the major powers. "If that were done," he predicted, "the whole reparation-debts problem would be at a different posture and the almost inevitable default soon to be declared . . . would receive a very different response."[61]

Hoover thought along similar lines. He made a sweeping disarmament proposal to the Geneva delegates during the 1932 campaign that focused upon a one-third cut in all armies, but the British and the French rejected it. Once these two countries announced their intention to default on war debts, however, and once the election had been lost, Hoover pursued the broader objectives first suggested to Laval. He proposed to achieve diplomatic immortality by shaping a comprehensive economic settlement that would resolve all outstanding issues—reparations, war debts, trade restrictions, and current stabilization—through the use of America's waning financial and political leverage. Frankfurter believed in this broad strategy. Unfortunately, Hoover's noble intentions came too late. In addition, they remained flawed by a naïve interpretation of the depression's causes, and by an awkward attempt to control the conduct of his successor.

Apart from the need to curb the occasional excesses of Wall Street speculators, Hoover believed in the soundness of the American economic order and the danger of drastic reforms. He placed the blame for the depression upon external economic dislocations: the draconian Versailles Treaty, Europe's profligacy, wasteful military spending, nationalistic trade barriers, and the abandonment of the gold standard by England and others. If these deformities could be corrected, he believed, and if Roosevelt could be induced to support his remedies for achieving international stability, the depression would end and America would be spared the uncertainties of the New Deal.

Guided initially by the Brains Trust and his own instinct for caution, Roosevelt refused to be trapped into a program of joint endeavors. He told Hoover on November 14 that the questions posed by the pending British and French defaults created "a responsibility which rests upon those now vested with executive and legislative authority." In a chilly meeting a week later with Hoover and his key advisers, F.D.R. and Moley turned down a plan that called for the president and the president-elect to cooperate in the appointment of a war debts commission to examine the existing obligations and to make recommendations about necessary revisions. Hoover saw the commission as the only way to diffuse congressional opposition to a reduction in war debts. If the United States made concessions, he believed, a quid pro quo might be secured from the Europeans on other issues, including freer trade and England's return to the gold standard.[62]

Roosevelt and Moley believed, on the contrary, that a war debts commission would inflame Congress and distract legislative energies from new domestic programs. It was much easier to exploit the nationalistic passions that treated the war debts as sacred obligations and the Europeans as ungrateful welshers. Roosevelt suspected as well that Hoover and his financial advisers hoped to thwart any efforts that the new administration might find necessary to devalue the American dollar in the interests of expanding trade and helping domestic recovery. F.D.R. insisted upon a statement that reaffirmed the nation's commitment to collect all its debts, rejected any collective resettlement, and affirmed the appropriateness of existing diplomatic channels for the resolution of all questions relating to this issue. In brief, he joined the nationalistic parade with a vengeance. "The positions taken," Moley wrote later, "made it clear that by keeping the debts as living obligations we were serving notice that European nations were not to count upon the United States as a potential war treasury in case the old hatreds and rivalries reappeared. . . . This was also warning that the foreign policy of the New Deal would not ally us with France and Britain as policemen of the world."[63]

The Roosevelt-Hoover impasse presented Frankfurter with a major dilemma. He rejected Hoover's interpretation of the depression totally and desired a major overhaul of the nation's economic system, including tax reforms, curbs on corporate bigness, and a more equitable distribution of income. He appreciated as well the political limitations under which Roosevelt operated with respect to Congress and the war debts issue. On the other hand, he feared Europe's drift toward the extreme Right and agreed with Stimson on the desirability of canceling all the "damn debts" that hung like an albatross around the neck of the Atlantic economy.

Ironically, this extreme position put him at odds with both Roosevelt and Hoover, but on the side of the great New York bankers, who believed that the tangled web of intergovernmental debts burdened their private credit remittances from Europe. Frankfurter cared little about Wall Street's ledgers, but he looked upon a constructive debt settlement as the linchpin of improved Anglo-American relations in a world that was lurching toward fascism, anti-Semitism, and war. The debts would have to be erased, he told Stimson on December 9, because of their "larger implication for a cooperative spirit between Great Britain and ourselves." But he refused to criticize Roosevelt's position on this issue, although it was more extreme than Hoover's. He told the president-elect that his handling of the negotiations with Hoover over the debts question had been "more than well adopted to the immediate situation" because it avoided a "sterile deadlock between the President and Congress," yet retained the possibility of future initiatives by the next chief executive. Behind the scenes, however, Frankfurter labored to narrow the gap between his own desires and Roosevelt's by bringing the latter into contact with Stimson.

After reviewing the entire situation with Feis in Cambridge, Frankfurter went to see Roosevelt in Albany near the end of December. He tried during this conversation to impress F.D.R. with the idea that Stimson "is a very different fellow from Hoover," suggesting that the secretary of state would not attempt to snare him into an awkward compromise that might jeopardize the New Deal. The suggestion worked. "Why doesn't Harry Stimson come up here and talk with me and settle this damn thing that nobody else seems to be able to do," Roosevelt asked. Frankfurter drafted the invitation.[64]

Much to the chagrin of Hoover and the Brains Trust, Roosevelt and Stimson met for nearly six hours at Hyde Park in early January. The president thought it foolish for his secretary of state to meet with this "very dangerous and contrary man," while Moley, Tugwell, and Berle feared Stimson's influence upon their boss and cursed Frankfurter. "I told him [F.D.R.] to remember that Stimson is rather slow-minded, methodical, single-trackminded like Wilson and not quick and darting as he is," Frankfurter wrote, "and that he will therefore have to give Stimson ample time to let him lay out all that is in his mind. He said he would."[65]

The two men discussed war debts, reparations, monetary policy, trade, and disarmament, but the only area of clear agreement seemed to be on Manchuria, where the president-elect endorsed Stimson's tough line with respect to Japan's economic and territorial ambitions. Even this limited agreement dismayed the Brains Trust, who also feared F.D.R.'s decision to meet once more with Hoover and Stimson in Washington before the inauguration. "What I feared then," Moley recalled, "was that Roosevelt, confronted by the skillful designs of Stimson, had abandoned the positions he had taken in November and December and had agreed to policies that would endanger his entire domestic program."[66]

In their panic, the Brains Trusters linked Frankfurter with an entire Hoover-Stimson strategy to forge a comprehensive foreign economic settlement and to frustrate the radical domestic experiments that might come after March 4. But no such grand design existed. Hoover and Stimson did not agree about debts, although both feared that Roosevelt might tamper with the currency unless he were tied down by strong international accords. Frankfurter, on the contrary, had no desire to limit F.D.R.'s innovations with respect to the currency or any other domestic program, but he did believe in the necessity for debt adjustment as a prelude to better relations with Great Britain. He shared only one of Stimson's motives and was not fully aware of the secretary's other intentions. He agreed with Stimson on the narrow issue of debt cancellation, but he certainly did not partake of the latter's anxiety about Roosevelt's anticipated reforms. Nonetheless, Moley and others believed that Frankfurter had become a key participant in an internationalists' plot to subvert the New Deal.

The members of the Brains Trust also believed that Frankfurter worked on behalf of Norman Davis's campaign to become the new secretary of state. This silver-haired veteran of the diplomatic establishment was intimately connected to the barons of Wall Street and had been serving as Hoover's representative at the faltering disarmament talks. In addition, he had become a major figure in efforts to organize the World Monetary and Economic Conference along the broadest possible lines that would focus simultaneously upon debts, tariffs, currency stabilization, and disarmament. Davis, for instance, urged Roosevelt to make a European trip after the election, and Moley talked darkly about "the Stimson-Davis-Frankfurter approach" to foreign affairs.[67] In fact, Frankfurter had been one of the strongest voices opposed to the foreign journey and he believed that Davis's conservative economic views disqualified him for any cabinet position. A "Stimson-Davis-Frankfurter approach" to foreign policy existed only in Moley's imagination.[68]

Despite Moley's worst nightmares and Stimson's best efforts, little came of the final Roosevelt-Hoover conversations on January 20. Even as to the British, F.D.R. rejected the concept of a unified conference dealing with war debts, currency stabilization, and trade. Each issue, he believed, could be dealt with seriatim through normal diplomatic channels. He did not oppose the forthcoming World Economic Conference, but he did not want war debts on the agenda. He neatly avoided the Hoover-Stimson trap of trading American concessions on war debts for England's promised return to the gold standard. He cared little about the gold standard or currency stabilization—a position that horrified Hoover and Stimson, who believed them to be a prerequisite for economic recovery.[69]

On the eve of the New Deal, Frankfurter had forged an intimate relationship with the most astute and enigmatic politician of his generation. But he had been unable to find a middle ground between two men he greatly admired: the president-elect, dedicated simultaneously to domestic reforms and the old clichés about war debts, and a retiring secretary of state, who had abandoned war debts but hoped to prevent too much domestic reform. Despite the Republican Party's newly found passion for international cooperation, Frankfurter discovered that the forces of autarky and chauvinism had become almost irreversible. That grim fact filled him with terrible foreboding about the fate of the world. Roosevelt's inauguration filled him with hope at least for America.

CHAPTER 12

NEW
DEALER

FRANKLIN ROOSEVELT ATTRACTED dozens of able and controversial people to his new administration—Tugwell, Moley, Ickes, Perkins, Hopkins, Wallace, Morgenthau, and Richberg. A few of them he armed with real power for a decade or more. Others savored it briefly. Around them all, however, there soon grew a dense thicket of political gossip, inuendo, and legend from which later scholars wove a history of the New Deal, that sometimes baffling collection of statutes, administrative decisions, and clashing personalities that profoundly changed the course of American life. Although he never held an official position in the government, Frankfurter sparked more debate than some cabinet officers, White House assistants, and congressional leaders. "People either loved or hated Felix," recalled William O. Douglas, another fiery New Dealer. He was "brilliant and able, friendly yet divisive."[1]

In a regime bubbling with political intrigue and sprinkled liberally with Machiavellian figures, Frankfurter ranked high on everyone's list of those who influenced Roosevelt, shaped policies, and pulled bureaucratic wires. General Hugh Johnson, the first head of the National Recovery Administration, declared flatly that he was "the most influential single individual in the United States." Some newspapers compared him with Iago, while others invoked the careers of Cardinal Richelieu or Rasputin for purposes of comparison. Moley called him the "patriarchal sorcerer" who cast dark spells of magic over the administration's young lawyers. "Felix more than any other person," wrote the journalist John Franklin Carter, "is the legal master-mind of the New Deal." He earned a special place in the demonology of the Right, where Westbrook Pegler denounced "the New Deal philosophy, which itself was derived from . . . Frankfurter, through his contamination of mischievous cub lawyers who, in turn, have polluted the thought of the government." Inside the administration, other Roosevelt advisers bemoaned "the Frankfurter group which is extremely powerful because it satisfies the President's desire for some personal villains," and even his Cambridge colleague, Calvert Magruder, spoke of Frankfurter's "Oriental guile" in managing Washington appointments.[2]

Against this portrait of almost superhuman influence and cunning can be placed Frankfurter's own description of his modest role during the New Deal. Although admitting to a special relationship with F.D.R. "of the utmost intimacy," he also claimed never to have made a suggestion or proposed an appointment without an invitation from the president first. "I've probably recommended more lawyers for Cravath and Henderson," he quipped, "than I have for any department of the government."[3] On the other hand, he told John Burns, a young law school graduate, that "I should be less than fair if I did not add my word about former students . . . when I know that they are otherwise under consideration," and in the case of his favorite student, Tommy Corcoran, he even confessed to making an exception to the rule of not "pestering the President about appointments."[4]

In truth, Frankfurter had far greater influence than he recalled in later life, but also somewhat less than he often desired or his enemies imagined. More than a casual visitor to the White House, he nonetheless exercised less sway over Roosevelt's day-to-day thinking than Morgenthau, Hopkins, Rosenman, and several others, largely because he refused to leave Harvard in 1933 and join the administration on a full-time basis.

The New Deal's conservative critics mistakenly lumped him with Tugwell as one of the administration's radicals who wished to impose a Soviet-style regime of centralized economic planning upon the country. Even as to Tugwell, who relished the concept of national planning, this was a wild exaggeration, but in the case of Frankfurter it bore absolutely no relationship to the truth. "Felix, a radical?" scoffed Thomas Reed Powell at a Cambridge cocktail party. "Hell! The damn fool is wearing out his heart trying to make capitalism live up to its pretensions."[5] As late as 1938, Berle complained that Frankfurter and his allies "propose recreating . . . in some fashion . . . thoroughly competitive machinery," a strategy that filled him with alarm, because in his opinion the nation needed "some very thorough-going overhauling of the economic system."[6] Frankfurter also believed in the necessity of restructuring the economic system, but not along the lines proposed by the Brains Trust or adopted by Roosevelt during the early years of the New Deal. Nor did he experience dazzling success initially in filling key administrative posts with people who shared his ideas.

Frankfurter's antidepression program drew heavily upon the prescriptions of Brandeis and Keynes. It emphasized a drastic attack upon financial and corporate bigness through progressive taxation and a huge expenditure of public funds to employ idle workers and resources, especially for conservation. In addition, he believed that the new administration would need to recruit the best legal talent available in order to defend its efforts in the nation's courts, the last bastion of institutionalized Republicanism following the party's crushing defeats in 1930 and 1932. F.D.R.'s initial programs bore little resemblance to the ones advocated by Brandeis, Keynes, or Frankfurter.

He undermined his own influence by declining Roosevelt's invitation to become solicitor general, a post crucial to shaping the administration's overall legal strategy and one where he could have been assured of large influence in the selection of other lawyers. In view of the importance that he placed on the government's need for able counsel and the dismal fate that soon befell the solicitor general's office, this refusal was indeed perverse. But Frankfurter balked at being limited to one bureaucratic task where his energies would be absorbed in the minutae of litigation. In addition, he had his heart set on becoming the Visiting Eastman Professor at Oxford in 1933.

In the end, his Anglophilia and intellectual interests triumphed over his political ambitions, despite Roosevelt's hint that it would be much easier to put a solicitor general on the Supreme Court than a Harvard professor. To do the task well, he told Roosevelt, required at least a sixteen-hour day, and "I could not have anything to do on any of the matters on which you would want my help and do my job as Solicitor General—it just can't be done."[7] A discerning critic of the

Supreme Court, Frankfurter also knew that the next solicitor general, whoever he might be, could expect a difficult time before that tribunal—especially if called upon to defend controversial legislation. Roosevelt's first choice for attorney general, Senator Thomas J. Walsh, had been cool to Frankfurter's appointment because he did not "want somebody in there who will lose cases in the grand manner." But even with the enthusiastic support of Homer Cummings, the eventual attorney general, Frankfurter could not have relished the idea of facing Justices Sutherland, Van Devanter, Butler, and McReynolds on a regular basis. The fact that Brandeis ridiculed the appointment as "absurd" probably clinched Frankfurter's decision, even in the face of Roosevelt's irritation that he had acted like "an independent prig" in spurning the job.[8]

Frankfurter had only himself to blame, therefore, when the solicitor general's office and the Justice Department fell into the hands of patronage mongers and second-rate lawyers. Cummings, a former Connecticut prosecutor and loyal party drayhorse, filled positions with more advice from Jim Farley than from the Harvard Law School. James Crawford Biggs, an affable country lawyer from North Carolina, became solicitor general and earned the distinction of losing ten out of seventeen cases during his first five months in office. Harold Stephens, whom Frankfurter dismissed contemptuously as "a C man," became Cummings's chief assistant. They assured Frankfurter of their complete confidence in his recommendations, but ignored most of them. The attorney general, complained Harold Ickes, had "apparently delivered himself into the hands of the place hunters," and "hardly anyone has any respect for the standing and ability of the lawyers over there."[9]

After turning down the solicitor general's position himself, Frankfurter worked tirelessly to secure the post for one of his favorite pupils and a former Brandeis clerk, Dean Acheson, but Cummings expressed "immediate, violent, and adverse" opinions about this fastidious young man, whose father, the Episcopal Bishop of Connecticut, had taken a dim view of the attorney general's multiple marriages.[10] Cummings also vetoed William A. Sutherland, another Frankfurter protégé and Brandeis clerk, who had built a thriving law practice in Atlanta and earned a distinguished reputation as a tax expert. Sutherland "would not meet the situation at all," Cummings told F.D.R. with some annoyance, "and it is rather too bad that this is so because, within certain limits, he is a man of very excellent attainments."

David Lilienthal, who quickly recruited Sutherland for the new legal division of the Tennessee Valley Authority, proved to be a more sagacious judge of legal abilities.[11]

Frankfurter did prevail upon Cummings and Stephens to retain two Hoover appointees, both his former students, Erwin N. Griswold and Paul D. Miller, but these lower-level additions in the solicitor's office did not improve its negative image. By the middle of the New Deal's first summer, both Justices Brandeis and Stone protested vehemently about the low quality of the administration's performance before the Supreme Court. Ickes lamented that Stephens, the "C man," had the reputation among Department of the Interior attorneys as "the best man in the whole [Justice] Department," a tribute that "makes me sick when I think of the way [he] handled our . . . case . . . last week."[12]

In view of the importance that he and Brandeis placed upon a bold fiscal policy and sweeping tax reforms to combat bigness, the Department of the Treasury assumed even greater importance than Justice, but Frankfurter's influence in the former became almost nil once Roosevelt named his Hyde Park neighbor, Henry Morgenthau, Jr., to the post vacated by the ailing William Woodin. The latter, who had once been a member of J.P. Morgan's "preferred list," was certainly not a fiscal or monetary heretic, but Frankfurter had enjoyed cordial relations with him. Woodin hired two of Frankfurter's smartest "boys," Acheson and Corcoran. Frankfurter's relations were anything but cordial with Woodin's replacement, who enjoyed intimate friendship with the president and, from Frankfurter's perspective at least, labored under the additional handicap of being the son of an old nemesis. "The Treasury I can do nothing with," he confessed to Brandeis, "H.M., Jr. is H.M., Sr."[13]

Frankfurter did the younger Morgenthau a considerable injustice. Although he shared his father's tepid enthusiasm for Zionism, Morgenthau remained more progressive than the latter on social and economic issues—especially in the area of taxation—and Frankfurter would be pleasantly surprised by this fact after 1935. In the early years of the New Deal, however, he found it almost impossible to cultivate a man he dismissed as "a disgrace," "a stupid bootlick," and a person anxious "not to be tarred by my stock and more generally not to be declared one of the 'liberal' Jews." Frankfurter objected above all to Morgenthau's cavalier attitude about wiretapping by Treasury agents.[14]

To compound their antagonisms, Frankfurter had a very low opinion of most of Morgenthau's assistants, especially the able general counsel, Herman Oliphant, a former Columbia professor with whom he had crossed swords during the legislative struggle over the Norris-La Guardia Anti-Injunction Act. He dismissed the department's chief tax expert, Roswell Magill, another Columbian, as "a bland, pleasant fellow, who will offend no one . . . a conventional, conservative mind."[15] And he wholly distrusted Morgenthau's two monetary advisers—James Harvey Rogers and George Warren—both of whom believed in currency devaluation as the key to economic recovery, an idea that Frankfurter considered puerile and diversionary.[16]

What little influence Frankfurter had in the treasury department vanished completely in the winter of 1933, when the Morgenthau forces ousted both Acheson and Corcoran. Acheson, who regarded Roosevelt as "a political trimmer, a skimper of problems, and an arrogant bully," resigned rather than implement the administration's gold purchase-devaluation scheme. Corcoran, a garrulous, ambitious, and somewhat ruthless Irishman, who had clerked for Holmes and functioned as staff sergeant in the Brandeis-Frankfurter guerrilla army, left with Acheson and returned to the Reconstruction Finance Corporation—a victim, according to Frankfurter, of Oliphant's jealousy and Morgenthau's suspicions. The "very small-minded people," he complained to Brandeis, "want everybody of Dean's crowd out."[17]

Corcoran's transfer back to the RFC proved to be a blessing in disguise for Frankfurter and his allies. That agency's freewheeling boss, Jesse Jones, and its general counsel, Stanley Reed, gave ample scope to Corcoran's insatiable political interests and his uncanny ability to find and recruit other good lawyers for the administration. The RFC, as Arthur Schlesinger noted, "furnished Corcoran the facilities he needed—the office space, the all-night secretaries, the long distance wires, the mimeograph machines. It supplied a means of bringing down new men, looking them over, and putting them on a payroll until something opened up for them.[18] Many of the "new men" just happened to be students of Felix Frankfurter.

F.D.R.'s secretary of the interior, the old Bull Mooser Harold Ickes, proved amenable to Frankfurter's blandishments, as did Frances Perkins, the secretary of labor, and the first woman to hold a cabinet post. Ickes, whose paranoia exceeded only his idealism and who revered Brandeis as "one of the greatest men of his generation," quickly hired Frankfurter's protégé, Nathan Margold, for the key position of department solicitor. Ickes also found a place at Frankfurter's urging for Louis Glavis, the venerable symbol of governmental recti-

tude during the Pinchot-Ballinger battle, although Glavis soon proved
to be a great disappointment because of his high-handed and reckless
investigative tactics.[19]

When Perkins told him, "I want to follow your advice with regard
to a Solicitor," Frankfurter put forward several names, including Paul
Freund, a recent Brandeis clerk, and Raymond Stevens, a veteran
progressive still serving on the Federal Trade Commission. In the
end, Perkins settled upon a third man, another Frankfurter student,
Charles Wyzanski, who had been Learned Hand's legal secretary. After squelching what he called Wyzanski's "undue modesty," Frankfurter helped to push the appointment through the Senate with the aid
of New York's Robert Wagner. With Wyzanski safely ensconced in
the solicitor's office, Frankfurter proceeded to ply him with the names
of desirable labor mediators. At one point, Frankfurter's list included
147 people.[20]

He could also count among his early triumphs the appointments of
Donald Richberg to the National Recovery Administration and David
Lilienthal to the Tennessee Valley Authority. Track star, song writer, novelist, and one-time Ickes law partner, Richberg had graduated
from the Harvard Law School in 1904, battled Chicago's machine
politicians, and represented the railway brotherhoods in important
litigation. Brandeis regarded him as one of the country's best lawyers,
and at Frankfurter's urging, Roosevelt met the Chicagoan shortly before the inauguration, "took quite a shine" to him, and later offered
Richberg the second most powerful post in the NRA.[21] Lilienthal had
landed his first job with Richberg's law firm through Frankfurter's
recommendation and served on the Wisconsin Public Service Commission throughout the late 1920s, where he constantly sought Frankfurter's advice on matters of legal strategy and regulatory policy.
When Lilienthal's nomination to the TVA passed the Senate, Frankfurter complimented Roosevelt on "a truly great appointment." "With
you, Ickes, and Lilienthal in seats of power," Brandeis told Richberg,
"it really looks like a New Deal."[22]

Ironically, the one administrative bailiwick where Frankfurter
placed most of his former students and friends was the one area of
public policy he knew least about—agriculture. The difference between winter wheat and other varieties, he once confessed to
Roosevelt, eluded him entirely. He did know good lawyers from bad
ones, however, and proceeded to bombard both the Department of
Agriculture and the new Agricultural Adjustment Administration
with lists of eligible candidates. In order to fill these posts, he had to

mend his fences with the undersecretary of agriculture, Tugwell. Following a meeting with the latter and Henry Wallace after the inauguration, he waxed eloquently that "the two of you are an admirable team and I left the Department . . . with a real sense of elation." Four days later, Tugwell received a letter from Cambridge which reminded him of the great legal abilities possessed by Max Lowenthal, William O. Douglas, and Acheson, an "admirable person." If Tugwell needed greater reassurance on these men, Frankfurter pointed out, Brandeis could also sing their praises. None of Frankfurter's initial suggestions worked out, but Tugwell did hire another of his nominees, Jerome Frank, thereby helping to launch one of the New Deal's stormier careers.[23]

"Jerry too often reminds me of Holmes in the reverse," Frankfurter once quipped. "You remember Holmes' remark: 'I don't know facts; I merely know their significance.' Jerry knows a helluvah lot of books, but not their significance." At the same time, he described Jerome Frank as "a first-class craftsman and one of the sweetest of men," who suffered from the verbal difficulties of "one who has messed around—I almost said mucked around—with psychoanalysis as much as he has."[24] Seven years Frankfurter's junior, high-strung, intellectual, fiercely liberal, Frank was another Chicagoan whose life blended urban politics, corporate law, legal philosophy, and the arts. A genius at corporate reorganizations, he earned a large income for Chadbourne, Stanchfield, and Levy in New York, but counted among his friends Carl Sandburg, Sherwood Anderson, and Max Eastman. He married a poet, Florence Kiper, who once remarked that "being married to Jerome is like being hitched to the tail of a comet," and along with Karl Llewellyn of Columbia University he helped to found the school of jurisprudence known as Legal Realism. In his 1930 book, *Law and the Modern Mind*, for instance, Frank suggested that most legal rules were little more than the arbitrary imposition of shifting prejudices manufactured by fallible and sometimes irrational judges. He and Llewellyn urged the law school to teach courses with less emphasis upon doctrinal hairsplitting and more upon how lawyers could influence judges, juries, and legal rules in the interests of liberal social policies.[25]

Frankfurter, who had urged a broadening of the law school curriculum since 1914, nonetheless abhorred the extreme realist doctrines, which, in his opinion, merely substituted for the old orthodoxy of judicial infallibility a new dogmatism of fashionable social science. Realism, moreover, threatened to discredit the ideal of disinterested, rational adjudication and to reduce the legal universe to one of brute force. "The neo-angels of light have excluded me from their church of 'realism,' " he confessed to Hand, and "regard me as a old fogy because I care too much about history."[26] "Church and chapel alike seem to be closed to me," he told Charles Clark of the Yale Law School. "Karl Llewellyn bars me from the realists but admits me among the sociological jurists. You now assure me that I have detached myself from the latter breed. I always suspected that I didn't really know what sociological jurisprudence was. And now I am sure of it, for one can hardly know a philosophy when one repudiates it unwittingly."[27]

He cared too much about the success of the New Deal to allow these intellectual disputes with Frank or the realists to cloud his estimate of the former's abilities and his usefulness to the administration. His recommendation brought Frank into the Triple A as its general counsel, where the prophet of legal realism developed a close relationship with Tugwell and became another placement officer in Frankfurter's network. "I have asked Tom Corcoran to talk with you about matters of personnel," he told Frank, shortly after his appointment. "He is a shrewd fellow generally and knows a good deal about Washington ways."[28]

The firm of Frankfurter, Brandeis, and Corcoran soon placed a large number of people in Frank's office, including Gardner Jackson, "a very dear friend of mine"; Nathan Witt, "a beautifully solid and serene lad"; Alger Hiss, "first-rate in every way"; and Lee Pressman, a recent graduate from the Harvard Law School, who earned forever a place in the folklore of the New Deal by once asking at a Triple A meeting what the agency planned to do for the nation's macaroni growers.[29] In addition to these young men, Frank also recruited Thurman Arnold, Abe Fortas, and Adlai Stevenson to create one of the best legal organizations in the city and probably the most radical, since Witt, Pressman, Hiss, and another colleague, John Abt, all belonged to the Communist Party.[30] Whatever their political views, they gave indigestion to the orthodox farm bloc politicians who ran the Triple A. "A plague of young lawyers settled on Washington," wrote one of them. "They all claimed to be friends of somebody or other and mostly of Felix Frankfurter and Jerome Frank. They floated airily into offices, took desks, asked for papers and found no end of things to be busy about. I never found out why they came, what they did or why they left."[31]

The Triple A appointments and Peek's caustic observations gave birth to one of the more enduring legends about Frankfurter and the

New Deal—the myth of his vast, cohesive, personal empire that spread throughout the executive branch, the White House, and the independent regulatory commissions, where hundreds of Harvard Law School graduates bowed before the shrine of Brandeis and jumped instantly to the command of their former professor. Frankfurter, according to Eliot Janeway, had become "the proprietor of an organization for filling government positions of every kind from a Cabinet post to a clerkship. . . . No ward heeler ever patrolled the neighborhood saloons as energetically and with as business-like sense of detail as Frankfurter did the nation's salons. . . . He was, in fact, a kind of alderman-at-large for the better element."[32]

Frankfurter himself cultivated an image as the administration's chief legal impresario with a famous 1936 *Fortune* magazine article, "The Young Men Go to Washington," in which he hailed the arrival in the capital of "the best men of the graduating classes of the leading law schools," and described them as a new class of selfless, dedicated public servants, "freed from complicated ramifications of private life . . . diverted by a minimum of vanities and jealousies . . . more resilient, more cooperative in taking orders . . . on the whole much better than . . . the generation that preceded [them]."[33] This article contained a good deal of wishful thinking on the part of a man who believed that through his efforts and those of others the foundations could be laid for a permanent, nonpolitical civil service modeled after Great Britain's.

Frankfurter's janissaries, "the best men of the graduating classes of the leading law schools," did not seem to be noticeably more cooperative, more resilient, less vain, or less petty than the lawyers who proceeded them to Washington. Because of the enormous growth in the public sector that took place after 1932, however, Washington became a magnet for many more of them, especially for young Jewish lawyers who faced severe discrimination in private firms. The New Deal, in Jerold Auerbach's apt phrase, remained preeminently "a lawyer's deal," but many of those lawyers who found work in Washington did so without Frankfurter's stamp of approval, and many of them gained power despite his opposition. He failed to prevent, for example, the appointment of Francis Biddle to the National Labor Board in 1934, although he considered him to be a poor substitute for the former chairman, Lloyd K. Garrison.[34]

Those who gained office through his influence and who later carried the sobriquet of Felix's "happy hot dogs" did not form a monolithic, ideologically coherent block of sentiment within the New Deal.

Many of them carried Harvard degrees and many of them had clerked for Holmes or Brandeis, but no single gospel of recovery bound together Dean Acheson, Pat Jackson, Tom Corcoran, Frederick Wiener, Herbert Feis, and Alger Hiss. One might distinguish them by the cut of their clothes and their fondness for Felix, but not by their devotion to one political creed.

❧❧❧

If Frankfurter experienced mixed success in filling administrative positions, he had even fewer triumphs when it came to the New Deal's first response to the depression. Under the influence of Tugwell, Berle, Peek, Wallace, and big businessmen such as Gerald Swope of General Electric and Henry I. Harriman of the Chamber of Commerce, Roosevelt's first program stressed the revitalization of the existing commercial banking structure, business-government cooperation, production controls for industry and agriculture, and a parsimonious budget. When these measures failed to generate recovery, F.D.R. turned to the half-baked monetary theories of Warren and Rogers. Very little in this strategy resembled Frankfurter's call for government spending, curbs on private capital, and greater economic democracy.

In the March 1933 issue of *Survey Graphic*, for example, Frankfurter outlined an antidepression program that emphasized huge government expenditures for public works, "even larger and more ambitious than the one [Senator Robert] Wagner sponsored," and a "socially sound taxing system" to help pay for it, based upon sharp increases in both estate and income levies on the very rich. He quoted Keynes liberally.[35] He urged upon Senator Burton K. Wheeler, the old progressive from Montana, a package of tax reforms that would limit the size of corporations and especially penalize holding companies.[36] These ideas all echoed Brandeis, who had urged Frankfurter to support a public works program of "great magnitude," financed at first through government deficits, but later with "high estate and income taxes."[37]

Frankfurter conveyed many of these suggestions to Moley with the added invitation that the latter see Brandeis immediately, because the justice wished "to have a talk with you about a public works program which seems to him . . . indispensable for recovery." Frankfurter then presented Moley with a bold plan to restructure Hoover's Reconstruction Finance Corporation along lines that would permit the agency to loan larger sums of money for a greater diversity of construction projects. His intention, quite obviously, was to expand greatly the fiscal capabilities of the federal government in anticipation of a major spending program by the president. "I hope you have had or will have that talk with Brandeis," he reminded Moley a few weeks later.[38]

The Moley-Brandeis meeting did not materialize until late April, and by then the New Deal had been fixed on a course very different from the one outlined by Frankfurter. He kept a cheerful façade in letters to Roosevelt, praised his messages on unemployment relief, lauded several appointments, and recommended many others, but there was little in the famous Hundred Days that truly delighted Frankfurter—except for the Securities Act, which he helped to draft, and the creation of the TVA, which provided employment for Lilienthal.

The banking reforms approved by Congress bore a closer resemblance to the views of Wall Street than to those of Brandeis. Worse yet, there was not a major spending program or effort at tax reform. The two centerpieces of F.D.R.'s recovery effort—the National Recovery Act and the Agricultural Adjustment Act—emphasized centralized planning, the promotion of cartels and monopolies, and economic retrenchment rather than economic expansion. Roosevelt seemed eager to appease the most reactionary economic interests at the expense of genuine structural reforms. The NRA symbolized this confusion.

Despite the public relations extravaganzas organized by Johnson and Richberg, the Blue Eagle never soared very high. The agency soon degenerated into a sprawling bureaucratic monster without clear lines of authority or defined methods of enforcement. Those businessmen who reached Washington first drew up so-called "codes of fair competition" for their industries, while late-arriving competitors, union representatives, and consumer groups remained isolated from the decision-making process. In his haste to spread the Blue Eagle logo everywhere, Johnson seldom questioned the composition of each code authority and wasted his energy on organizing codes in areas with little economic impact. Roosevelt signed whatever documents Johnson brought to the White House.[39]

Labor violence soon flared between workers who were eager to capitalize on the provisions of Section 7a, and employers who were determined to resist the spread of unions. Within a year, big business denounced the NRA for excessive government regulation; small busi-

nessmen raged against monopolists. Both fought against labor and
used the NRA machinery to boost prices before any general recovery
had taken place. Ickes, entrusted with spending $3.3 billion for public
works under the law, ladled out the dollars with an eye to preventing
graft, not employing a maximum of idle workers. On top of all these
problems, most of the administration's best lawyers doubted that the
law could survive a constitutional test.[40]

With its sweeping but empty pretensions to centralized economic
management and its cozy relationship between big business and government, the NRA quickly stimulated Frankfurter's opposition, although Johnson had begged him to become the agency's chief counsel.
The NRA might provide a momentary advantage to particular
groups, Frankfurter complained, but it could do little to spur "genuine recovery except as it serves to increase the interchange of goods
and services in this country." Production restrictions and price increases seemed to him self-defeating without "increasing the effective
demand for goods and services," and that demand could be generated
only by means of a redistribution of income or substantial government
spending. Roosevelt was committed to neither one.[41]

From his former student, Fred Wiener, an assistant to Ickes in the
Public Works Administration, he received a depressing portrait of
how Honest Harold spent the small appropriation under Title II of
the NRA. This money, Wiener noted, had been "turned into a Defi-
ciency Appropriation Act by whatever department can put up a big
enough howl" and the secretary of the interior made certain that every
cent was carefully spent. Ickes "may be a great man," Wiener concluded, "sound on oil, Indians and Interior . . . but he has still to
learn . . . that the Administrator of a three billion [dollar] fund hasn't
time to check every typewriter requisition."[42] While Ickes fought
graft, the unemployed begged for work.

As for the NRA statute itself, Wyzanski pronounced it "so far
beyond the bounds of constitutionality . . . [as to] be useless." The
code-writing powers granted to private industrial groups and to the
president seemed to him "entirely too broad" to withstand judicial
scrutiny.[43] Except for the NRA's labor provisions, Brandeis regarded
the program with horror because of "the impossibility of enforcement,
the dangers to the small industries, [and] the inefficiency of the big
unit, be it governmental or private." The agency, he declared, had "a
terrible record in putting men back to work," and real progressives
should work for its "early liquidation."[44] Frankfurter shared all of
these reservations about the program and hotly denounced "the ro-

mantic simplicity of some of our friends, particularly . . . the younger lawyers," who believed in "a partnership with industry." They were, he said, "so bitten with a touching confidence in regulation, and with a strange inability to understand the difficulty of regulating powerful forces."[45]

Although many of his friends and former students worked for the Agricultural Adjustment Administration, Frankfurter had very mixed feelings about its recovery effort as well. Moley believed that he harbored "a deep antipathy" to the Triple A, but that is probably too strong a characterization. On the one hand, he knew that something had to be done to curb surplus farm production and to boost farm income. On the other hand, he recognized that the Triple A benefits, financed by a tax on food processors, merely taxed consumers to pay farmers without boosting the nation's total purchasing power. Despite Wallace's encomiums to "grass-roots democracy," Frankfurter also knew that the Triple A bureaucracy had been captured by a tiny elite of landowners, extension service managers, and farm machinery executives.

The AAA, he told Roosevelt, had been made necessary by the "terrible conditions" in rural America, and it had brought "important benefits" to these areas, but he seldom spoke with greater enthusiasm about the agency and remained mindful of Brandeis's warning that "this whole AAA production curtailment policy will prove disastrous." The New Deal's agricultural policy, the justice believed, retarded recovery and represented "sham democracy" because it excluded most sharecroppers, tenants, and migrant workers.[46]

Frankfurter's lack of enthusiasm for the NRA and the Triple A—programs that symbolized the ascendancy of Moley, Tugwell, and Berle—did not prevent him from responding to Moley's cry for assistance when the administration's efforts to regulate the nation's securities industry ran aground in the House and Senate. He had spurned Roosevelt's and Johnson's pleas to join the New Deal in an official legal capacity, but he could not pass up the opportunity to write a major statute, win favor with Moley, a key White House adviser, and promote the careers of two young associates. "Typically," complained Berle, "F.F. comes in at the last minute with many ideas, some very good, none of which could be got into legislative shape in less than a year or got by this Congress. . . . His opposition has been brilliant, but his ideas have never been brought to fruition—except over his protest."[47] The passage of the Securities Act in 1933 proved how wrong Berle could be. It was a vintage performance by Frankfurter

✗ with far-reaching consequences—not the least of which was the arrival in Washington of James McCauley Landis and Benjamin V. Cohen.

Roosevelt had pledged during the campaign that the New Deal would adopt legislation "to inspire truth telling" in the marketing of securities and also fumigate the stock exchanges which many people held responsible for the financial panic and depression. In the administration's rush to bail out the banking industry, salvage farm mortgages, organize the NRA, and curb farm surpluses, however, securities legislation did not receive top priority from either the White House or Congress. F.D.R. and Moley had given the task of writing a bill to the secretary of commerce, Daniel Roper, who in turn had delegated the actual work to several minor bureaucrats in his department and to the former chairman of the Federal Trade Commission, Huston Thompson.

Thompson's bill required corporations wishing to sell securities in interstate commerce to file a registration statement with the FTC, permitted the commission to revoke approval of any issue it believed "not based upon sound principles," and imposed absolute civil liability upon both the vendor of the securities and officers of the company for all errors or misrepresentations in the statement. In this form, the measure came under withering attack by legislators, businessmen, and investment bankers, all of whom predicted that it would "paralyze business entirely," cause "great injury to the public," and produce a "mass exodus" from the corporate board rooms of America. Congressman Sam Rayburn of Texas, the chairman of the House Committee on Interstate and Foreign Commerce, told Moley bluntly that the bill could not pass without major revisions. Two days later, with Landis and Cohen in tow, Frankfurter arrived in Washington to attempt the rescue of what Lilienthal called "a pretty amateurish piece of drafting."[48]

The two men who set up headquarters with Frankfurter at the Hotel Carlton were anything but amateurs. The hawklike Landis, Frankfurter's youngest colleague on the law school faculty, specialized in legislation and statutory construction. A coiled spring of concentrated intellectual power, who chain-smoked cigarettes and lost his temper easily, Landis has been raised in a family of Presbyterian missionaries and earned a Phi Beta Kappa key at Princeton before taking the Harvard Law School by storm in the early 1920s. At age thirty-four, he was idealistic, impatient, somewhat naïve about politics, but very ambitious for himself and for the new class of university-trained lawyers he epitomized.[49]

At the University of Chicago, faculty members rated Cohen as one of the most brilliant undergraduates in the school's history. He had clerked for Judge Julian Mack after finishing graduate studies at Harvard, battled at Frankfurter's side throughout the Zionist struggles of the Wilson era, and finally earned a reputation in New York City as a lawyer's lawyer who specialized in corporate reorganizations and worked on the side for the National Consumers League. Now approaching forty, Cohen was one of the best legal technicians in the country, a man whose mild, gentle exterior and sometimes melancholy nature cloaked the heart of a progressive lion. After examining Thompson's creation, he and Landis pronounced it "partly innocuous and partly unconstitutional," while Frankfurter described it to Moley as "really a very bad bill."[50]

Gulping coffee and napping when they could, Landis, Cohen, and Corcoran drew up a new securities law over the weekend of April 8, while Frankfurter attended to "other political duties" in Washington and while, in the suite of rooms above them, J.P. Morgan and his lawyers plotted their counterstrategy. To Landis' great pleasure, they sometimes rode silently in the same elevator with the titan of Wall Street, "happy that our burrowing into the structure of that empire had no noticeable reverberations above."[51] Their labors, however, were no more palatable to Wall Street than Thompson's had been.

Frankfurter's draftsmen limited the liability of corporate officers and underwriters to a standard of "due care" rather than strict liability, but they extended these provisions as well to accountants, engineers, lawyers, and other experts who prepared the registration statements. In addition, the new bill intensified the law's disclosure requirements and expanded the discretionary authority of the Federal Trade Commission. They tailored the law to the complex institutional realities of modern business and finance and gave the FTC ample powers to cope with unforeseen regulatory problems in the future. They eliminated the harsh revocation language that threatened to make the commission a virtual insurer against all financial risks, but they added a thirty-day "cooling off" period between registration and sale, during which time the FTC could demand changes or additions to the statement.[52]

On Monday morning, after a quick briefing by Landis, Cohen, and Corcoran, Frankfurter led Rayburn's committee paragraph by paragraph through the text of what he euphemistically called "perfecting amendments" in order to soften the blow for Thompson and the other architects of the original measure. He easily convinced the committee, but before the new legislation passed both houses of Congress at the end of May, Frankfurter and his allies had to turn back a series of attacks from the servants of Wall Street, who alleged that the revisions were more draconian than the first version, and from Thompson and others, who regarded the changes as a total capitulation to the securities industry. Frankfurter believed that his group had found a reasonable compromise. "To impose . . . an insurer's liability," he told Rayburn, "is to put to serious hazard the constitutionality of the measure. . . . There is ample protection to the public without securing that public interest through vindictive features which the Courts might resent and most likely would not sustain."[53]

Nonetheless, Wall Street lawyers who cheered Frankfurter's arrival in April denounced his efforts by the beginning of May. They especially resented the fact that he, Landis, and Cohen kept them at arm's length during the last stages of bill drafting, despite Moley's frantic efforts to insinuate them into the process. Without much success, lawyers such as John Foster Dulles and Arthur Dean attempted to water down the liability provisions still further and to reduce the disclosure requirements to a minimum. Unless these changes were made, they threatened, the capital markets of the nation would dry up. Even his old friend and patron, Henry Stimson, blasted Frankfurter for his "excess of crusader's zeal." At the opposite end of the political spectrum, some House and Senate members actually believed that the revisions had been approved by Wall Street. "Investment bankers would be satisfied with the Frankfurter . . . definition of responsibility," Thompson fumed during one stormy White House meeting, "it would never work."[54]

Ignoring these extremes, Rayburn and Senate Majority Leader Joe Robinson mustered large majorities for the final bill and Roosevelt signed it into law on May 27. "Rayburn did not know whether the bill passed so readily because it was so damned good," Cohen quipped, "or so damned incomprehensible." He noted that "the better educated [law] offices in New York are becoming reconciled. . . . I only hope that the boys have not discovered some of the holes that we neglected to plug."[55] Frankfurter had thrashed Wall Street's best lawyers in the legislative arena, but he offered the olive branch of peace once the battle had been won. "Conservative investment banking, within its appropriate function," he wrote, "has nothing to fear and everything to gain from the Securities Act." He assured Stimson that he had been "a moderating influence" among the bill's draftsmen, but Stimson probably didn't believe him.[56]

New York's financial and legal establishment took the defeat hard, as if they had been conquered by radicals in the opening round of a real revolution. They took little comfort in Frankfurter's "moderating influence" or in Roosevelt's quick appointment of Landis to the Federal Trade Commission once the Securities Act went into effect. Nor were they pleased to learn that Cohen and Corcoran were hard at work on additional legislation to regulate the stock exchanges fully and to dismantle public utility holding companies. Wall Street sighed with relief when the Frankfurters sailed for England in the fall of 1933.

CHAPTER 13

THE HIGH
TIDE
OF REFORM

FRANKFURTER LEFT THE UNITED STATES at a curious time, when his own influence soared as a consequence of the Securities Act triumph and while the programs of the New Deal drifted toward crisis and incoherence in late 1933 and early 1934. That he kept his date at Oxford, despite these developments, suggests that he was something more than the Iago of legend, a man interested solely in building a personal political empire and aggrandizing bureaucratic power. Frankfurter was above all an academician and an intellectual, who relished ideas for their own sake, and who, as he told Learned Hand, looked upon the Eastman Professorship "as a great adventure in adult education—for it is my education that I expect most to be improved." In addition, he could savor the prestige of the appointment, cultivate the British establishment, lobby on behalf of Zionist interests, and, finally, indulge to the utmost his Anglomania, what Isaiah Berlin described as his "childlike passion for England, English institutions, Englishmen . . . for the liberal and constitutional traditions that before 1914 were so dear to the hearts and imaginations especially of those brought up in Eastern or Central Europe."[1]

Before departing, he deputized Corcoran as his official liaison with the White House and praised the young man's virtues to F.D.R.'s chief secretary. Tommy the Cork, he assured Missy LeHand, was "a most valuable public servant and one of the most indefatigable workers for the success of the administration," who "from time to time . . . may come to you about matters." She soon discovered that "from time to time" meant at least once a week as the trans-Atlantic cable business boomed between Oxford and Washington.[2]

He arrived in England at a moment in history when the confidence of Zionists in the promises of the <u>Balfour Declaration</u> had been deeply shaken by publication and then partial repudiation of Lord Passfield's famous White Paper of 1930. Written largely in response to violent anti-Jewish rioting in Palestine by Arab extremists, the report by the Colonial Secretary recommended a prohibition on future Zionist land purchases in the Holy Land as well as a suspension of all Jewish immigration into the region until unemployment had been eliminated among the Arab population. The British set forth these harsh proposals despite mounting evidence that Jewish economic development increased employment opportunities among Palestinian Arabs and that the region's full economic potential had not been tapped. They came despite evidence of rising anti-Semitism in Europe and the hopeless situation faced by millions of Jewish refugees.[3]

Frankfurter had been unsparing in his denunciation of the White Paper. Passfield, he told Felix Warburg, had written "unheard of conditions" into the Palestine Mandate. The rights of non-Jews should be protected, he wrote, but the Balfour Declaration became a dead letter if the rate of Jewish immigration depended upon the level of unemployment among the Arabs: "When is an Arab 'unemployed'? When is he 'employed'? You know very well that even with our very advanced economic state there are continuing controversies . . . as to what constitutes 'unemployment'." A high rate of Arab unemployment, he pointed out, could be maintained forever as a result of migration from Transjordania and elsewhere by the poorest bedouins, eager to participate in Palestine's prosperity. On the basis of these arguments, he helped to mobilize American Zionists against the White Paper, and he wrote a critique of the British position for the influential journal, *Foreign Affairs*.[4]

The cogency and the vehemence of the Zionists' response—led in England by Weizmann and in America by Brandeis and Frankfurter—forced the Labour government to back down from the Passfield proposals, although Laski, who had been asked by Prime Minister Ramsay MacDonald to negotiate a settlement, found it almost impossible to locate common ground with his American friends. "If it were not for my deep affection for them [Frankfurter and Brandeis]," he told Holmes, angrily, "I think I would have told them long ago to go to hell."[5] Never had their relationships been more strained.

Finally, MacDonald issued a clarification of the White Paper, which reaffirmed Great Britain's devotion to the Balfour Declaration and endorsed Jewish immigration into Palestine with the proviso that the land would be able to absorb them. The tone had been softened, but not the original substance of the White Paper, which marked a major shift in British policy with a decided anti-Zionist bias. Frankfurter blasted MacDonald's remarks as "a futile piece of dialectic," but he held out little hope for more immediate concessions. At Oxford, therefore, he attempted to influence the views of Reginald Coupland, the Beit Professor of Colonial History, and others on Palestine, while privately he expressed great pessimism about England's ultimate intentions in the Middle East.[6]

Not even the White Paper imbroglio could dampen Frankfurter's zest for the intellectual and social life of Great Britain during the early 1930s, or lessen the enthusiasm that he generated among the country's elite lawyers, judges, journalists, politicians, economists, and intellectuals. Formally, the Eastman Professor imparted his wisdom in a series of lectures on American politics and law while dressed in full academic regalia. "There is no doubt that he has made a profound impression," Laski reported. "I hear that alike from the dons and students in Oxford; and the others he meets, here and elsewhere, are all captured at once by his personality."[7] Somewhat less formally, he also taught seminars for more advanced students and supervised the writing of theses. Frankfurter met these obligations, but from many accounts, his most profound teaching came during long, impromptu gatherings in the dining halls.

"Felix Frankfurter had an uncommon capacity for melting reserve," Berlin recalled, "breaking through inhibitions, and generally emancipating those with whom he came into contact." During one such session in All Souls, "he talked copiously, with an overflowing gaiety and spontaneity which conveyed the impression of great natural sweetness; his manner contrasted almost too sharply with the reserve, solemnity and, in places, vanity and self-importance of some of the highly placed persons who seated themselves around him." Frankfurter, he noted, seemed to prefer the company of the junior fellows and the students.[8]

Of course, he cultivated the higher circles as well—Geoffrey Dawson, editor of *The Times;* Sir John Simon, the famous jurist; the Archbishop of Canterbury; the Astronomer Royal; Lord Hugh Cecil; the Asquiths; and Nancy Astor. He relished Grand Day at the Inner Temple, which included "a grand meal and a grand series of grand wines," plus "a lot of the legal bigwigs . . . the Master of the Rolls, two of the Law Lords . . . three or four judges of the High Court, et al." He enjoyed "a Cambridge feast" and "spending the night with Keynes" when "all that has been dark about American finance" suddenly became illuminated. Spring brought the famous Eights Week regatta to Oxford, when "everything is subordinated to parties and affairs and celebrations of every variety . . . into which art and finance and government and science and wisdom and beauty are drawn to play their mystic share." At each of these events, he told Reed Powell, "I have been struck with the variety and the volume of drinking, even less than with the moderation in its use." When it came to grand wines, Frankfurter held his own.[9]

Intellectually, the high point of his stay came in the famous Chatham House debate with Sir William Beveridge and George Bernard Shaw and in his long talks with Keynes and other British economists on the pros and cons of Roosevelt's recovery program. At Chatham House he skewered both England's greatest living dramatist and the head of the London School of Economics, who revealed their profound ignorance of the American Constitution and the role of the Supreme Court. "Beveridge was really pathetic," he told Powell, "because he would come back for punishment three or four times, exposing himself each time to that tragedy when a big theory collides with a little fact." Shaw, although profoundly uninformed about American law, remained "charmingly irrelevant and tartly gay . . . extraordinarily handsome . . . looking like a very beautiful tall white pine." But he failed to understand, as he told Hand, why "those innocents expose themselves when they had not even a fig leaf."[10]

After a session with Oxford economists, including Roy Harrod, he communicated their views to Roosevelt. "We lay stress on the increase of incomes by contrast with (1) an increase of money in circulation and (2) an increase in the liquidity of corporation assets," they told the president of the United States. "We believe that the principal weapon in raising prices should be a great campaign of Public Works" financed by means of borrowed money.[11] Keynes, after a long conversation with Frankfurter, conveyed the same message to Roosevelt in his famous "open letter" of December 31, which the president received from Oxford before it appeared in the *New York Times*. "Some people seem to infer," Keynes wrote, "that output and income can be raised by increasing the quantity of money. But this is like trying to get fat by buying a larger belt. In the United States today your belt is plenty big enough for your belly. It is a most misleading thing to stress the quantity of money, which is only a limiting factor, rather than the volume of expenditure, which is the operative factor."[12]

Since both the Harrod and Keynes letters contained direct attacks on two of Roosevelt's pet programs—the NRA and the gold-purchase scheme—the president expressed some annoyance at Frankfurter for becoming the instrument of their criticism. "You can tell the professor [Keynes] that in regard to public works we shall spend in the next fiscal year nearly twice the amount we are spending in this fiscal year," he said, "but there is a practical limit to what the Government can borrow—especially because the banks are offering passive resistance in most of the large centers." Reflecting upon Ickes's cautious performance, Frankfurter could only shake his head in sadness and disbelief. When Roosevelt finally met Keynes in person five months later at Frankfurter's initiative, the results were hardly more positive. "He left a whole rigamarole of figures," F.D.R. complained to Frances Perkins. "He must be a mathematician rather than a political economist."[13]

Emotionally, the highlight of his year abroad was not Oxford, Cambridge, London, or Keynes, but a spring visit to the Middle East. "For a brief space I should like to be the boss of the universe," he told Holmes. "I would transplant you, for a short stay, to Palestine." The land of David, Solomon, Elijah, and Balfour's Declaration pierced the heart of "a pedestrian, unimaginative lawyer," above all its "endless fields of red, luscious anemones" and "glorious, passionate poppies." He marveled at the idealism, the heroism, and the practical achievements of the Jewish settlers. "There is something poignant and magical about Palestine in its very air," he wrote, "that makes one feel that the utterance of the prophets, the songs of the ancient poets were indigenous, they could not have come from any other soil, they are *there* now." His visit to this place of "magical beauty," where "man's efforts . . . are not unworthy of nature" swelled his pride in being Jewish, and steeled his resolve to work for a modification of British policy.[14]

❧❧❧❧❧

Whatever his own reservations about Roosevelt's programs in 1933, Frankfurter had left behind a president and an administration filled with optimism. When he returned to New York a year later, he found a regime wracked by internal discord and mired in uncertainty about the future. Despite NRA, AAA, PWA, CCC, TVA, banking reform, and securities regulation, business still languished, farmers went broke, consumers did not buy, and millions of workers lived on the edge of destitution. Furthermore, no consensus had emerged among Roosevelt's senior advisers about what could or should be done to break the stalemate.

Instead of becoming an engine for recovery and a model of cooperation among business, labor, and the government, the National Recovery Administration spawned confrontations between employers and employees in key industries such as automobiles and steel, generated a torrent of litigation, and provoked accusations of government-sanctioned price gouging by big business. The Triple A, although it had raised the income of some farmers, boiled with conflict among large landowners and sharecroppers, food processors and consumers. Bankers, lawyers, and stock brokers blamed the Securities Act and "socialistic experiments" such as the TVA for the drought of new private investment. Wall Street also expressed horror at the administration's gold-purchase and inflation panaceas, while the inflationists complained that Roosevelt had not gone far enough. Ickes spent PWA funds too slowly to stimulate employment. Hopkins spent money so rapidly through the improvised Civil Works Administration that the president ordered the program shut down.

One group of advisers, led by Tugwell and Jerome Frank's allies in the Triple A, wanted the president to jettison the pretense of cooperation with big business and opt for a program of full-scale nationalization. "The Tugwell crowd," Corcoran reported to Frankfurter, "has been pushed by its enemies—and its own loose talk—away over to the left." Another group, headed by Moley, whose relationship with Roosevelt had deteriorated since the London Economic Conference, urged Roosevelt to continue his détente with business, a strategy which Corcoran described as "vacillating considerably toward the right."[15]

Corcoran placed himself, Brandeis, and other Frankfurter lawyers somewhere in the middle, "militant and impatient" between these two factions. On the one hand, they believed that cooperation with business was impossible except on terms acceptable to business and hostile to Roosevelt's other programs. But they rejected Tugwell's solutions as utopian. Frankfurter, Corcoran warned, would now find himself "strangely straddled between Isaiah [Brandeis] on one side who wants to ride ahead hard with his full program, completely contemptuous of political obstacles—and Ray on the other side, who is afraid of Isaiah's belligerence, quite through with the agony and sweat of reforming, and wearily eager to settle down to a false security of sweet reasonableness."[16]

Until Frankfurter returned, F.D.R. seemed to tilt toward Moley's position of "sweet reasonableness." He dropped Warren's monetary experiments that Wall Street abhorred; watered down the Cohen-Corcoran stock exchange bill that attempted to curb the influence of the market's insiders; accepted amendments to the Securities Act that softened its liabilities and loosened registration requirements; named Joseph P. Kennedy rather than Jim Landis to the chairmanship of the new SEC; killed the Civil Works Administration; and endorsed a balanced budget. He spoke warmly about free enterprise and the profit motive and approved of Moley's efforts to bring corporate leaders and New Dealers together through a series of dinners.[17]

But the dividends from this approach proved meagre. Despite assurance from Wall Street insiders that private capital would burst forth once the Securities Act had been amended, the volume of new issues remained pathetically small. Corporate leaders continued to fight the NRA and the TVA. They organized the American Liberty League, bankrolled by the duPonts, the Pews, and the barons of General Motors, to resist the New Deal throughout the length and breadth of the nation's judicial system. Roosevelt's "sweet reasonableness," meanwhile, earned him only the enmity and suspicion of progressives, labor, small farmers, and consumers. When Frankfurter sat down with Roosevelt at the end of August, he found a president anxious for new departures.

For nearly five hours on August 29 and 30, Frankfurter talked with Roosevelt alone in the White House. In one fundamental sense, he agreed with Tugwell and the radicals: the New Deal, he told the president, faced an "irrepressible conflict" with big business that would have to be faced sooner or later. The president did not need to declare war verbally, Frankfurter added, but he should "recognize that there is war and act on that assumption." It was absolutely vital, he continued, for the administration to begin a bold spending program—especially for housing and "large public works"—because the prospect of four or five million permanently unemployed citizens "is intolerable and destructive of American institutions." Roosevelt said he agreed with Frankfurter's analysis of the "irrepressible conflict," but continued to express annoyance at his friend's grandiose fiscal ideas. He simply could not borrow $3 billion a year for ten years, he said, without bankrupting the nation and committing political suicide.[18]

The NRA, Roosevelt confided, had not met his expectations, but he hoped to salvage some of its important reforms that benefitted labor. He assured Frankfurter that he would not push for federal incorporation of big business and wished to maintain a large role for the states in the area of business regulation. Despite his militant mood, Roosevelt agreed that some members of his administration—Farley, Tugwell, and Hopkins—had been writing and talking too much. He promised to shut them up and singled out Frankfurter's young men for high praise. "He knows all about Tom and Ben," Frankfurter rejoiced, "values them greatly and has important plans."[19]

Seldom one to lose the initiative, Frankfurter continued to drive home his point of view in a series of letters and visits to the White House during the fall of 1934. He blasted the fiscal conservatism of the great bankers, especially J.P. Morgan's chief political operator, Russell Leffingwell, whose advice to F.D.R. consisted of pleas for less government regulation of banking and the stock exchanges. Frankfurter ridiculed these suggestions as "the same old cliches, the same old incantations." Finally, in November from Warm Springs, Roosevelt confided to him that he was hard at work on several new messages to Congress and "from present indications," he noted, "the liberals will get more comfort out of them than the Tories."[20]

Frankfurter's activities bore fruit shortly before Christmas, when Henry Morgenthau, Jr. called to ask for assistance in drafting new tax legislation. The president, according to Morgenthau, had suggested that he use Corcoran and Cohen for the job. Frankfurter could hardly contain his enthusiasm. "I really think," he told Brandeis, "that F.D.'s needs and Tom's and Ben's abilities may give us a real opportunity." The second Hundred Days had begun.[21]

From the spring of 1935 until the late summer, Roosevelt and the Seventy-fourth Congress enacted into law the most sweeping changes in American society since the Civil War. These months saw the adoption of a $4.8 billion work relief program, the single largest peacetime appropriation in the nation's history. The National Labor Relations

Act guaranteed industrial workers the right to form unions and to bargain collectively. The Social Security Act provided old-age pensions, unemployment compensation, and federal money for the care of dependent mothers, the blind, and the disabled. The Banking Act concentrated greater regulatory authority over the commercial banks in the Federal Reserve Board to be appointed by the president. The Revenue Act raised the maximum surtax on personal incomes to 75 percent, hiked estate taxes upon the very rich, and levied a graduated tax on corporations.

In addition to these landmark measures, Congress passed and Roosevelt signed legislation creating the Resettlement Administration to assist small farmers, sharecroppers, migrants, and others of the rural poor. The Rural Electrification Administration began to finance low-interest government loans for the construction of power plants and transmission lines. The Guffey-Snyder Bituminous Coal Act created a commission to regulate wages, hours, and prices for the soft coal industry; and the Public Utility Holding Company Act limited the size and activities of these behemoth firms. Conservatives howled with indignation and liberals cheered as the New Deal moved left to succor the weak and to curb the powerful. After a meeting with congressional progressives at the end of May, Frankfurter reported that "Bob Wagner . . . said . . . F.D.R. . . . was in [a] real fighting spirit such as he had not been for some time."[22]

It would be, of course, a gross simplification to attribute Roosevelt's new zeal for reform solely to Frankfurter's influence or to see in "the wonderful year" of the New Deal a complete fulfillment of his ideas with respect to recovery. Roosevelt had little choice but to join the liberals in 1935, given the disaffection of key business groups, the impatience of urban Democrats in the Congress, and the threat posed to his own political future by the redistributionist panaceas of Huey Long, Francis Townsend, Upton Sinclair, and others. Either Roosevelt attempted to lead the revolt on his left or he risked becoming its victim. Frankfurter, however, played a critical role in reinforcing this shift. He became a source of almost constant intellectual stimulation pushing the president leftward and he placed his personal mark upon more pieces of legislation in 1935 than any other adviser.

He, Corcoran, and Cohen became permanent fixtures in the Oval Office during the spring and summer of 1935—especially Tommy the Cork, who joined Roosevelt's official staff in March. "The Boys (Ben and Tom) are a legion," Frankfurter reported to Brandeis. "They were "admirably composed," their reputations "have been much enhanced," and the president "is very, very fond of Tom."[23] It was important for him to see Roosevelt at "reasonably frequent intervals," Frankfurter believed, in order to reinforce "the indispensability of aggressive action," as well as "the hopelessness of Social mindedness from the Aldriches et al." He longed for big business to become "still more articulate in its true feelings towards F.D.R. so that even [his] genial habits would see the futility of hoping anything from [them] in '36." And on every occasion, he emphasized to the president that they faced an "irrepressible conflict" with the business establishment.[24]

Frankfurter did more than intensify Roosevelt's suspicions about the Aldriches and the Leffingwells. With Cohen and Corcoran he became a principal author of the legislative outlines of the Social Security Act, the Revenue Act, and the Public Utility Holding Company Act. These three statutes—although they had little cumulative impact upon economic recovery—best exemplified Frankfurter's commitment to localism and his hostility to concentrated economic power, a position that infuriated both big businessmen and those New Dealers like Tugwell who remained wedded to other ideals of national planning.

In the case of unemployment insurance, a key factor of the Social Security Act, he became a spokesman for Brandeis's ideas which critics later singled out as the program's worst defect: its emphasis upon decentralized administration and individual responsibility. Quite properly, Brandeis regarded himself as the intellectual architect of the nation's first unemployment compensation plan adopted in Wisconsin in 1932 through the efforts of his daughter, Elizabeth, and his son-in-law, Paul A. Raushenbush. The Wisconsin plan placed the financial burden squarely upon each employer, who was required to build up unemployment reserves for his own workers and to pay insurance premiums based upon his own success at maintaining steady employment. Brandeis hoped to extend the Wisconsin model throughout the nation by means of a federal tax deduction for employers who participated in approved state programs. Brandeis's critics denounced the idea of individual company reserves and merit ratings as anachronistic; they favored joint employee-employer contributions, pooled insurance funds, and direct federal subsidies to promote more uniformity in state benefits.[25]

In the White House and in Congress, Frankfurter worked for the Brandeis formula and against what he branded as "the grandiose proposals" pushed by Tugwell and Wallace.[26] He warned Roosevelt of "the constitutional obstacles in the way of an all-embracing national

scheme" and quoted Holmes on the virtues of social experiments conducted "in the insulated chambers of the individual States." Unemployment compensation, he added, provided an excellent example
"not of state's rights but of state opportunities."[27] Tugwell, on the
other hand, lamented that he had done everything possible to sway
Roosevelt in the direction of federal subsidies and national standards
for the program, "but the Frankfurter and Brandeis influence has just
been too strong."[28] He neglected to add that Roosevelt's own prejudices lay in this direction, too, and that sentiment against the national
plan remained intense in Congress. As a result, the final statute became, in the words of one historian, "a crazy-quilt unemployment
compensation system, with widely varying benefits distributed under
divergent standards by forty-eight separate state agencies." Even supporters of the Brandeis-Frankfurter plan soon doubted the wisdom of
such federal passivity.[29]

"I wish you had seen Brandeis's face light up when I gave him
your message about . . . tax policy," Frankfurter told the president.
"His eyes became glowing coals of fire, and shone with warm satisfaction."[30] Frankfurter seldom had kind words to say about Henry
Morgenthau, Jr., but even he reported that "tax matters are really
moving and here is ideal determination on part of F.D. I must say
Treasury is also good."[31] The revenue bill of 1935—hammered out by
Morgenthau's staff with the advice and encouragement of Frankfurter, Corcoran, and Cohen—proposed a sharp increase in individual
surtax levies on the rich, an inheritance tax, a graduated corporation
tax scaled to penalize bigness, and a tax on intercorporate dividends
designed to discourage holding companies. The Hearst newspapers
labeled it a "soak the successful" program, while the Philadelphia *In-
quirer* denounced the president for attempting to lure "the something-
for-nothing followers of Huey Long . . . and the whole tribe of false
prophets."[32]

House and Senate committees soon watered down the measure's
more radical provision, but the Revenue Act of 1935 remained the
most progressive fiscal statute in a generation. Frankfurter, who had
played a key role in its formation, believed that the legislative struggle
brought out the best in Roosevelt and the worst in the New Deal's
wealthy opponents who "are correspondingly more and more bitter"
while the president's "fighting qualities are being ever more
aroused."[33] Brandeis looked upon its passage as a tribute to Frankfurter's healthy influence upon Roosevelt and a foretaste of even more
sweeping tax reforms in the future. "You have rendered a great service," he concluded, "F.D. comes out on top."[34]

The legislative battle over the Revenue Act paled in comparison with that spawned by the Public Utility Holding Company Act. The New Deal's attempt to limit the size of corporate properties brought forth one of the most brazen lobbying campaigns in history, charges of illegal searches and seizures against Senator Hugo Black, and accusations that Corcoran had used blackmail to gain a congressman's vote for the bill's controversial "death sentence" provision. "The presure on F.D. re holding cos. is terrific," Frankfurter reported from the scene of battle. "It *will* be a test of him." It was a test for everyone.[35]

As originally drafted by Corcoran and Cohen, the legislation authorized the Securities and Exchange Commission to break up "unnecessarily complicated" holding-company structures, but it did not contain a rigid timetable for divestiture and provided some tax incentives to hasten the process. Frankfurter advised Roosevelt to proceed with caution. "They cannot be eliminated over night," he warned, "and therefore the policy would seem to be temporary stiff regulation and taxation, with the defined objective of elimination." But Roosevelt, his Dutch temper aroused by Frankfurter's constant call to arms and by mounting attacks in the press, refused to compromise. He wanted the SEC to begin to dismantle the companies after three years, and he wanted a flat prohibition against all holding companies in the public utility field unless they could prove their existence "necessary for the operation of a geographically and economically integrated . . . system." When Frankfurter spoke out against this formula, he informed Stimson, "I got rapped for it." The president, he told Brandeis, seemed "wholly untouched by all the ballyhoo of the utility crowd" and bent upon "drastic action."[36]

In this form, however, the measure passed the Senate by a single vote and moved nowhere in the House, where many Democrats broke party ranks under pressure from the utilities, denounced the legislation as communistic, and equated the administration's techniques with "mob murder" and "the lynching bee." Representative Ralph Brewster of Maine, an opponent of the "death sentence," alleged that Corcoran had threatened to stop the construction of a dam in his district unless he changed his vote, an accusation that proved groundless because Corcoran seldom threatened something he could not deliver, but Brewster's charges embarrassed the administration and diverted attention from the legislation for weeks. "Tom has borne himself with great skill and restraint and acquitted himself," Frankfurter reported, while Roosevelt "has been sweet and strong in his support of Tom — as a general should be of his subordinate, but so often they are not."

The Brewster incident, he hoped, would "stiffen F.D.'s fibre and make him realize . . . that it's the same old gang." [37]

Frankfurter's cunning, not Roosevelt's fibre, however, finally broke the impasse after attempts to reconcile the Senate and House versions failed during most of July and August. The Senate insisted upon the "death sentence" with statutory language that restricted holding companies to a single "geographically and economically integrated . . . system" operating in "contiguous states." The House demanded only an "integrated public-utility system" which critics claimed would permit the continued abuse of holding companies controlling two or more scattered systems in many states. Frankfurter, working out of the White House, finally drafted a compromise that the Senate leadership sold to the lower chamber.

Shrewdly, he retained the House's pet phrase of an "integrated public-utility system," but he further defined the concept as constituting "a single integrated . . . system" and one "not so large . . . as to impair the advantages of localized management, efficient operation, or the effectiveness of regulation." No one quite knew what that meant, except perhaps Frankfurter, who thought the courts would construe it in favor of the Senate and the SEC. Die-hard conservatives in the House also believed that his language favored the Senate, and they denounced the "different shroud . . . in which death has been newly wrapped." Grumpily, Roosevelt finally accepted the compromise, although he teased Frankfurter for behaving like John W. Davis.[38]

The momentum of reform, generated with Frankfurter's assistance, continued into the election year of 1936, especially in the area of taxation, where the administration pushed for the adoption of an undistributed profits tax designed to discourage tax avoidance by the well-to-do and to generate new investment as well.[39] With Corcoran and Frankfurter now playing major roles, moreover, the content of Roosevelt's reelection campaign presented a sharp contrast to the rhetoric of 1932. There was much less talk about cooperation with business, national planning, and government by consensus. Greater emphasis was placed upon the necessity for social justice, income redistribution, and reducing the power of big business.

In a long memorandum for Roosevelt on the substance of the Democratic Party platform, Frankfurter urged an all-out war upon concentrated economic power, represented by "interlocking directors, interlocking bankers, and interlocking lawyers." "There is no practical way to regulate the economic oligarchy of autocratic, self-constituted and self-perpetuating groups," he told F.D.R. "It is necessary to destroy the roots of economic fascism in this country, if we wish to remove the dangers of political fascism, which engulf freedom in other lands."[40] It was the most radical document that Frankfurter ever authored.

Throughout the fall campaign, Roosevelt elaborated upon the basic themes in Frankfurter's memorandum. He likewise denounced "economic royalists" and the dangers posed to American democracy by the "new industrial dictatorship." The power of "organized money," he told the party faithful, "are unanimous in their hate for me—and I welcome their hatred." With his crushing defeat of Landon in November, the forces of American liberalism seemed to gather even more momentum.[41]

Frankfurter never exercised greater influence over Roosevelt than during the years of 1935 and 1936, yet he could hardly claim a complete ideological and political victory over his opponents inside or outside of the administration. Roosevelt, for example, continued to be niggardly with public works expenditures, and his timidity subverted the cornerstone of Frankfurter's program for genuine economic recovery. The terrible recession of 1937 indicated just how little influence Frankfurter had in the critical area of fiscal policy, despite his own stature and that of Keynes as well.

The tax reforms of 1935—1936 proved to be ephemeral once businessmen screamed loud enough and once conservatives in Congress regained the initiative. He watched as many of his friends, including Frank, Hiss, and Jackson, were fired from the Triple A for displaying too much solicitude for the rights of sharecroppers and tenant farmers. He denounced Wallace's "weak behavior" during the struggle and his capitulation to "administrative exigencies," but also confessed to Brandeis that "our liberal friends have not been the wisest in temperament and action."[42] Despite his close identification with Brandeis and the war against bigness and centralized planning, finally, many of the measures that Frankfurter supported—including the TVA, the SEC, and even the Public Utility Holding Company Act—contributed to the spread of institutional giantism.

In the golden days of 1935 and 1936, however, these setbacks and contradictions seemed less crucial than the sweetness of other legislative achievements and the biggest electoral mandate in American history. With a single exception, symbolized by nine men in black robes, Roosevelt, Frankfurter, and the New Deal reigned triumphant.

CHAPTER 14

THE CONSTITUTIONAL REVOLUTION

ONE DAY IN 1936, Justice Harlan Fiske Stone met a former student from the Columbia Law School on the streets of Washington, D.C.

"How are you getting on, John?" inquired Stone.

"Pretty good, Mr. Justice," replied the young man. "I was with the legal division of the NRA last year, then I transferred to the AAA, and now I am in the legal division of the Securities and Exchange Commission."

Stone smiled.

"I see," he said, "keeping just one jump ahead of us."[1]

The Great Depression brought to a sudden climax the intellectual and political struggle over the constitutional system that had begun at the end of the nineteenth century when a majority of the members of the Supreme Court asserted their broad authority to shape the nation's economic value by means of the Fourteenth Amendment and the commerce clause. By 1936, that struggle had become a full-blown crisis that pitted president, Congress, and forty-eight state legislatures—all attempting to cope with the manifold social problems generated by the depression—against a majority of the justices, whose narrow constitutional vision threatened the institution of judicial review itself.

The sudden death of Chief Justice Taft in 1930 and the retirement soon thereafter of Justice Sanford raised the hopes of many liberals that their replacements would speed the day when the Court governed marginally rather than absolutely. But Hoover's nomination of Charles Evans Hughes to the Taft seat spread gloom in the progressive ranks, and his choice of John J. Parker to fill the Sanford vacancy produced stunned disbelief. Although Hughes had authored several due process and commerce clause opinions before 1916 that shocked conservatives, twenty-six senators voted against his confirmation and denounced the New Yorker's close ties with Wall Street and big business. "No man in public life," declared Senator Norris, "so exemplifies the influence of powerful combinations in the political and financial world as does Mr. Hughes."[2]

Frankfurter shared Norris's skepticism about the appointment. He had been unsparing in his criticism of Hughes's lucrative retainers during the 1920s and uncertain about the latter's fidelity to liberal causes. On the one hand, Hughes earned a handsome income defending railroads, banks, insurance companies, and utilities; on the other, he condemned debt peonage and efforts to purge socialists from the New York legislature. Was he, as some critics argued, "the man on the flying trapeze," who swung back and forth between liberal and conservative platforms, torn between his desire for historical immortality and his patrician's fear of sweeping economic reforms? Frankfurter thought so. "I have very mingled feelings about Hughes," he confided to Hand, "and little of enthusiasm."[3]

He had favored Stone, the former law school dean, for the chief justiceship, but believed that Hughes would be an improvement upon Taft, despite the fact that he seemed too "comfortable with the world . . . suspicious of L.D.B. [Brandeis] and really not penetrating." He hoped that the new chief justice would lead the Court away from "the sedulously cultivated notion that in its decisions . . . [it is] deciding law as you are deciding law in passing upon a contract of marine insurance." Perhaps, he reasoned, the angry Senate debate had made an impression upon "Charles the Baptist," who would now "summon detachment and try to understand the legitimate solicitude for the public welfare that found expression [there]."[4]

Parker's obtuseness and antilabor record horrified him even more.

The man seemed to be "just a kitchen knife," he told Hand, after digesting his opinions, "one of those long quoters of the obvious—he writes as though he were paid by space. He belongs to the Sutherland School of jurists." If Parker had, as Hoover claimed, "legal ability of the highest order," Frankfurter concluded, "then judges like Cardozo, Mack and B. Hand are super-gods." To his great relief, even moderates in the Senate found Parker's credentials too repugnant, and he failed to be confirmed.[5]

In his place, Hoover chose another member of the Eastern legal establishment, Owen J. Roberts, a plump Philadelphian, who usually represented corporate clients, but who earned high marks from many progressives for his tenacious prosecution of the Teapot Dome criminals. Roberts's nomination, which the Senate quickly approved, impressed Frankfurter as "a real gain" in comparison with Hoover's initial selection, and he praised the newest justice in letters to Stone and others. "I do not believe there are any skeletons in his mental closet," he reported. "Facts will find a ready access to his mind."[6] Frankfurter's optimism was not shared by all of his friends, including Joe Cotton, who warned that "anyone who takes Owen Roberts for a liberal is going to be mistaken."[7]

Frankfurter, however, insisted upon seeing Roberts as another Stone, who had also come to the court after extensive Wall Street practice, but quickly fell under the influence of Holmes and Brandeis. Frankfurter took credit for helping the transition. "Stone is in a different class from Butler and McReynolds," he told Hand. "The latter haven't the slightest desire to be thought well of, let us say, by the *New Republic*. Stone has—but he also wants to be thought well of by those who regard the general direction of the *New Republic* as subversive."[8] Almost weekly, he bombarded Stone with letters that stroked his ego and heaped damnation upon the Court's conservatives. "If he didn't get a letter of praise by Wednesday on a Monday opinion that he thought I ought to approve," Frankfurter recalled, "he would grouch to L.D.B."[9] After Roberts joined the Court, Frankfurter gave him the same treatment.

"There is a good deal of loose talk about 'conservative' and 'liberal,' " he told Roberts, but these labels "hardly describe anybody since we are all a compound of both. What divides men much more decisively is the extent to which they are free—free from a dogmatic outlook on life, free from fears. And that is what cheers me so about your appointment." Despite what others might say, Frankfurter assured the newest justice, he believed that Hoover had selected a man who was "a servant neither of a blind traditionalism nor of blind indifference to historic wisdom." With Roberts now on the Court, he informed Hand, "I expect considerable improvement and detect signs even in Hughes of pulling in horns. . . . And you don't have to go far on that Court to be 'liberal.' "[10]

Joe Cotton proved to be a more discerning student of Owen Roberts's judicial behavior than Felix Frankfurter. Despite the addition of Cardozo in 1932, the Hughes Court began to operate in ways that filled Frankfurter with alarm even before Roosevelt launched the New Deal. He became distressed by the tendency of Roberts and Hughes to vote with the Four Horsemen of the Apocalypse—Butler, McReynolds, Sutherland, and VanDevanter.

From Frankfurter's perspective, the first ominous signs appeared less than a year after Hughes became chief justice in a complex railroad bankruptcy case involving the Chicago, Milwaukee, St. Paul, and Pacific Company. Relying upon its powers in the Transportation Act of 1920, the ICC had approved the issuance of new securities for the financially troubled company with the proviso that the reorganization managers not pay their own expenses and those of their lawyers until the courts and the commission investigated the reasonableness of these stupendous fees. Since the reorganization expenses were to be paid out of a special assessment levied against the stockholders, the ICC reasoned that the size of these fees would have a permanent, long-term impact upon the railroad's financial health.

With Roberts voting in the majority, Justice Sutherland stripped the commission of any jurisdiction over the reorganization fees on the theory that they constituted a wholly private contract beyond the ICC's authority to protect the public interest. In a pungent dissent, endorsed by Holmes and Brandeis, Stone pointed out that this cramped statutory interpretation would undermine public confidence in the nation's economic system.[11]

Roberts's vote in the *St. Paul* case shook Frankfurter's confidence in the newest justice, but he continued to believe that the latter would soon follow Hughes and adopt a more tolerant attitude with respect to local economic regulations. The *St. Paul* decision was "outrageous," he told Hand, but Roberts's vote did not come as a complete surprise. "I think that is the way he will be pulled whenever such financial questions will arise. I think on the whole he believes in the boys, and as time goes on is apt to grow more conservative than otherwise."[12] Very soon, however, his faith that Hughes could guide Roberts in a progressive direction also collapsed.

First, in the *Car-hire* case, Hughes and Roberts joined Sutherland and the other conservatives in overturning another ICC regulation that required most railroads to pay a one dollar per diem rental fee for the use of one another's freight cars, but exempted all short lines from such payment when they returned the cars within two days. After years of investigation, the ICC had determined that the two-day exemption amounted to a reasonable compensation for the short lines because of their higher terminal and switching expenses. The Court majority, nevertheless, ridiculed the ICC's ruling as confiscatory, arbitrary, and unreasonable. Unless the commission imposed the same fee structure on all the roads, Sutherland announced, its actions constituted a taking of property prohibited by the Fifth Amendment.[13]

A week later, the same majority, now speaking through the tortured prose of Justice McReynolds, slapped down the ICC again—this time by holding that because the agency's first attempt to fix a rate retroactively had been illegal, the charges prescribed in the order also could not take effect thirty days later, although the Interstate Commerce Act specifically permitted such a result. The effort to apply the rate retroactively, McReynolds argued, dammed the entire order and required the commission to begin the hearing process over again from square one.[14] On the same day, Roberts and Hughes displayed their toleration for state economic regulation by voting to invalidate a section of the Wisconsin income tax laws that assessed a husband on the basis of his own as well as his spouse's income. Because other Wisconsin laws gave husbands no interest in or control over a spouse's property, Roberts reasoned, the taxation scheme violated the due process and equal protection clauses of the Fourteenth Amendment, which apparently required perfect symmetry in a state's statutes.[15]

Frankfurter was not the only one who was shocked by these decisions. "In some States, if not in all," wrote Holmes sarcastically, "the husband became the owner of the wife's chattels, on marriage, without any trouble from the Constitution. . . . It is said that Wisconsin has taken away the former characteristics of the marriage state. But it has said in so many words that it keeps this one."[16] Joseph B. Eastman, one of Frankfurter's liberal friends on the ICC, complained that "it seemed as if the intelligence of the Chief Justice and Justice Roberts would save the situation in many instances, but now there seems little certainty that this will be the result."[17]

Frankfurter poured out his frustrations to Hand. That both Hughes and Roberts had resisted Stone's powerful dissent in the *Car-hire* case, he wrote, "is almost too much for me to understand. . . . I am aware of the caveat that Joe [Cotton] uttered about Roberts. But what about the Chief?"[18] Stone, who had once been optimistic as well about the addition of Hughes and Roberts, confessed his own bafflement to Frankfurter. "What troubles me," he wrote, "is that the gentlemen . . . do not want for intelligence. What is the answer? . . . I have been really hoping that someone would point out that my own presentation of the matter involved was defective."[19]

St. Paul, Car-hire, and *Hoeper* did not augur well, but as the depression worsened and the forces of political protest intensified after 1932, Hughes and Roberts occasionally joined Stone, Brandeis, and Cardozo to form a majority that sanctioned many governmental efforts at the state level to battle the economic problems of the nation. This majority, for example, sustained laws regulating commissions paid to fire insurance agents, the amount of oil to be produced by privately owned wells, mortgage foreclosures, and also the retail price of milk in New York State.[20] Even Frankfurter had to admit that Hughes's masterful opinion in the Minnesota mortgage moratorium case represented an ingenious reformulation of the contracts clause that permitted extraordinary relief to hard-pressed debtors. In fact, he expressed some admiration for Sutherland's plaintive dissent.[21]

He cheered Roberts's opinion in the *Nebbia* case as the most liberal construction of the due process clause in a generation and one that seemed destined to afford the states ample authority to experiment with many social and economic regulations. "He swept away all the rubbish that had accumulated around *Munn* v. *Illinois*," Frankfurter wrote, "showed what an empty husk 'affected with a public interest' really is and didn't even give decent Christian burial to the Sutherland-Butlerian concoction that price-fixing is forbidden by the Constitution."[22]

With the chief justice blazing the way, the Court also won praise from liberals for a series of civil liberties decisions that limited the power of state officials to punish subversive speech, to ban the publication of irritating newspapers, or to railroad Negroes into the electric chair without effective legal counsel.[23]

Beneath this progressive veneer, a careful student of the Court's behavior such as Frankfurter could discern, however, an abiding conservatism on the part of both Hughes and Roberts that found expression in their frequent alliance with the Four Horsemen on many economic questions—especially those that touched upon the authority of administrative experts to regulate big business or that challenged the prerogatives of corporate management. Hughes and Roberts, for instance, rejected legislative efforts to restrict the spread of giant chain stores or to protect small businessmen from destructive competition.[24] In *Cowell* v. *Benson* they voted to give the judicial branch sweeping authority to reverse the factual determinations of administrative tribunals and in *Rogers* v. *Guaranty Trust Company*, they closed the federal courts to dissenting stockholders who attempted to prevent the looting of company coffers by entrenched directors.[25]

The decision in *Cowell*, Frankfurter said, "makes me wonder whether law is really my beat. . . . I could hardly have believed that disciplined legal minds would reach the conclusion which the majority reached."[26] Stone, who dissented with Brandeis and Cardozo in both cases, was especially furious about *Rogers*, which he saw as a symbol of "the blindness of those who have the big stake in our present system. . . . It is the story of the Bourbons over again."[27]

Certain decisions of the Hughes Court such as *Nebbia* and *Blaisdell* offered hope for the experimental legislation generated by the New Deal and by the states, but dozens of other rulings, highlighted by *Hoeper*, *Cowell*, *Rogers*, and *Car-hire*, exemplified a cramped constitutional vision and a fierce judicial distrust of reforms that attempted to redistribute wealth, arm regulatory officials with greater power, and curb the abuses of big business. It is not surprising that Frankfurter hoped to delay for as long as possible a final confrontation between the Roosevelt administration and the justices.

꘎꘎꘎

Frankfurter had other reasons for prudence in addition to his mounting skepticism about Hughes and Roberts. After a close reading of early New Deal statutes, he and many other lawyers had been shocked by their sloppy language, especially with respect to the scope of claimed federal authority and the administrative discretion vested in executive officers, including the president. This statutory anarchy, he feared, invited judicial mutilation. Portions of the National Recovery Act, Wyzanski told him bluntly, "which allow either an industry itself or the President on his own initiative to set up a code of fair competition are entirely too broad."[28] Very soon, the Court would echo this indictment. Frankfurter had no enthusiasm for the Blue Eagle, but he had not criticized the measure in Roosevelt's presence either. He hoped that the president would see the error of his ways without tasting the judicial lash.

Brandeis presented Frankfurter with another dilemma because he nursed negative feelings about the initial programs of the New Deal and would probably vote with the Four Horsemen in several cases. That would not raise the justice's influence with F. D. R., and it might undermine Frankfurter's as well at a time when he hoped to guide Roosevelt away from his infatuation with centralized economic planning and big business. Brandeis had become almost irrational on the issues of excessive federal power, congressional abdication, and the dangers of presidential usurpation. He denounced Roosevelt's effort to break up the London Economic Conferences as "a manifestation of the disintegrating effect of absolute power on mind and character" and warned Frankfurter that the nation would not be entirely safe until Congress reconvened.[29]

Although not wedded to the orthodoxy of the gold standard, Brandeis also condemned the government's decision to abrogate the gold clause in its own financial instruments as "terrifying in its implications," violating a "solemn obligation," and exhibiting a cowardly attitude with respect to taxation.[30] The president's gold-purchase program, he told Frankfurter, showed F.D.R.'s "aberrations and plunges" and confirmed the "inescapable penalties paid for conferring absolute power."[31]

Frankfurter, who had made a profession out of watching the Court since the Fuller era, advised the administration's lawyers to avoid litigation at all costs. Given what he knew about the early statutes, about Brandeis's grim mood, about the dogmatism of the Four Horsemen, and the vacillating behavior of Hughes and Roberts, this was not bad advice. The administration, he believed, risked a humiliating defeat on several issues. A further wedge would be driven between two men he admired in public life—Roosevelt and Brandeis—and he would be placed in the disagreeable position of having to choose between them and the institutions they represented. His fears were soon confirmed in the first New Deal case to reach the Supreme Court, when eight justices, including Brandeis, declared the so-called "hot-oil" provisions of the National Recovery Act unconstitutional for improper delegation of legislative authority to the president.[32] The administration won a narrow victory in the gold clause cases, thanks largely to Hughes's doctrinal sleight of hand, but the heart of the New Deal— including NRA and AAA—had yet to be tested.[33]

In the spring of 1935, therefore, Frankfurter urged Roosevelt and Stanley Reed, the solicitor general, not to appeal an adverse ruling on the NRA's lumber code. He made a similar plea with respect to the live poultry code, where the government had won a partial victory from the Second Circuit Court of Appeals. Through Corcoran, he told F.D.R. that it was "most impolitic and dangerous to yield . . . because fundamental situation of Court not changed."[34] That message never reached Roosevelt, a fact which Frankfurter and Corcoran blamed upon the attorney general and others who had been urging the president to appeal the *Schechter* case. Frankfurter's strategy of delay, argued Homer Cummings, General Johnson, and Donald Richberg, could not be pursued indefinitely without inflicting great damage upon the administration. The NRA statute might expire within two months, they pointed out, but meanwhile the agency's morale sagged, code violations soared, and the public equated the administration's refusal to litigate with unconstitutionality. These powerful arguments finally persuaded Roosevelt to permit the appeal. A confrontation with the justices, if kept within reasonable limits, might work to his political advantage—an idea that had not apparently occured as yet to Frankfurter.

Once a unanimous Court killed the NRA on May 27, the eager supporters of the appeal attempted to place the onus for defeat upon Frankfurter. They spread the false story through Arthur Krock of the *New York Times* that Harvard's chief constitutional lawyer had used his influence to hasten the appeal. Frank Buxton, editor of the *Boston Herald*, finally convinced Krock that this fairy tale, manufactured chiefly by Richberg, represented little more than "the inborn American right of alibiing and second guessing. . . . It was not Frankfurter who threw the overalls into General Johnson's chowder."[35] Richberg himself soon repented and apologized for "his attempt to escape responsibility by trying to unload on others. He was very nice about it and confessed error."[36]

But the damage had been done. On "Black Monday," May 27, in addition to toppling the entire NRA for improper legislative delegation and finding the wages and hours provisions of the live poultry code beyond Congress's authority to regulate interstate commerce, the justices also united to invalidate the Frazier-Lemke Farm Relief Act and to curtail sharply the president's ability to remove members of the independent regulatory agencies without congressional approval.[37]

Brandeis, who joined the *Schechter* majority, wrote the opinion for the Court in *Radford*, and saw his dissenting views become law in the removal case, delivered a stern lecture to Corcoran after leaving the bench. "This is the end of this business of centralization," he warned, "and I want you to go back and tell the President that we're not going to let this government centralize everything. It's come to an end. As for your young men, you call them together and tell them to get out of Washington—tell them to go home, back to the states. That is where they must do their work." [38]

Several weeks before *Schechter*, the Four Horsemen and Roberts had dealt the president and Congress another punishing blow by striking down the Railroad Retirement Act of 1934, which had created a mandatory pension system for the employees of all interstate lines. In the past, the Court had granted Congress sweeping authority to regulate all aspects of the interstate railroad business, including wages, rates, safety standards, and labor relations, but Roberts and his four colleagues now found the pension program to fall beyond the federal commerce power and to be, in addition, a coercive taking of property prohibited by the Fifth Amendment. [39]

Precisely why the Constitution permitted Congress to impose mandatory rates but not mandatory pensions was not made clear by Roberts. The opinion was so dreadful in terms of logic and history that Hughes wrote a scathing dissent for himself, Brandeis, Stone, and Cardozo. "The Railroad Retirement Act decision," fumed Stone, "was, I think, about the worst performance of the Court since the Bake Shop case. . . . How arrogant it must all seem to those unaccustomed to judicial omniscience in the interpretation of the Constitution." [40] Roosevelt took these defeats very hard. He met reporters in a fighting mood at the end of May.

With Marion Frankfurter and his own wife in attendance, the president compared the *Schechter* decision to the *Dred Scott* case—not one of the Court's happiest moments—chided the justices for relegating the nation to "the horse-and-buggy definition of interstate commerce," and gave them a short lesson in constitutional law. Congress could not regulate wages and hours in the live poultry industry, Hughes had written, because such matters touched interstate commerce "indirectly" rather than "directly," but Roosevelt cited many occasions on which the Court had ignored that subtle distinction—including cases where injunctions had been issued against striking workers. "This case . . . seems to be a direct reversal," he noted, dryly, "in that the shoe is on the other foot and that where you try to improve wages and hours of miners the coal suddenly becomes a purely local . . . matter and you can't do anything about it." [41]

"Black Monday" and Roosevelt's press conference put Frankfurter into an uncomfortable position between a prophet and a president. Brandeis believed that "our Court did much good for the country," and he urged Ben Cohen to give Frankfurter a blunt message: "You must see that Felix understands the situation and explains it to the President. You must explain it to the men Felix brought into the Government. They must understand that these three decisions change everything. The President has been living in a fool's paradise."[42] After Frankfurter huddled with F.D.R., however, the latter seemed more defiant than ever, accused the Court of living in the nineteenth century, and suggested that it favored big business at the expense of labor. He told reporters that he had received many ideas about how to deal with the situation, including some that "go all the way from abolishing the Supreme Court to . . . I think abolishing the President." Brandeis was not amused by the remark.

In early June, Frankfurter attempted to mollify Brandeis with the observation that F.D.R "gave me no intimation whatever that he was going to do the press conference talk. I knew nothing of it until Marion told me just as we were coming to lunch with you." With rumors flying that the Congress might pass a constitutional amendment to limit the Court's jurisdiction, Frankfurter told Brandeis "that all this . . . talk will run into the sand, with the Borahs and Joe Robinsons et al also opposing it." He felt certain that the Court would in time modify its views on the commerce clause and that the *Schechter* opinion would have been done "very differently" if Hughes had given the assignment to Brandeis or Cardozo. He praised Brandeis's own opinion in the Frazier-Lemke case as "magnificent" and "beautifully delivered."[43] Frankfurter did not tell Brandeis that he had done very little to curb Roosevelt's anger about the Court and a great deal to inflame it.

Frankfurter urged Roosevelt to follow a strategy that would, as he put it, allow him to "accumulate popular grievances against the Court on issues so universally popular that the Borahs, the Clarks, the Nyes and all the currents of opinion they represent will be with you in addition to the support you have today." They should push forward with legislation for old-age pensions, a ban on holding companies, and Senator Wagner's collective bargaining bill. "Put *them* up to the Supreme Court," Frankfurter urged. "Let the Court strike down any or all of them next winter or spring, especially by a divided Court. Then propose a Constitutional amendment giving the national Government adequate power to cope with national economic and industrial problems." But he also warned F.D.R. against "a general attack on the Court, unlimited in the changes it may cause." The once cautious advocate of delay had now become the militant apostle of confrontation. Emotionally and politically, Frankfurter had sided with the president against Brandeis, but he had not conveyed this information to the latter, who despite his sympathy for social security and the Wagner bill, would not have endorsed the plan of battle proposed to the president.[44]

Tugwell also reported that Frankfurter endorsed a constitutional amendment in discussions with Roosevelt, "but thought that we had to have some more adverse Supreme Court decisions before we got to it."[45] As an immediate response to the *Schechter* decision, however, Frankfurter advised the president to seek new legislation that would permit him to attach fair labor clauses to all federal contacts as well as a new law extending the principles of the Webb-Kenyon Act to areas such as child labor. That 1913 statute, already sustained by the Court, prohibited the interstate shipment of liquor into states that banned such imports, but whether the principle could be applied to labor policies was not at all certain in the wake of *Panama Refining Co.* At the same time, it encouraged reforms at the state level that Brandeis surely endorsed.[46]

Throughout the frantic summer of 1935, Frankfurter worked almost daily on the legislative program of the second Hundred Days, helped Stanley Reed recruit better lawyers for the solicitor general's office, and supervised the preparation of legal briefs for the next round of litigation. He kept Brandeis informed on many of these matters, especially taxation and holding companies, but he did not mention his theory of confrontation with the Court or the fact that he had displayed enthusiasm for a constitutional amendment.[47] He hoped for the best and expected the worst, but even he did not anticipate the Court's reckless conduct in 1936.

❧❧❧

From early January until early June, five and sometimes six members of the Court advanced theories of constitutional law so barren of historical principles, so blind to contemporary political realities, and so contemptuous of both Congress and the state legislatures that Brandeis, Stone, and Cardozo—all of whom had voted against the New Deal a year before—openly revolted. "We are getting new doctrine now faster than I can absorb it." Stone told Frankfurter, even before the most imaginative decisions had been handed down.[48]

First, speaking through Roberts, the majority struck down the Triple A in an opinion that upheld the authority of Congress to tax and spend broadly for the general welfare, but simultaneously limited that authority in the case at hand with the Tenth Amendment. Roberts sang a rhapsody on the scope of congressional power, then denounced the program as coercive, confiscatory, and an invasion of the states' control over agricultural production.[49] Stone, unable to contain his anger, branded the performance "contradictory and destructive," a "tortured construction of the Constitution" that produced "absurd consequences" for the nation.[50]

A month later, brushing aside the Tenth Amendment restrictions announced in *Butler* and upholding the federal government's right to sell electric power, the majority handed the New Deal's enemies a powerful new weapon by permitting stockholders' law suits against corporate officers who collaborated with agencies such as the Tennessee Valley Authority.[51] On April 6, the Four Horsemen plus Hughes and Roberts denounced the Securities and Exchange Commission for attempting to probe the affairs of a notorious stock swindler who had withdrawn his registration statements in an effort to stop the commission's inquiry. The majority's opinion, Cardozo wrote, gave comfort to "knaves intent upon obscuring and suppressing the knowledge of their knavery."[52]

The same six justices scuttled the Guffey Coal Act by finding its taxation, price fixing, and labor provisions in violation of the Fifth Amendment and beyond Congress's authority under the commerce clause. The nation's glut of bituminous coal, they reasoned, should be left to local regulation along with the surpluses of wheat, cotton, and tobacco—a solution that even Brandeis found absurd. "The liberty protected by the Fifth Amendment," Cardozo wrote for the three dissenters, "does not include the right to persist in this anarchic riot."[53]

Having curtailed the New Deal's ability to fight the depression, the majority turned its doctrinal guns against the states as well. With Hughes and Roberts joining the Four Horsemen again, the Court struck down a section of Vermont's income tax law on the extraordinary grounds that it violated the privileges and immunities clause of the Fourteenth Amendment to levy a tax on the interest earned on loans made outside the state while exempting the interest earned on loans made within Vermont.[54] They also overturned a North Dakota tax assessment of railroad properties as "arbitrary" and "grossly excessive," but without any evidence that the figure had been discriminatory in comparison with the tax burdens placed upon other property owners in the state.[55]

In the *Mayflower Farms* case, the same six justices toppled a provision of New York's Milk Control Act that permitted dealers without well-known brand names to sell their milk for one penny less than their better-known competitors. This penny differential, intended to protect the industry's weakest members, violated the equal protection clause according to Roberts, although Cardozo noted that "hardships, great or little, were inevitable. . . . The legislature, and not the court, has been charged with the duty of determining their comparative extent."[56]

On the last day of the term, Roberts and the Four Horsemen reaffirmed the decision in *Adkins* by declaring invalid New York's minimum-wage law for women. Any legislative effort to coerce employers into making such payments, Butler wrote, amounted to confiscation of their property without due process of law.[57] Even former President Hoover expressed shock over the *Morehead* result and urged that "something . . . be done to give back to the states the powers they thought they already had."[58]

Frankfurter believed that the Court's reckless use of the Fourteenth Amendment represented a greater menace to democratic values than its animus toward the New Deal. The majority had now spun a web of constitutional doctrine that permitted them to veto all governmental programs, whether federal or state, that attempted to redistribute income or socialize the losses arising from the depression. Few decisions in the Court's entire history seemed to him more unjustified than the *Colgate* case. "I thought of all the stock mishaps—Lochner, Adair, Burns Baking Co., Ribnic . . . and all the rest," he told Stone. "But, honestly, the disinterment of 'privileges and immunities' and their perversion to the use put in the Colgate decision, seems to me the end of the limit."[59]

Roberts and Hughes, he complained later, "reached terrible depths in the *Mayflower* case. Plainly now, a statute must . . . prove itself in accord [with] what five men think wise. . . . J.B. Thayer must be turning in his grave—and so Miller, J."[60] And Hughes's endorsement of Butler's opinion in the *Great Northern* case seemed to him inexplicable in light of what the chief justice had written in the past with respect to railroad valuation questions. "Something deep in me just balks at that assumption of obtuseness in Hughes," he told Stone. "And so I am driven to the alternative which makes the matter worse."[61]

For a brief moment following the *Ashwander* decision, Frankfurter believed that the Court might display some flexibility in the face of controversial new programs. He deplored Hughes's opinion that encouraged more stockholder's suits, but advised Roosevelt that the decision "created sufficient confusion in the public mind" so that other adverse rulings "would come in the atmosphere of goodwill for the

Court." He and Corcoran urged Roosevelt to avoid an immediate test of the PWA's housing program — which they expected to lose — where the political dividends generated by a negative decision would not be very large. "Any benefit from further decisions against constitutionality," Corcoran argued, "must derive from a specific and well organized class feeling directly and specifically aggrieved."[62]

The Court's spring offensive against both the administration and the states paid large dividends in the form of protest from coal miners, congressmen, and angry local politicians. Frankfurter lost all hope of compromise. The *Morehead* decision, he told Stone, "leaves me numb," because the majority "demonstrated anew the versatility, or at least the resources, of unreason and folly. . . . This fateful term is over, but its ghosts will walk for many a day."[63] "Aren't the Mastiffs wonderful," he wrote to Hand. "There are MEN for you — Due Process and the Eternal Truths are, nothing daunted, election or no election, safe in their keeping."[64] He saved his sharpest barbs for Roberts, who had once seemed to be a promising addition to Brandeis, Stone, and Holmes. "Roberts proves that a man may be, as he is, a most engaging and fearless fellow . . . even be a good slugger in a thing like the Teapot Dome business," he observed, "and yet not be adequately equipped for the task of statesmanship that Commerce Clause and Due Process require."[65]

Whatever the justifications and excuses later advanced by Hughes and some historians, Frankfurter knew that the behavior of six justices had discredited the Court and invited political retribution from the administration and others. Sutherland, McReynolds, Butler, and Van Devanter lived in an idealized constitutional universe, oblivious to the pressing needs of millions of Americans. Owen Roberts, after flirting with the liberalism of Stone, Brandeis, and Cardozo, had been driven into alliance with the Four Horsemen on the great issues of the commerce clause, taxation, and due process — largely because of his fear of radical economic panaceas and his lifelong devotion to the Republican Party. The chief justice, "liberal through expedience . . . conservative by inclination," had joined that alliance as well — partly because of his own hostility to redistributive legislation, partly because of his desire to avoid embarrassing five to four decisions, and partly because of his unwillingness to fight the Court's main bullies, Sutherland and McReynolds.[66]

By Christmas, a month after Roosevelt's stunning reelection victory, Frankfurter and his allies had prepared several constitutional amendments designed to limit the Court's veto over federal legislation. One proposal, which enjoyed Reed's support and was similar to others introduced in Congress, permitted "an unchallengeable reenactment" by Congress of any law declared invalid on constitutional grounds. Frankfurter knew that this measure faced enormous political obstacles, but he also saw "the need for constitutional reform" in the wake of the Court's dismal performance in 1936. He had long urged confrontation upon Roosevelt, but not the one chosen by the president's bombshell on February 5, 1937.[67]

❧❧❧

"Very confidentially," Roosevelt told him in January, "I may give you an awful shock in about two weeks. Even if you do not agree, suspend judgment and I will tell you the story."[68] F.D.R.'s "awful shock," prepared secretly by Attorney General Cummings and a small coterie of advisers, asked Congress not to amend the Constitution—a strategy endorsed by the party's 1936 platform—but to permit the president to appoint new federal judges for every present judge who waited more than six months after his seventieth birthday to retire or resign. This legislation, Roosevelt argued, would "vitalize the courts" by reducing overcrowded dockets. It would hasten appeals through the infusion of more and younger jurists. His frontal assault on the Court shocked conservatives. His disingenuous defense of the plan appalled even his allies. "Boys," remarked one congressman, "here's where I cash in my chips."[69]

In addition to Cummings and lawyers in the Justice Department, Roosevelt had consulted Edward S. Corwin, a professor of jurisprudence at Princeton and one of the Court's most trenchant critics. He had consulted neither party leaders in Congress nor Felix Frankfurter. His reluctance to take Frankfurter into his confidence on the most explosive legislative proposals of the decade is not difficult to understand when one recalls that Roosevelt distrusted Brandeis in the wake of the *Schechter* and *Myers* cases, sensed Frankfurter's divided sympathies, and could not count upon his support for the plan in advance. "Brandeis, as he got older," Roosevelt remarked to Ickes, "was losing sight of the fundamentals." The president had given up hope that Brandeis, "our Cape Code friend," as he told Norman Hapgood, could "help us find ways of answering the people who . . . say either 'don't do it' or 'you can't do it' whenever constructive action of any kind is proposed."[70]

Roosevelt knew, in addition, that although Frankfurter willingly gave advice on a constitutional amendment, he had written an article in 1934 which argued that "to enlarge the size of the Supreme Court would be self-defeating."[71] Frankfurter had also warned the Court's critics to avoid what he called "mechanical contrivances" when thinking about how to change its jurisprudence. "The ultimate determinant," he wrote, "is the quality of the Justices."[72] Fearing negative comments, the president had shunned congressional advice before proposing the plan, and these same apprehensions no doubt led him to exclude Frankfurter from the secret deliberations.

Roosevelt must have been surprised by Frankfurter's encouraging reply on February 7. He complimented the president on "the deftness of the general scheme," blasted the Court for "a long series of decisions not defensible in the realm of reason," and confessed that "some major operation was necessary" in order "to save the Constitution from the Court and the Court from itself."[73] Roosevelt not only incorporated that phrase into his fireside chat of March 9, but he drew upon other Frankfurter suggestions as well. "People have been taught to believe that when the Supreme Court speaks it is not they who speak but the Constitution," Frankfurter told F.D.R., "whereas, of course, in so many vital areas, it is *they* who speak and not the Constitution." The justices, he added, "have identified the Constitution with their private social philosophy." He urged Roosevelt to become more candid with the American people about the reasons for his plan. This could be done by deemphasizing the issues of judicial efficiency and stressing the Court's abuse of power.[74]

Not once over the next five months, as Roosevelt pursued his futile course, ruptured the progressive coalition, and wasted his political leverage, did Frankfurter propose a more cautious strategy. Both in letters and in person, he plied F.D.R. with encouragement and advice on how to wage the battle more effectively. At his suggestion, Henry M. Hart, Jr., a recent protégé, wrote a favorable article in the *Harvard Alumni Bulletin*. At the same time, he never endorsed the president's plan openly and declined to be drawn into public debate over its merits. "Foolish folks (enemies of yours)," he told F.D.R., "are doing their damndest to make me attack the court so as to start a new line of attack against your proposal. They miss their guess. I shan't help them to divert the issue. . . . There are various ways of fighting a fight."[75]

Frankfurter's behind-the-scenes encouragement coupled with his public silence have generated considerable criticism. Some people theorize that he despised the plan, but went along with Roosevelt out of blind loyalty and self-interest. According to this interpretation, he behaved like a hypocrite by keeping his true feelings hidden from Roosevelt. Others, including Joseph Lash, argue that Frankfurter had a duty to the public to speak out against the president's nefarious scheme, which would have destroyed the Court. The evidence for the first theory is not entirely convincing, while the second criticism ignores the fact that Frankfurter probably viewed the Court's abuse of power as a greater threat than Roosevelt's.

Jim Landis, for one, reported that he "caught hell" from his former mentor for supporting the Court-packing bill shortly after he became the new dean at Harvard, succeeding Roscoe Pound. Acheson believed that Frankfurter remained "dead against" the president's plan, although he never said so. Reed Powell recalled that after studying Roosevelt's message to Congress, Frankfurter expressed shock at "the longevity point" and added: "You may think it sentimental of me, but I have a real feeling of reverence for old age."[76]

His stern advice to Landis, however, can be seen in the light of his fastidious concern to keep the Harvard Law School officially out of the conflict. Powell also recalled that Frankfurter quickly urged F.D.R. to adopt "an alternative proposal" which ignored the longevity-efficiency arguments and stressed the point that the justices "had long wielded control to thwart governmental policies." Frankfurter himself had second thoughts on the longevity argument. "The mere fact that men dispatch business does not mean they dispatch it wisely or are capable of adequate intake of the relevant considerations," he told Powell, citing the research on aging done by his friend, Alfred Cohn, "who I suspect knows more about senescence than anybody on either side of the Atlantic."[77]

Frankfurter's public silence probably sprang more from careful political calculation than from cowardice, doubt, or hypocrisy. Endorsement of the president's plan by the notoriously radical Professor Frankfurter would not generate much support for the measure. Seldom one to avoid exploiting a political asset, Roosevelt never asked for Frankfurter's public support. Other, more positive evidence suggests that he supported the spirit if not the substance of the president's plan and came very close to an open break with Brandeis over the issue.

When New York Governor Lehman, a liberal Democrat, came out against the proposal, Frankfurter sharply criticized his desertion.[78] He became even more furious when Hughes, Brandeis, and Van Devanter, supposedly speaking for all of the justices, sent a letter to the Senate Judiciary Committee which rejected all of Roosevelt's arguments on the necessity for reorganization. He immediately dashed off a tart letter to Brandeis, which remains the fullest exposition of his views:

> Tampering with the Court is a very serious business. Like any major operation it is justified only by the most compelling considerations. But no student of the Court can be blind to its long course of misbehavior. I do not relish some of the implications of the President's proposal, but neither do I relish victory for the subtler but ultimately deeper evils inevitable in the victory for Hughes and the Butlers and their successors. . . . It is a complicated situation and an unhappy one that F.D.R. has precipitated, but the need, it seems to me, more important than any is that in a handful of men . . . the fear of God should be instilled so that they may walk humbly before their Lord.[79]

Frankfurter never mailed it. When his anger cooled he recognized that the letter would only rupture an already strained relationship with Brandeis and not accomplish anything, because the latter's opposition to Roosevelt's plan was well known.[80] Whatever his reservations about "some of the implications of the President's proposals," they paled in comparison with what he called the "deeper evils inevitable in the victory for Hughes and the Butlers and their successors." In the final analysis, Roosevelt's attack, however clumsy, seemed to him no more "political" than the behavior of several justices, above all, Hughes and Roberts.

The truth of that observation became abundantly clear when the two men suddenly capitulated in the spring of 1937. They did so in such a blatantly cynical manner that Frankfurter despaired over the Court's tarnished reputation even while he savored the New Deal's victories. One week after the Hughes-Brandeis-Van Devanter letter reached the Senate, the Court upheld a minimum-wage law similar to the one vetoed nine months earlier. The vote was five to four, with Hughes and Roberts in the majority.[81] Two weeks later, the same coalition put its stamp of approval on the National Labor Relations Act in a sweeping commerce clause opinion written by the chief justice himself.[82]

Hughes did his best to disguise Robert's retreat in the minimum-wage case with the argument that New York had never asked the Court to overrule *Adkins*. This statement flatly contradicted the state's original petition for certiorari as well as its petition for rehearing. It also ignored the obvious point, spelled out in Stone's dissent, that the justices did not have to overrule *Adkins* in order to decide in New

York's favor. They simply had to follow Roberts's own analysis in *Nebbia*.[83]

Roberts's "somersault," Frankfurter told Stone, was "incapable of being attributed to a single factor relevant to the professed judicial process. Everything that he now subscribes to he rejected not only on June first last, but as late as October twelfth. . . . I wish either Roberts or the Chief had the responsibility of conducting the class when we shall reach this case shortly. It is very, very sad business."[84] Frankfurter later modified his views on Roberts's behavior, but this first assessment had been the correct one. Roosevelt's reorganization plan played no part in "the big switch," but his resounding reelection victory surely did.[85]

The Hughes-Roberts capitulation in the *Labor Board* cases proved to be an even greater embarrassment, because not even the most cunning doctrinal hair splitters could easily reconcile their earlier views on the commerce clause with the newest version. "In order to reach the result which was reached in these cases," Stone remarked, "it was necessary for six members of the Court either to be overruled or to take back some things they subscribed to in the Guffey Coal Act case."[86] Frankfurter, who cheered the result, deplored the method. "After today," he told F.D.R., "I feel like finding some honest profession to enter."[87] Wyzanski, who argued the cases before the Court, quipped to Isador Lubin that "the President's castor oil seemed to work." "Yes," replied Lubin, "after some labor pains the Court gave birth to quintuplets."[88]

On May 18, Justice Van Devanter announced his retirement. A week later, in another five to four decision, the justices upheld both the unemployment compensation and old-age pension provisions of the Social Security Act.[89] These two events sealed the fate of Roosevelt's reorganization plan, although the recriminations continued until August, when both sides finally agreed upon a face-saving compromise that gave the president a bill to sign without any provision for the appointment of additional justices.

In his suggestions for Roosevelt's Constitution Day address on September 17, Frankfurter spoke of the "temporarily complete" victory of Congress and president over the Court. Wholesome governmental programs had been frustrated in the past, he noted, "not because of anything the Constitution says but because men with axes to grind have chosen to put their lawyers' own notions of policy upon the silence or the vagueness of the Constitution." Now was the time to invoke "the whole Constitution," not simply those parts "which . . .

serve the purposes of certain limited interests." Now was the time to form "a more perfect Union, establish Justice, insure domestic tranquility, provide for the common defense, promote the general Welfare, and secure the Blessings of Liberty to ourselves and our Posterity."[90]

Not even Frankfurter's eloquence could arrest the confusion and doubt that now enveloped the nation's political institutions in the aftermath of the constitutional revolution. At considerable cost to his own and the judiciary's reputation, Hughes had been able to preserve the substance of judicial review, while giving up the more grandiose ambition to check the New Deal and the forces of social reform. A year after the *Parrish* case, Stone drove the last nails into the coffin of substantive due process, but no one could now say with certainty what role the Court of John Marshall, Roger Taney, and Oliver Wendell Holmes would play in the future.[91]

"To me it is all painful beyond words," Frankfurter told Wyzanski, "the poignant grief of one whose life has been dedicated to faith in the disinterestedness of a tribunal and its freedom from responsiveness to the most obvious immediacies of politics. . . . It all . . . gives one the sickening feeling which is aroused when moral standards are adulterated in a convent."[92] At equally great cost to his own political coalition, Roosevelt had saved the heart of the New Deal and modern liberalism, but lost the momentum for further reforms. The Court-packing battle had left deep wounds upon president, party, and Congress. Roosevelt's enemies had been emboldened by his defeat; his friends remained divided. The future of the Supreme Court as well as the future of American liberalism never seemed more problematic.

MR. JUSTICE
FRANKFURTER

IN MARCH OF 1938, German soldiers paraded through the streets of Vienna celebrating the triumph of Adolf Hitler's *Anschluss* and the extinction of Austrian independence. Briefly, Vienna's new masters imprisoned one of the city's most distinguished Jewish scholars, Solomon Frankfurter, for what Lady Nancy Astor described as "some unguarded remarks." Ten months later, Franklin Roosevelt nominated the scholar's nephew, also a Vienna-born Jew, to the Supreme Court of the United States. Europe's descent into lawlessness and barbarism, already well advanced by events in Ethiopia and Spain, gathered fresh momentum from the first event. American liberals, scarred by the Court-packing battle, the recession of 1937, and the debacle of Munich, took heart from the second—although Frankfurter's appointment arose more from simple friendship than from the symbolic exigencies of international and domestic policies.[1]

The fact that he was a Jew, an Easterner, a liberal, and an internationalist almost kept Frankfurter off the Court, despite F.D.R.'s broad hint in 1933 that he would find it much easier to put a solicitor general than a Harvard professor on the bench. He had not left Harvard, but his fidelity to Roosevelt might have compensated for that had the Court-packing fight not strained his relationship with Brandeis. He and Marion dined with the justice shortly after the Senate killed the reorganization bill, but their correspondence fell off sharply in 1938 and 1939, even with respect to critical Zionist issues where Frankfurter had always been Brandeis's chief confidant and adviser. Clearly, the latter had been deeply offended by Frankfurter's defection to F.D.R. on the reorganization bill and by the behavior of his protégés, above all, Corcoran.[2]

As the administration's hatchet-man during the reorganization fight, Corcoran remained unforgiving toward Brandeis for his opposition, and he spread his resentments all over Washington. "I am not going to see him [Brandeis]," he told Ben Cohen, tartly. "He did not shoot straight with us last year, and it is best not to renew the relationship. The Skipper is very bitter, and I think it is best that he should not think we are in touch with him." Corcoran also expressed great annoyance that Brandeis had not stepped down from the Court in order to make way for Frankfurter's appointment. When these rumors reached Brandeis, he observed that "he was not sure that Frankfurter could not do more by teaching the younger generation," a reply that suggested he had no intention of retiring for anyone, including Felix Frankfurter. If Brandeis did not retire before Roosevelt left office, Ickes snapped, he "will have something to answer for to the liberals of the country."[3]

With both Brandeis and Cardozo on the Court, of course, there was little hope for Frankfurter. The Van Devanter and Sutherland vacancies both went to Southerners—Hugh Black of Alabama and Stanley Reed of Kentucky—but this left the Court in 1938 with an underrepresentation of the West. Even if Brandeis or Cardozo stepped down, Roosevelt hinted, he probably could not appoint Frankfurter. "Whom do you think I should appoint—Landis or Frankfurter?" the president asked Henry Morgenthau, Jr., who expressed his preference for Landis "by all means," but F.D.R. seemed to favor the latter, although he noted, "I think I would have a terrible time getting Frankfurter confirmed."[4]

When Cardozo's sudden death and not Brandeis's resignation created a new vacancy in the summer of 1938, Roosevelt broke the bad news to Frankfurter at Hyde Park. After lunch in his "little bit of a dinky hole" study, a nervous and embarrassed president told his friend that the Holmes seat would have to go to a Westerner, because "I've given very definite promises to Senators and party people that the next appointment to the Court would be someone west of the

Mississippi." Frankfurter expressed some astonishment that Roosevelt felt compelled to explain his decision, and, characteristically, he began to rattle off a long list of possible nominees who met the president's geographical requirements.[5]

Outwardly over the next few months, Frankfurter behaved like the good soldier. He wrote reports for Roosevelt on the judicial opinions of several candidates and, through his extensive network of informants, gathered personal information on at least one of them, Wiley Rutledge, then dean of the law school at the University of Iowa. This cheerful façade, however, camouflaged considerable disappointment and frustration at not getting the appointment as well as a reluctance to give up the battle entirely. He could not, of course, lobby for his own nomination, but friends could do it for him. By December, F.D.R. reported to Jim Farley that "Felix Frankfurter wants to get on [the Supreme Court] in the worst way. Some months ago I had to tell him at Hyde Park that I just couldn't appoint him for many reasons. In the first place the appointment has to go west. In the second place, I told Felix that I could not appoint another Jew."[6] Roosevelt, very annoyed, felt the heat coming from Frankfurter's friends, especially Corcoran and his allies.

Later in life, Frankfurter always maintained that he had been totally surprised by Roosevelt's telephone call on the evening of January 4, when the president finally offered him the nomination. This image of Frankfurter, clad only in undershorts, struck dumb by Roosevelt's change of heart, has a certain romantic appeal—but it is wholly false. Joe Rauh, Jr., then one of Corcoran's assistants and later a Frankfurter law clerk, recalls a different version of events in December and January. Tommy the Cork kept the phone lines busy between Washington and Cambridge each evening, bringing his mentor up to date on the shifting battle scene. Corcoran and his supporters kept friendly senators supplied with damaging information about other potential candidates, and they organized an impressive letter-writing campaign on Frankfurter's behalf. Wavering senators, for instance, found their mailboxes stuffed with pro-Frankfurter wires from Harvard Law School alumni, old progressives, law professors, and leaders of local bar associations.[7]

In addition to gaining the endorsement of Senator Norris, a key Westerner, the Corcoran forces received important support for Frankfurter from Hopkins, Robert Jackson, the new solicitor general, and Ickes, all of whom argued that Roosevelt might forever lose the opportunity to put his friend on the Court unless he did it now. "If you appoint Felix," Ickes told F.D.R., "his abilities and learning are such that he will dominate the Supreme Court for fifteen or twenty years to come. The result will be that probably after you are dead, it will still be your Supreme Court." Only Frankfurter, argued Jackson, had the legal resources "to face Chief Justice Hughes in conference and hold his own in discussion," a point reinforced by Justice Stone, who also urged F.D.R. to name Frankfurter, because he could help contain the wily chief justice.[8]

Frankfurter's opponents mobilized a powerful counterattack. Still smarting from the Court-packing fight, Cummings insisted that the nomination would provoke a bitter confirmation debate and plunge the administration into more controversy. Morgenthau, perhaps the president's closest adviser, kept up a steady drumfire of anti-Frankfurter criticism, as did a group of other prominent Jews, headed by Arthur Hays Sulzberger of the *New York Times*, who warned Roosevelt that putting a second Jew on the Court would play into the hands of anti-Semites at home and abroad. Sometime in early January, despite these objections, despite his own irritation at the organized campaign for Frankfurter, and despite the fact that Brandeis remained on the Court, Roosevelt changed his mind. No one ingredient seems to have been decisive, but several circumstances taken together probably explain the shift.

Roosevelt found it difficult to ignore the opinion of Norris, Stone, Jackson, and Ickes that Frankfurter was, after all, the most qualified candidate by virtue of intellect and experience and the one appointment most likely to bring stability as well as new luster to the Court. Whatever else they had brought to the high bench, neither of Roosevelt's first two justices brought the distinction associated with Holmes, Brandeis, Hughes, or Stone. Faithful New Dealers, Black and Reed were both noted for their intense political partisanship and mediocre legal abilities. Black, in addition, had been tarred with the brush of past membership in the Ku Klux Klan. Reed's appointment did not generate much enthusiasm among either administration loyalists or students of the Court. Justice Stone, for example, described the Kentuckian as "honest, straightforward . . . a hard worker, and I think a sound lawyer," but these words did not describe someone in the mold of Marshall, Story, or Field.[9]

Black's quixotic behavior had already provoked alarm among other justices on a Court whose reputation had been badly damaged by accusations of expediency and incompetence during the rapid doctrinal shifts in 1937 and 1938. In one of his first dissents, Roosevelt's first appointee called on the Court to reverse over fifty years of precedent by excluding business corporations from the protection of the Fourteenth Amendment.[10] "He needs guidance from someone who is more familiar with the workings of the judicial process than he is," Stone complained about Black's sledgehammer tactics. "There are enough present day battles of importance to be won without wasting our effort to remake the Constitution *ab initio*, or using the judicial opinion as a political tract."[11] Frankfurter, the loyal New Dealer, could be expected to defend the social and economic gains of the decade. Frankfurter, the scholar, the student of the Court's past, would also add ballast to a vessel now running in uncertain waters and very much in need of experienced helmsmen.

By putting Frankfurter on the Court, Roosevelt also made a symbolic gesture of support for American Zionists at a time when even symbolic gestures had become important to their hopes. The Peel Report of July 1937 had recommended the partition of Palestine into two states—one Arab and one Jewish—and while this particular solution had been shelved a year later, the British had set a course designed to restrict new Jewish immigration into Palestine and to limit the area of their settlements. Frankfurter and Brandeis had both spoken forcefully to F.D.R. about the injustice of British policy; the president expressed sympathy, but he was not prepared to apply diplomatic pressure to Great Britain—even in the wake of the *Anschluss*, Munich, and the Nazis' murderous anti-Semitic campaigns. Unable and perhaps unwilling to support the Zionists on the most important issue, he nonetheless named one of them to the nation's highest court.[12]

By early January, in addition, Brandeis's failing health made it clear that he could not long continue on the bench. Grippe, followed by a heart attack, brought his letter of retirement five weeks after Roosevelt sent Frankfurter's name to the Senate. The political problem of two Jewish justices, both from Massachusetts, serving at the same time, became moot.

Perhaps above all, there was the friendship. However much he complained about Frankfurter's intrigues, his many importunities, and his garrulousness, Roosevelt liked him enormously. Frankfurter's devotion to the New Deal was unquestionable, and his adoration of Roosevelt, seemingly unquenchable, bordered upon the obsequious. Roosevelt had hated to turn down Frankfurter in October. He clearly relished appointing him three months later and even joked to Missy

LeHand about "a little bunch of conspirators" who, he claimed, put Frankfurter on the Court.[13] At the end of January, the president received the first of many notes written on Supreme Court stationery: "Dear Frank: In the mysterious ways of Fate, the Dutchess County American and the Viennese American have for decades pursued the same directions of devotion to our beloved country. And now, on your blessed birthday I am given the gift of opportunity for service to the Nation which, in any circumstances would be owing, but which I would rather have had at your hands than at those of any other President barring Lincoln."[14]

Forty-four days later, Hitler absorbed all of Czechoslovakia.

NOTES

INTRODUCTION

1. Frankfurter to Oliver Wendell Holmes, December 1, 1921, Box 30, File 17, Holmes Papers, Harvard Law School (hereafter cited as OWHP).
2. Frankfurter to Holmes, ibid., March 2, 1914, Box 30, File 15.

Chapter 1. YOUNG MAN FROM THE PROVINCES

1. Harold Laski to Oliver Wendell Holmes, July 20, 1925, *Holmes-Laski Letters*, I, ed. Mark De Wolfe Howe (Cambridge, MA: Harvard University Press, 1953), p. 766.
2. John Mason Brown, "The Uniform of Justice," *The Saturday Review 37* (October 30, 1954): 46.
3. Matthew Josephson, "Jurist," *The New Yorker 16* (November 30, 1940): 25.
4. Lionel Trilling, *The Liberal Imagination: Essays on Literature and Society* (New York: Doubleday, 1953), p. 58.
5. Allan Janik and Stephen Toulmin, *Wittgenstein's Vienna* (New York: Simon & Schuster, 1973), p. 67; Carl E. Schorske, "Politics and the Psyche in *fin de siecle* Vienna: Schnitzler and Hofmannsthal," *American Historical Review 66* (February 1961): 930–946; Schorske, "Cultural Hothouse," *New York Review of Books* (December 11, 1975), pp. 39–44.
6. Carl E. Schorske, "Politics in a New Key: An Austrian Triptych," *The Journal of Modern History 39* (December 1967): 343–386; P.G.J. Pulzer,

The Rise of Political Anti-Semitism in Germany and Austria (New York: John Wiley & Sons, 1964), pp. 184–216.

7. Janik and Toulmin, *Wittgenstein's Vienna*, pp. 55–58; Schorske, "Politics in a New Key," pp. 375–380 and *passim*.
8. Liva Baker, *Felix Frankfurter* (New York: Coward-McCann, 1969), p. 18.
9. C. Vann Woodward, "The Populist Heritage and the Intellectuals," *The American Scholar 21* (Winter 1959–1960): 55–72; Moses Rischin, *The Promised City: New York's Jews, 1870–1914* (Cambridge, MA: Harvard University Press, 1962), pp. 261–262.
10. Rischin, *The Promised City*, p. 93; Felix Frankfurter, Oral History Transcript, May 1953, Frankfurter Papers, Library of Congress (hereafter cited as FFLC).
11. Frankfurter, ibid., October 1953; Matthew Josephson, "Jurist," *The New Yorker 16* (December 7, 1940): 35.
12. Frankfurter, Oral History Transcript, October 1953, FFLC.
13. Harlan B. Phillips, ed., *Felix Frankfurter Reminisces* (New York: Reynal, 1960), pp. 6–7.
14. Frankfurter, Oral History Transcript, October 1953, FFLC; Wallace Mendelson, ed., *Felix Frankfurter: A Tribute* (New York: Reynal, 1964), p. 49.
15. Quoted in Ronald Sanders, *The Downtown Jews: Portraits of an Immigrant Generation* (New York: Harper & Brothers, 1969), pp. 259–260.
16. Frankfurter, Oral History Transcript, October 1953, FFLC; Mendelson, ed., *Felix Frankfurter: A Tribute*, pp. 82–83.
17. Quoted in Melvin I. Urofsky, *American Zionism from Herzl to the Holocaust* (New York: Doubleday, 1975), p. 59.
18. Frankfurter, Oral History Transcript, May 1953, FFLC; Morris R. Cohen, *A Dreamer's Journey* (Boston: Little, Brown, 1949), pp. 89–99.
19. Frankfurter, Oral History Transcript, May and November 1953, FFLC.
20. Ibid.
21. *The Law Quarterly Review 3* (1887): 123–124.
22. Ibid.
23. Lawrence M. Friedman, *A History of American Law* (New York: Simon & Schuster, 1973), pp. 530–536.
24. Arthur E. Sutherland, *The Law at Harvard: A History of Ideas and Men, 1817–1967* (Cambridge, MA: Harvard University Press, 1967), pp. 215–216.
25. Frankfurter, Oral History Transcript, November 1953, FFLC.
26. Louis Brandeis to William H. Dunbar, February 2, 1893, *Letters of Louis D. Brandeis*, I, ed. Melvin I. Urofsky and David Levy (Albany: State University of New York Press, 1971), pp. 106–107; Martin Mayer, *Emory Buckner: A Biography* (New York: Harper & Row, 1968), pp. 4–5.
27. Phillips, *Frankfurter Reminisces*, pp. 31–32.

28. Oliver Wendell Holmes, *The Common Law*, ed. Mark De Wolfe Howe (Boston: Little, Brown, 1963), p. 5; Holmes, "The Path of the Law," *Harvard Law Review 10* (1897): 469.
29. Morris R. Cohen and Felix S. Cohen, *Readings in Jurisprudence and Legal Philosophy* (Boston: Little, Brown, 1951): 407 – 415.
30. James B. Thayer, "The Origin and Scope of the American Doctrine of Constitutional Law," *Harvard Law Review* 7 (October 1893): 129 – 142.
31. See, for example, *United States* v. *E. C. Knight Co.*, 156 U.S. 1 (1895); *In Re Debs*, 158 U.S. 564 (1895); *Pollock* v. *Farmers Loan and Trust Co.*, 158 U.S. 601 (1895); *Chicago, Milwaukee & St. Paul Railway Co.* v. *Minnesota*, 134 U.S. 418 (1890) and *Smyth* v. *Ames*, 169 U.S. 466 (1898).
32. *Lochner* v. *New York*, 198 U.S. 45 (1905), 49 – 57, 62.
33. Louis D. Brandeis, "The Opportunity in the Law," *American Law Review 39* (July – August 1905): 559 – 561.
34. Frankfurter, Oral History Transcript, February 1954, FFLC.

Chapter 2. THE MAKING OF A REFORMER

1. Mark Sullivan, *Our Times*, III (New York: Charles Scribner's Sons, 1930), pp. 70 – 71; Henry Adams, *The Education of Henry Adams* (New York: Random House, 1931), p. 417.
2. Frankfurter to Philip L. Miller, June 20, 1912, Box 84, FFLC; Frankfurter to Learned Hand, March 12, 1912, Learned Hand Papers, Harvard Law School (hereafter cited as LHP).
3. The literature on Roosevelt, his administration, and the progressive movement in general is voluminous. For this account I have relied especially upon the following: George E. Mowry, *The Era of Theodore Roosevelt and the Birth of Modern America* (New York: Harper & Row, 1958), pp. 85 – 142, 197 – 225; John M. Blum, *The Republican Roosevelt* (Cambridge, MA: Harvard University Press, 1954), pp. 7 – 124; Robert H. Wiebe, *Businessmen and Reform: A Study of the Progressive Movement* (Cambridge, MA: Harvard University Press, 1962), pp. 16 – 100; William H. Harbaugh, ed., *The Writings of Theodore Roosevelt* (New York: Bobbs-Merrill, 1967), pp. xvii – xliv; Gabriel Kolko, *The Triumph of Conservatism: A Reinterpretation of American History, 1900 – 1916* (New York: Free Press, 1963), pp. 57 – 158; Samuel P. Hays, *Conservation and the Gospel of Efficiency: The Progressive Conservation Movement, 1890 – 1920* (Cambridge, MA: Harvard University Press, 1959); William H. Harbaugh, *Power and Responsibility: The Life and Times of Theodore Roosevelt* (New York: Colliers, 1961).
4. *Employers' Liability Cases, First*, 207 U.S. 463 (1908).
5. *Adair* v. *United States*, 208 U.S. 161 (1908).

6. *Loewe* v. *Lawlor*, 208 U.S. 274 (1908).

7. Quoted in Alfred H. Kelley and Winfred A. Harbison, *The American Constitution: Its Origins and Development*, 5th ed. (New York: W. W. Norton, 1976), p. 596.

8. Elting E. Morison, *Turmoil and Tradition: A Study of the Life and Times of Henry L. Stimson* (New York: Atheneum, 1964), pp. 3–60.

9. Ibid., 77.

10. Frankfurter to Marion Denman, n.p.n.d., but probably 1917, Box 5, FFLC; Mendelson, ed., *Felix Frankfurter: A Tribute*, p. 38.

11. Henry L. Stimson and McGeorge Bundy, *On Active Service in Peace and War* (New York: Harper & Brothers, 1947), p. 7; Martin Mayer, *Emory Buckner*, pp. 4, 28–29, 32.

12. See, for example, *United States* v. *Wimsatt*, 161 Federal Reporter, 586 (1908).

13. Morison, *Stimson*, p. 81.

14. Phillips, *Frankfurter Reminisces*, pp. 42–43.

15. *New York Central and Hudson River Railroad Company* v. *United States*, 212 U.S. 481 (1909).

16. *United States* v. *Morse*, 161 Federal Reporter, 429 (1908); and *United States* v. *Heinze*, 161 Federal Reporter, 425 (1908).

17. Henry Stimson, "Report on Investigation into Various Fraudulent Practices at the New York Custom House," Box 51, FFLC.

18. Ibid.; *Heike* v. *United States*, 227 U.S. 131 (1912).

19. *Harriman* v. *Interstate Commerce Commission*, 211 U.S. 407 (1908). Holmes, who usually voted to uphold governmental efforts to regulate wages, hours, and working conditions, became very squeamish about assaults against the titans of big business. He deplored the antitrust laws and generally assisted in judicial efforts to narrow their scope. See for example, his opinion in the United Shoe Machinery case, *United States* v. *Winslow*, 227 U.S. 202 (1913).

20. Phillips, *Frankfurter Reminisces*, pp. 46–47.

21. Morison, *Stimson*, pp. 92–93.

22. Dewey Grantham, Jr., "The Progressive Movement and the Negro," *The South Atlantic Quarterly 54* (October 1955): 461–477.

23. John D. Weaver, *The Brownsville Raid* (New York: W. W. Norton, 1970), p. 140. See also Ann J. Lane, *The Brownsville Affair: National Crisis and Black Reaction* (Port Washington, NY: Kennikat Press, 1971), p. 104 and *passim*.

24. *Reid* v. *United States*, 161 Federal Reporter, 469 (1908), at 472; *Reid* v. *United States*, 211 U.S. 529 (1909).

25. Phillips, *Frankfurter Reminisces*, pp. 45–46, 48–49.

26. Theodore Roosevelt, *The New Nationalism* (New York: Peter Smith, 1910), pp. 3–33.

27. Morison, *Stimson*, pp. 103–105.

28. Ibid., p. 116.

29. Phillips, *Frankfurter Reminisces*, p. 52.

Chapter 3. EMPIRE, ARMAGEDDON, AND HARVARD

1. Frankfurter to Buckner, December 26, 1911, Box 30, FFLC.

2. Frankfurter, Diary, October 20, 24, and 25, 1911, ibid., Box 1.

3. Winfred Denison to Emma Frankfurter, October 28, 1912, ibid., Box 51.

4. Frankfurter, Diary, November 3, 1911, ibid., Box 1.

5. Frankfurter to Buckner, February 13, 1912, ibid., Box 30.

6. Holmes to Laski, July 12, 1921, *Holmes-Laski Letters*, I. p. 346.

7. Morison, *Stimson*, pp. 117–121.

8. Frankfurter to Buckner, February 12, 1912, Box 30, FFLC.

9. Morison, *Stimson*, pp. 129–139; Frankfurter, Diary, November 5 and 6, 1911, Box 1, FFLC.

10. Frankfurter to Buckner, January 17, 1912, ibid., Box 30.

11. Frankfurter to Pound, November 23, 1911, RG 350, Records of the Bureau of Insular Affairs, National Archives (hereafter cited as BIA).

12. Frankfurter, Diary, November 3, 1911, Box 1, FFLC.

13. Frankfurter to Foster V. Brown, December 29, 1911, RG 350, BIA.

14. *Porto Rico* v. *Rosaly y Castillo*, 227 U.S. 270 (1913), 271–272, 275.

15. *Tiaco* v. *Forbes*, 228 U.S. 549 (1913), 556–557.

16. Morison, *Stimson*, p. 139.

17. Frankfurter to Foster V. Brown, December 29, 1911, RG 350, BIA.

18. Frankfurter, "Memorandum for the Secretary of War, Re: Government and Administration of the Philippine Islands," April 11, 1913, Box 189, FFLC.

19. Denison to Frankfurter, March 8, 1914, ibid., Box 51.

20. See Arthur Link, *Woodrow Wilson and the Progressive Era* (New York: Harper & Row, 1954), pp. 227–228.

21. R.L. Clute, "Report on Conditions in Porto Rico," January 2, 1917, File 1175-34, RG 350, BIA.

22. "We are trying to overcome the party spirit among the teachers themselves by creating a professional spirit," the head of the Insular Board of Education noted at the turn of the century. "It will be only in the course of time and with the gradual introduction of more lady teachers . . . that we can secure the same attitude on the part of a teacher toward his school that public opinion in the States demands — that he look upon the exercise of his profession as a professional career and not as an opportunity for political intrigue." Victor S. Clark to the Secretary of War, September 20, 1899, File 451-10, RG 350, BIA.

23. Stimson, "Confidential Report on His Trip to the West Indies," September 9, 1911, ibid., File 23436-4, RG 350; Frankfurter to Feline, September 21, 1911, ibid., RG 350; Frankfurter to Edwards, September 19, 1911, ibid., File 451-74.

24. Frankfurter, Diary, October 26, 1911, Box 1, FFLC; C.R. Edwards to George Colton, September 21, 1911, File 451-75, RG 350, BIA; Stimson to Taft, September 13, 1911, File 451-73, RG 350, BIA.

25. Frankfurter to Bloomfield, October 12, 1911, File 14525-10, RG 350, BIA.

26. Ratner to Colton, January 8, 1912, ibid., File 451-83, RG 350.

27. Bloomfield, "Report of Visit to Porto Rico," 1912, ibid. File 451-85, RG 350.

28. Ibid.

29. Frankfurter to Stanley King, January 3, 1912, and King to Frankfurter, January 5, 1912, ibid., File 24245, RG 350.

30. Arthur Yager to Frank McIntyre, November 25, 1915, ibid., File 3377-234; and Philander Betts to McIntyre, March 3, 1919, ibid., File 1493-171, RG 350.

31. Frankfurter, Diary, November 22, 1911, Box 1, FFLC; Phillips, *Frankfurter Reminisces*, p. 65.

32. Frankfurter, Diary, October 26, 1911, Box 1, FFLC.

33. Frankfurter to Buckner, April 20, 1912, ibid., Box 30.

34. Frankfurter, Diary, November 6, 1911, ibid., Box 1.

35. Phillips, *Frankfurter Reminisces*, pp. 105–106. On Valentine, see Milton J. Nadworney, *Scientific Management and the Unions, 1900–1932* (Cambridge, MA: Harvard University Press, 1955), pp. 74–77, 80–82; and Samuel Haber, *Efficiency and Uplift: Scientific Management in the Progressive Era. 1890–1920* (Chicago: University of Chicago Press, 1964), pp. 33–34. Valentine resigned from the administration in 1912, assisted Roosevelt's campaign, and then opened an office as an industrial relations counselor in Boston. In 1914, he helped to resolve a bitter strike by the Typographical Union against the Plimpton Press that resulted in a contract providing for collective bargaining and a preferential union shop. In return, the union accepted several management proposals for greater efficiency. The preferential union shop concept outraged traditional advocates of scientific management such as Taylor, but Brandeis used the same framework to resolve the protracted strike in New York's garment industry. With Brandeis's encouragement, Valentine became a member of that industry's Board of Protocol Standards in 1915, a few months before his death.

36. Holmes to Frederick Pollock, October 31, 1926, *Holmes-Pollock Letters*, II, ed., Mark De Wolfe Howe (Cambridge, MA: Harvard University Press, 1961), p. 191. On Brandeis generally, see Melvin I. Urofsky, *A Mind of One Piece: Brandeis and American Reform* (New York: Charles

Scribner's Sons, 1971), pp. 152–161, Nadworny, *Scientific Management*, pp. 34–37; Richard Abrams, "Brandeis and the New Haven-Boston & Maine Merger Battle Revisited," *Business History Review 36* (1962): 408–430.

37. Brandeis to Frankfurter, January 28, 1913, Box 26, FFLC.
38. *Standard Oil Company of New Jersey* v. *United States*, 221 U.S. 1 (1911); and *United States* v. *American Tobacco Company*, 221 U.S. 106 (1911).
39. Frankfurter, Diary, October 27, 1911, Box 1, FFLC; Brandeis to Robert M. LaFollette, May 17, 1911, *Brandeis Letters*, II, p. 435.
40. Frankfurter, Diary, November 3, 1911, Box 1, FFLC.
41. On the steel suit and Roosevelt's relationships with the company during his presidency, see Kolko, *Triumph of Conservatism*, pp. 114–117.
42. Frankfurter to Buckner, August 2, 1912, Box 40, FFLC.
43. Frankfurter to Philip Miller, June 20, 1912, ibid., Box 84.
44. Theodore Roosevelt, "The Trusts, the People, and the Square Deal," *Outlook 99* (November 18, 1911): 649–656; Kolko; *Triumph of Conservatism*, p. 199.
45. Woodrow Wilson, *The New Freedom* (New York: Charles Scribner's Sons, 1913), p. 187.
46. On Brandeis's views, see Brandeis to Wilson, September 30, 1912; Brandeis to Norman Hapgood, September 14 and October 2, 1912, *Brandeis Letters*, II, pp. 686–694, 672–673, 695.
47. Frankfurter to Hand, April 11, 1912, Box 104, LHP.
48. Hand to Frankfurter, April 4, 1912, Box 198, Felix Frankfurter Papers, Harvard Law School (hereafter cited as FFPH); Hand to Frankfurter, April 11, 1912, ibid.
49. Frankfurter to Philip Miller, July 15, 1912, Box 84, FFLC; Frankfurter to Hand, September 23, 1912, ibid., Box 63.
50. Ibid.
51. Ibid. Following Wilson's victory, Brandeis in fact endorsed the idea of a federal regulatory commission with powers similar to those proposed by the Progressive Party. See Urofsky, *Brandeis*, pp. 71–92.
52. Root quoted in Morison, *Stimson*, p. 112.
53. Frankfurter to Hand, July 8, 1913, Box 104, LHP.
54. Frankfurter to Buckner, January 6, 1912, Box 30, FFLC.
55. Frankfurter to Philip Miller, March 11, 1913, ibid., Box 84.
56. Frankfurter to Hand, April 11, 1911, Box 104, LHP.
57. Hand to Frankfurter, February 26, 1911, Box 198, FFPH.
58. The Lowenthal quotation is from Mendelson, ed., *Felix Frankfurter: A Tribute*, pp. 89–90. Frankfurter's speech, "The Zeitgeist and the Judiciary," is reprinted in *Law and Politics: Occasional Papers of Felix Frankfurter, 1913–1938*, ed., Archibald MacLeish and E.F. Prichard, Jr. (New York: Harcourt, Brace, 1939), pp 3–9.
59. Frankfurter to Hand, April 2, 1912, Box 104, LHP.

60. Frankfurter to Pound, April 9, 1912, Box 37, Roscoe Pound Papers, Harvard Law School (hereafter cited as RPP). On Pound's ideas and their impact upon legal education, see David Wigdor, *Roscoe Pound: Philosopher of Law* (Westport, CT: Greenwood Press, 1974), pp. 161–205; Sutherland, *The Law at Harvard*, pp. 236–240.
61. Frankfurter to Hand, April 2, 1912, Box 104, LHP.
62. Denison to Edward H. Warren, June 12, 1913, Box 51, FFLC.
63. Warren to Denison, June 16, 1913, ibid., Box 51.
64. Erza Thayer to Stimson, June 24, 1913, ibid., Box 103.
65. Stimson to Frankfurter, June 28, 1913, ibid.
66. Brandeis to Denison, July 12, 1913, *Brandeis Letters*, III, p. 134.
67. Phillips, *Frankfurter Reminisces*, p. 78.
68. Hand to Frankfurter, July 3, 1913, Box 198, FFLC.
69. Frankfurter to Hand, July 8, 1913, Box 104, LHP.
70. Frankfurter to Walter Meyer, September 25, 1913, Box 79, FFLC.
71. Frankfurter to Hand, June 28, 1913, Box 104, LHP. See also Brandeis to Jacob Schiff, November 3, 1913, *Brandeis Letters* III, p. 207.

Chapter 4. LEGAL PROGRESSIVE

1. Hand to Frankfurter, July 31, 1914, Box 104, LHP.
2. Percy to Frankfurter, May 23, 1915, Box 89, FFLC.
3. The quotation is from Dalton Trumbo's *Johnny Got His Gun* (New York: Bantam, 1970), p. 240.
4. Frankfurter to Hand, April 24, 1914, Box 104, LHP. Stevens, a New Hampshire congressman, helped Brandeis draft proposals to revise the antitrust laws and fashion the Federal Trade Commission statute. Kent was a conservation-minded congressman from California. On Wilson and the Mexican Revolution, see the discussion in Link, *Woodrow Wilson and the Progressive Era*, pp. 107–144.
5. Frankfurter to Hand, May 5, 1914, Box 104, LHP.
6. Percy to Frankfurter, August 29, 1916, Box 89, FFLC.
7. Frankfurter to Hand, September 17, 1915, Box 104, LHP.
8. Frankfurter to Buckner, October 28, 1914, Box 30, FFLC.
9. Frankfurter to Holmes, n.p.n.d., but probably July 1914, File 13, Box 30, OWHP.
10. Frankfurter to Holmes, September 6, 1913, ibid., File 15, Box 30.
11. Holmes to Frankfurter, March 24, 1914, ibid., File 2, Box 29.
12. Ernest Brown, "Professor Frankfurter," *Harvard Law Review* 78 (June 1965): 1523–1525. The Plimpton poem is from his *Reunion Runes*.
13. Laski to Holmes, December 16, 1916, *Holmes-Laski Letters*, I, pp. 43–44.
14. Frankfurter to Sofy Buckner, n.p.n.d., but probably 1914, Box 30, FFLC.

15. Frankfurter to Emory Buckner, May 30, 1915, ibid.
16. Frankfurter to Pound, July 11, 1916, Box 37, RPP.
17. Frankfurter to Holmes, March 2, 1914, File 15, Box 30, OWHP.
18. Frankfurter, "The Republic," Box 159, FFLC. This memorandum was probably written in 1913 or 1914.
19. Croly to Frankfurter, October 10, 1913 and March 3, 1914, Box 159, FFLC.
20. Laski to Holmes, November 7, 1916, *Holmes-Laski Letters*, I, p. 35.
21. Holmes to Frankfurter, January 21, 1915, File 2, Box 29, OWHP.
22. Holmes to Einstein, August 12, 1916, *The Holmes-Einstein Letters*, ed. James Bishop Peabody (New York: St. Martin's Press, 1964), p. 136.
23. *Chicago, Burlington & Quincy Railroad Company* v. *McGuire*, 219 U.S. 459 (1911); and *Baltimore & Ohio Railroad* v. *Interstate Commerce Commission*, 221 U.S. 612 (1911).
24. *Chicago, Burlington & Quincy Railroad* v. *McGuire*, 219 U.S. 549, at 567.
25. Frankfurter to Hand, March 2, 1911, Box 104, LHP.
26. On Pitney, see his opinion in *Jonas Glass Company* v. *Glass Bottle Blowers Association*, 77 N.J. Eq. 219 (1908); and the sketch by Fred Israel in *The Justices of the United States Supreme Court, 1789 – 1969*, III ed. Leon Friedman and Fred Israel (New York: Chelsea House, 1969), pp. 2001 – 2009. Lurton is quoted by James F. Watts, Jr., "Horace H. Lurton," ibid., p. 1855.
27. *Coppage* v. *Kansas*, 236 U.S. 1 (1915), 15 – 19, 26 – 27.
28. Hand to Frankfurter, October 9, 1914, Box 198, FFPH.
29. Frankfurter to Hand, February 18, 1915, Box 104, LHP.
30. Thomas W. Gregory to R.L. Batts, March 1, 1916, Box 1, Gregory Papers, Library of Congress.
31. Frankfurter to Ludington, May 12, 1916, Box 79, FFLC.
32. See *The New Republic 16* (March 11, 1916): 139. On the nomination fight, see A.L. Todd, *Justice on Trial: The Case of Louis D. Brandeis* (New York: McGraw-Hill, 1964).
33. Frankfurter to Hand, January 30, 1916, Box 104, LHP.
34. Frankfurter to Root, March 17, 1916, Box 128, FFLC.
35. See the *Brandeis Letters*, IV, pp. 25 – 210.
36. Frankfurter to Buckner, November 6, 1914, Box 30, and Frankfurter to Buckner, June 30, 1916, Box 31, FFLC; Frankfurter to Hand, December 12, 1915, Box 104, LHP.
37. Frankfurter to Pound, January 5, 1916, Box 37, RPP.
38. Frankfurter to Hand, January 4, 1916, Box 104, LHP.
39. Frankfurter to Buckner, January 5, 1916, Box 31, FFLC.
40. Frankfurter to Pound, September 6, 1916, Box 37, RPP; and Phillips, *Frankfurter Reminisces*, pp. 94 – 95.
41. Ibid., p. 101.
42. *The Nation 104* (March 15, 1917): 320.

43. *Penn Bridge Co.* v. *United States,* 29 App. Cas. (D.C.), 452.

44. *Holden* v. *Hardy,* 169 U.S. 366 (1898).

45. *Muller* v. *Oregon,* 208 U.S. 412 (1908); and *Bosley* v. *McLaughlin,* 236 U.S. 385 (1915).

46. *Adair* v. *United States,* 208 U.S. 161 (1908), at 169.

47. *Stettler* v. *O'Hara,* 69 Ore. 519 (1914), 524 – 525.

48. Quoted in *Brandeis Letters,* IV, p. 364.

49. Phillips, *Frankfurter Reminisces,* p. 102.

50. *Bunting* v. *Oregon,* 243 U.S. 426 (1917).

51. *Stettler* v. *O'Hara* and *Simson* v. *O'Hara,* 243 U.S. 629 (1917).

52. *Wilson* v. *New,* 243 U.S. 332 (1917). Holmes voted with the majority in this case, but he complained bitterly to Frankfurter about the power of the railroad unions. "Patriotism is the demand of the territorial club for priority," he said, "over such tribal groups as the churches and trade unions. I go the whole hog for the territorial club — and I don't care a damn if it interferes with some of the spontaneities of the other groups. I think the Puritans were quite right when they whipped the Quakers." See Holmes to Frankfurter, March 27, 1917, File 4, Box 29, OWHP.

53. *Hitchman Coal & Coke Company* v. *Mitchell,* 245 U.S. 229 (1917), 232 – 262.

54. Frankfurter to Holmes, April 19, 1920, File 16, Box 30, OWHP.

55. Frankfurter to Marion Denman, April 29, 1919, Box 7, FFLC.

56. Frankfurter to Holmes, December 1916, File 9, Box 30, OWHP.

57. Quoted in Liva Baker, *Felix Frankfurter,* p. 50.

58. Marion Denman to Frankfurter, n.p.n.d., but probably 1915, Box 5, FFLC.

59. Denman to Frankfurter, early October, 1916, ibid.

60. Denman to Frankfurter, n.p.n.d., but probably 1916, ibid.

61. Frankfurter to Denman, June 21, 1917, ibid.

62. See Link, *Woodrow Wilson and the Progressive Era,* pp. 145 – 167.

63. Frankfurter to Katherine Ludington, June 8, 1915, Box 79, FFLC.

64. Frankfurter to Hand, July 29, 1915, Box 104, LHP.

65. Frankfurter to Ludington, June 9, 1915, Box 79, FFLC.

66. Frankfurter to Ludington, June 13, 1915, ibid.

67. Frankfurter to Ludington, January 21, 1916, ibid.

68. Frankfurter to Ludington, May 15, 1916 and October 26, 1916, ibid.

69. Frankfurter to Hand, July 3, 1916, Box 104, LHP.

70. Frankfurter to Ludington, February 5 and 7, 1917, Box 79, FFLC.

71. Frankfurter to Ludington, April 10, 1917, ibid.

72. On *The New Republic* and the war, see Charles Forcy, *The Crossroads of Liberalism: Croly, Weyl, Lippmann, and the Progressive Era, 1900 – 1925* (New York: Oxford University Press, 1961), pp. 221 – 315.

Chapter 5. BISBEE AND MOONEY

1. Elsie Douglas to Alexander Bickel, July 22, 1964, Box 206, File 14, FFPH.
2. Laski to Holmes, September 5, 1917, *Holmes-Laski Letters*, I, p. 98.
3. National War Labor Board, "Executive Minutes," May 11, 1918, Box 1, Records of the National War Labor Board, National Archives.
4. Frankfurter to Hand, May 24, 1917, Box 104, LHP.
5. *Congressional Record*, 65th Congress, 1st Session, 55 (Washington, D.C.: U.S. Government Printing Office, 1917), pp. 212–214.
6. The Wilson and Gregory quotes are from Robert J. Goldstein, *Political Repression in Modern America* (New York: Schenkman, 1978), pp. 107–108.
7. The Immigration Act of 1917, for instance, provided for the deportation of any alien, who after entry into the country "shall be found advocating or teaching the unlawful destruction of property or advocating or teaching anarchy or the overthrow by force or violence of the government of the United States." The Trading with the Enemy Act required all foreign-language newspapers to submit to censorship by the Postmaster General and the Espionage Act of 1917 provided up to twenty years in jail for those who "caused or attempted to cause insubordination, disloyalty, mutiny or refusal to duty" in the armed forces or who made false statements with the intent "to interfere with the operation or success of the military or to promote the success of its enemies." A year later, the draconian Sedition Act made it a federal crime to speak, print, or publish any "disloyal, profane, scurrilous or abusive language about the form of government of the United States or the constitution of the United States, or the military or naval forces of the United States or the flag of the United States or the uniform of the army or navy" or any language intended to bring these institutions into "contempt, scorn, contumely or disrepute." See Goldstein, *Political Repression*, pp. 108–109. On popular repression of war protestors, see Joan Jensen, *The Price of Vigilance* (New York: Rand McNally, 1968), pp. 33–82.
8. Frankfurter to Baker, February 8, 1917, Box 23, FFLC.
9. See "Preliminary Report of the Committee on Clothing Contracts," August 13, 1917, Box 1, Newton D. Baker Papers, Library of Congress. On the Baker-Gompers accord, see Alexander M. Bing, *War Time Strikes and Their Ajustment* (New York, 1921; reprint, New York: Arno, 1971), pp. 14–19.
10. Frankfurter to Baker, April 3, 1917, Box 23, FFLC.
11. Phillips, *Frankfurter Reminisces*, p. 114.
12. Frankfurter, "Memorandum for the Secretary of War," August 18, 1917, Box 1, Baker Papers.

13. The Morgenthau episode is recalled with appropriate humor, sarcasm, and indignation in Phillips, *Frankfurter Reminisces*, pp. 145–153.
14. Frankfurter to Baker, August 7, 1917, Box 189, FFLC.
15. Robert Lansing to Wilson, August 13, 1917, Box 166; House to Wilson, September 20 and October 3, 1917, Box 168, Woodrow Wilson Papers, Library of Congress.
16. Frankfurter to Marion Denman, October 1, 1917, Box 5, FFLC.
17. Frankfurter to Ludington, October 28, 1917, ibid., Box 79.
18. Walter Doudna to George P. Hunt, October 31, 1915, File 33-1116, Records of the Federal Mediation and Conciliation Service, Federal Records Center, Suitland, Maryland (hereafter cited as FMCS).
19. Joseph Myers to William B. Wilson, November 5, 1915; Hywell Davies and Myers to Wilson, December 10, 1915; George Hunt to Wilson, December 24, 1915, all File 33-116, FMCS. On the strikes, see also *The Survey 36* (May 6, 1916: 143–146; *The Outlook 112* (February 2, 1916): 250–252; and *The New Republic 5* (March 18, 1916): 186–187.
20. Arizona State Federation of Labor, *Proceedings of the Sixth Annual Convention* (1916), pp. 3–9. On the difficulties of the IUMMSW, see Vernon Jensen, *Heritage of Conflict: Labor Relations in the Nonferrous Metals Industry Up to 1930* (Ithaca: Cornell University Press, 1950), pp. 160–368. On the IWW, see Melvyn Dubofsky, *We Shall Be All: A History of the Industrial Workers of the World* (Chicago: Quadrangle, 1969), pp. 36–170.
21. Moyer to Gompers, April 20 and June 29, 1917, Western Miners File, AFL-CIO Archives, Washington, D.C.; Moyer to James Lord, August 3, 1917, File 33-438A, FMCS.
22. Baruch to William B. Wilson, June 30, 1917, Day File, Baruch Papers, Princeton University.
23. Thomas Flynn to Thomas Gregory, April 12, 1917, and Gregory to Flynn, April 13, 1917, File 9-53373, Records of the Department of Justice, National Archives.
24. William Preston, Jr., *Aliens and Dissenters* (New York: Harper & Row, 1963), pp. 104–105; J. E. Lewis to Commanding Officer, Arizona District, September 3, 1917, Abraham Glasser File, Box 1, Records of the Department of Justice.
25. Walter Douglas to A.J. Thompson, June 29, File 186813-31, Department of Justice Records; "General Parker's Census of Men Held at Columbus," August 6, 1917, File 33-438B1, FMCS.
26. "Minutes of Conference Between Governor Campbell and Citizens Committee from Bisbee," July 23, 1917, File 186813-31, Department of Justice Records.
27. Louis G. Whitney to Wilson, July 12, 1917, File 400C, Series 4, Woodrow Wilson Papers, Library of Congress.
28. Frankfurter to Baker, September 4, 1917, Box 1, Baker Papers.

29. Quoted in Simeon Larson, *Labor and Foreign Policy: Gompers, the AFL, and the First World War, 1914–1918* (Cranbury, NJ: Fairleigh Dickinson University, 1975), pp. 24–25.
30. Frankfurter to Baker, September 4, 1917, Box 1, Baker Papers.
31. Gompers to Wilson, August 10, 1917, Box 166, Series 2, Wilson Papers; Gompers to William B. Wilson, August 27, and William B. Wilson to Woodrow Wilson, August 31, 1917, both File 20-473, Box 82, Records of the Department of Labor, National Archives; E. David Cronon, ed., *The Cabinet Diaries of Josephus Daniels, 1913–1921* (Lincoln: University of Nebraska Press, 1963), p. 196.
32. Quoted in Mendelson, ed., *Felix Frankfurter: A Tribute*, p. 128.
33. Frankfurter to Marion Denman, October 1, 1917, Box 5, FFLC; Frankfurter to Hand, November 6, 1917, Box 104, LHP.
34. See Frankfurter to Stanley King, October 16, 1917; King to Frankfurter, October 18 and October 26, 1917, all Fragmentary Records of the President's Mediation Commission, National Archives; Frankfurter to King, October 27, 1917, and October 30, 1917, File 33-438A2, FMCS; King to Arthur Willert, October 17, 1917, Box 5, Records of the War Labor Policies Board, National Archives.
35. Frankfurter to Robert Szold, October 15, 1917; Frankfurter to Sam Rosensohn, October 16 and October 21, 1917; Eugene Meyer to Frankfurter, October 22, 1917, all Box 5, Records of the War Labor Policies Board; Frankfurter to Meyer, October 22, 1917, File 33-438A2, FMCS.
36. Frankfurter to Hand, November 6, 1917, Box 104, LHP.
37. Frankfurter to Brandeis, October 20 and November 7, 1917, Box 29, FFLC.
38. See Eugene Meyer to Frankfurter, October 31, 1917, Box 173, Records of the War Industries Board, Suitland, Maryland; Frankfurter to Meyer, October 31, 1917, File 33-438A2, FMCS.
39. See, for example, Department of Labor, "Decision and Order of the President's Mediation Commission to the Employers and Employees of the Clifton-Morenci-Metcalf District," October 30, 1917, Vol. 4, Mediation Commission Fragments.
40. Frankfurter to Brandeis, November 7, 1917, Box 29, FFLC. See also *Report on the Bisbee Deportation Made by the President's Mediation Commission to the President of the United States* (Washington, D.C.: U.S. Government Printing Office, 1918), 5–7.
41. President's Mediation Commission, "Proceedings at Bisbee," pp. 610–611.
42. Unidentified letter from Bisbee, November 25, 1917, File 33-438A2, FMCS.
43. Joseph Myers to William B. Wilson, November 2, 1917, File 33-438A3, FMCS.

44. William Scarlett to Frankfurter, May 20, 1918, Box 101, FFLC.
45. "Meeting of the President's Mediation Commission," January 12, 1918, File 33-438A6, FMCS.
46. Frankfurter to Marion Denman, October 9 and October 27, 1917, Box 5, FFLC; Frankfurter to Brandeis, October 20, 1917, Box 29, FFLC.
47. Thomas Croaff to William B. Wilson, March 29, 1918, File 33-438A7, FMCS; T.E. McCoy to Gompers, February 1, 1918, Box 1012, Records of the War Industries Board.
48. Ibid.
49. Frankfurter to Scarlett, May 28, 1918, Box 101, FFLC.
50. On the telephone and meat-packing settlements, see Phillips, *Frankfurter Reminisces*, pp. 122 – 129, and "Packing File," Box 192, Records of the War Labor Policies Board.
51. Frankfurter to Brandeis, November 28, 1917, Box 29, FFLC.
52. Frankfurter to Brandeis, December 1917, ibid.
53. Frank Walsh to Ann Sloan, December 2, 1916, Box 132, Walsh Papers, New York Public Library.
54. This and later discussions of the case are based upon Richard Frost's patient study, *The Mooney Case* (Stanford, CA: Stanford University Press, 1968), especially pp. 103 – 226. Frost concluded, based largely on interviews with Earl Hatcher, a Sacramento rancher with whom Oxman had been staying on July 22, 1916, that the latter probably did not arrive in the city on that day in time to see the bombing or the parade. The prosecutors, including Fickert, may also have doubted Oxman's story, because they did not call him to testify during the trial of Mooney's alleged coconspirators.
55. Phillips, *Frankfurter Reminisces*, pp. 130 – 134.
56. "Report on the Mooney Dynamite Cases in San Francisco Submitted by President Wilson's Mediation Commission," *Official Bulletin of the United States Committee on Public Information* (pamphlet), January 18, 1918, especially pp. 14 – 15.
57. George S. Arnold to Frankfurter, April 4, 1918, and Arnold to William D. Stephens, April 15, 1918, both Box 154, FFLC.
58. James Beck to Herbert Croly, February 2, 1922; Croly to Frankfurter, February 3, 1922, ibid., Box 255.
59. Theodore Roosevelt to Frankfurter, December 19, 1917, ibid., Box 154.
60. Frankfurter to Roosevelt, January 7, 1918, ibid.
61. Frankfurter to Roosevelt, January 7, 1918, ibid.
62. Roosevelt to Frankfurter, January 18, 1918, ibid.
63. Quoted in Frost, *The Mooney Case*, pp. 304 – 305.
64. Walsh to Dante Baron, May 25, 1917, Box 133, Walsh Papers.
65. William D. Stephens to Paul Scharrenberg, November 29, 1919, Box 155, FFLC.
66. Walsh to Mooney, November 30, 1918, Box 349, Walsh Papers.

Chapter 6. THE CZAR OF LABOR

1. Quoted in Daniel R. Beaver, *Newton D. Baker and the American War Effort, 1917−1919* (Lincoln: University of Nebraska Press, 1966), p. 89.
2. Ibid., pp. 50−78.
3. Frankfurter to Brandeis, December 1917, Box 29, FFLC.
4. Edward House, Diary, January 9, 1918, House Papers, Yale University.
5. Frankfurter, "Memorandum for the Secretary of War," January 7, 1918, Box 189, FFLC.
6. Ibid.
7. Brandeis to House, January 9, 1918, ibid., Box 189; House, Diary, January 9, 1918, House Papers.
8. Beaver, *Newton D. Baker*, pp. 106−108; Robert D. Cuff, *The War Industries Board: Business-Government Relations during World War I* (Baltimore: Johns Hopkins Press, 1973), especially pp. 148−190.
9. Report and Recommendation of the War Labor Conference Board," March 29, 1918; and William B. Wilson to Woodrow Wilson, April 4, 1918, both File 19F, Series 4, Wilson Papers.
10. See, for example, Taft to Walsh, October 20, 1918, Vol. 78, Series 8, William Taft Papers, Library of Congress; Bing, *War-Time Strikes*, pp. 116−125.
11. "Report and Recommendations of the War Labor Conference Board," March 29, 1918, File 19F, Series 4, Wilson Papers.
12. Robert Woolley to Wilson, April 19, 1918, ibid., File 4341, Series 4.
13. Woolley to Wilson, April 25, 1918, ibid.
14. Frankfurter to Baker, April 30, 1918, Box 5, Baker Papers.
15. Wilson to Wooley, April 27, 1918, File 4341, Series 4, Wilson Papers.
16. Eleanor Roosevelt to Sara Delano Roosevelt, May 12, 1918, Eleanor Roosevelt Papers, Hyde Park, New York.
17. Frankfurter to Pound, May 3, 1917, Box 37, RPP.
18. Samuel Lavit to Frank Walsh, n.p.n.d., but probably May 1918, Box 22, Walsh Papers.
19. Quoted in Bing, *War-Time Strikes*, p. 313.
20. See "Memorandum of Conference at the office of Felix Frankfurter with Employers in the Metal Trades," August 6, 1918, Box 190, FFLC.
21. See "Minutes of Conference with Employers," August 6, 1918; "Conference of Metal Trades of the American Federation of Labor," August 10, 1918; "Proposed Tentative Agreement for the Establishment of a Metal Trades Board," all ibid., Box 190; "Conference of Mr. Frankfurter with Building Trades Unions," July 12, 1918, ibid., Box 189.
22. War Labor Policies Board, "Minutes," September 20, 1918, ibid., Box 191.
23. See "Report of the Conference Committee of National Labor Adjustment Agencies," October 14, 1918, Box 425, Series 4, Wilson Papers;

"Minutes of Meeting of Representatives of Various Governmental Wage Fixing Boards," September 25, September 26, and October 1, 1918, Box 190, FFLC.

24. War Labor Policies Board, "Minutes," October 11, 1918, and "Sanitary Code for the Explosives Industry," both ibid., Box 191.

25. "Report of the Chairman on the Stimulation of Production," October 11, 1918, ibid., Box 191.

26. Frankfurter to Wilson, September 6, 1918, ibid., Box 190. Placed in charge of the Western Union Company, the Postmaster General of the United States displayed an antilabor attitude comparable to the company's own dismal record.

27. Frankfurter to Walsh, August 30, 1918, ibid.

28. Walsh to Frankfurter, September 16, 1918, ibid.

29. George P. West to Walsh, October 10, 1918, Box 24, Walsh Papers.

30. Frankfurter to Hand, January 21, 1919, Box 104, LHP.

31. See Frankfurter to Gary, July 9, 1918, and Gary to Frankfurter, July 19, 1918, Box 190, FFLC.

32. Fankfurter to William H. Taft, October 16, 1918, Box 425, Series 3, Taft Papers.

33. Frankfurter to House, March 12, 1918, House Papers.

34. Frankfurter to House, March 24, 1918, Box 189, FFLC.

35. Frankfurter to House, June 21, 1918, House Papers.

36. Quoted in Ronald Radosh, *American Labor and United States Foreign Policy* (New York: Random House, 1969), p. 146. For a discussion of Henderson, the Europe left, and Wilsonian diplomacy, see pp. 122–184.

37. Frankfurter to Hudson, January 13, 1918, File 20, Box 35, Manley Hudson Papers, Harvard Law School.

38. Frankfurter to Lippmann, January 13, 1919, Box 79, FFLC.

39. Frankfurter to William B. Wilson, November 11, 1918, ibid., Box 189.

40. Newton D. Baker to Woodrow Wilson, November 30, 1918, Box 8, Baker Papers.

41. Walsh to Victor Olander, December 4, 1918, Box 26, Walsh Papers.

42. "Minutes of Meeting of Conference of Adjustment Agencies," December 9, 1918, Box 190, FFLC.

43. Frankfurter to Hand, January 21, 1919, Box 104, LHP.

44. Frankfurter to Lippmann, January 13, 1919, Box 79, FFLC.

Chapter 7. THE RED SCARE

1. Quoted in Goldstein, *Political Repression*, pp. 148, 150, 158–159.

2. Ibid., p. 157.

3. The full horror of these sixteen months is told in Robert K. Murray's

classic study, *Red Scare: A Study in National Hysteria, 1919–1920* (New York: McGraw-Hill, 1955).

4. Brandeis to Alice G. Brandeis, June 13 and 14, 1919, *Brandeis Letters*, IV, pp. 398, 400.
5. Frankfurter to Pound, June 3, 1919, Box 37, RPP.
6. Philip H. Burt to Frankfurter, November 28, 1919, Box 89, FFLC. Burt's letter included a stenographic copy of notes taken at the Faneuil Hall meeting.
7. Frankfurter to Hand, December 9, 1919, Box 104, LHP.
8. Perkins to Frankfurter, November 26, 1919, Box 89, FFLC.
9. Frankfurter to Perkins, November 25, 1919, ibid.
10. Frankfurter to Perkins, November 28, 1919, ibid.
11. Holmes to Frankfurter, December 4, 1919, File 5, Box 29, Holmes Papers.
12. Hand to Frankfurter, December 3, 1919, Box 198, FFPH.
13. Frankfurter to Hand, December 4, 1919, Box 104, LHP.
14. Frankfurter to Hand, May 20, 1920, ibid.
15. Frankfurter to Hudson, November 20, 1919, File 34, Box 7, Hudson Papers.
16. Frankfurter to Hand, November 4, 1919, Box 104, LHP.
17. Hand to Frankfurter, November 8, 1919, Box 198, FPH.
18. Laski to Holmes, November 14, 1919, *Holmes-Laski Letters*, I, p. 221.
19. Laski to Holmes, January 14, 1920, ibid., p. 233.
20. Brandeis to Alice G. Brandeis, April 20, 1920, *Brandeis Letters*, IV, pp. 458–459.
21. Quoted in Joseph Lasch, *From the Diaries of Felix Frankfurter* (New York: W. W. Norton, 1975), p. 30. See also Liva Baker, *Felix Frankfurter*, pp. 89–90; Mendelson, *Felix Frankfurter: A Tribute*, pp. 52–54.
22. Frankfurter to Holmes, April 19, 1920, File 16, Box 30, Holmes Papers.
23. Holmes, *The Common Law*, p. 115.
24. *Michaels* v. *Hillman*, 183 N.Y. 197 (1920), at 198.
25. Phillips, *Frankfurter Reminisces*, pp. 171–173; Martin Mayer, *Emory Buckner*, pp. 168–170.
26. *Colyer* v. *Skeffington*, 265 Fed. Rep. 17 (1920), pp. 43–49, 58–59, 62–63, 79–80.
27. Quoted in Phillips, *Frankfurter Reminisces*, p. 174.
28. A. Mitchell Palmer to Frankfurter, June 4, 1919, Box 127, FFLC.
29. See Frankfurter to Harry Weinberger, March 10, 1920, Weinberger Papers, Yale University. Weinberger had been one of the defense attorneys in the *Abrams* case.
30. Sutherland, *The Law at Harvard*, pp. 251–259
31. Hand to Frankfurter, July 27, 1921, Box 198, FFPH.
32. See, for example, Goldstein, *Political Repression*, p. 159.
33. Frankfurter to Hand, December 4, 1919, Box 104, LHP.

Chapter 8. ZIONIST

1. Frankfurter to Ludington, September 16, 1917, Box 79, FFLC.
2. Frankfurter recalled this incident in a later letter to Jerome Frank, May 3, 1946, Jerome Frank Papers, Yale University.
3. Before the United States Immigration Commission in 1909, for example, Julian Mack deplored the government's practice of distinguishing between Jewish and non-Jewish Russian immigrants. This practice, he said, fomented anti-Semitism and tended to set Jews apart as a separate nationality, a concept he abhorred. "The newest element of Jews in this country who largely are not yet American citizens, recognize that division," Mack said, "and claim there is a Jewish race. They want to re-create it as a nation. . . . I would disclaim that. I do not recognize the Jewish race. There are Jews who do. I do not." Quoted in Harry Barnard, *The Forging of an American Jew: The Life and Times of Judge Julian W. Mack* (New York: Herzl Press, 1974), p. 96.
4. Lowenthal to Frankfurter, October 22, 1914, Box 79, FFLC.
5. Melvin Urofsky, *American Zionism From Herzl to the Holocaust* (New York: Doubleday, 1975), p. 24.
6. Ibid., pp. 23, 43, 101.
7. Ibid., p. 33. See also Yonathan Shapiro, *Leadership of the American Zionist Organization, 1897–1930* (Urbana: University of Illinois Press, 1971).
8. Quoted in Urofsky, *American Zionism*, p. 75.
9. The Kallen quote is from Barnard, *The Forging of an American Jew*, p. 181. On the rise of anti-Semitism in America during these years, see John Higham, *Send These to Me: Jews and Other Immigrants in Urban America* (New York: Atheneum, 1975), pp. 152–153; Higham, *Stranger in the Land: Patterns of American Nativism, 1890–1925* (New York: Atheneum, 1970), pp. 160–161; and E. Digby Baltzell, *The Protestant Establishment: Aristocracy & Caste in America* (New York: Vintage, 1966), pp 109–196.
10. Higham, *Send These to Me*, p. 135; Urofsky, *American Zionism*, p. 76; Louis D. Brandeis, *Brandeis on Zionism: A Collection of Addresses and Statements* (Washington, D.C.: Zionist Organization of America, 1942), pp. 54–55.
11. Leonard Dinnerstein, *The Leo Frank Case* (New York: Columbia University Press, 1968), pp. 1–109, 114–129, 136–147, *passim*; Barnard, *The Forging of an American Jew*, pp. 160–161; *Frank* v. *Mangum*, 237 U.S. 309 (1915), at 350.
12. Higham, *Send These to Me*, pp. 174–186.
13. Brandeis's speech is reprinted in Jacob deHaas, *Louis D. Brandeis: A Biographical Sketch* (New York, 1929), pp. 163–170.
14. Brandeis, *Brandeis on Zionism*, p. 28.
15. Ibid., p. 68. See also Brandeis to Nathan D. Kaplan, November 27, 1914, *Brandeis Letters*, III, p. 371.

16. Brandeis, *Brandeis on Zionism*, pp. 39–40.
17. Brandeis to David Lubin, September 29, 1918, *Brandeis Letters*, IV, p. 356.
18. Brandeis, *Brandeis on Zionism*, p. 35.
19. Quoted in *Brandeis Letters*, III, p. 317.
20. Frankfurter to deHaas, January 29, 1918, Roll 37, Frankfurter Zionist Papers, Harvard Law School (hereafter cited as FFZ).
21. Ibid.
22. Brandeis to Alfred Brandeis, October 21, 1914, *Brandeis Letters*, III, p. 334.
23. *New York Times*, March 11, 1916.
24. Urofsky, *American Zionism*, p. 173.
25. On the Congress battle, see ibid., pp. 164–194.
26. Brandeis to deHaas, November 22, 1917, *Brandeis Letters*, IV, p. 322.
27. Frankfurter to Wise, September 20, 1917, Roll 37, FFZ.
28. See House, Diary, September 23, 1917, House Papers; Brandeis to Mack and deHaas, September 3, 1918, *Brandeis Letters*, IV, 354–355. On the Balfour Declaration, see Leonard Stein, *The Balfour Declaration* (New York: Simon & Schuster, 1961); and Isaiah Friedman, *The Question of Palestine, 1914–1918* (New York: Schocken Books, 1973).
29. Frankfurter to David Amram, May 14, 1918, Roll 37, FFZ.
30. Szold to Frankfurter, undated, but probably late 1918, ibid., Roll 37.
31. Weizmann to Balfour, July 17, 1918, ibid., Roll 37.
32. Brandeis to deHaas, April 24, 1917, *Brandeis Letters*, IV, p. 283.
33. Frankfurter to deHaas, April 1, 1918, Roll 37, FFZ.
34. Frankfurter to Mack, April 9 and April 12, 1918, ibid.
35. Frankfurter to deHaas, April 9, 1918, ibid.
36. See Brandeis to Frankfurter, June 5 and June 9, 1919, *Brandeis Letters*, IV, pp. 396–397.
37. Frankfurter to Brandeis, March 23, 1919, Roll 37, FFZ.
38. Frankfurter to Szold, April 7, 1919, ibid.
39. Frankfurter to Mack, July 1, 1919, ibid.
40. See Barnard, *The Forging of an American Jew*, p. 242; Phillips, *Frankfurter Reminisces*, pp. 156–157.
41. Frankfurter to Brandeis, March 23, 1919, Roll 37, FFZ.
42. Frankfurter to Szold, April 7, 1919, ibid.
43. Frankfurter to Brandeis, January 3, 1919, ibid.
44. Frankfurter to Brandeis, March 23, 1919, ibid.; Frankfurter to House, April 30, 1919, House Papers.
45. Frankfurter to House, April 14, 1919, House Papers; Urofsky, *American Zionism*, pp. 236–237.
46. Freidenwald to Frankfurter, May 2, 1919, Roll 1, FFZ.
47. Frankfurter to Brandeis, March 23, 1919, ibid., Roll 37.
48. Brandeis to Alice Goldmark Brandeis, August 15 and 20, 1919, *Brandeis Letters*, IV, pp. 422–423.

49. Brandeis to deHaas, October 24, 1919, *Brandeis Letters*, IV, p. 433.
50. See Chaim Weizmann, *Trial and Error* (New York: Harper & Brothers, 1949), p. 249.
51. Weizmann to Frankfurter, August 27, 1919, Roll 37, FFZ. Ferdinand Lasalle was the renowned European socialist who, unlike Karl Marx, believed it possible to improve the conditions of the working class without violent revolution.
52. Urofsky, *American Zionism*, pp. 276–277; Brandeis to Mack, Wise, et al., February 6, 1921, *Brandeis Letters*, IV, p. 530.
53. Quoted in Barnard, *The Forging of an American Jew*, p. 266.
54. Quoted in Urofsky, *American Zionism*, p. 272.
55. See Brandeis to Abba Hillel Silver, October 24, 1920, *Brandeis Letters*, IV, p. 494; Barnard, *Forging of an American Jew*, p. 267.
56. Brandeis to Mack, Wise, Frankfurter, et al., March 19, 1921, *Brandeis Letters*, IV, pp. 544–545.
57. Frankfurter to Brandeis, October 2 and December 2, 1920, Box 29, FFLC.
58. Brandeis to Mack, Wise, Frankfurter, et al., January 13, 1921, *Brandeis Letters*, IV, pp. 524–525.
59. Frankfurter to Brandeis, April 14, 1921, Box 29, FFLC.
60. Frankfurter to Brandeis, May 23, 1920, ibid.

Chapter 9. SCHOOL AND SCHOLAR

1. Frankfurter to Alice Hamilton, January 24, 1924, Box 62, FFLC.
2. Frankfurter to Feis, July 15, 1925, Box 34, Herbert Feis Papers, Library of Congress.
3. Frankfurter to Maley O. Hudson, October 27, 1919, Box 7, File 34, Hudson Papers.
4. Pound to Frankfurter, November 30 and December 14, 1925, Box 188, FFPH. Pound's temper became legendary among students and faculty. James Landis recalled that as a student he had prepared a note on equity for the *Harvard Law Review* and showed it to the dean, who not only objected to the piece, but lost his temper and began throwing pencils out the window to demonstrate his displeasure. James Landis, Oral History, p. 150, Columbia University. For a more sympathetic view of Pound's deanship, see Arthur E. Sutherland, *The Law at Harvard*, pp. 243–298.
5. Frankfurter to Holmes, November 4, 1923, Box 30, File 11, OWHP. Harvard, according to Brandeis, should become the "mother of law schools" by maintaining high academic standards, training professors for other schools, and serving as an example of excellence. He once quoted to Chafee the famous line from Goethe: *"In der Beschrankung zeigt sich Erst der Meister"* — "It is in restraint that the master primarily reveals himself."

See Melvin I. Urofsky, "Brandeis on Legal Education," *The American Journal of Legal History 23* (July 1978): 198.

6. Frankfurter to Chafee, August 12, 1930, Box 4, File 12, Chafee Papers.
7. Frankfurter to Hand, January 16, 1930, Box 104, LHP.
8. Frankfurter to Warren, November 19, 1925, Box 185, FFPH.
9. Pound, Diary, October 25, 1927. See also Diary, February 28, 1933, both Box 38, RPP.
10. Frankfurter to Pound, December 9, 1925, Box 64, File 11, RPP.
11. Frankfurter to Chafee, December 23, 1926, Box 4, File 11, Chafee Papers.
12. Frankfurter to Hand, October 3, 1924, Box 198, FFPH.
13. Frankfurter to Hand, October 7, 1929, ibid.
14. Frankfurter, "Some Observations on Third Year Work," May 12, 1932; and "Theses in Administrative Law and Federal Jurisdiction," both Box 188, FFPH.
15. Frankfurter, "Some Observations on Third Year Work," ibid.
16. Mrs. Howe quoted in Lasch, *From the Diaries of Felix Frankfurter*, p. 54.
17. Barnard, *The Forging of an American Jew*, pp. 291–300.
18. Farnkfurter to Pound, September 8, 1923, Box 22, RPP.
19. Pound, Diary, March 13, 1923 and May 20, 1924, ibid., Box 38.
20. Frankfurter to Pound, August 28, 1921, ibid., Box 22.
21. Harry Bates to Pound, September 17, 1927, and Pound to Bates, September 19, 1927, ibid., Box 7, File 1.
22. Quoted in Jerold Auerbach, *Unequal Justice: Lawyers and Social Change in Modern America* (New York: Oxford University Press, 1976), p. 186.
23. On the Margold controversy, see Frankfurter, Diary, January 3, February 1, February 10, February 21, and March 3, 1928, Box 1, FFLC; Pound, Diary, February 18, 20, and 21, 1928, Box 38 RPP; Frankfurter to Chafee, September 21, 1928, Box 4, File 18, Chafee Papers.
24. Pound, Diary, January 7, 11, 12, 28, and April 26, 1929, Box 38, Pound Papers; Frankfurter, Diary, February 10, 1928, Box 1, FFLC.
25. Pound, Diary, June 16, 19, 1933, Box 38, RPP.
26. Frankfurter to Chafee, July 7 and August 24, 1932, Box 4, File 13, Chafee Papers.
27. Laski to Holmes, November 7, 1916, *Holmes-Laski Letters*, I, p. 35.
28. Laski to Holmes, March 30, 1918 and Laski to Holmes, February 18, 1920, ibid., pp. 145, 245.
29. Ibid.
30. See Felix Frankfurter, *Mr. Justice Holmes and the Supreme Court* (New York: Atheneum, 1965), especially pp. 45–73.
31. Felix Frankfurter, "The Present Approach to Constitutional Decisions on the Bill of Rights," *Harvard Law Review 28* (1915): 790–793; Frankfurter, "The Law and the Law Schools," *American Bar Association Journal 1* (1915): 532–535; Frankfurter, "Hours of Labor and Realism in Consti-

tutional Law," *Harvard Law Review* 29 (1916): 353–364; Frankfurter, "Constitutional Opinions of Justice Holmes," *Harvard Law Review* 29 (1916): 683–710.

32. W. Barton Leach, "Felix," in *Harvard Law School Bulletin* (March 1968), p. 9.

33. James Landis to Jean P. Smith, August 2, 1925, Landis Papers, Harvard Law School.

34. David Lilienthal to Frank Walsh, May 15, 1921, and Lilienthal to Frankfurter, May 1, 1921, both Box 47, David Lilienthal Papers, Princeton University.

35. Brandeis to Frankfurter, November 25, 1920, *Brandeis Letters*, IV, pp. 509–510.

36. Holmes to Frankfurter, January 28, 1930, Box 29, File 12, OWHP.

37. See, for example, Paul Freund, "Justice Brandeis: A Law Clerk's Remembrance," *American Jewish History*, 68 (September 1978): 7–18.

38. Dean Acheson to Frankfurter, April 22, 1921. See also Acheson to Frankfurter, April 11 and March 2, 1921, all Box 19, FFLC.

39. See, for instance, *Lochner* v. *New York*, 198 U.S. 45 (1905), at 75 (dissenting opinion); *Coppage* v. *Kansas*, 236 U.S. 1 (1915), at 26 (dissenting opinion); and *Bloch* v. *Hirsh*, 265 U.S. 135 (1921), 56; *Buck* v. *Bell*, 274 U.S. 200 (1927); and *Bartels* v. *Iowa*, 262 U.S. 404 (1922), at 412 (dissenting opinion). On Holmes's jurisprudence generally, see G. Edward White, *The American Judicial Tradition: Profiles of Leading American Judges* (New York: Oxford University Press, 1976), pp. 150–165; and John T. Noonan, Jr., *Persons and Masks of the Law* (New York: Farrar, Straus & Giroux, 1976), pp. 65–110.

40. Holmes to Frankfurter, March 25, 1930, Box 29, File 13, OWHP.

41. Holmes to Frankfurter, January 4, 1922, Box 29, File 7, and Holmes to Frankfurter, October 24, 1920, Box 29, File 5, both ibid. One limerick went: "There was a young lady of Joppa/ Who came a Society cropper/ She went to Ostend/ With a military friend/ The rest of the story is not proper." Holmes to Frankfurter, December 23, 1930, Box 29, File 13, OWHP.

42. Holmes to Frankfurter, September 10, 1928, ibid., Box 29, File 12.

43. Holmes to Frankfurter, November 12, 1932, ibid., Box 29, File 13.

44. Brandeis to Frankfurter, January 1, 1925, *Brandeis Letters*, V, p. 156.

45. Brandeis to Laski, September 21, 1921, ibid., p. 17.

46. Brandeis to Frankfurter, January 16, 1921, *Brandeis Letters*, IV, p. 528.

47. Compare, for example, Brandeis's views in *Pennsylvania Coal Co.* v. *Mahon*, 260 U.S. 393 (1922), at 400–401 (dissenting), with *Whitney* v. *California*, 274 U.S. 357 (1927), at 372–379 (concurring). See also White, *American Judicial Tradition*, pp. 165–177.

48. Frankfurter, "Conversation with Brandeis," August 11, 1922, Box 29, FFLC.

49. Frankfurter, "Conversation with Brandeis," November 30, 1922, ibid.

50. Despite section 20, which clearly prohibited injunctions in labor disputes, "between an employer and employees, or between employers and employees involving or growing out of a dispute concerning terms or conditions of employment," the Duplex Printing Company had secured an injunction against the machinists' union which had struck against the company's factory in Michigan and instructed its members not to install Duplex presses in New York. The Taft majority upheld the injunction by limiting section 20 to labor disputes between employers and their *immediate* employees, making it virtually impossible for national unions to attack open-shop firms. *Duplex Printing Co.* v. *Deering*, 254 U.S. 443 (1921). See Frankfurter's unsigned editorial, "The 'Law' and Labor," in *The New Republic* (January 26, 1921), p. 14.

51. "To the mere layman," Frankfurter wrote after the *Truax* decision, "this result must appear as incredible as the process by which it is reached is mysterious. . . . It involves the power of the Supreme Court of the United States to translate its views of social policy into the law of each of the forty-eight States. Nor will the layman's bewilderment be lessened by the fact that this appalling result is reached by the votes of five men as against the votes of four men." See Frankfurter, "Taft and the Supreme Court," in *Felix Frankfurter on the Supreme Court: Extrajudicial Essays on the Court and the Constitution*, ed. Philip H. Kurland (Cambridge, MA: Harvard University Press, 1970), pp. 55–56. This unsigned editorial series first appeared in *The New Republic* for October 27, 1920, January 18, 1922, and January 25, 1922. For Brandeis's scathing dissent, see *Traux* v. *Corrigan*, 257 U.S. 312 (1921), at 366–368.

52. *Jay Burns Baking Co.* v. *Bryan*, 264 U.S. 504 (1924); *Tyson & Bros.* v. *Banton*, 273 U.S. 418 (1927); *Ribnik* v. *McBride*, 277 U.S. 350 (1928).

53. *United Railways* v. *West*, 280 U.S. 234 (1930); *Wolff Packing Co.* v. *Court of Industrial Relations*, 262 U.S. 522 (1923).

54. *Adkins* v. *Children's Hospital*, 261 U.S. 525 (1925), at 530–533.

55. Frankfurter to Hand, April 11, 1923, Box 198, FFPH. For Frankfurter's role in preparing the *Adkins* case, see his extensive correspondence with Mary Dewson, Jesse Adkins, Dean Acheson, and Florence Kelley, Box 153, FFLC.

56. Frankfurter, "The Red Terror of Judicial Reform," in *Felix Frankfurter on the Supreme Court*, p. 167. The unsigned editorial first appeared on October 1, 1924.

57. *Meyer* v. *Nebraska*, 262 U.S. 390 (1923), at 401.

58. *Bartels* v. *Iowa*, 262 U.S. 404 (1923), at 412.

59. Frankfurter to Hand, June 5, 1923, Box 198, FFPH.

60. *Pierce* v. *Society of Sisters*, 268 U.S. 510 (1925).

61. Frankfurter, "Can the Supreme Court Guarantee Toleration?" in *Felix Frankfurter on the Supreme Court*, p. 174. The editorial first appeared in *The New Republic* on June 17, 1925.

62. Holmes rejected the state's contention that the Kohler Act constituted a valid exercise of the police power similar to zoning or health laws that did not require compensation when the value of property was reduced as a result of the regulation. In this case, he reasoned, the state had gone too far and would have to pay compensation if it prevented the company from mining on its own property. See *Pennsylvania Coal Co.* v. *Mahon*, 260 U.S. 393 (1922), at 396–397, 401–403. He remained unmoved as well by criticism of the decision, including a sharp rejoinder in *The New Republic* written by Acheson. Holmes lectured Frankfurter on "the distinction between the rights of the public generally and their rights in respect of being in a particular place where they have no right to be at all except so far as they have paid for it." See Holmes to Laski, January 13, 1923, *Holmes-Laski Letters*, I, p. 473; and Holmes to Frankfurter, February 14, 1923, Box 29, File 8, OWHP. Brandeis attributed Holmes's views to the aging process that heightened his respect for property rights. "They caught him when he was weak," he told Frankfurter, following a painful prostate operation "and played him to go whole hog." See Frankfurter, "Conversation with Brandeis," August 11, 1923, FFLC.

63. *Pennsylvania Coal Co.* v. *Mahon*, 260 U.S. 393 (1922), at 401.

64. *Wolff Packing Company* v. *Court of Industrial Relations*, 262 U.S. 522 (1923).

65. Frankfurter, "Exit the Kansas Court," in *Frankfurter on the Supreme Court*, p. 140. The unsigned editorial first appeared in *The New Republic* on June 27, 1923.

66. Frankfurter to Holmes, April 18, 1921, Box 30, File 16, OWHP.

67. Frankfurter, "The American Judge," in *Frankfurter on the Supreme Court*, pp. 150–151. This essay first appeared as a book review of Andrew Bruce's *The American Judge* in *The New Republic* for April 23, 1924.

68. Frankfurter, "Hughes on the Supreme Court," in *Frankfurter on the Supreme Court*, p. 209.

69. See *Pennsylvania Coal Co.* v. *Mahon*, at 396–397, as well as *Gitlow* v. *New York*, 268 U.S. 652 (1925).

70. See, for example, his concurring opinion in *Whitney* v. *California*, 274 U.S. 357 (1927).

71. Frankfurter, "The Paradoxes of Legal Science," in *Frankfurter on the Supreme Court*, p. 204.

72. Brandeis to Frankfurter, November 8, 1920, *Brandeis Letters*, IV, pp. 498–499.

73. Felix Frankfurter and James M. Landis, "The Compact Clause of the Constitution—A Study in Interstate Adjustments," *Yale Law Journal 34* (May 1925): 701–707.

74. Ibid., pp. 708, 717, 727, 729.

75. Felix Frankfurter and James M. Landis, *The Business of the Supreme Court: A Study in the Federal Judicial System* (New York: Macmillan, 1927). Frankfurter later condensed these views in the "Distribution of Judicial Power Between United States and State Courts," *Cornell Law Quarterly, 13* (June 1928): 499–530.

76. Frankfurter, "Distribution of Judicial Power," pp. 506–517. See also Felix Frankfurter and Thomas G. Corcoran, "Petty Federal Offenses and the Constitutional Guaranty of Trial by Jury," *Harvard Law Review 39* (June 1926): 917–1019.

77. *Swift* v. *Tyson*, 16 Pet. 1 (U.S. 1842). The Supreme Court carried this doctrine to an absurd length in 1928 by upholding the freedom of the federal court sitting in Kentucky to ignore thirty-five years of precedent in that state relating to questions of land use and zoning. Holmes, Brandeis, and Harlan Stone dissented. See *Black & White Taxi Co.* v. *Brown and Yellow Taxi Co.*, 276 U.S. 518 (1928).

78. Frankfurter, "Distribution of Judicial Power," p. 526.

79. Frankfurter, "The Labor Injunction Must Go," in *Frankfurter on the Supreme Court*, p. 107. The unsigned editorial first appeared in *The New Republic* on September 22, 1922.

80. Ibid., p. 106.

81. Frankfurter and Greene, *The Labor Injunction* (New York: Macmillan, 1930), especially pp. 199–228.

82. Over the biting dissent of Holmes and Brandeis, the Supreme Court affirmed the conviction. Holmes thought the sentence was "more than an abuse of power. I think it should be found wholly void." *Craig* v. *Hecht*, 263 U.S. 255 (1923), at 280–281. See Frankfurter, "Lese Majeste Mayer," in *Frankfurter on the Supreme Court*, p. 146. This unsigned editorial first appeared in *The New Republic* for December 12, 1923.

83. Felix Frankfurter, "Power of Congress Over Procedure in Criminal Contempts in 'Inferior' Federal Courts—A Study in Separation of Powers," *Harvard Law Review 36* (June 1924), p. 1058.

84. Frankfurter, "Hours of Labor and Realism in Constitutional Law," pp. 367, 370.

85. Felix Frankfurter, "A Note on Advisory Opinions," *Harvard Law Review 37* (June 1925): 1002.

86. Roscoe Pound and Felix Frankfurter, eds., *Criminal Justice in Cleveland: Report of the Cleveland Foundation Survey of the Administration of Criminal Justice in Cleveland, Ohio* (Cleveland: Cleveland Foundation, 1922), especially pp. 559–652.

87. Frankfurter to E.F. Gay, February 1, 1927, Box 22, RPP.

88. Frankfurter, "Progress Report for Members of Crime Survey," ibid.

89. Ibid.

90. *Truax* v. *Corrigan*, 257 U.S. 312 (1921), at 366–368.

91. Frankfurter to Hand, November 22, 1923, Box 198, FFPH.

Chapter 10. THE TWO ITALIANS

1. Roberta Strauss Feuerlicht, *Justice Crucified: The Story of Sacco and Vanzetti* (New York: Farrar, Straus & Giroux, 1977), p. 409. On the demonstrations, see the *New York World* and the *New York Times*, August 23, 1927; Francis Russell, "Sacco-Vanzetti: The End of the Chapter," *National Review* 23 (May 5, 1970): 454.
2. Learned Hand, Oral History Memoir, 101, Columbia University.
3. Matthew Josephson, "Jurist-II," *New Yorker* (December 7, 1940), p. 44; Gardner Jackson, Oral History Memoir, pp. 295–296, Columbia University.
4. On Marion's illness, see Brandeis to Frankfurter, January 28 and February 11, 1928, *Letters of Louis D. Brandeis*, V, pp. 320, 323.
5. Felix Frankfurter, "Case of Sacco and Vanzetti," *Atlantic Monthly* 139 (March 1927): 409–432. It was shortly republished in book form as *The Case of Sacco and Vanzetti: A Critical Analysis for Lawyers and Laymen* (Boston: Little, Brown, 1927).
6. Taft to Elihu Root, May 12, 1927, Taft Papers.
7. Francis Russell, "The 'Second Trial' of Sacco and Vanzetti," *Harvard Magazine* 80 (May–June 1978): 52; Russell, "Sacco-Vanzetti: The End of the Chapter," p. 454.
8. William F. Buckley, Jr., "Sacco-Vanzetti, Again," *American Legion Magazine* 69 (October 1960): 50.
9. John Dos Passos, *The Big Money* (New York: New American Library, 1969), p. 469.
10. Frankfurter to Pound, August 31 and May 9, 1927, Box 64, File 12, RPP.
11. A major source for the case remains the six volumes known as the Holt Record: *The Sacco-Vanzetti Case: Transcript of the Record of the Trial of Nicola Sacco and Bartolomeo Vanzetti in the Courts of Massachusetts and Subsequent Proceedings, 1920–1927*, 5 Vols. *With a Supplemental Volume on the Bridgewater Case* (New York: Holt, 1928–1929). Hereafter, all references will be to the volume and page number of this collection.
12. At the time of the attempted robbery in Bridgewater, according to several witnesses, Vanzetti had been selling eels in Plymouth for the traditional Christmas eve feast. On April 15, according to others, he had been selling fish as usual in the town and purchasing cloth for a new coat. Holt Record, Supp. vol., pp. 227–231, 259–261; Vol. II, pp. 1496, 1587. Sacco had taken the day off from his factory job on April 15 in order to secure a passport from the Italian consulate in Boston. A clerk there recalled that he came in around 2 P.M. with an unusually large and unsuitable photograph. Other witnesses reported having lunch with him in Boston that day and Sacco himself recalled seeing one specific commuter on the Boston-to-Stoughton railroad who later testified that he

was on the train at about the time of the South Braintree holdup. Holt Record, Vol. II, pp. 1162, 1645, 1993 – 1995, 2015 – 2016, 2021 – 2022, 2266b – 2266d.

13. Holt Record, Supp. vol., p. 219.
14. Holt Record, Vol. V, p. 5253; Vol. IV, p. 3579.
15. Holt Record, Vol. II, pp. 1867 – 1873.
16. Holt Record, Vol. II, pp. 1874 – 1875.
17. Feuerlicht, *Justice Crucified*, p. 202; Holt Record, Vol. V, pp. 4964 – 4965.
18. Holt Record, Vol. II, p. 2239.
19. Holt Record, Vol. V, pp. 5065 – 5066.
20. Holt Record, Vol. V, pp. 5067 – 5068.
21. Holmes to Laski, September 1, 1927, *Holmes-Laski Letters*, II, p. 975.
22. Holt Record, Vol. I, pp. 292 – 295, 333 – 338, 425 – 427, 595 – 597.
23. Holt Record, Vol. I, pp. 807 – 822, 920; Vol. II, pp. 1418 – 1419.
24. Holt Record, Vol. I, pp. 842 – 848; Vol. II, pp. 2197 – 2198.
25. Holt Record, Vol. II, p. 2237.
26. Nunzio Pernicone, "Carlo Tresca and the Sacco-Vanzetti Case," *Journal of American History 66* (December 1979): 535 – 547.
27. Herbert B. Ehrmann, *The Case That Will Not Die: Commonwealth vs. Sacco and Vanzetti* (Boston: Vanguard Press, 1969), pp. 250 – 251. On Moore, see Francis Russell, *Tragedy in Dedham: The Story of the Sacco-Vanzetti Case* (New York: Harper & Row, 1962), pp. 108 – 111.
28. *Frankfurter Reminisces*, pp. 209 – 211; Russell, "Sacco-Vanzetti: The End of the Chapter," p. 459.
29. *Frankfurter Reminisces*, p. 211.
30. Holt Record, Vol. IV, pp. 3641 – 3643.
31. Holt Record, Vol. II, pp. 2182, 2254.
32. Holt Record, Vol. IV, p. 3681.
33. Holt Record, Vol. V, p. 5055.
34. Holt Record, Vol. V, p. 5084
35. Holt Record, Vol. V, p. 4975.
36. Holt Record, Vol. IV, pp. 3699 – 3704.
37. Ehrmann's complete story is told in *The Untried Case* (New York: Vanguard, 1933), and again in *The Case That Will Not Die*, pp. 404 – 432. Madeiros's full confession may be found in Holt Record, Vol. V, pp. 4416 – 4418.
38. Holt Record, Vol. V, pp. 4726 – 4777.
39. Holt Record, Vol. V, pp. 4893, 4357.
40. See, for instance, John Beffel, "Eels and the Electric Chair," *New Republic 25* (December 29, 1920): 127 – 129.
41. *Frankfurter Reminisces*, pp. 214 – 215.
42. Frankfurter, *The Case of Sacco and Vanzetti*, p. 46.
43. Ibid., p. 104.

44. Ibid., p. 88.
45. Ibid., pp. 90–91.
46. Frankfurter to Hill, August 6, 1927, Box 207, FFPH.
47. Pound, Diary, February 28, 1927, Box 38, RPP.
48. Pound, Diary, October 11, 1927, ibid.
49. Frankfurter to Pound, August 22 and 23, 1927, ibid., Box 64, File 12.
50. Perkins to Frankfurter, April 27, May 9, 1927; Frankfurter to Perkins, April 27, May 11, 1927, all Box 197, FFPH.
51. Frankfurter to Seligman, May 14, 18, 1927, ibid., Box 208.
52. Frankfurter to Franklin Hichborn, June 20, 1927, ibid., Box 197.
53. Quoted in Russell, *Tragedy in Dedham*, p. 371. On April 11, two weeks before Wigmore's initial attack, the *New York Times* quoted Judge Thayer as saying that "in reference to the articles published by Professor Frankenstein [sic] of Harvard in *The Atlantic Monthly*, I would say that these will be answered by one of the best authorities in the United States at the proper time." See Frankfurter to Seligman, May 14, 1927, Box 208, FFPH.
54. Brandeis to Frankfurter, April 29, 1927, *Brandeis Letters*, V, p. 283.
55. *Frankfurter Reminisces*, pp. 216–217.
56. Minutes of Meeting of Citizens of Committee, April 7, 1927, p. 3, Box 208, FFPH.
57. Ibid., p. 8.
58. Ibid., pp. 10–12.
59. Russell, *Tragedy in Dedham*, pp. 364–373.
60. Frankfurter to Hapgood, April 13, 1927, Box 197, FFPH; Frankfurter to Ehrmann, July 14, 1927, Box 2, Herbert Ehrmann Papers, Harvard Law School.
61. *The New Republic*, August 3, 1927.
62. Jackson, Oral History Memoir, p. 280.
63. Russell, *Tragedy in Dedham*, p. 375; Holmes to Laski, April 25, 1927, *Holmes-Laski Letters*, II, p. 938.
64. Thompson's theory of substitution, which Frankfurter shared, is set out in his letter to the latter, October 3, 1927, Box 197, FFPH, and more fully in Ehrmann's book, *The Case That Will Not Die*, pp. 284–287. It rests upon a number of curious circumstances surrounding the so-called mortal bullet and fatal shell. The prosecutors conceded that only one of the six bullets recovered from the bodies after an autopsy could have been fired from Sacco's .32 Colt and only one of the four shells found near the scene of the crime could have come from such a gun. Yet eye witnesses who identified Sacco as the highwayman firing at the guard and paymaster swore that he pumped at least two and perhaps as many as four bullets into the paymaster. In his opening statement to the jury, moreover, the assistant district attorney stated that Sacco "was standing in front of Berardelli with a pistol, and fired two shots at the prostrate man." Why then had only one bullet and one shell been recovered that

could be linked to Sacco's gun? Why had Katzmann stipulated that the government would not attempt to connect any particular bullet to any particular gun until the eighteenth day of the trial — following the tests at Lowell — although Captain Proctor had been examining these same bullets, cartridges, and weapons for more than a year? Why had Proctor testified so ambiguously at the trial? Finally, during the Goddard tests, Ehrmann and others noticed that the so-called mortal bullet had been marked with a different metal instrument than the one used to identify the other three — again suggesting the possibility of a substitution after the autopsy. But critics of the substitution theory point to their own set of anomalies. The different identification markings, they argue, probably resulted from the different surgical instruments used during the autopsy. Eye-witness testimony about the number of bullets fired could be unreliable. And if Proctor created the mortal bullet and shell in order to convict Sacco, why had he not been more positive about his own creations on the witness stand? And why did he later attempt to help the defense with his affidavit? See James Grossman, "The Sacco-Vanzetti Case Reconsidered," *Commentary* 34 (January 1962): 36–38.

65. Holt Record, Vol. V, pp. 5378c–5378h.
66. Holt Record, Vol. V, p. 5378m.
67. Holt Record, Vol. V, pp. 5378w–5378x.
68. Ehrmann, *The Case That Will Not Die*, pp. 511–512. James Grossman has argued that because Katzmann did not exploit this similarity at the trial, the defense claims about a forged bullet must collapse. Why would the prosecutors go to the extreme of faking evidence, but then rely upon "the shrewdness of the jury to note the identity of type and to the defense to bring out the obsoleteness?" See Grossman, "The Sacco-Vanzetti Case Reconsidered," p.38. The defense, however, never suggested that Katzmann knew of the substitution, only that Captain Proctor had probably done it and later, during the trial and before his death, experienced remorse.
69. Hapgood to Ehrmann, August 31, 1928, Box 208, FFPH.
70. Frankfurter, Diary, December 16, 1927, Box 1, FFPLC.
71. Frankfurter to Thompson, August 22, 1927, Box 208, FFPH.
72. Frankfurter to Pound, August 22, 23, 1927, Box 64, File 12, RPP.
73. Katherine Ann Porter, "The Never-Ending Wrong" *Harper's, 187* (November 1978): 38–64.
74. Both the wiretap logs and the reports of informants are available from the Massachusetts Department of Public Safety, hereafter cited as MDPS.
75. Frankfurter-Jackson Telephone Conversation; Frankfurter-Cook Telephone Conversation, both August 10, 1927, Wiretap Logs, MDPS.
76. Frankfurter-Kellogg Telephone Conversation, August 13, 1927, Wiretap Logs, ibid.

77. Felix Frankfurter-Marion Frankfurter Telephone Conversation, August 18, 1927, Wiretrap Logs, ibid.
78. Frankfurter-Ludington Telephone Conversation, August 13, 1927, Wiretap Logs, ibid.
79. Frankfurter-Hill Telephone Conversation, August 20, 1927, Wiretap Logs, ibid; Frankfurter to Hill, August 8, 1927, Box 207, FFPH.
80. Frankfurter-Ehrmann Telephone Conversation; Frankfurter-Mears Telephone Conversation, both August 16, 1927, Wiretap Logs, MDPS.
81. Frankfurter-Jackson Telephone Conversation, August 20, 1927, Wiretap Logs, ibid.
82. Michael Musmanno, *After Twelve Years* (New York, 1939), pp. 294, 311–312.
83. Holt Record, Vol. V, p. 5532.
84. Holt Record, Vol. V, p. 5516.
85. Frankfurter-F. Lauriston Bullard Telephone Conversation, August 15, 1927, Wiretap Logs, MDPS.
86. Holmes to Laski, August 18, 1927, *Holmes-Laski Letters*, II, p. 971. Four years earlier, Holmes had written the opinion for a near-unanimous Court that threw out the murder conviction of a Negro condemned by an all-white jury, but the entire trial had been intimidated by a mob and the opinion cautioned plaintiffs about seeking broad relief in the federal courts from alleged misconduct by state tribunals. See *Moore* v. *Dempsey*, 261 U.S. 86 (1923).
87. Holmes to Laski, August 24, September 1, 1927, *Holmes-Laski Letters*, II, pp. 974–975.
88. Frankfurter-Sherman Telephone Conversation, August 21, 1927, Wiretap Logs, MDPS. For a sample of Brandeis's negative remarks about the case and Judge Thayer, see Brandeis to Frankfurter, April 29, May 22, 1927, *Brandeis Letters*, V, pp. 283, 287.
89. Brandeis to Frankfurter, August 5, 24, 1927, ibid., pp. 299–300.
90. Frankfurter-Jackson Telephone Conversation, August 21, 1927, Wiretap Logs, MDPS.
91. See, for example, Frankfurter to William M. Bullitt, April 23, 1929, Box 208, FFPH; Frankfurter to Charles C. Burlingham, June 24, 1953, Box 36, FFPLC.
92. Pernicone, "Carlo Tresca and the Sacco-Vanzetti Case," 536; Grossman, "The Sacco-Vanzetti Case Reconsidered," p. 40; Eric Foner, "Sacco and Vanzetti," *The Nation 225* (August 20, 1977): 135–141.

Chapter 11. PROFESSOR AND PRESIDENT

1. Frankfurter to Thomas Reed Powell, September 4, 1927, Box A, File 1, Thomas Reed Powell Papers, Harvard Law School.
2. Brandeis to Frankfurter, December 11, 1927, *Brandeis Letters*, V, p. 316.

3. Frankfurter to Hand, June 4, 1930, Box 104, Hand Papers; Frankfurter to Powell, November 17, 1933, Box A, File 6, Powell Papers.
4. Frankfurter to Hand, December 10, 1931, Box 198, FFPH; Frankfurter to Hand, January 30, 1932, Box 105, LHP.
5. Frankfurter to Chafee, July 19, 1928, Box 4, File 18, Chafee Papers.
6. Oscar Handlin, *Al Smith and His America* (New York: Little, Brown, 1927), pp. 3–11; Norman Hapgood and Henry Moskowitz, *Up from the City Streets* (New York, 1927), pp. 165–217.
7. Frankfurter to Holmes, September 9, 1928, Box 30, File 17, OWHP.
8. Frankfurter, "Mr. Hoover on Power Control," *New Republic 56* (October 1928): 240–243; Frankfurter to Chafee, July 19, 1928, Box 4, File 18, Chafee Papers.
9. Brandeis to Frankfurter, October 21, 1928, *Brandeis Letters*, V, p. 361.
10. Holmes to Laski, November 13, 1928, *Holmes-Laski Letters*, II, p. 1109; Brandeis to Laski, November 29, 1928, *Brandeis Letters*, V, p. 364. On the Smith-Hoover election and its significance, see Samuel Lubell, *The Future of American Politics* (New York: Vintage, 1952), pp. 34–41, and Richard Hofstadter, "Could a Protestant Have Beaten Hoover in 1928?" *Reporter 22* (March 17, 1960): 31–33.
11. Brandeis to Frankfurter, November 6 and 14, 1928, *Brandeis Letters*, V, pp. 361, 363.
12. Brandeis to Frankfurter, November 4, 1928, ibid., p. 364.
13. Frankfurter to Roosevelt, November 8, 1928, *Roosevelt & Frankfurter: Their Correspondence, 1928–1945*, ed., Max Freedman (Boston: Little, Brown 1967), p. 39.
14. Felix Frankfurter, *The Public & Its Government* (New Haven: Yale University Press, 1930), pp. 151–155.
15. Ibid., pp. 159–160.
16. Roosevelt to Frankfurter, August 7, 1932, *Roosevelt & Frankfurter Correspondence*, p. 82.
17. Frankfurter to Roosevelt, January 5, April 19, June 27, September 17, 1929, Microfilm Roll 11, FFPH. See also Frank Freidel, *Franklin D. Roosevelt: The Triumph* (Boston: Little, Brown, 1956), pp. 100–119.
18. Frankfurter to Roosevelt, August 5, 1932, *Roosevelt & Frankfurter Correspondence*, pp. 80–81; Grace Tully, *F.D.R. My Boss* (New York: Charles Scribner's Sons, 1949), p. 140.
19. Hand to Frankfurter, November 9, 1930, Box 198, FFPH.
20. Hand to Frankfurter, February 3, 1932, ibid.
21. Walter Lippmann, *Interpretations, 1931–1932*, ed. Allan Nevins (New York: Harper & Row, 1932), pp. 261–262, 273.
22. Frankfurter to Lippman, October 23, 1930, *Frankfurter & Roosevelt Correspondence, p. 52*.
23. Frankfurter to Feis, September 30, 1932, Box 34, Herbert Feis Papers, Library of Congress.
24. Frankfurter to Hand, November 9, 1932, Box 105, LHP.

25. Frankfurter to Sedgwick, February 10, 1932 and Frankfurter to Smith, October 24, 1932, both Box 164, FFPLC.
26. Arthur M. Schlesinger, Jr., *The Crises of the Old Order* (Boston: Houghton Mifflin, 1957), p. 416; Brandeis to Frankfurter, October 11, 1932, Box 28, FFLC.
27. Frankfurter to Chafee, July 19, 1928, Box 4, File 18, Chafee Papers.
28. Frankfurter to Hand, January 9, 30, 1932, Box 105, LHP.
29. Frankfurter to Hand, February 12, January 30, 1932, ibid.
30. Frankfurter to Hand, January 30, 1932, ibid.
31. Schlesinger, *Crises of the Old Order*, pp. 398 – 399.
32. Frankfurter to Pound, September 7, 1924, Box 64, File 12, Pound Papers; Elliott A. Rosen, *Hoover, Roosevelt, and the Brains Trust: From Depression to New Deal* (New York: Viking, 1977), pp. 115 – 130.
33. John Franklin Carter, *The New Dealers* (New York: Literary Guild, 1934), pp. 330 – 331; John McCarter, "Atlas With Ideas," *New Yorker* (January 18, 1943), p. 23; Frankfurter to Max Lerner, March 20, 1953, Box 76, FFPLC.
34. Schlesinger, *Crises of the Old Order*, pp. 400 – 401.
35. Adolph A. Berle, Jr. and Gardner C. Means, *The Modern Corporation and Private Property* (New York: Macmillan, 1933), pp. 1 – 44.
36. Berle to Brandeis, February 19, 1932, Container S.C. 11, Brandeis Papers, University of Louisville.
37. Quoted in Schlesinger, *Crises of the Old Order*, p. 401.
38. Samuel I. Rosenman, ed., *The Papers and Addresses of Franklin D. Roosevelt*, I (New York: Random House, 1938), pp. 630 – 632.
39. Ibid., p. 642.
40. Quoted in Schlesinger, *Crises of the Old Order*, p. 401.
41. Frankfurter to Lippmann, March 11, 1933, Box 78, FFLC.
42. Brandeis to Alfred Brandeis, February 18, 1925, *Brandeis Letters*, V, p. 163.
43. See Brandeis's opinions in *New State Ice Co.* v. *Liebmann*, 285 U.S. 262, 302 – 303 (1932) and *Liggett Co.* v. *Lee*, 288 U.S. 517, 580 (1933).
44. Thomas H. Eliot to Brandeis, November 13, 1936, Box 8, Folder 1, Brandeis Papers.
45. Harry Shulman, "Memorandum of Talk with Louis D. Brandeis," December 8, 1933, Box 188, File 8, FFPH.
46. Brandeis to Elizabeth Brandeis Raushenbush, November 19, 1933, *Brandeis Letters*, V, p. 527.
47. Frankfurter to Moley, November 16, 1935, Roll 4, Frankfurter Microfilm, FFPH.
48. Frankfurter to Douglas, January 16, 1934, Box 10, FFPLC.
49. Frankfurter to Ely, June 29, 1932, *Roosevelt & Frankfurter Correspondence*, pp. 72 – 73.
50. Berle to Lilienthal, July 13, 1932, Box 55, Lilienthal Papers.

51. Frankfurter to Brandeis, August 7, 1932, Box 29, FFLC; Brandeis to Frankfurter, July 14, 1928, *Brandeis Letters*, V. p. 348.

52. Berle, Memorandum, August 5, 1932, reprinted in *Navigating the Rapids, 1918—1971: From the Papers of Adolf A. Berle, Jr.*, ed. Beatrice Bishop Berle and Travis Beal Jacobs (New York: Harcourt, Brace, 1973), pp. 53—54.

53. Berle to Frankfurter, August 6, 1932, and Frankfurter to Berle, August 8, 1932, both Box 164, FFLC.

54. Rosenman, ed., *Public Papers*, I, pp. 680—681.

55. Ibid., p. 749.

56. Rexford G. Tugwell, *The Brains Trust* (New York: Viking, 1968), pp. 461—462.

57. Rexford G. Tugwell, "Notes for a New Deal Diary," p. 13, Franklin D. Roosevelt Library, Hyde Park, New York.

58. Berle to Moley, February 2, 1966; Berle to Roosevelt, January 11, 1933, both in *Navigating the Rapids*, pp. 79, 83.

59. Frankfurter to Feis, November 9, 1931, Box 34, Feis Papers.

60. Frankfurter to Feis, December 16, 1931, ibid.

61. Frankfurter to Feis, June 10, 1932, ibid.

62. Raymond Moley, *After Seven Years* (New York: Harper, 1939), pp. 72—77; Raymond Moley, *The First New Deal* (New York: Harcourt, Brace, 1966), pp. 29—36.

63. Moley, *First New Deal*, p. 35.

64. Frankfurter, Memorandum, January 4, 1933, *Roosevelt & Frankfurter Correspondence*, pp. 101—103; Morison, *Turmoil and Tradition*, pp. 362—363.

65. Frankfurter, Memorandum, January 4, 1933, *Roosevelt & Frankfurter Correspondence*, pp. 101—103.

66. Moley, *First New Deal*, p. 51.

67. Ibid. pp. 45—59.

68. Frankfurter to Roosevelt, November 12, 1932; Frankfurter to Lippman, January 10, 1933, both *Roosevelt & Frankfurter Correspondence*, pp. 94, 103.

69. Moley, *First New Deal*, pp. 51—56.

Chapter 12. NEW DEALER

1. William O. Douglas, *Go East Young Man: The Early Years* (New York: Random House, 1977), p. 397.

2. Freedman, ed., *Roosevelt & Frankfurter Correspondence*, pp. 7—9; Moley, *After Seven Years*, p. 285; Carter, *The New Dealers*, p. 317; Berle, *Navigating the Rapids*, p. 176; Magruder to Frankfurter, October 10, 1933, Box 80, FFPLC.

3. Phillips, *Frankfurter Reminisces, pp. 235 – 248.*

4. Frankfurter to Burns, May 24, 1935, Box 135, and Frankfurter to Marguerite A. LeHand, March 9, 1935, Box 97, both FFPLC.

5. Quoted in Michael E. Parrish, *Securities Regulation and the New Deal* (New Haven: Yale University Press, 1970), p. 2.

6. Berle, *Navigating the Rapids*, p. 176.

7. Frankfurter, Memorandum of a Visit with Roosevelt, March 8, 1933, *Roosevelt & Frankfurter Correspondence*, p. 112.

8. Roosevelt to Frankfurter, April 5, 1933, ibid., p. 124.

9. Arthur Schlesinger, Jr., *The Politics of Upheaval* (Boston: Houghton Mifflin, 1960), p. 261; Frankfurter to Learned Hand, December 4, 1939, Box 64, FFPLC; Harold Ickes, *The Secret Diary of Harold L. Ickes: The First Thousand Days, 1933 – 1936* (New York: Simon & Schuster, 1953), p. 243.

10. Brandeis to Frankfurter, March 13, 1933, Box 28, FFPLC; Dean Acheson, *Morning and Noon* (Boston: Houghton Mifflin, 1965), pp. 161 – 162.

11. Brandeis to Frankfurter, May 28, 1933, Box 28, FFPLC; Sutherland to Frankfurter, July 2 and 7, 1933, Box 6, Folder 2, Louis D. Brandeis Papers, University of Louisville; Cummings to Roosevelt, July 14, 1933, OF 10, Franklin D. Roosevelt Papers, Hyde Park; Frankfurter to Roosevelt, July 10, 1933, *Roosevelt & Frankfurter Correspondence*, pp. 139 – 140.

12. Frankfurter to Roosevelt, July 10, 1933, *Roosevelt & Frankfurter Correspondence*, p. 139; Harlan Stone to Frankfurter, May 15, 1933, Box 105, FFPLC; Brandeis to Frankfurter, June 13, 1933, Box 28, FFPLC; Ickes quoted in Schlesinger, *Politics of Upheaval*, p. 261.

13. Carter, *The New Dealers*, pp. 281 – 283; Frankfurter to Brandeis, November 28, 1934, Box 9, Folder 2, Brandeis Papers.

14. Frankfurter to Brandeis, December 9, 28, 1933 and January 7, 1934, all Box 9, Folder 2, Brandeis Papers; Frankfurter to Brandeis, October 16, 1933, Box 29, FFPLC.

15. Frankfurter to Brandeis, December 4, 1933 and November 28, 1934, Box 9, Folder 2, Brandeis Papers.

16. Frankfurter to Brandeis, September 12, 1933, Box 29, FFPLC.

17. Corcoran to Frankfurter, December 30, 1933, Box 49, and Frankfurter to Brandeis, September 12, 1933, Box 29, both ibid.

18. Schlesinger, *Politics of Upheaval*, p. 228.

19. Ickes, *Secret Diary*, pp. 8, 39; Frankfurter to Ickes, March 16, 23, 1933, Box 149, FFPLC.

20. Perkins to Frankfurter, March 18, 1933; Frankfurter to Perkins, April 11 and May 2, 1933; Frankfurter to Wagner, May 8, 1933, all Box 150, ibid; Brandeis to Frankfurter, March 22 and 25, 1933, Box 28, ibid; Donald Richberg, Memorandum, 1933, Folder 1933, Donald Richberg Papers, Library of Congress; Frankfurter to Wyzanski, July 18, 1933, Box 113, FFPLC.

21. Carter, *The New Dealers*, pp. 38–39; Thomas E. Vadney, *The Wayward Liberal: A Political Biography of Donald Richberg* (Lexington: University of Kentucky Press, 1970), pp. 172–173; Brandeis to Frankfurter, September 16, 1923, *Brandeis Letters*, V, p. 100; David Lilienthal, *The TVA Years, 1939–1945* (New York: Harper & Row, 1964), p. 30.

22. Thomas K. McGraw, *Morgan vs. Lilienthal* (Chicago: University of Chicago Press, 1970), p. 19; Frankfurter to FDR, June 10, 1933, Box 9, Folder 2, Brandeis Papers; Brandeis to Richberg, August 18, 1933, Box 1, Folder 1933, Richberg Papers.

23. Frankfurter to Tugwell, March 11 and 15, 1933, Box 125, FFPLC.

24. Frankfurter to Learned Hand, December 11, 1947, Box 64, ibid.; Frankfurter to Hand, March 25, 1941, Box 105, LHP.

25. Carter, *The New Dealers*, pp. 96–97; Arthur Schlesinger, Jr., *The Coming of the New Deal* (Boston: Houghton Mifflin, 1958), 49–50; Grant Gilmore, *The Ages of American Law* (New Haven: Yale University Press, 1977), pp. 78–90.

26. Frankfurter to Hand, March 14, 1932, Box 198, File 17, FFPH.

27. Frankfurter to Clark, June 4, 1932, Box 183, File 30, ibid.

28. Frankfurter to Frank, April 24, 1933, Box 125, FFPLC.

29. Frankfurter to Nathan Margold, March 11 and 30, 1933, Box 149, ibid.; Nathan Witt to Frankfurter, June 14, 1933, Box 5, General Correspondence, James M. Landis Papers, Library of Congress; Schlesinger, *The Coming of the New Deal*, p. 51.

30. Allen Weinstein, *Perjury: The Hiss-Chambers Case* (New York: Knopf, 1978), pp. 132–157.

31. George N. Peek, "In and Out: The Experiences of the First AAA Administrator," *The Saturday Evening Post* (May 16, 1936), p. 7.

32. Eliot Janeway, *Struggle for Survival* (New Haven: Yale University Press, 1951), pp. 140–141.

33. Frankfurter, "The Young Men Go to Washington," reprinted in Frankfurter, *Law and Politics*, pp. 238–249.

34. There was, Frankfurter told Wyzanski, "a la de da quality to Biddle which is not merely sartorial but psychic." Frankfurter to Wyzanski, October 22, 1934, Box 113, FFPLC.

35. Felix Frankfurter, "What We Confront in American Life," *Survey Graphics* (March 1933), pp. 133–136.

36. Frankfurter to Wheeler, March 30, 1932, Box 111, FFPLC.

37. Brandeis to Frankfurter, January 31, 1933 and February 5, 1933, Box 28, ibid.

38. Frankfurter to Moley, February 9, 10, and 23, 1933, Box 84, ibid.

39. Ellis W. Hawley, *The New Deal and the Problem of Monopoly* (Princeton, NJ: Princeton University Press, 1966), pp. 19–71; Schlesinger, *The Coming of the New Deal*, pp. 87–102.

40. Hawley, *The New Deal and the Problem of Monopoly*, pp. 111–146; Schlesinger, *The Coming of the New Deal*, pp. 152–176.

41. Frankfurter to Alfred E. Cohn, October 30, 1935, *Roosevelt & Frankfurter Correspondence*, pp. 288–289; Frankfurter, Memorandum of NRA, May 30, 1933, Box 159, FFPLC.
42. Wiener to Frankfurter, August 31, 1933, Box 111, FFPLC.
43. Wyzanski to Frankfurter, May 24, 1933, Box 159, ibid.
44. Brandeis to Frankfurter, September 22, 1934, February 21, 1934, and September 29, 1934, all ibid., Box 28. When General Johnson later declared that he had been in "constant touch" with Brandeis during the initial days of the NRA, the justice became apoplectic: "It must have been more than 'liquor' — what he said of me was not only an indiscretion but a lie." Brandeis to Frankfurter, September 14, 1934, ibid.
45. Frankfurter to James M. Landis, March 17, 1934, ibid., Box 117.
46. Frankfurter to Roosevelt, November 15, 1933, *Roosevelt & Frankfurter Correspondence*, p. 294; Brandeis to Frankfurter, February 24, 27, 1935, Box 28, FFPLC; Milo Perkins, Memorandum, June 5, 1935, Rexford Tugwell Papers.
47. Berle to Roosevelt, January 11, 1933, reprinted in *Navigating the Rapids*, p. 83.
48. See Michael E. Parrish, *Securities Regulation and the New Deal*, pp. 42–56.
49. Donald A. Ritchie, *James M. Landis: Dean of the Regulators* (Cambridge, MA: Harvard University Press, 1980), pp. 6–42.
50. Parrish, *Securities Regulation*, p. 66.
51. James M. Landis, "The Legislative History of the Securities Act of 1933," *George Washington Law Review* 28 (October 1959): 34, 38–39.
52. Parrish, *Securities Regulation*, pp. 63–64.
53. Ibid., p. 68.
54. Ibid., p. 69; Stimson to Frankfurter, January 26, 1934, Box 103, FFPLC.
55. Cohen to Landis, May 5 and June 7, 1933, Box 4, Landis Papers.
56. Parrish, *Securities Regulation*, pp. 71, 42.

Chapter 13. THE HIGH TIDE OF REFORM

1. Frankfurter to Hand, September 27, 1933, Box 104, Hand Papers. The Berlin quotation is from Mendelson, ed., *Felix Frankfurter: A Tribute*, p. 30.
2. Frankfurter to Marguerite LeHand, September 24, 1933, *Roosevelt & Frankfurter Correspondence*, p. 156.
3. Urofsky, *American Zionism*, pp. 380–383.
4. Frankfurter to Warburg, August 6, 1930, Roll 2, FFZ; Felix Frankfurter, "The Palestine Situation Revisited," *Foreign Affairs* 9 (April 1931): 409–434.
5. Laski to Holmes, November 30, 1930, *Holmes-Laski Letters*, II, pp. 1298–1299.

6. Frankfurter to Laski, November 2, 1930, Roll 2, and Frankfurter to Brandeis, November 30, 1930, Roll 37, FFZ.

7. Laski to Holmes, December 17, 1933, *Holmes-Laski Letters*, II, p. 1458.

8. Mendelson, *Felix Frankfurter: A Tribute*, pp. 24–25.

9. Frankfurter to Thomas Reed Powell, November 17, 1933 and May 18, 1934, Box A, File 16, Powell Papers; Frankfurter to Hand, November 29, 1933, Box 104, LHP.

10. Frankfurter to Powell, February 20, 1934, Box A, File 16, Powell Papers; Frankfurter to Hand, March 15, 1934, Box 104, LHP.

11. Frankfurter to Roosevelt, November 23, 1933, *Roosevelt & Frankfurter Correspondence*, pp. 167–173.

12. Ibid., pp. 180–181.

13. Roosevelt to Frankfurter, December 22, 1933; Frankfurter to Roosevelt, May 7, 1934; Frankfurter to Marguerite LeHand, May 7, 1934, all *Roosevelt & Frankfurter Correspondence*, pp. 183, 213, 214–215; Frances Perkins, *The Roosevelt I Knew* (New York: Viking Press, 1946), pp. 225–226.

14. Frankfurter to Holmes, May 7, 1934, Box 30, File 18, OWHP; Frankfurter to Stimson, April 15, 1934, Stimson Papers.

15. Corcoran to Frankfurter, June 18, 1934, *Roosevelt & Frankfurter Correspondence*, pp. 224–225.

16. Ibid.

17. Parrish, *Securities Regulation*, pp. 108–144, 179–198; Schlesinger, *The Coming of the New Deal*, pp. 496–500.

18. Frankfurter to Brandeis, August 31, 1934, Box 25, FFPLC.

19. *Ibid.*

20. Frankfurter to Roosevelt, October 3 and November 21, 1934; Roosevelt to Frankfurter, November 27, 1934, all *Roosevelt & Frankfurter Correspondence*, pp. 237, 240–242, 245.

21. Frankfurter to Brandeis, December 20, 1934, Box 29, FFPLC.

22. Frankfurter to Brandeis, May 21, 1935, ibid.

23. Frankfurter to Brandeis, June 14, and July 17, 1935, ibid.

24. Frankfurter to Brandeis, May 6, 21, 22, 1935, all *ibid.* Winthrop Aldrich, an old friend of Roosevelt's, was the head of the Chase National Bank and the self-appointed spokesman for so-called Wall Street "liberals."

25. Paul Rauschenbush, "Starting Unemployment Compensation in Wisconsin," *Unemployment Insurance Review* 4 (April–May 1967): 18–23; Daniel Nelson, *Unemployment Insurance: The American Experience, 1915–1935* (Madison: University of Wisconsin Press, 1969); Abraham Epstein, "Enemies of Unemployment Insurance," *New Republic* (September 6, 1933), pp. 94–96.

26. Frankfurter to Brandeis, July 18, 1934, Box 9, Folder 2, Brandeis Papers.

27. Frankfurter to Roosevelt, undated, Box 224, FFPLC.

28. Tugwell, "New Deal Diary," December 28, 1934, Tugwell Papers.
29. Schlesinger, *The Coming of the New Deal*, pp. 313 – 314.
30. Frankfurter to Roosevelt, May 16, 1935, *Roosevelt & Frankfurter Correspondence*, p. 271.
31. Frankfurter to Brandeis, June 14, 1935, Box 9, Folder 2, Brandeis Papers.
32. John M. Blum, *From the Morgenthau Diaries: Years of Crisis, 1928 – 1938* (Boston: Houghton Mifflin, 1959), pp. 299 – 305; William E. Leuchtenberg, *Franklin D. Roosevelt and the New Deal* (New York: Harper & Row, 1963), p. 152.
33. Frankfurter to Brandeis, July 21, August 15, 1935, Box 9, Folder 2, Brandeis Papers.
34. Brandeis to Frankfurter, August 30, 1935, Box 28, FFPLC.
35. Frankfurter to Brandeis, April 13, 1935, ibid., Box 29.
36. Parrish, *Securities Regulation*, pp. 153 – 159; Frankfurter to Brandeis, December 20, 1934, and January 22, 1935, both Box 9, Folder 2, Brandeis Papers.
37. Frankfurter to Brandeis, July 10, 1935, Box 28, FFPLC.
38. Parrish, *Securities Regulations*, pp. 175 – 177; Moley, *After Seven Years*, p. 316n.
39. Blum, *From the Morgenthau Diaries*, pp. 308 – 319.
40. Frankfurter to Roosevelt, July 11, 1936, *Roosevelt & Frankfurter Correspondence*, pp. 345 – 354.
41. Quoted in Leuchtenberg, *Franklin D. Roosevelt*, pp. 183 – 184.
42. Frankfurter to Brandeis, February 9, 1935, Box 29, FFPLC. Brandeis had given considerable financial and moral support to the sharecroppers' cause. On the conflicts within the Triple A, see Donald H. Grubbs, *Cry From the Cotton: The Southern Tenant Farmers' Union and the New Deal* (Chapel Hill: University of North Carolina Press, 1971); and Schlesinger, *The Coming of the New Deal*, pp. 77 – 81.

Chapter 14. THE CONSTITUTIONAL REVOLUTION

1. Drew Pearson and Robert S. Allen, *The Nine Old Men* (New York: Vanguard Press, 1936), p. 44.
2. *Congressional Record*, 71 Cong., 2nd Session, LXXII, 3373.
3. Frankfurter to Hand, February 4, 1930, Box 104, LHP.
4. Frankfurter to Hand, February 14, 1930, ibid.
5. Frankfurter to Hand, March 22 and May 15, 1930, ibid.; William Burris, *The Senate Rejects a Judge: A Study of the John J. Parker Case* (Chapel Hill: University of North Carolina Press, 1962).
6. Frankfurter to Hand, May 26, 1930, Box 104, LHP; Frankfurter to Stone, May 22, 1930, Box 171, FFPH.

7. Hand to Frankfurter, May 27, 1931, Box 104, LHP.
8. Frankfurter to Hand, March 10,1926, ibid.
9. Herbert Wechsler to Frankfurter, July 12, 1946, Box 172, FFPH. Handwritten note by Frankfurter on the original.
10. Frankfurter to Roberts, May 10, 1930, ibid., Box 171; Frankfurter to Hand, May 31, 1930, Box 104, LHP.
11. *United States* v. *Chicago, Milwaukee, St. Paul and Pacific Railroad Company*, 282 U.S. 311 (1931), 331–344.
12. Frankfurter to Hand, January 13, 1931, Box 198, FFPH.
13. *Chicago, Rock Island and Pacific Railway Co.* v. *United States*, 284 U.S. 80 (1931), 87–100.
14. *United States* v. *Baltimore and Ohio Railroad Co.*, 284 U.S. 195 (1931), 198–204.
15. *Hoeper* v. *Tax Commission of Wisconsin*, 284 U.S. 206 (1931), 212–218.
16. Ibid., at 220.
17. Eastman to Frankfurter, December 12, 1931, Box 171, FFPH.
18. Frankfurter to Hand, December 10, 1931, ibid., Box 198.
19. Stone to Frankfurter, December 16, 1931, ibid., Box 171.
20. See, for instance, *O'Gorman and Young* v. *Hartford Insurance Co.*, 282 U.S. 251 (1931); *Bandini Petroleum Co.* v. *Superior Court*, 284 U.S. 8 (1931); *Home Building and Loan Assn.* v. *Blaisdell*, 290 U.S. 398 (1934); and *Nebbia* v. *New York*, 291 U.S. 502 (1934).
21. Frankfurter to Thomas R. Powell, January 27, 1934, Box A, File 6, Powell Papers.
22. Frankfurter to Hand, March 15, 1934, Box 104, LHP.
23. *Stromberg* v. *California*, 283 U.S. 359 (1931); *Near* v. *Minnesota*, 283 U.S. 697 (1931); and *Powell* v. *Alabama*, 287 U.S. (1932).
24. *New State Ice Co.* v. *Liebmann*, 285 U.S. 262 (1932); *Liggett* v. *Lee*, 288 U.S. 517 (1932).
25. *Cowell* v. *Benson*, 285 U.S. 48 (1932); *Rogers* v. *Guaranty Trust Company of New York*, 288 U.S. 123 (1932).
26. Frankfurter to Stone, February 29, 1932, Box 171, FFPH.
27. Stone to Frankfurter, February 17, 1933, ibid.
28. Wyzanski to Frankfurter, May 24, 1933, Box 159, FFPLC.
29. Brandeis to Frankfurter, July 8, 1933, ibid., Box 28.
30. Brandeis to Frankfurter, June 13, 1933, ibid.
31. Brandeis to Frankfurter, November 6, 1933, ibid., Box 115.
32. *Panama Refining Co.* v. *Ryan*, 293 U.S. 388 (1935).
33. *Norman* v. *Baltimore and Ohio Railroad Co.*, 294 U.S. 240 (1935); *Nortz* v. *United States*, 294 U.S. 317 (1935); *Perry* v. *United States*, 294 U.S. 330 (1935). See also John P. Dawson, "The Gold-Clause Decisions," *Michigan Law Review* 33 (1935): 647–684.
34. See Frankfurter, "Memorandum on the Belcher Case," undated, Box 98, FFPLC; *U.S.* v. *Belcher*, 294 U.S. 736 (1935); Corcoran to Roosevelt, April 4, 1935, in *Roosevelt & Frankfurter Correspondence*, p. 260.

35. Frank Buxton to Frankfurter, November 27, 1935, and Buxton to Krock, December 2, 1935, both Box 38, FFPLC.
36. Frankfurter to Stanley Reed, March 25, 1936, Box 170, FFPH.
37. *Louisville Bank* v. *Radford*, 295 U.S. 555 (1935); *Humphrey's Executor* v. *United States*, 295 U.S. 602 (1935).
38. Quoted in Schlesinger, *The Politics of Upheaval*, p. 280.
39. *Railroad Retirement Board* v. *Alton Railroad Co.*, 295 U.S. 330 (1935), 344 – 374.
40. Stone to Frankfurter, May 9, 1935, Box 171, FFPH.
41. *Complete Presidental Press Conferences of Franklin D. Roosevelt*, Vol. V. pp. 309 – 337. He failed to mention that only a year before the *Schechter* decision, the Hughes Court had sustained a federal antitrust indictment against local marketmen, teamsters, and butchers in the same live poultry industry – a contradiction that led at least one scholar to question the difference "in the constitutional power to protect interstate commerce against unduly high prices, as in the Sherman Act, and excessively low prices, as in the New Deal legislation." See *Local 167* v. *United States*, 291 U.S. 293 (1934); and Robert L. Stern, "The Commerce Clause and the National Economy, 1933 – 1946," *Harvard Law Review 59* (May 1946): 651.
42. Harry Hopkins, "A Statement to Me by Thomas Corcoran Giving His Recollection of the Genesis of the Supreme Court Fight," April 3, 1939, Harry Hopkins Papers, Roosevelt Library.
43. Frankfurter to Brandeis, June 3, 1935, Box 35, FFPLC.
44. Frankfurter to Roosevelt, May 29, 1935, *Roosevelt & Frankfurter Correspondence*, pp. 273 – 274.
45. Tugwell, Diary, May 31, 1935, Tugwell Papers.
46. Frankfurter to Roosevelt, May 30, 1935, *Roosevelt & Frankfurter Correspondence*, p. 275.
47. Frankfurter to Brandeis, July 21, 1935, Box 25, FFPLC.
48. Stone to Frankfurter, May 27, 1935, Box 171, FFPH.
49. *United States* v. *Butler*, 297 U.S. 1 (1936), 53 – 78.
50. Ibid., at 85 – 87.
51. *Ashwander* v. *Tennessee Valley Authority*, 297 U.S. 288 (1936), with Brandeis concurring at 341 – 356.
52. *Jones* v. *Securities and Exchange Commission*, 298 U.S. 1 (1936), at 33.
53. *Carter* v. *Carter Coal Co.*, U.S. 238 (1936), at 331.
54. *Colgate* v. *Harvey*, 296 U.S. 404 (1936).
55. *Great Northern Railway Co.* v. *Weeks*, 297 U.S. 135 (1936).
56. *Mayflower Farms, Inc.* v. *Ten Eyck*, 297 U.S. 269 (1936), at 276 – 278.
57. *Morehead* v. *New York ex rel. Tipaldo*, 298 U.S. 587 (1936), 611 – 614.
58. Quoted in Schlesinger, *The Politics of Upheaval*, p. 489.
59. Frankfurter to Stone, December 19, 1935, Box 171, FFPH. Stone himself blamed the decision on what he called "that inventive genius

[Hughes C.J.] which has so often of late distorted the body of our law. If the inventor would only sponsor his invention in public, I think, I could write a really effective dissent, but prudence seems to warn against any unnecessary exposure to attack." Stone to Frankfurter, December 23, 1935, Box 171, FFPH.

60. Frankfurter to Stone, February 12, 1936, Box 13, Stone Papers.

61. Frankfurter to Stone, February 14, 1936, Box 171, FFPH.

62. Frankfurter to Roosevelt, February 25, 1936 and Corcoran to Frankfurter, February 21, 1936, both Box 256, FFPLC.

63. Frankfurter to Stone, June 2, 1936, Box 13, Stone Papers.

64. Frankfurter to Hand, November 20, 1936, Box 105, LHP.

65. Frankfurter to Hand, November 28, 1936, ibid. Justice Stone, who found himself again and again in dissent that spring, poured out his frustrations to Frankfurter. "I think there has never been a time in the history of the Court," he wrote, "when there has been so little intelligible, recognizable pattern in its judicial performance. . . . The worst of it is that the one that you find it most difficult to understand [Hughes] is the one chiefly responsible." Stone to Frankfurter, February 17, 1936, Box 171, FFPH. He described Sutherland's opinion in the *Jones* case as "written for morons, and such will no doubt take comfort from it. But I can hardly believe that intelligent people, trained in the law, will swallow such buncombe." Stone to Frankfurter, April 7, 1936, Box 171, FFPH. After the majority killed the Guffey Coal Act, with Hughes concurring in Sutherland's cramped interpretation of the commerce clause, Stone protested that "perhaps when you have read it all you will tell me what it was the Chief thought should be decided and why." Stone to Frankfurter, May 18, 1936, Box 171, FFPH.

66. Hughes argued that the New Dealers had only themselves to blame for the Court's negative attitude. "The laws have been poorly drafted, the briefs have been badly drawn and the arguments have been poorly presented," he complained to Senator Wheeler in 1937. "We've had to be not only the Court but we've had to do the work that should have been done by the Attorney General," Quoted in William F. Swindler, *Court and Constitution in the 20th Century: The New Legality, 1932-1968* (Indianapolis and New York: Bobbs-Merrill, 1970), p. 72. While this defense seems somewhat creditable with respect to the "hot-oil" decision, *Radford,* and *Schechter,* it is not a reasonable interpretation of the administration's misfortunes in cases such as *Butler, Carter Coal,* and *Jones.* It is a preposterous explanation for the Court's behavior with respect to the state laws invalidated in *Morehead, Colgate, Great Northern,* and *Mayflower.*

67. Frankfurter to Reed, December 14, 1936; Reed to Frankfurter, December 17, 1936; and Frankfurter to Cohen, December 17, 1936, all Box 170, FFPH.

68. Roosevelt to Frankfurter, January 15, 1937, *Roosevelt & Frankfurter Correspondence*, p. 377.
69. William E. Leuchtenberg, "The Origins of Franklin D. Roosevelt's 'Court-Packing' Plan," *The Supreme Court Review* (Chicago, 1966), pp. 352–399; Leuchtenberg, "Franklin D. Roosevelt's Supreme Court 'Packing' Plan," in *Essays on the New Deal*, ed. Harold M. Hollingsworth (Austin: University of Texas Press, 1969), pp. 75–115; Joseph Alsop and Turner Catledge, *The 168 Days* (New York: Doubleday, 1938), pp. 32–37.
70. Ickes, Diary, November 13, 1935; Roosevelt to Hapgood, July 22, 1935, Special XGP, 31, Roosevelt Papers.
71. Felix Frankfurter, "The Supreme Court of the United States," in the *Encyclopedia of Social Sciences*, 45 (New York: Macmillan, 1934), reprinted in Archibald MacLeish and E. F. Prichard, eds., *Law and Politics*, p. 28.
72. Felix Frankfurter, "The Supreme Court and the Public," *Forum* (June 1930), p. 334.
73. Frankfurter to Roosevelt, February 7, 1937, *Roosevelt & Frankfurter Correspondence*, pp. 380–381.
74. Frankfurter to Roosevelt, February 18, 1937, ibid., pp. 383–387; Rosenman, ed., *The Public Papers of Franklin D. Roosevelt*, VI, pp. 122–133.
75. Frankfurter to Roosevelt, March 30 1937, *Roosevelt & Frankfurter Correspondence*, p. 392.
76. Leuchtenberg, "Origins of Franklin D. Roosevelt's 'Court-Packing' Plan," p. 347; Dean Acheson, *Morning and Noon*, p. 202; Liva Baker, *Felix Frankfurter*, pp. 182–183; Thomas Reed Powell to Frankfurter, December 20, 1937, Box A, File 6, Powell Papers.
77. Powell to Frankfurter, December 20, 1937, and Frankfurter to Powell, December 17, 1937, both Box A, File 6, Powell Papers.
78. Frankfurter to Roosevelt, July 20, 1937, *Roosevelt & Frankfurter Correspondence*, p. 403.
79. Frankfurter to Brandeis, March 26, 1937, Box 28, FFPLC.
80. Robert Sherwood, *Roosevelt and Hopkins* (New York: Harper, 1948), p. 90; Brandeis to Frankfurter, February 6, 1937, Box 28, FFPLC.
81. *West Coast Hotel Company* v. *Parrish*, 300 U.S. 379 (1937).
82. *National Labor Relations Board* v. *Jones and Laughlin Steel Corporation*, 301 U.S. 1 (1937).
83. *Morehead* v. *New York, ex rel. Tipaldo*, 298 U.S. 587 (1936), at 636; John W. Chambers, "The Big Switch: Justice Roberts and the Minimum-Wage Cases," *Labor History* (Winter 1969), pp. 51–56, 68–109.
84. Frankfurter to Stone, March 30, 1937, Box 13, Stone Papers.
85. See Felix Frankfurter, "Mr. Justice Roberts," *University of Pennsylvania Law Review 104* (December 1955): 313–316. Cf. Michael E. Parrish, "The Hughes Court, the Great Depression, and the Historians," *The Historian 40* (February 1978): 286–308.

86. Quoted in Alpheus T. Mason, *Harlan Fiske Stone: Pillar of the Law* (New York: Viking, 1956), 459. For a contrary, but unconvincing opinion, cf. Samuel Hendel, *Charles Evans Hughes and the Supreme Court* (New York: Russell & Russell, 1951), pp. 260–265; and Paul Freund, "Charles Evans Hughes," *Harvard Law Review 81* (November 1967): 34.
87. Frankfurter to Roosevelt, April 12, 1937, *Roosevelt & Frankfurter Correspondence*, p. 397.
88. Wyzanski to Frankfurter, April 14, 1937, Box 1, File 11, Wyzanski Papers.
89. *Steward Machine Company* v. *Davis*, 301 U.S. 548 (1937); and *Helvering* v. *Davis*, 301 U.S. 619 (1937).
90. Frankfurter's memorandum and Roosevelt's address may be found in *Roosevelt & Frankfurter Correspondence*, pp. 409–417, and in Rosenman, ed., *Public Papers*, VI, pp. 359–367.
91. See *United States* v. *Carolene Products Co.*, 304 U.S. 144 (1938).
92. Frankfurter to Wyzanski, April 13, 1937, Box 1, File 11, Wyzanski Papers.

Epilogue: MR. JUSTICE FRANKFURTER

1. The Nazis released Frankfurter's uncle after Lady Astor interceded on his behalf with German officials in London. Frankfurter, however, never told Roosevelt of his uncle's plight until after Solomon's death in 1941. See Nancy Astor to Frankfurter, May, 1938, and Frankfurter to Roosevelt, October 24, 1941, both *Roosevelt & Frankfurter Correspondence*, pp. 473–474, 619.
2. Frankfurter to Charles C. Burlingham, September 9, 1937, Box 34, FFPLC.
3. Benjamin V. Cohen to Frankfurter, October 11, 1937, ibid., Box 45; Ickes, *Diary*, July 16 and September 18, 1938.
4. Henry Morgenthau, Memorandum, May 24, 1937, Morgenthau Diaries, p. 69, Roosevelt Library.
5. Phillips, *Frankfurter Reminisces*, pp. 280–281; Samuel Spencer's Notes of Frankfurter-Grenville Clark Conversation, Summer 1947, p. 8, Box 195, FFPH.
6. Jim Farley, *Jim Farley's Story: The Roosevelt Years*, (New York: McGraw-Hill, 1948), pp. 161–162.
7. Joe Rauh, Jr., interview with author, August 12, 1975.
8. Ickes, *Diary*, January 2, 15, 1939; Eugene Gerhart, *America's Advocate: Robert Jackson* (Indianapolis: Bobbs-Merrill, 1938), p. 166; Mason, *Harlan Fiske Stone*, p. 482.
9. Stone to Frankfurter, January 20, 1938, Box 171, FFPH.
10. *Connecticut General Life Insurance Co.* v. *Johnson*, 303 U.S. 77 (1938).
11. Stone to Frankfurter, February 8, 1938, Box 171, FFPH.

12. Urofsky, *American Zionism*, pp. 403 – 416; Brandeis to Bernard Flexner, October 12, 1938, Brandeis to Frankfurter, October 16, 1938, and Brandeis to Robert Szold, November 11, 1938, all *Brandeis Letters*, V, pp. 602-605.
13. Ickes, *Diary*, January 15, 1939.
14. Frankfurter to Roosevelt, January 30, 1939, *Roosevelt & Frankfurter Correspondence*, p. 485.

INDEX